THE COMPLETE
CANADIAN LIVING
BAKING BOOK

Transcontinental Books
1100 René-Lévesque Boulevard West
24th floor
Montreal, Que. H3B 4X9
Tel.: (514) 340-3587
Toll-free: 1-866-800-2500
www.canadianliving.com

Bibliothèque et Archives nationales du Québec and Library and Archives Canada cataloguing in publication

Baird, Elizabeth, 1939-
The Complete Canadian Living Baking Book : The Essentials of Home Baking
Includes index.
ISBN 978-0-9809924-2-7
1. Pastry. 2. Baking. I. Canadian Living Test Kitchen. II. Canadian Living. III. Title.

TX763.B34 2008   641.8'65   C2008-941319-9

Project editor: Christina Anson Mine
Copy editor: Karen Campbell-Sheviak
Inputters: Austen Gilliland, Miriam Osborne, James Doyle
Indexer: Gillian Watts
Art direction and cover design: Michael Erb
Designer: Roy Gaiot
Production coordinator: Erin Poetschke

Printed in Canada
© Transcontinental Books, 2008
Legal deposit – 3rd quarter 2008
3rd print, February 2012
National Library of Quebec
National Library of Canada
ISBN 978-0-9809924-2-7

We acknowledge the financial support of our publishing activity by the Government of Canada through the BPDIP program of the Department of Canadian Heritage, as well as by the Government of Quebec through the SODEC program Aide à la promotion.

For information on special rates for corporate libraries and wholesale purchases, please call 1-866-800-2500.

Canadian Living

THE COMPLETE CANADIAN LIVING BAKING BOOK

BY ELIZABETH BAIRD & THE CANADIAN LIVING TEST KITCHEN

Transcontinental Books

Home-Baked Is Always Better

❯ Sometimes you have to stand back to see the obvious: Canadians are the most skilled and talented home bakers. It's true, French patisseries and *boulangeries* are world famous, and professional bakers from Denmark, Austria and Portugal, just to name a few countries, create extraordinary baked goods. But where do the inhabitants of these countries go when it's time to welcome guests or celebrate birthdays? To the bake shop. Canadians, on the other hand, are more likely to head to the fridge for eggs and a pound of butter, check the cupboard for chocolate and nuts, and bake a cake – a good-looking, fine-tasting cake. Or a pan of squares, or a batch of cookies, or a flaky fruit pie….

This comfort and ease we have with baking must have something to do with an important collective rite of passage. No, not the learning-to-skate one. Rather, the making-of-cookies-with-a-caring-adult one. This ritual includes everything required to imprint the joy of baking on young minds: shared love; techniques that are easy for little ones; the sensuality of delicious aromas, sticky hands and that first sweet taste; and, best of all, success. No wonder so many of us got hooked as kids and have taken every opportunity since to hone our skills. Divvying up the goods with the people we love (or hoarding a few treats for ourselves) just adds to the bliss.

Then think of the school teams that sport spiffy new uniforms, clubs that enjoy field trips, and the religious and community institutions that can repair roofs and replace worn carpets, all because of a significant offshoot of Canadians' baking prowess: the bake sale. And don't forget the holiday event that unites friends, family, colleagues and neighbours: the cookie exchange.

It's so personally satisfying to measure out, mix and transform raw ingredients into something splendid, leaving your own stamp on its success. To feed that pleasure, The Canadian Living Test Kitchen has built on our collective baking passion and heritage. It's our day's work to create recipes for Canadian kitchens, using ingredients you will find in your local grocery store. You can count on us to deliver the goods via our tested-till-perfect recipes, and we guarantee that you will have a good time getting there.

As Canadians, we bake to support our communities, to share, for our own pleasure and sense of accomplishment, to celebrate joyous occasions, to comfort when life's tough times need smoothing, and to tickle the fancy of our favourite people. Canadians are hardwired to bake. There's no use resisting. It's time to roll up your sleeves, head into the kitchen and get your hands on some dough!

Elizabeth Baird

An Introduction to Baking

Cookies, Bars & Squares

Cakes

Pies & Pastries

Yeast Breads

Quick Breads

Spoon Desserts

Sauces & Garnishes

Secrets of Great Baking from The Canadian Living Test Kitchen

❯ Buy the best ingredients possible: the freshest butter, eggs, nuts, spices, yeast, baking powder and baking soda; the plumpest raisins; the finest chocolate; and real vanilla.

❯ Invest in good baking equipment. Start with the basics – a heavy rimless baking sheet if you like making cookies, for example – and add only the highest-quality equipment, one piece at a time, as you go along. Resist the temptation to buy sets, especially if the price is too good to be true. Avoid nonstick, except for fancy Bundt pans.

❯ Read the recipes all the way through before you start. This will give you a clear idea of the time, ingredients and equipment you need.

❯ Before you begin, get out all the equipment and ingredients you need for the recipe. If you wisely prep and measure out the ingredients before you start to mix, you are less likely to forget one. Chill the ingredients that need to be cold and set the ones that should be at room temperature out on the counter.

❯ Prepare the pans first. Whether you're lining them with parchment paper or greasing the sides, or simply setting them out before you mix, you'll ensure that they're ready when you are.

❯ Set the oven rack to the right position, according to the recipe.

❯ Allow about 10 minutes for the oven to preheat before baking.

❯ Keep a pencil and pad handy so you can make notes and clip them to the recipe. The next time you use it, you can build on your observations and experience.

The Baker's Pantry and Fridge

❯ Baked goods are only as fresh as the ingredients that go into them. Here's everything you need to know about ingredients, from buying to storing to testing whether they're at their peak.

❯ Baking Powder

In Canada, baking powder is continuous action. That means it creates bubbles and lightness from the moment liquid touches it and continues bubbling when exposed to heat in the oven. A word of advice: with such quick leavening action, get your cakes and quick breads into the oven as soon as they are in their pans.

To leaven, count on 1 to 1¼ tsp (5 to 6 mL) baking powder for each 1 cup (250 mL) flour. But be careful: increasing the amount of baking powder does not make a lighter, higher product. Quite the contrary: excessive baking powder produces large bubbles that rise to the surface, where they break, depriving the recipe of their leavening powder. You'll end up with a stodgy, straight-to-the-trash result.

If you're a frequent baker, buying a large container of baking powder is a good idea. If not, choose a smaller container or envelopes. Stored in a cool, dark, dry spot, baking powder will last for two years from the date of manufacture. But once it's opened, it loses its strength after about six months. To test for freshness, stir 1 tsp (5 mL) baking powder into 1 cup (250 mL) hot water; if the mixture bubbles, the baking powder is active. If not, get a fresh package, making sure that the best-before date gives you plenty of leeway to suit your baking style.

Baking Soda

This leavener is often used when a recipe calls for acidic ingredients, such as buttermilk and chocolate. It begins leavening as soon as wet and dry ingredients meet. Like baking powder, baking soda requires you to get quick breads into pans and into the oven ASAP.

An open box of baking soda stored in a cool, dark, dry spot can last for up to one year. To test for effectiveness, add ¼ tsp (1 mL) baking soda to 2 tsp (10 mL) white vinegar. If the mixture foams on contact, it is active. If not, it's time for a new box.

Butter

The Canadian Living Test Kitchen generally uses regular salted butter in baking, except where it would give a noticeably salty result, such as in a buttercream icing. However, many bakers prefer unsalted butter. If you do, compensate for the missing salt, adding a small pinch per each 1 cup (250 mL) butter.

Chocolate

The different types of chocolate depend on the proportions of chocolate liquor, cocoa butter and other ingredients, such as sugar. The Canadian Living Test Kitchen creates and tests chocolate recipes using popular Canadian brands. Fair Trade chocolate, grown and processed in a way that is beneficial to communities, is increasingly available and offers consumers good choices. Here are the types of chocolate you'll use frequently for baking.

- **Unsweetened chocolate:** Also called baking chocolate, this is pure, unsweetened chocolate liquor cooled and moulded into blocks. It is bitter and cannot be used interchangeably with semisweet or bittersweet chocolate.

- **Bittersweet and semisweet chocolate:** These chocolates contain pure chocolate liquor, cocoa butter, sugar, vanilla and lecithin. In baking, both types are interchangeable, although the bittersweet has a more pronounced chocolate flavour. Some quality brands now offer bittersweet chocolate with varying amounts of cocoa solids. A higher percentage is not always better. The Test Kitchen prefers baking with bittersweet chocolate in the 70 per cent range.

- **Sweet chocolate:** This contains the same ingredients as semisweet but has a higher sugar content.

- **Milk chocolate:** This chocolate has dry or concentrated milk added to the same base as semisweet, bittersweet and sweet chocolate. It's popular to eat out of hand.

- **White chocolate:** This type does not actually contain any chocolate liquor, just cocoa butter. Good-quality white chocolate is ivory- or cream-coloured, unlike white chocolate confectionery coating, which contains vegetable fats instead of cocoa butter and is starker white.

- **Cocoa powder:** Made of ground, partially defatted cocoa solids, cocoa powder comes in two types: natural (usually labelled unsweetened cocoa powder and used with baking soda) and Dutch-process, which has been treated to neutralize its natural acidity and is generally used with baking powder. Cocoa should not be replaced with sweetened or hot chocolate powders.

- **Storage:** Wrap chocolate and store in a cool, dry place, making sure to use it within two years. When storage temperatures are too warm, the cocoa butter in chocolate separates from the solids, leaving a harmless white discolouration, called bloom, on the surface.

Eggs

Canadian Living recipes use large eggs.

❯ Flour

The Canadian Living Test Kitchen tests all of its recipes using widely available, standard brands of flour to ensure that home bakers get the same results in their kitchens that we get in ours. Here are the most common types you'll need in your kitchen.

• **All-purpose flour:** A combination of milled hard and soft wheat that is bleached, **regular all-purpose** flour requires no sifting before measuring. It works in most baking recipes, from biscuits to cookies to cakes to pies. There are two other types of all-purpose flour: an **unbleached** version, which is cream-coloured and becoming more available and popular, and a **whole wheat** version. Both can be used cup for cup in place of regular all-purpose flour and require no sifting before measuring.

• **Bread flours:** For yeast breads and buns, there are hard wheat flours that may contain increased gluten. They come in versions including white, multigrain and whole wheat. They require no sifting and can be replaced, cup for cup, by all-purpose flours.

• **Cake-and-pastry flour:** Recipes for cakes and pastry often call for – you guessed it – cake-and-pastry flour, which is milled from softer wheat. Always sift this type of flour before measuring. If a recipe calls for all-purpose flour, you can substitute 1 cup (250 mL) plus 2 tbsp (25 mL) cake-and-pastry flour for each 1 cup (250 mL) all-purpose flour. If a recipe calls for cake-and-pastry flour, you can substitute 1 cup (250 mL) minus 2 tbsp (25 mL) regular or unbleached all-purpose flour for each 1 cup (250 mL) cake-and-pastry flour.

• **Rye flour:** This whole grain flour comes in two versions – dark and light – which you can use interchangeably, depending on the strength of flavour you're looking for.

• **Shelf life:** The shelf life for white flours is 12 months from the date of manufacture. Store them in airtight containers in a cool, dry spot. Whole grain and whole wheat flours, and those that contain added bran, have a shelf life of nine months. Store them in the freezer to keep them fresh.

Wondering where to find the date of manufacture on your bag of flour? One popular brand available across Canada has a code number stamped on the top of the bag. You only need the first few digits of it, though. Flour processed in October 2008, for example, will have 8 and 10 as the first two sets of numbers in the code.

❯ Nuts

Whenever possible, buy whole nuts or nut halves rather than chopped, which tend to be rancid (especially in the case of walnuts). The one exception is almonds; slivered and sliced almonds are reliably fresh and a real time-saver. Store nuts in the freezer for up to one year. At room temperature, their high fat content can cause them to go rancid.

❯ Spices

Ground spices lose their flavour after about six months. To prolong their oomph, store in airtight containers in a cool, dark spot (make sure you date the containers). Dedicating a drawer away from heat to spices and herbs is a good idea. If you have a spice grinder, mortar and pestle, or coffee grinder, buy whole spices to grind to order. Clean the grinder between uses to prevent spice flavours from mingling. For nutmeg, buy whole nutmegs and use a small hand grater or the fine side of a box grater.

❯ Sugar

A basic baker's pantry requires just a few sweeteners. The following are the ones you'll need for most of the recipes in this book.

• **Granulated sugar:** Snowy white regular granulated sugar is the right choice for most baking. Coarser granulated sugars (including sanding sugar used for decorating) are found at cake decorating and some bulk food stores.

• **Superfine sugar:** Finely granulated sugar, which is used in drinks and some baking recipes, is available in boxes under a variety of names including fruit, berry, ultrafine, instant-dissolving and superfine. In the U.K., this sugar is known as caster sugar.

• **Icing sugar:** This powdery granulated sugar is blended with about 3 per cent cornstarch to keep it from caking. It blends smoothly into icings and glazes of all kinds.

• **Brown sugar:** Made from a combination of white granulated sugar and molasses, this moist sugar should be enclosed in its original bag and stored in an airtight container to keep it from becoming rock-hard. In our dry houses during the winter, you may need to add a water-soaked terra-cotta disc or figure to the sugar to keep it moist and ready to use. Or cover the surface of the sugar with foil and place a moistened piece of paper towel, or a slice of fresh bread or raw apple, on top. Let soften for two to three days.

• **Specialty brown sugars:** These include Demerara and turbinado sugars, which are golden brown coarse crystal sugars often used to garnish breads or pastries or to sweeten coffee or tea. Muscovado sugar is finer than Demerara and turbinado and can be used like regular brown sugar. All of these have a pleasant molasses flavour.

❯ Vanilla

Most *Canadian Living* recipes use pure vanilla extract. It's readily available and made by percolating vanilla beans with ethyl alcohol and water. While imitation or artificial vanilla extract is usually scorned in the press, and is not a first choice for custards, it can take the heat and is often preferable in baked goods such as pound cake.

To use the real McCoy – vanilla beans – slit the bean in half lengthwise. Scrape out the seedy pulp and use in cake batters and custards. One whole bean yields the equivalent of 2 to 3 tsp (10 to 15 mL) vanilla extract. The pod can be added to custards as well, but remove it before serving. You can recycle the pod by adding it to a canister of granulated sugar or to a fruit compote.

❯ Yeast

Make sure to buy the freshest yeast you can find, with a far-away expiry date, to ensure the highest-rising breads.

• **Active dry yeast:** We use this tried-and-true yeast most frequently in the Test Kitchen. It is easy to find and requires two rises. To activate, combine a bit of sugar with water that's just a tad warmer than lukewarm (100°F to 110°F/38°C to 43°C); sprinkle yeast over water and let stand for 10 minutes. If it froths and bubbles, it's ready to use.

• **Quick-rising (instant) dry yeast:** The smaller granules of this yeast are designed to be incorporated into the dry ingredients and activated by adding warmer water, about 120°F to 130°F (49°C to 54°C). It can be used interchangeably with both active dry and bread machine yeast.

• **Bread machine yeast:** Similar to quick-rising (instant) dry yeast, this type is finely granulated and has ascorbic acid added to increase the volume of the finished bread. Use interchangeably with quick-rising yeast, adding it directly to dry ingredients.

• **Handling and storage:** Use a dry measuring spoon when working with yeast. Store unopened packages in a cool, dry spot. Once opened, enclose the yeast in its original packaging in an airtight container and store at the back of the refrigerator, where the temperature is constant. Use within three to four months, before the expiry date.

The Baker's Basic Equipment

❯ When outfitting your kitchen for baking, these are the tools you can't do without. For equipment you need for a specific category of baked goods, such as cookies, cakes, pies and so on, see the introduction to that particular chapter.

- Three or more stainless-steel bowls, from small to large
- Measuring cups: nesting dry measures in ¼-cup (50 mL), ⅓-cup (75 mL), ½-cup (125 mL) and 1-cup (250 mL) capacities; and liquid measures in 1-cup (250 mL), 2-cup (500 mL), 4-cup (1 L) and 8-cup (2 L) capacities
- Measuring spoons: ¼ tsp (1 mL), ½ tsp (2 mL), 1 tsp (5 mL) and 1 tbsp (15 mL)
- Knives: chef's, paring and serrated with long blade
- Oven thermometer
- Two metal cooling racks
- Heatproof silicone (rubber) spatulas
- Wooden spoons (reserve for sweet baking and keep away from savoury, spicy dishes)
- Parchment paper, waxed paper, heavy-duty aluminum foil and microwaveable plastic wrap
- Large wooden cutting board
- Box grater and/or rasp
- Citrus juicer (reamer)
- Kitchen shears
- Ruler
- Two natural-bristle pastry brushes, each about 1 inch (2.5 cm) wide
- Flexible lifter or wide spatula
- Offset metal spatulas: 1 large and 1 small
- Sieve: 1 small with fine mesh, 1 medium with medium-fine mesh
- Pastry blender
- Two stainless-steel sauce whisks, each 8 inches (20 cm) long
- One small stainless-steel sauce whisk, about 4 inches (10 cm) long
- Long metal spoon
- Piping bag with selection of tips, including plain fine tip for writing or outlining and larger plain and star tips for whipped cream and profiteroles
- Oven mitts or pot holders
- Double boiler, or shallow heatproof bowl wide enough to rest on rim of saucepan and grip with oven-mitt-covered hand
- Hand mixer
- Food processor or food mill

Measuring for Success

❯ For dry or thick ingredients, always use dry measuring cups, or dry measures. These nesting metal or plastic cups usually come in ¼-cup (50 mL), ⅓-cup (75 mL), ½-cup (125 mL) and 1-cup (250 mL) capacities.

● **All-purpose and bread flours, granulated sugars, icing sugar and cocoa powder:** Working over canister or container, lightly spoon dry ingredients into dry measure until heaping. Push straight edge of metal spatula or knife across top to level, letting excess fall back into canister. Do not pack down or tap on counter to level.

● **Cake-and-pastry flour:** Sift flour before filling dry measure to overflowing; level with metal spatula or straight edge of knife.

● **Brown sugar:** Pack into dry measure until level with top of cup and firm enough that sugar holds its shape when turned out.

● **Baking powder, baking soda, salt and spices:** Use standard measuring spoon. Fill to top; level with flat edge of knife. For a pinch, use what you can hold between tips of thumb and index finger, or about $\frac{1}{16}$ tsp (0.25 mL).

• **Butter:** Use butter measuring guide or markings on foil wrapper. Or use this guide: 1 lb (454 g) butter is 2 cups (500 mL). Cut butter in half for 1 cups (250 mL), quarters for $\frac{1}{2}$ cups (125 mL), sixths for $\frac{1}{3}$ cups (75 mL), or eighths for $\frac{1}{4}$ cups (50 mL).

• **Yogurt, sour cream, ricotta, cottage cheese and often cream cheese:** Spoon into dry measure just until overflowing; level with knife, returning any excess to container.

❯ For liquid ingredients, always use liquid measuring cups, or liquid measures. These are glass or clear plastic with a spout. They range in size from 1 cup (250 mL) to 8 cups (2 L). Imperial and metric divisions are clearly marked on the measure.

• Place glass measure on work surface. Bend down so your eye is level with the marking on the cup while filling.

• For small amounts of liquids, such as vanilla, fill measuring spoon to top.

• For a dash, add about $\frac{1}{8}$ tsp (0.5 mL).

Substitutions

❯ Sometimes what you need just isn't in the cupboard or fridge. Here are some handy substitutions that just might save your baking.

• **1 tsp (5 mL) baking powder =** $\frac{1}{2}$ tsp (2 mL) cream of tartar plus $\frac{1}{4}$ tsp (1 mL) baking soda

• **1 tsp (5 mL) cream of tartar (when beating egg whites) =** 1 tsp (5 mL) white vinegar or lemon juice

• **1 cup (250 mL) sifted cake-and-pastry flour =** 1 cup (250 mL) minus 2 tbsp (25 mL) unsifted all-purpose flour

• **1 cup (250 mL) unsifted all-purpose flour =** 1 cup (250 mL) plus 2 tbsp (25 mL) sifted cake-and-pastry flour

• **1 cup (250 mL) self-rising flour =** 1 cup (250 mL) all-purpose flour plus 1 tsp (5 mL) baking powder plus $\frac{1}{4}$ tsp (1 mL) salt

• **1 egg (in muffins or quick breads) =** $\frac{1}{2}$ tsp (2 mL) additional baking powder plus $\frac{1}{4}$ cup (50 mL) additional liquid (use same liquid as called for in recipe)

• **1 cup (250 mL) granulated sugar =** 1 cup (250 mL) packed brown sugar

• **1 cup (250 mL) buttermilk =** 1 tbsp (15 mL) lemon juice or white vinegar plus enough whole milk to make 1 cup (250 mL); let stand for 5 minutes

• **1 cup (250 mL) plain yogurt =** 1 cup (250 mL) buttermilk

• **1 cup (250 mL) 2% or whole milk =** $\frac{1}{3}$ cup (75 mL) instant powdered milk plus 1 cup (250 mL) water OR $\frac{1}{2}$ cup (125 mL) evaporated milk plus $\frac{1}{2}$ cup (125 mL) water

• **Bittersweet chocolate =** equal amount of semisweet chocolate

Convection Ovens

❯ Equipped with a fan that keeps hot air flowing, convection ovens are a boon for cooks and bakers. We've found that, generally, they produce an evenly baked product about 25 per cent faster than a radiant heat oven.

They're great for cookies but not for some light, airy baked goods (such as meringues) or loose batters (such as for cupcakes), which can be blown out of shape by the moving air. For more information, see page 23.

Chapter 1

Cookies, Bars & Squares

Cookies are the simplest and most pleasurable introduction to baking – just ask anyone who has a passion for it. Chances are this love was born during childhood over a bowlful of cookie dough beside a patient adult.

Count on cookies to be mouth-satisfying, with a huge range of textures – tender, crisp, crunchy, chewy, soft, moist or brittle. And their mouth-watering variety is nearly infinite, thanks to a whole baking aisle of flavourings and add-ins in your supermarket.

This chapter is organized by method, starting with easy drop cookies. They're a great place for the novice to begin: they mix up in one bowl, don't require forming or rolling, and bake quickly. Yet they give all the satisfaction of a fancy baked item as they fill the kitchen with sweet aromas that forever link cookies with good times.

Second come an assortment of shaped, or hand-rolled, cookies, followed by slice-and-bake (a.k.a. refrigerator or icebox) cookies. We finish with rolled-out-and-cut cookies, which require only slightly more skill and patience. For variety, we've also included biscotti and some delicious representatives from the bar, square and brownie/blondie family.

Our recipes are representative of Canada's favourite cookies and include some international inspirations for the adventurous baker. So have fun, fill the cookie jar and make some memories – all at once.

Use the Best Ingredients

❯ Buy the best – cookies are only as good as the ingredients that you put into them.

● **Butter:** This gives cookies the best flavour. Be sure to let it come to room temperature before starting. If butter is hard and cold, here's a trick to soften it quickly: cut it into small cubes or grate on the coarsest holes of a box grater, then spread in a mixing bowl and let stand until softened. Our recipes are tested with salted butter, so use that unless otherwise noted. If you prefer unsalted, add one pinch salt per each 1 cup (250 mL) butter to compensate.

● **Salt:** Use fine salt. Coarse sea salt does not dissolve well in flour mixtures. Save it to top Soft Pretzels (recipe, page 228) or grilled food.

● **Sugar:** Should you use granulated or brown? Granulated sugar produces crisper cookies. Using brown sugar, with its molasses content, results in chewier, softer cookies. In a pinch, you can substitute one for the other.

● **Eggs:** Like butter, these need to be at room temperature. To quickly warm up fridge-cold eggs, let stand in a bowl of warm water for 10 minutes.

Easy Mixing

❯ An electric mixer makes short work of beating butter with sugar. There's no need to beat them for as much time as you would for a cake – just enough to blend into a creamy mixture. In the Test Kitchen, we like to stir in both the dry ingredients and add-ins, such as chips or nuts, with a wooden spoon. You can continue with the electric mixer at low speed for the flour mixture, but the add-ins are too lumpy and risk being crushed, so switch to a wooden spoon for those.

EQUIPMENT FOR COOKIES, BARS & SQUARES

● Shiny metal rimless baking sheets

● Straight-sided shiny metal cake pans: 8-inch (2 L) square, 9-inch (2.5 L) square and 13- x 9-inch (3.5 L)

● Rolling pin

● Cookie cutters: sets and singles

● Silicone baking mat(s)

● Ice-cream scoop (disher) with release mechanism: 1¼-inch (3 cm) for 1-tbsp (15 mL) portions, and larger sizes as desired

● Metal cookie storage tins

Drop Cookies

❯ Drop cookie dough is the softest of all types. While these doughs may have similar consistencies, they may be handled differently. For example, the recipe might call for chilling the dough. Why? The cooler the dough, the better it keeps its shape and the thicker the cookie. If you like thicker drop cookies, scoop and chill the dough before baking.

To make uniform-size cookies, scoop and level dough in a measuring spoon, using a second spoon from your cutlery drawer to push the dough onto the baking sheet. You can also use two regular spoons, or a small ice cream scoop with a release mechanism (scrape against rim of bowl to level).

Space out cookies so they can expand without touching as they bake. The usual distance is 1 to 2 inches (2.5 to 5 cm), but doughs vary in how much they spread, so check each recipe.

Shaped Cookies

❯ This dough is slightly firmer than that of drop cookies, which allows you to shape it into round, thumbprint, crescent or other forms. Piped cookies also fall under this category. The dough is often chilled before shaping, both to make it a less sticky job and to help the cookies keep their shape when baked. The recipe might also tell you to chill the shaped dough before baking.

To ensure that all cookies are as close to the same size as possible, do the same as you would for drop cookies: scoop and level the dough using a measuring spoon and a second spoon, or a small ice cream scoop. You can scoop and shape as you go or scoop all the cookies, then do the shaping.

Shaping often starts with rolling balls of dough between your palms. Keep the touch light but decisive. For some recipes, having a light dusting of flour (or cocoa powder for chocolate cookies) on your hands will keep the dough rolling and not sticking.

Slice & Bake Cookies

❯ Firmer like shaped cookie dough, slice-and-bake dough is first roughly shaped by hand. Then, with the support of waxed paper and an even, steady back-and-forth motion, it's rolled into a neat log. Be sure to measure the log – it should be the exact length or diameter called for in the recipe to ensure that the baking time works and the yield matches. To keep the log bottoms from flattening, reroll a couple of times as they chill and firm up.

Simply twist the ends of the waxed paper around the dough to store slice-and-bake logs in the refrigerator (replacing the icebox, the heritage home cooler that gave these cookies one of their aliases). You may want to freeze a stash of the logs – it's handy to have one or two on hand for fresh on-demand cookies or to give as a gift to wanna-be bakers. For short-term refrigerator storage, place logs in an airtight container; for longer-term freezer storage, overwrap logs in heavy-duty foil and enclose in an airtight container, such as a freezer bag or rigid container.

Rolled Cookies

❯ This firm dough is usually chilled, then rolled out between two sheets of waxed paper or on a lightly floured work surface. We recommend waxed paper because it keeps the cookies from absorbing additional flour and hardening. If cookie dough softens excessively in a hot kitchen, slip the waxed paper–enclosed dough onto a baking sheet and chill before continuing.

Cut the cookie shapes as close together as possible. This results in fewer scraps and less dough handling. Gathering and rerolling the scraps once is usually fine, but cookies toughen with every reroll. If the scraps are too soft to roll, flatten them into a disc and chill before continuing. Keep cookies from the first rolling separate from subsequent ones, serving the tenderest cookies to the people you love the most or want to impress with your rolling pin prowess.

To prevent cookie cutters from sticking and clogging up with dough, dip them regularly into a bowl of flour. Tap the cutter on the rim after each dip to avoid flour residue on the finished cookies. For chocolate cookies, use cocoa powder.

Transfer the cut shapes from the work surface to prepared baking sheets using a metal spatula with a thin, flexible blade.

The Big Cookie Secret: Measuring

❯ Nowhere in baking is measuring more important than with cookies. This is especially true for the flour – a little extra will turn chewy, crisp cookies into dry, tough little pucks, and too little will let cookies spread out and lose their shape. So remember, working over the canister, spoon flour into dry measuring cup until overflowing, then sweep off excess with the back of a knife to make it level with the rim. No shaking the cup, packing it down or making do with a liquid measuring cup. For more tips, see Measuring for Success, page 12.

GOLD STANDARD RECIPE

Chocolate Chip Cookies

Here's one fine chocolate chip cookie recipe with lots of variations to ensure that you never tire of this über-popular treat.

1 cup	butter	250 mL	1 tsp	baking soda	5 mL
1 cup	packed brown sugar	250 mL	½ tsp	salt	2 mL
½ cup	granulated sugar	125 mL	2 cups	semisweet chocolate chips	500 mL
2	eggs	2	1 cup	chopped walnut halves or pecans	250 mL
1 tbsp	vanilla	15 mL			
2⅓ cups	all-purpose flour	575 mL			

ICE-CREAM SANDWICH COOKIES

❯ Sandwich a scoop of ice cream between two favourite drop or rolled cookies and press gently to push ice cream to edges. If desired, roll edges in sprinkles or mini coloured chocolate chips. For make-ahead occasions, wrap each sandwich in plastic wrap, then enclose in airtight container and freeze for up to 1 week.

Line 2 rimless baking sheets with parchment paper or grease; set aside.

In bowl, beat together butter and brown and granulated sugars until fluffy. Beat in eggs, 1 at a time; beat in vanilla. In separate bowl, whisk together flour, baking soda and salt; stir into butter mixture. Stir in chocolate chips and walnuts.

Drop by rounded tablespoonfuls (15 mL), about 2 inches (5 cm) apart, onto prepared baking sheets. With fork, flatten to ½-inch (1 cm) thickness. Bake in top and bottom thirds of 375°F (190°C) oven, rotating and switching pans halfway through, until edges are golden and centres are still slightly underbaked, 8 to 9 minutes. Let cool on pans on racks for 5 minutes. Transfer to racks; let cool. **(Make-ahead: Layer between waxed paper in airtight container and store at room temperature for up to 5 days or freeze for up to 2 weeks.)**

Makes about 48 cookies. | PER COOKIE: about 132 cal, 1 g pro, 8 g total fat (3 g sat. fat), 15 g carb, 1 g fibre, 14 mg chol, 72 mg sodium. % RDI: 1% calcium, 4% iron, 2% vit A, 4% folate.

VARIATIONS

Reverse Chocolate Chip Cookies: Substitute cocoa powder for ⅓ cup (75 mL) of the flour, sifting with flour before adding to dough; use white chocolate chips or 6 oz (175 g) white chocolate, chopped, instead of semisweet chocolate chips. Bake as directed.

Sour Cherry Chocolate Chunk Cookies: Replace chocolate chips and walnuts with 6 oz (175 g) bittersweet chocolate, chopped, and ¾ cup (175 mL) dried sour cherries. Bake as directed.

Hazelnut Chocolate Chip Bars: Reduce flour to 2 cups (500 mL). Replace chocolate chips and walnuts with 1½ cups (375 mL) each jumbo chocolate chips and hazelnuts, toasted, skinned and chopped. Chill dough for 15 minutes. Press evenly into parchment paper–lined 15- x 10-inch (40 x 25 cm) rimmed baking sheet; bake until just firm to touch in centre, 18 to 20 minutes. Cut into bars while still warm.

Dark and Dangerous Triple Chocolate Cookies

These intensely chocolaty cookies are just the thing when you want a chocolate fix. Team them up with your beverage of choice: milk, tea, chai or cappuccino.

1 cup	butter	250 mL	½ cup	cocoa powder	125 mL
1 cup	granulated sugar	250 mL	1 tsp	baking soda	5 mL
½ cup	packed brown sugar	125 mL	¼ tsp	salt	1 mL
2	eggs	2	1 cup	semisweet chocolate chips	250 mL
1 tsp	vanilla	5 mL	1 cup	white chocolate or milk chocolate chips	250 mL
2 cups	all-purpose flour	500 mL			

↝ Line 2 rimless baking sheets with parchment paper or grease; set aside.

↝ In large bowl, beat together butter and granulated and brown sugars until fluffy. Beat in eggs, 1 at a time; beat in vanilla. In separate bowl, sift or whisk together flour, cocoa, baking soda and salt. Stir into butter mixture in 2 additions. Stir in semisweet and white chocolate chips.

↝ Drop by heaping tablespoonfuls (15 mL), about 2 inches (5 cm) apart, onto prepared baking sheets.

↝ Bake in top and bottom thirds of 350°F (180°C) oven, rotating and switching pans halfway through, until firm to the touch and no longer glossy, about 12 minutes. Transfer to racks; let cool. (Make-ahead: Layer between waxed paper in airtight container and store at room temperature for up to 5 days or freeze for up to 2 weeks.)

Makes about 48 cookies. | PER COOKIE: about 120 cal, 1 g pro, 6 g total fat (4 g sat. fat), 15 g carb, 1 g fibre, 21 mg chol, 82 mg sodium. % RDI: 1% calcium, 4% iron, 4% vit A, 4% folate.

VARIATION

Apricot Pecan White Chocolate Cookies: Instead of semisweet chocolate chips, add 1 cup (250 mL) each chopped pecans and dried apricots.

Candied Ginger and White Chocolate Hermits

The humble look of these easy drop cookies belies their luscious flavour combination of ginger, white chocolate and dried apricots.

SCOOP-AND-FREEZE DROP COOKIES

❯ Make your favourite drop cookie dough and chill until slightly firm. Scoop amounts according to recipe onto waxed paper–lined baking sheets. Freeze until firm; layer between waxed paper in airtight container. Freeze for up to 1 month. To bake from frozen, follow recipe, increasing baking time by up to 2 minutes, if necessary, unless longer time is specified in recipe.

1 cup	butter, softened	250 mL	½ tsp	baking soda	2 mL
⅔ cup	packed brown sugar	150 mL	½ tsp	each ground nutmeg and allspice	2 mL
½ cup	granulated sugar	125 mL	1 cup	finely chopped crystallized ginger	250 mL
2	eggs	2			
2¼ cups	all-purpose flour	550 mL	6 oz	white chocolate, chopped	175 g
1 tsp	baking powder	5 mL			
¾ tsp	ground ginger	4 mL	1 cup	chopped dried apricots	250 mL

❧ Line 2 rimless baking sheets with parchment paper or grease; set aside.

❧ In large bowl, beat together butter and brown and granulated sugars until fluffy; beat in eggs, 1 at a time. In separate bowl, whisk together flour, baking powder, ground ginger, baking soda, nutmeg and allspice; stir into butter mixture in 2 additions. Stir in chopped ginger, white chocolate and apricots.

❧ Drop by level tablespoonfuls (15 mL), 2 inches (5 cm) apart, onto prepared baking sheets. **(Make-ahead: Freeze on sheets. Layer between waxed paper in airtight container and freeze for up to 1 month. Bake frozen.)**

❧ Bake in top and bottom thirds of 350°F (180°C) oven, rotating and switching pans halfway through, until bottoms are golden, 10 to 12 minutes. (Or bake frozen in 325°F/160°C oven for 20 minutes.) Let cool on pans on racks for 5 minutes. Transfer to racks; let cool. **(Make-ahead: Layer between waxed paper in airtight container and store at room temperature for up to 5 days or freeze for up to 1 month.)**

Makes about 72 cookies. | PER COOKIE: about 80 cal, 1 g pro, 4 g total fat (2 g sat. fat), 11 g carb, trace fibre, 9 mg chol, 32 mg sodium. % RDI: 2% calcium, 6% iron, 3% vit A, 2% vit C, 2% folate.

VARIATION

Pecan Cherry Chocolate Hermits: Omit crystallized ginger, white chocolate and apricots. Add 1¼ cups (300 mL) each toasted chopped pecans, dried cherries and chocolate chips.

Anzac Bickies

Chef James Smith, Australian to the core, introduced this simple crisp "biscuit" to *Canadian Living* readers. The bickies have few ingredients, boast a long shelf life and are loved by Australians all over the world.

1 cup	all-purpose flour	250 mL	1 cup	packed brown sugar	250 mL
1 cup	large-flake rolled oats	250 mL	½ cup	butter	125 mL
1 cup	unsweetened desiccated coconut	250 mL	3 tbsp	Lyle's golden syrup	50 mL

- Line rimless baking sheet with parchment paper or grease; set aside.
- In large bowl, whisk together flour, oats, coconut and brown sugar; set aside.
- In saucepan, heat together butter, syrup and 2 tbsp (25 mL) water over medium-low heat until butter is melted; stir into dry ingredients.
- Drop by rounded tablespoonfuls (15 mL), 2 inches (5 cm) apart, onto prepared baking sheet.
- Bake in centre of 350°F (180°C) oven until light golden on bottoms, about 15 minutes. Let cool on pan on rack for 2 minutes. Transfer to rack; let cool. (**Make-ahead: Layer between waxed paper in airtight container and store at room temperature for up to 1 week or freeze for up to 1 month.**)

Makes about 24 cookies. | PER COOKIE: about 129 cal, 1 g pro, 5 g total fat (4 g sat. fat), 19 g carb, 1 g fibre, 12 mg chol, 52 mg sodium. % RDI: 1% calcium, 5% iron, 4% vit A, 4% folate.

OVEN RACK PLACEMENT

❯ What type of oven you have determines the optimal rack placement during baking.

● **Regular, a.k.a. radiant or thermal heat, ovens:** The optimum position for cookies is on the centre rack. This allows good air circulation around the cookies and devotes all the heat to that pan. However, when baking a big batch or two, you can speed up the operation by using two baking sheets at a time, positioning them on the racks just above and below the centre position. Halfway through the suggested baking time, switch and rotate pans.

● **True convection ovens:** These have a third element and a fan that circulates the hot air. Reduce the temperature by 25°F (13°C) and use up to three racks simultaneously, spacing them evenly apart. Check cookies a few minutes before the time suggested in the recipe. Make a note of the final baking time for future reference.

Farmland Flax Cookies

When we went looking for a back-to-school lunch box treat, Linda Braun, executive director of the Saskatchewan Flax Development Commission, obliged us with this recipe. Originally a winning entry from chef B. Gerwing in a cooking contest held by the Association of Saskatchewan Home Economists, these cookies have become the signature cookie of the commission.

COOLING COOKIES

Many cookies need a few minutes to cool down and firm up on the baking sheet before you transfer them to the cooling rack. Use a spatula with a thin, flexible blade to make the transfer.

½ cup	butter, softened	125 mL	1 cup	all-purpose flour	250 mL
½ cup	packed brown sugar	125 mL	¾ cup	quick-cooking rolled oats	175 mL
⅓ cup	granulated sugar	75 mL			
1	egg	1	⅔ cup	flaxseeds	150 mL
½ tsp	vanilla	2 mL	1 tsp	baking soda	5 mL

❧ Line 2 rimless baking sheets with parchment paper or grease; set aside.

❧ In bowl, beat together butter and brown and granulated sugars until fluffy; beat in egg and vanilla. In separate bowl, whisk together flour, oats, flaxseeds and baking soda; stir into butter mixture to make soft dough.

❧ Drop by level tablespoonfuls (15 mL), 2 inches (5 cm) apart, on prepared baking sheets. Bake in top and bottom thirds of 350°F (180°C) oven, rotating and switching pans halfway through, until golden, about 12 minutes. Let cool on pans on racks for 2 minutes. Transfer to racks; let cool. **(Make-ahead: Layer between waxed paper in airtight container and store at room temperature for up to 5 days or freeze for up to 1 month.)**

Makes about 40 cookies. | PER COOKIE: about 69 cal, 1 g pro, 3 g total fat (2 g sat. fat), 9 g carb, 1 g fibre, 11 mg chol, 57 mg sodium. % RDI: 1% calcium, 4% iron, 2% vit A, 5% folate.

Tropical Coconut Macaroons

This ultimate macaroon is chewy and dense, with a heavenly combo of coconut and tropical fruit. Drizzle a little melted dark chocolate over the cooled cookies if you like the contrast.

THE CHOCOLATE DRIZZLE

❯ Arrange cookies, such as macaroons or biscotti, close together in a single layer on baking sheet. Melt enough chocolate to come about 1 inch (2.5 cm) up side of small bowl. Holding bowl close to cookies, dip tines of dinner fork into chocolate; lift and drizzle back and forth over cookies. Let cool until firm before packing. Store in a cool spot to keep chocolate drizzle from melting.

⅔ cup	sweetened condensed milk	150 mL	2½ cups	sweetened shredded or flaked coconut	625 mL
1	egg white	1	½ cup	each slivered candied pineapple and mango or papaya	125 mL
Pinch	salt	Pinch			

↝ Line 2 rimless baking sheets with parchment paper or grease; set aside.

↝ In bowl, whisk together condensed milk, egg white and salt. Add coconut, pineapple and mango; stir to coat evenly.

↝ Drop by rounded teaspoonfuls (5 mL) onto prepared baking sheets. Bake, 1 sheet at a time, in centre of 325°F (160°C) oven until golden and no longer sticky, 15 to 20 minutes. Let cool on pan on rack for 5 minutes. Transfer to rack; let cool. **(Make-ahead: Layer between waxed paper in airtight container; store for up to 5 days or freeze for up to 1 month.)**

Makes about 50 cookies. | PER COOKIE: about 55 cal, 1 g pro, 3 g total fat (3 g sat. fat), 6 g carb, trace fibre, 1 mg chol, 8 mg sodium. % RDI: 1% calcium, 1% iron, 3% vit C.

VARIATIONS

Ginger Coconut Macaroons: Add ¼ cup (50 mL) chopped crystallized ginger to batter.

Tropical Coconut Macaroons with White Chocolate: Dip macaroons into melted white chocolate to coat bottom or half of each.

Brazil Nut Snaps

This classy cookie dresses up ice cream, sorbets and macerated fruit. Almonds, hazelnuts, macadamia nuts or pecans are fine alternatives to the Brazil nuts.

½ cup	butter	125 mL	1 tsp	ground ginger	5 mL
½ cup	packed brown sugar	125 mL	Pinch	salt	Pinch
½ cup	corn syrup	125 mL	1 cup	all-purpose flour	250 mL
1 tsp	each lemon juice and vanilla	5 mL	½ cup	finely chopped Brazil nuts	125 mL

↝ Line 2 rimless baking sheets with parchment paper; set aside.

↝ In saucepan, melt butter, brown sugar, corn syrup, lemon juice and vanilla, stirring until sugar is dissolved. Remove from heat. Stir in ginger and salt, then flour and nuts.

❧ Drop by level teaspoonfuls (5 mL), about 6 at a time and 3 inches (8 cm) apart, onto prepared baking sheets. Round batter with tip of spoon. Wipe paper between batches.

❧ Bake, 1 sheet at a time, in centre of 325°F (160°C) oven until caramel brown, 8 minutes. Let cool on pans for 5 minutes. Transfer to racks; let cool. (**Make-ahead: Layer between waxed paper in airtight container and store at room temperature for up to 1 week or freeze for up to 2 weeks.**)

Makes about 80 cookies. | PER COOKIE: about 32 cal, trace pro, 2 g total fat (1 g sat. fat), 4 g carb, 0 g fibre, 4 mg chol, 15 mg sodium. % RDI: 1% iron, 1% vit A, 1% folate.

Corkscrew Tuiles

The tuiles are hot and pliable when they come out of the oven and, if you work quickly, they are easy to shape. Use two wooden spoons so one tuile cools while you shape another. If they begin to harden before shaping, return the pan to the oven briefly to soften.

1	egg white	1	2 tbsp	butter, melted	25 mL
⅓ cup	all-purpose flour	75 mL	1 tsp	water	5 mL
¼ cup	granulated sugar	50 mL	½ tsp	vanilla	2 mL

❧ Line 2 rimless baking sheets with silicone baking mats; set aside.

❧ In large bowl, whisk together egg white, flour, sugar, butter, water and vanilla just until blended. Refrigerate until firm, about 15 minutes.

❧ Transfer batter to piping bag fitted with ¼-inch (5 mm) plain tip. Pipe four 8-inch (20 cm) long lines of batter, 2 inches (5 cm) apart, onto each baking sheet.

❧ Bake, 1 sheet at a time, in centre of 350°F (180°C) oven until edges are just beginning to brown, about 10 minutes.

❧ Remove from oven. While still hot, carefully wrap hot tuile around handle of wooden spoon into corkscrew shape. Let stand until slightly hardened and set, about 30 seconds. Gently slide off spoon onto rack; let cool. (**Make-ahead: Store in airtight container at room temperature for up to 5 days.**)

Makes about 14 cookies. | PER COOKIE: about 40 cal, 1 g pro, 2 g total fat (1 g sat. fat), 6 g carb, 0 g fibre, 4 mg chol, 15 mg sodium. % RDI: 1% iron, 1% vit A, 3% folate.

VARIATION

Almond Tuiles: Reduce flour to 3 tbsp (50 mL). Do not refrigerate batter. Spoon by level teaspoonfuls (5 mL) onto prepared baking sheets. Using offset spatula, spread each out into 3-inch (8 cm) circle. Using ¾ cup (175 mL) sliced almonds, sprinkle each round with a few almonds. Reduce baking time to 8 minutes. Shape over wine bottle or leave flat.

Crisscross Peanut Butter Cookies

There's something about the delicious aroma of freshly baked peanut butter cookies that lingers in our memories long after the last cookie has disappeared. Instead of plain peanuts, you can use chopped honey-glazed peanuts.

TOASTING NUTS, SEEDS AND COCONUT

> SMALL AMOUNTS:
Warm dry skillet over medium heat; toast nuts, seeds or coconut, swirling pan regularly to brown evenly.

> LARGER AMOUNTS FOR COOKIE OR CAKE BAKING: Preheat toaster oven or regular oven to 350°F (180°C). Spread nuts, seeds or coconut evenly on rimmed baking sheet (or in metal cake pan for smaller amount). Bake, stirring occasionally to prevent overbrowning at edges, for 3 to 4 minutes for seeds, 6 to 8 minutes for chopped nuts, or 10 minutes for larger whole or halved nuts. Remove toasted items from oven and spread on separate, cool baking sheet to stop browning; let cool.

½ cup	butter, softened	125 mL	½ tsp	vanilla	2 mL
½ cup	granulated sugar	125 mL	1½ cups	all-purpose flour	375 mL
½ cup	packed brown sugar	125 mL	½ tsp	salt	2 mL
1	egg	1	½ tsp	baking soda	2 mL
1 cup	smooth peanut butter	250 mL	1 cup	unsalted peanuts, coarsely chopped	250 mL

Line 2 rimless baking sheets with parchment paper or grease; set aside.

In large bowl, beat together butter and granulated and brown sugars until fluffy; beat in egg, peanut butter and vanilla. In separate bowl, whisk together flour, salt and baking soda; stir into peanut butter mixture in 3 additions. Stir in peanuts.

Drop by level tablespoonfuls (15 mL), 2 inches (5 cm) apart, onto prepared baking sheets; flatten in crisscross pattern with fork, dipping into flour if necessary to prevent sticking. Bake in top and bottom thirds of 375°F (190°C) oven, rotating and switching pans halfway through, until light golden brown, about 10 minutes. Transfer to racks; let cool. (**Make-ahead: Layer between waxed paper in airtight container and store at room temperature for up to 4 days or freeze for up to 1 month.**)

Makes about 42 cookies. | PER COOKIE: about 111 cal, 3 g pro, 7 g total fat (2 g sat. fat), 10 g carb, 1 g fibre, 10 mg chol, 89 mg sodium. % RDI: 1% calcium, 3% iron, 2% vit A, 8% folate.

Mostaccioli

If you've never made these spiced chocolate cookies, put it off no longer. They are from web food editor Christine Picheca, who describes them as incredibly in demand when Canadians of Italian heritage get together to fête a bride-to-be.

¼ cup	unsalted butter	50 mL		⅓ cup	milk	75 mL
½ cup	granulated sugar	125 mL		1 cup	semisweet chocolate chips	250 mL
1	egg	1		⅓ cup	chopped walnut halves	75 mL
1¼ cups	all-purpose flour	300 mL		**GLAZE:**		
¼ cup	cocoa powder	50 mL		1¼ cups	icing sugar	300 mL
1 tsp	cinnamon	5 mL		¼ cup	brewed coffee	50 mL
½ tsp	each baking powder and baking soda	2 mL		½ tsp	vanilla	2 mL
¼ tsp	each ground cloves and salt	1 mL				

❧ Line 2 rimless baking sheets with parchment paper or grease; set aside.

❧ In bowl, beat butter with granulated sugar until light and fluffy; beat in egg. In separate bowl, sift together flour, cocoa, cinnamon, baking powder, baking soda, cloves and salt; sift again. Add to butter mixture alternately with milk, making 2 additions of each and scraping down bowl between additions.

❧ Stir in chocolate chips and chopped walnuts. Cover and refrigerate until firm, about 2 hours.

❧ Roll by rounded tablespoonfuls (15 mL) into 1-inch (2.5 cm) balls. Place, 2 inches (5 cm) apart, on prepared baking sheets. Bake in top and bottom thirds of 350°F (180°C) oven, rotating and switching pans halfway through, until tops begin to crack, about 12 minutes. Transfer to racks; let cool.

❧ GLAZE: Place rack on baking sheet. In bowl, whisk together sugar, coffee and vanilla; spoon 1 tsp (5 mL) onto each cookie. Let stand until set. (Make-ahead: Layer between waxed paper in airtight container and store at room temperature for up to 5 days or freeze for up to 2 weeks.)

Makes about 34 cookies. | PER COOKIE: about 95 cal, 1 g pro, 4 g total fat (2 g sat. fat), 15 g carb, 1 g fibre, 9 mg chol, 43 mg sodium. % RDI: 1% calcium, 4% iron, 2% vit A, 6% folate.

BIG-BATCH COOKIE PREP

❯ When a big baking project is on the horizon, get a head start by measuring out dry ingredients and combining them where suitable; e.g., whisking together dry ingredients (flour, leavening and spices), combining add-ins and measuring out sugar. Store in separate airtight containers with the recipe until it's time to soften the butter, let the eggs come to room temperature and bake.

Gluten-Free Chocolate Glitter Cookies

These satisfy both people on special diets and anybody who enjoys a simply superb cookie. For another scrumptious gluten-free cookie, try Basler Brunsli (recipe, page 57).

6 oz	bittersweet chocolate, chopped	175 g
3 tbsp	butter	50 mL
2	eggs	2
¼ cup	granulated sugar	50 mL

¼ cup	liquid honey	50 mL
2 cups	ground almonds	500 mL
Pinch	salt	Pinch
¼ cup	coarse sugar	50 mL

❧ Line 2 rimless baking sheets with parchment paper or grease; set aside.

❧ In heatproof bowl over saucepan of hot (not boiling) water, melt chocolate with butter, stirring occasionally. Let cool to room temperature.

❧ In bowl, beat together eggs, granulated sugar and honey until foamy; fold in chocolate. In separate bowl, whisk almonds with salt; fold into chocolate mixture. Cover and refrigerate until firm, about 1 hour. **(Make-ahead: Refrigerate for up to 1 day.)**

❧ Roll by rounded tablespoonfuls (15 mL) into balls; roll each in coarse sugar. Place, 2 inches (5 cm) apart, on prepared baking sheets. Freeze until firm, about 15 minutes.

❧ Bake in top and bottom thirds of 325°F (160°C) oven, rotating and switching pans halfway through, until bottoms are darkened, about 16 minutes. Let cool on pans on racks for 5 minutes. Transfer to racks; let cool. **(Make-ahead: Layer between waxed paper in airtight container and store at room temperature for up to 5 days or freeze for up to 1 month.)**

Makes about 36 cookies. | PER COOKIE: about 88 cal, 2 g pro, 6 g total fat (2 g sat. fat), 8 g carb, 1 g fibre, 13 mg chol, 10 mg sodium. % RDI: 2% calcium, 4% iron, 1% vit A, 1% folate.

Barazek

This generations-old Lebanese recipe is a festive season specialty. But don't wait until December rolls around to try it.

3 cups	shelled natural pistachios (12 oz/375 g)	750 mL	1 tbsp	butter, melted	15 mL
1⅔ cups	icing sugar	400 mL	1 tsp	rose water	5 mL
1	egg	1	2 tbsp	sesame seeds, toasted	25 mL
2	egg yolks	2	1 tbsp	granulated sugar	15 mL

❧ Line 2 rimless baking sheets with parchment paper or grease; set aside.

❧ In food processor, pulse pistachios with icing sugar just until ground, being careful not to turn into paste.

❧ In bowl, whisk egg with yolks; stir in pistachio mixture, ½ cup (125 mL) at a time, to form sticky dough. Add butter and rose water; knead gently to combine and make very sticky dough. Roll by level tablespoonfuls (15 mL) into balls; place, 3 inches (8 cm) apart, on prepared baking sheets.

❧ In small bowl, stir sesame seeds with granulated sugar. Dip flat bottom of damp glass into seed mixture; press ball to flatten to ½-inch (1 cm) thickness. Repeat with remaining sesame seed mixture and balls.

❧ Bake in top and bottom thirds of 300°F (150°C) oven, rotating and switching pans halfway through, until bottoms are golden, 20 to 25 minutes. Transfer to racks; let cool. **(Make-ahead: Layer between waxed paper in airtight container and store at room temperature for up to 4 days or freeze for up to 1 month.)**

Makes about 40 cookies. | PER COOKIE: about 84 cal, 2 g pro, 6 g total fat (1 g sat. fat), 7 g carb, 1 g fibre, 16 mg chol, 6 mg sodium. % RDI: 1% calcium, 5% iron, 1% vit A, 2% vit C, 4% folate.

Pignoli

Chewy and crunchy, these sweet morsels are all about the pine nuts, with lots of help from the marzipan.

12 oz	marzipan, crumbled	375 g	2	egg whites	2
1 cup	icing sugar	250 mL	¼ cup	all-purpose flour	50 mL
½ cup	granulated sugar	125 mL	2 cups	pine nuts	500 mL

❧ Line 2 rimless baking sheets with parchment paper or grease; set aside.

❧ In bowl, beat together marzipan, icing and granulated sugars, and egg whites until smooth. Stir in flour to make smooth, thick paste.

❧ Place nuts in shallow bowl. With wet hands, roll dough by level tablespoonfuls (15 mL) into balls; roll in nuts, pressing to make nuts stick. Place, 2 inches (5 cm) apart, on prepared baking sheets.

❧ Bake, 1 sheet at a time, in centre of 325°F (160°C) oven until golden brown, 20 minutes. Let cool on pans on racks for 5 minutes. Transfer to racks; let cool. **(Make-ahead: Layer between waxed paper in airtight container and store at room temperature for up to 3 days.)**

Makes about 36 cookies. | PER COOKIE: about 120 cal, 2 g pro, 8 g total fat (1 g sat. fat), 12 g carb, 2 g fibre, 0 mg chol, 4 mg sodium. % RDI: 2% calcium, 6% iron, 5% folate.

Spice Mice

Kids can help search through the dried chow mein noodles for the ones that will make the most curvaceous tails.

¾ cup	unsalted butter, softened	175 mL	¼ tsp	ground allspice	1 mL
1 cup	packed brown sugar	250 mL	Pinch	each ground cardamom and salt	Pinch
1	egg	1	96	sliced unblanched almonds (about ¼ cup/50 mL)	96
1 tsp	vanilla	5 mL			
2½ cups	all-purpose flour	625 mL	48	currants, halved (about 1 tbsp/15 mL)	48
½ tsp	each baking powder and cinnamon	2 mL	48	dried chow mein noodles (about ¼ cup/50 mL)	48

❧ Line 2 rimless baking sheets with parchment paper or grease; set aside.

❧ In large bowl, beat butter with brown sugar until fluffy; beat in egg and vanilla. In separate bowl, whisk together flour, baking powder, cinnamon, allspice, cardamom and salt; stir into butter mixture in 3 additions.

❧ Form by scant tablespoonfuls (15 mL) into egg shapes. Place, 2 inches (5 cm) apart, on prepared baking sheets. Insert 2 almond slices for ears and 2 currant halves for eyes at narrow end. Insert 1 chow mein noodle for tail at wide end. Refrigerate until firm, about 15 minutes.

❧ Bake, 1 sheet at a time, in centre of 350°F (180°C) oven until light golden and firm, 15 to 18 minutes. Let cool on pans on racks for 5 minutes. Reinsert almond ears if necessary. Transfer to racks; let cool. **(Make-ahead: Store in single layers in airtight containers for up to 1 week.)**

Makes about 48 cookies. | PER COOKIE: about 73 cal, 1 g pro, 3 g total fat (2 g sat. fat), 10 g carb, trace fibre, 11 mg chol, 8 mg sodium. % RDI: 1% calcium, 4% iron, 3% vit A, 6% folate.

KEEPING BROWN SUGAR SOFT

❯ Brown sugar hardens in a dry, warm kitchen – a typical condition during cold Canadian winters. To help it stay soft, keep it in its original bag, closed with a twist tie, and store in an airtight container.

If your brown sugar hardens anyway, you can fix it: Transfer to an airtight container and place a square of foil on sugar. Top with a piece of damp paper towel or a soaked terra-cotta figure designed for this purpose. Reseal container. In a few days, the molasses in the brown sugar will absorb the moisture, and the sugar will return to a usable state. Redampen the towel as needed. Or skip the towel and use a piece of bread or a slice of apple, changing them every few days.

For quick results, place hard brown sugar in microwaveable container; cover and microwave on high for a few seconds or just until soft enough to measure. Use it right away, before it hardens.

Thumbprint Cookies

There are a host of variations for these cookies: almonds, pecans, Brazil nuts or pistachios instead of the walnuts; for the currant jelly, substitute raspberry or blackberry jam.

½ cup	butter, softened	125 mL	Pinch	salt	Pinch
⅓ cup	granulated sugar	75 mL	1 cup	all-purpose flour	250 mL
1	egg, separated	1	¾ cup	finely chopped walnut halves	175 mL
½ tsp	vanilla	2 mL	2 tbsp	red currant jelly (approx)	25 mL

↜ Line 2 rimless baking sheets with parchment paper or grease; set aside.

↜ In bowl, beat butter with sugar until fluffy. Beat in egg yolk, vanilla and salt. Stir in flour, blending with hands if necessary.

↜ Shape by rounded teaspoonfuls (5 mL) into 36 balls. In shallow bowl, beat egg white lightly. Place walnuts in separate bowl.

↜ Using spoons to hold balls, dip into egg white, letting excess drip off; roll in walnuts. Place, 2 inches (5 cm) apart, on prepared pans. Press thimble or top of small bottle cap into each cookie to make indentation.

↜ Bake, 1 sheet at a time, in centre of 350°F (180°C) oven for 5 minutes. Remove from oven; press hole again and fill with small dab of jelly. Bake until golden, about 12 minutes longer. Let cool on pans on racks for 2 minutes. Transfer to racks; let cool. **(Make-ahead: Layer between waxed paper in airtight container and store at room temperature for up to 3 days or freeze for up to 1 month.)**

Makes 36 cookies. | PER COOKIE: about 64 cal, 1 g pro, 4 g total fat (2 g sat. fat), 6 g carb, trace fibre, 13 mg chol, 28 mg sodium. % RDI: 1% iron, 3% vit A, 3% folate.

VARIATIONS

Cherry Thumbprint Cookies: Bake cookies as directed, but do not fill holes with jelly. When cookies are finished baking, re-press holes; press candied cherry half into each cavity while cookies are still hot.

Chocolate Thumbprint Cookies: Bake cookies as directed, but do not fill holes with jelly. When cookies are finished baking, re-press holes; add a small chocolate kiss or chunk of chocolate to each cavity while cookies are still hot.

PREPARING BAKING SHEETS

❯ The preparation depends on the cookie, and each recipe offers the preferred method right up front. Generally, a sheet of parchment paper or a silicone baking mat is the best liner.

You can use the same piece of parchment paper several times if you wipe it clean with a damp cloth after each use. To store it between uses, just dry and roll up. Wash silicone mats in hot soapy water and rinse. Let dry, then fold or roll up to store.

For many cookies, you can lightly grease a rimless baking sheet with butter instead. For especially buttery cookies, such as shortbread, leave the sheet ungreased.

Oatmeal Cookies

Whether you eat them on their own as or sandwich them together with the thick date filling in the variation, you won't find a better version of this great Canadian classic. When making the cookies but not the filling, feel free to play with add-ins. Currants, raisins, toasted nuts, white and dark chocolate, peanut butter chips, toffee chips and dried cranberries or cherries are all delicious. Use up to 1 cup (250 mL).

⅔ cup	butter, softened	150 mL		1 cup	all-purpose flour	250 mL
1 cup	packed brown sugar	250 mL		½ tsp	each baking powder and baking soda	2 mL
1	egg	1		¼ tsp	salt	1 mL
1 tbsp	vanilla	15 mL				
1½ cups	large-flake rolled oats	375 mL				

❧ Line 2 large rimless baking sheets with parchment paper or grease; set aside.

❧ In large bowl, beat butter with brown sugar until fluffy; beat in egg and vanilla. In separate bowl, whisk together oats, flour, baking powder, baking soda and salt; stir into butter mixture in 4 additions until blended. Cover and refrigerate for 30 minutes. **(Make-ahead: Refrigerate for up to 1 day.)**

❧ Shape by heaping tablespoonfuls (15 mL) into 24 balls. Place, 2 inches (5 cm) apart, on prepared baking sheets. Bake in top and bottom thirds of 350°F (180°C) oven, rotating and switching pans halfway through, until golden, edges are crispy and centres are still soft, 12 to 15 minutes. Transfer to racks; let cool.

Makes 24 large cookies. | PER COOKIE: about 125 cal, 2 g pro, 6 g total fat (3 g sat. fat), 17 g carb, 1 g fibre, 21 mg chol, 100 mg sodium. % RDI: 1% calcium, 5% iron, 5% vit A, 6% folate.

VARIATION

Oatmeal Date Sandwich Cookies: In small heavy saucepan, combine 2 cups (500 mL) pitted dates, chopped; 1 tbsp (15 mL) grated orange rind; ⅔ cup (150 mL) orange juice; and ⅓ cup (75 mL) water; bring to boil over medium heat, stirring often. Reduce heat to low; cover and simmer, stirring occasionally, until dates are very soft, about 45 minutes. Uncover and cook, stirring constantly, until thickened and sticky, about 5 minutes. Let cool. **(Make-ahead: Refrigerate in airtight container for up to 2 days.)**

❧ Spread date purée evenly over smooth side of 12 of the cookies; sandwich with remaining cookies, smooth side down. Makes 12 large cookies.

COOL BAKING SHEETS

❯ If you put cookie dough on a warm baking sheet, it will spread as it starts to cook, resulting in poorly shaped and unevenly baked cookies. So if you're reusing a baking sheet when making cookies, be sure to let it cool completely before filling it with more dough.

To speed things up, you can chill the sheet in the fridge, the freezer or a sinkful of cold water. You can also keep placing dough on parchment paper or a silicone mat, then slide it onto the baking sheet when it's cool. Bake on!

Witches' Fingers

Sometimes even cookies as creepy as these are so delicious you just have to try a batch! That's what the Test Kitchen thought back in the early 1990s, when reader Emilie Dore sent in this inventive recipe she devised for Halloween "finger food." Somehow we lost track of Emilie's letter, and the credit for the great success of these cookies did not go to her. But it should be known that Emilie started it all: the recipe caught on and has been popular with our readers ever since.

1 cup	butter, softened	250 mL	1 tsp	baking powder	5 mL
1 cup	icing sugar	250 mL	1 tsp	salt	5 mL
1	egg	1	¾ cup	whole blanched almonds	175 mL
1 tsp	almond extract	5 mL	1	tube (19 g) red decorator gel	1
1 tsp	vanilla	5 mL			
2¾ cups	all-purpose flour	675 mL			

⌁ Line 2 rimless baking sheets with parchment paper or grease; set aside.

⌁ In bowl, beat together butter, sugar, egg, almond extract and vanilla until smooth. In separate bowl, whisk together flour, baking powder and salt. Stir into butter mixture. Cover and refrigerate for 30 minutes.

⌁ Working with one-quarter of the dough at a time and keeping remaining dough refrigerated, roll heaping teaspoonful (5 mL) into elongated oval. Press almond firmly into 1 end for nail. Press in centre to create knuckle shape. Using paring knife, make slashes in several places to form knuckle. Place on prepared baking sheets.

⌁ Bake, 1 sheet at a time, in centre of 325°F (160°C) oven until pale golden, 20 to 25 minutes. Let cool on pans on racks for 3 minutes.

⌁ Lift up almond; squeeze red decorator gel onto nail bed and press almond back in place so gel oozes out from underneath. Transfer to racks; let cool. (Make-ahead: Layer between waxed paper in airtight container and store at room temperature for up to 5 days or freeze for up to 2 weeks.)

Makes about 60 cookies. | PER COOKIE: about 68 cal, 1 g pro, 4 g total fat (2 g sat. fat), 7 g carb, trace fibre, 11 mg chol, 72 mg sodium. % RDI: 1% calcium, 2% iron, 3% vit A, 6% folate.

Golden Walnut Sticks

It's the melt-in-your-mouth texture of these cookies that keeps you reaching for just one more. Try the sticks with pecans instead of walnuts.

3½ cups	walnut halves	875 mL	2 cups	all-purpose flour	500 mL
1 cup	butter, softened	250 mL	½ tsp	salt	2 mL
1 cup	icing sugar	250 mL	GARNISH:		
1½ tsp	vanilla	7 mL	1 tbsp	icing sugar	15 mL

✾ Line 2 rimless baking sheets with parchment paper or leave ungreased; set aside.

✾ Spread walnuts on rimmed baking sheet; toast in 350°F (180°C) oven until fragrant, about 8 minutes. Let cool. In food processor, pulse walnuts until crumbly. Transfer 1¾ cups (425 mL) to shallow dish and set aside for coating.

✾ In large bowl, beat butter with sugar until fluffy; beat in vanilla. Stir in flour, remaining walnuts and salt. Cover and refrigerate until firm, about 30 minutes.

✾ Shape by level tablespoonfuls (15 mL) into 2-inch (5 cm) long logs; roll in reserved walnuts to coat, pressing gently if necessary. Place, 1 inch (2.5 cm) apart, on prepared baking sheets. Bake in top and bottom thirds of 325°F (160°C) oven, rotating and switching pans halfway through, until light golden, about 18 minutes. Transfer to racks; let cool.

✾ GARNISH: Dust with icing sugar. (Make-ahead: Layer between waxed paper in airtight container and store at room temperature for up to 1 week or freeze for up to 1 month.)

Makes about 55 cookies. | PER COOKIE: about 97 cal, 2 g pro, 8 g total fat (3 g sat. fat), 7 g carb, 1 g fibre, 9 mg chol, 45 mg sodium. % RDI: 1% calcium, 3% iron, 3% vit A, 7% folate.

TIME TO CHECK
❯ Check cookies often near the end of the suggested baking time – even 1 minute can make the difference between too soft in the centre and too brown to serve. The best way to check is to lift a cookie to see if the bottom is golden brown or simply darkened, depending on the colour of the unbaked dough.

Candy Cane Kisses

The trick to making these meringue stripes look like candy canes is so easy you won't believe it. Read on!

ONE STRIPE OR TWO?

❯ For red-and-green-striped kisses, add 2 stripes of green food colouring beside the stripes of red.

2	egg whites	2	½ cup	granulated sugar	125 mL
Pinch	cream of tartar	Pinch		Red paste food colouring	
¼ tsp	peppermint extract	1 mL			

❧ Line 2 rimless baking sheets with silicone baking mats, parchment paper or grease; set aside.

❧ In large bowl, beat egg whites with cream of tartar until soft peaks form; beat in peppermint extract. Beat in sugar, about 2 tbsp (25 mL) at a time, until stiff glossy peaks form.

❧ Fit pastry bag with ¼-inch (5 mm) plain tip. Using small clean paintbrush or cotton swabs, brush inside of bag with 2 stripes of red food colouring opposite each other.

❧ Spoon meringue into bag. Pipe 1-inch (2.5 cm) kisses, 1 inch (2.5 cm) apart, onto prepared baking sheets. Bake in top and bottom thirds of 200°F (100°C) oven, rotating and switching pans halfway through, until dry, about 1½ hours. Turn off oven; let stand in oven for 30 minutes. Transfer to rack; let cool. **(Make-ahead: Layer between waxed paper in airtight container and store at room temperature for up to 1 week.)**

Makes about 70 cookies. | PER COOKIE: about 6 cal, trace pro, 0 g total fat (0 g sat. fat), 1 g carb, 0 g fibre, 0 mg chol, 1 mg sodium.

Orange Sesame Biscotti

Pepitas (green pumpkin seeds) and sesame seeds add crunch to these bite-size biscotti.

½ cup	butter, softened	125 mL
⅔ cup	packed brown sugar	150 mL
½ cup	liquid honey	125 mL
2 tbsp	sesame oil	25 mL
3	eggs	3
2 tbsp	grated orange rind	25 mL
4 tsp	orange-flavoured liqueur or orange juice	20 mL

1 tsp	vanilla	5 mL
3¼ cups	all-purpose flour	800 mL
¾ cup	sesame seeds	175 mL
1 tsp	each baking powder and cinnamon	5 mL
¼ tsp	each baking soda and salt	1 mL
½ cup	pepitas	125 mL

Line 2 rimless baking sheets with parchment paper or grease; set aside.

In bowl, beat butter with brown sugar until fluffy; beat in honey and oil. Beat in 2 of the eggs, 1 at a time. Reserving remaining egg white, beat in remaining yolk. Beat in orange rind, liqueur and vanilla.

In separate bowl, whisk together flour, all but 1 tbsp (15 mL) of the sesame seeds, the baking powder, cinnamon, baking soda and salt; stir into batter in 2 additions to form slightly sticky dough. Stir in pepitas.

Divide dough into thirds. On lightly floured surface, roll each into 12-inch (30 cm) long log. Place, 2 inches (5 cm) apart, on prepared baking sheet; press to flatten slightly.

Beat reserved egg white with 2 tsp (10 mL) water; brush all over logs. Sprinkle with remaining sesame seeds. Bake in centre of 325°F (160°C) oven until light golden and just firm to the touch, about 30 minutes. Let cool on pan on rack for 10 minutes.

Transfer logs to cutting board. Cut into ½-inch (1 cm) thick slices. Stand slices up, about ½ inch (1 cm) apart, on baking sheet.

Bake, 1 sheet at a time, in centre of 325°F (160°C) oven until almost dry, about 20 minutes. Transfer to rack; let cool. (Make-ahead: Layer between waxed paper in airtight container and store at room temperature for up to 1 week or freeze for up to 1 month.)

Makes about 72 cookies. | PER COOKIE: about 63 cal, 1 g pro, 3 g total fat (1 g sat. fat), 9 g carb, trace fibre, 11 mg chol, 29 mg sodium. % RDI: 1% calcium, 4% iron, 2% vit A, 6% folate.

FREEZING COOKIES

❯ You can freeze almost any baked cookies except meringues. Cookies that need glazing, icing and/or filling are best frozen unadorned, ready to finish after thawing and closer to serving time. Here's how to freeze with ease.

● Layer completely cooled cookies between waxed paper in an airtight container. Top with a layer of crumpled waxed paper to keep the cookies steady and to avoid contact with ice crystals.

● Seal, label and date the container.

● Include baking instructions if freezing unbaked cookies, and/or finishing instructions for baked cookies that need a final step.

Double Chocolate Hazelnut Biscotti

These long and elegant biscotti are superb to dunk in espresso or enjoy with your favourite latte. You can dip into or drizzle with melted white or bittersweet chocolate – see page 26 for how-tos.

CUTTING AND BAKING BISCOTTI

As soon as the baked logs are cool enough to handle, transfer to cutting board and cut decisively with a chef's or serrated knife. Use a ruler to make identical-size slices. Cut straight across for shorter biscotti or on the diagonal to make longer biscotti with coffee shop allure.

Arrange biscotti standing up as shown. Or arrange lying on one cut side, turning the biscotti over halfway through baking.

1 cup	hazelnuts	250 mL	½ cup	cocoa powder	125 mL
1⅓ cups	granulated sugar	325 mL	1 tsp	baking powder	5 mL
⅔ cup	butter	150 mL	½ tsp	baking soda	2 mL
2	eggs	2	¼ tsp	salt	1 mL
1 tsp	vanilla	5 mL	½ cup	semisweet chocolate chips	125 mL
2 cups	all-purpose flour	500 mL			

❧ Line large rimless baking sheet with parchment paper or grease; set aside.

❧ Spread hazelnuts on separate rimmed baking sheet. Bake in centre of 350°F (180°C) oven until fragrant, about 10 minutes. Transfer to tea towel and rub briskly to remove as much of the skins as possible. Let cool.

❧ In food processor, pulse ½ cup (125 mL) of the hazelnuts with ⅓ cup (75 mL) of the sugar until finely ground; set aside. Coarsely chop remaining hazelnuts; set aside.

❧ In large bowl, beat butter with remaining sugar. Beat in ground hazelnut mixture until fluffy. Beat in eggs, 1 at a time, then vanilla. In bowl, sift together flour, cocoa powder, baking powder, baking soda and salt; stir into butter mixture in 2 additions. Stir in chopped hazelnuts and chocolate chips.

❧ Divide dough in half. On lightly floured surface, roll each into 14-inch (35 cm) long log. Place, 3 inches (8 cm) apart, on prepared baking sheet. Press to flatten slightly. Bake in centre of 350°F (180°C) oven until firm to the touch, about 30 minutes. Let cool on pan on rack for 15 minutes.

❧ Transfer logs to cutting board; cut crosswise on slight diagonal into ¾-inch (2 cm) thick slices. Stand slices up, 1 inch (2.5 cm) apart, on baking sheet.

❧ Bake in centre of 300°F (150°C) oven until almost dry, about 20 minutes. Let cool.

(Make-ahead: Layer between waxed paper in airtight container and store for up to 1 week or freeze for up to 1 month.)

Makes about 36 cookies. | PER COOKIE: about 127 cal, 2 g pro, 7 g total fat (3 g sat. fat), 16 g carb, 1 g fibre, 19 mg chol, 70 mg sodium. % RDI: 1% calcium, 5% iron, 3% vit A, 9% folate.

Kamishbrot

These crunchy, not-too-sweet cookies, also known as mandelbrot and kamish, are a Jewish cookie that's double-baked like Italian biscotti. Enjoy them dunked in tea or coffee.

3	eggs	3	1 cup	chocolate chips	250 mL
1 cup	granulated sugar	250 mL	1 cup	chopped walnut halves	250 mL
1 cup	vegetable oil	250 mL	½ cup	sweetened shredded or flaked coconut	125 mL
1 tsp	vanilla	5 mL			
3 cups	all-purpose flour	750 mL	CINNAMON SUGAR:		
2 tsp	baking powder	10 mL	⅓ cup	granulated sugar	75 mL
1 tsp	cinnamon	5 mL	2 tsp	cinnamon	10 mL
½ tsp	salt	2 mL			

❧ Line 2 rimless baking sheets with parchment paper or grease; set aside.

❧ In large bowl, beat eggs with sugar until light and fluffy; beat in oil and vanilla. In separate bowl, whisk together flour, baking powder, cinnamon and salt; stir into egg mixture. Fold in chocolate chips, walnuts and coconut. Cover and refrigerate for 30 minutes. Divide into quarters.

❧ CINNAMON SUGAR: In small bowl, stir sugar with cinnamon; sprinkle half onto waxed paper. On sugared paper, shape each quarter of dough into 12-inch (30 cm) log. Place, 2 inches (5 cm) apart, on prepared baking sheets. Bake in top and bottom thirds of 350°F (180°C) oven, rotating and switching pans halfway through, until golden and firm, 15 to 20 minutes. Let cool for 15 minutes.

❧ Cut each log into 15 slices. Return slices, cut side down, to paper-lined baking sheets. Sprinkle with half of the remaining cinnamon sugar. Reduce heat to 325°F (160°C); bake for 20 minutes. Turn cookies over; sprinkle with remaining sugar mixture. Bake until golden and firm, about 20 minutes longer. Let cool on pans on racks. (Make-ahead: Layer between waxed paper in airtight container and store at room temperature for up to 5 days or freeze for up to 1 month.)

Makes about 60 cookies. | PER COOKIE: about 107 cal, 1 g pro, 6 g total fat (1 g sat. fat), 12 g carb, 1 g fibre, 9 mg chol, 35 mg sodium. % RDI: 1% calcium, 4% iron, 8% folate.

White Chocolate Lemon Cookies

Unblanched almonds bring contrasting colour to these golden gems.

1 cup	butter, softened	250 mL	2 cups	all-purpose flour	500 mL
½ cup	granulated sugar	125 mL	½ tsp	salt	2 mL
½ cup	packed brown sugar	125 mL	¼ tsp	baking soda	1 mL
2	eggs	2	6 oz	white chocolate, finely chopped	175 g
1 tbsp	grated lemon rind	15 mL	½ cup	finely chopped unblanched almonds	125 mL
½ tsp	vanilla	2 mL			

❧ Line 2 rimless baking sheets with parchment paper or grease; set aside.

❧ In large bowl, beat together butter and granulated and brown sugars until fluffy. Beat in eggs, 1 at a time, then lemon rind and vanilla. In separate bowl, whisk together flour, salt and baking soda. Add to butter mixture; stir until combined. Stir in white chocolate and almonds. Refrigerate for 30 minutes.

❧ Scrape dough onto work surface; divide into quarters. One at a time, shape on waxed paper into 10-inch (25 cm) log. Roll up in waxed paper; refrigerate until firm, rerolling to maintain shape, about 2 hours. **(Make-ahead: Refrigerate in airtight container for up to 3 days or freeze for up to 2 weeks.)**

❧ One at a time, slice logs into ¼-inch (5 mm) thick rounds; place, 1 inch (2.5 cm) apart, on prepared baking sheets. Bake in top and bottom thirds of 350°F (180°C) oven, rotating and switching pans halfway through, until edges start to turn golden, about 11 minutes. Let cool on pans on racks for 5 minutes. Transfer to racks; let cool. **(Make-ahead: Layer between waxed paper in airtight container and store at room temperature for up to 5 days or freeze for up to 2 weeks.)**

Makes about 96 cookies. | PER COOKIE: about 50 cal, 1 g pro, 3 g total fat (2 g sat. fat), 5 g carb, trace fibre, 10 mg chol, 38 mg sodium. % RDI: 1% calcium, 1% iron, 2% vit A, 2% folate.

CHOOSE THE RIGHT LENGTH

A 10-inch (25 cm) long log will make about 36 cookies. You can cut the logs shorter to suit your baking style and needs and to fit better into airtight containers. Wrapped logs of cookie dough are a thoughtful present to friends, neighbours and colleagues.

A Multitude of Slice &Bake Cookies

When you need a lot of cookies, make up this yummy cookie dough. It's easy to divide and bake into three different-looking cookies. Both the dough and the cookies can be made well ahead of time.

CLEAN CUTS
> When slicing cookie logs, wipe the knife clean with a damp cloth between cuts.

Vanilla and Chocolate Doughs:

4 oz	unsweetened chocolate, chopped	125 g	2	eggs	2
1 cup	butter, softened	250 mL	2 tbsp	vanilla	25 mL
2 cups	granulated sugar	500 mL	4 cups	all-purpose flour	1 L
			1 tsp	baking soda	5 mL
			1 tsp	salt	5 mL

❧ In heatproof bowl over saucepan of hot (not boiling) water, melt chocolate, stirring occasionally. Let cool to room temperature.

❧ In large bowl, beat butter with sugar until fluffy. Beat in eggs, 1 at a time; beat in vanilla. In separate bowl, whisk together flour, baking soda and salt; stir into butter mixture in 3 additions, using hands if too stiff to stir.

❧ Scrape half of the dough into separate bowl; stir in chocolate. Divide vanilla and chocolate doughs each into thirds; shape into rectangles. **(Make-ahead: Wrap each and refrigerate for up to 3 days.)**

Makes enough for about 144 cookies.

Two-Tone Wraparounds

Third	Vanilla Dough (recipe, above)	Third	Third	Chocolate Dough (recipe, above)	Third
1	egg white, beaten	1			

❧ Line 2 rimless baking sheets with parchment paper or grease; set aside.

❧ Between waxed paper, roll out half of the Vanilla Dough into 10- x 5-inch (25 x 12 cm) rectangle. Remove top paper; cut into 8- x 3½-inch (20 x 9 cm) rectangle, reserving scraps. Brush with egg white.

❧ Divide Chocolate Dough in half; roll one half into 8-inch (20 cm) long log. Place log in centre of rectangle. Bring sides of vanilla dough over log to meet in centre; press edges together. Repeat with remaining dough, forming chocolate on outside and vanilla on inside. Wrap in waxed paper; refrigerate until chilled, 1 hour. **(Make-ahead: Overwrap in heavy-duty foil; freeze in airtight container for up to 3 weeks. Thaw for 20 minutes.)**

❧ Cut each roll into ¼-inch (5 mm) thick slices; arrange, 1 inch (2.5 cm) apart, on prepared baking sheets.

↶ Bake in top and bottom thirds of 375°F (190°C) oven, rotating and switching pans halfway through, until firm to the touch, about 8 minutes. Let cool on pans on racks for 1 minute. Transfer to racks; let cool. **(Make-ahead: Layer between waxed paper in airtight container and store at room temperature for up to 1 week or freeze for up to 2 weeks.)**

Makes about 60 cookies. | PER COOKIE: about 32 cal, trace pro, 1 g total fat (1 g sat. fat), 5 g carb, trace fibre, 5 mg chol, 31 mg sodium. % RDI: 1% iron, 1% vit A.

....

VARIATION

Walnut Crunch Slices: Roll one-third of the Chocolate or Vanilla Dough into 10-inch (25 cm) long log. Brush with lightly beaten egg white; roll in ½ cup (125 mL) finely chopped walnut halves. Wrap, store, cut and bake as directed. Makes about 40 cookies.

PERFECT ROUNDS
❯ To keep cookie dough logs smooth and round, reroll them several times as they firm up in the fridge.

Black-and-White Spirals

Third	Vanilla Dough (recipe, opposite)	Third	1	egg white, beaten	1
Third	Chocolate Dough (recipe, opposite)	Third			

↶ Line 2 rimless baking sheets with parchment paper or grease; set aside.
↶ Between waxed paper, roll out Vanilla Dough into 14- x 8-inch (35 x 20 cm) rectangle. Repeat with Chocolate Dough. Remove top papers. Brush vanilla dough with egg white. Holding chocolate dough by paper, turn over onto vanilla dough. Roll lightly with rolling pin; remove top sheet of paper.
↶ With sharp knife, trim edges to neaten. Using bottom sheet of paper as support, tightly roll up from long edge; roll back and forth to seal seam. Wrap in waxed paper; refrigerate until chilled, at least 1 hour. **(Make-ahead: Overwrap in heavy-duty foil; freeze in airtight container for up to 3 weeks. Thaw for 20 minutes.)**
↶ Place roll seam side down; cut into ¼-inch (5 mm) thick slices. Arrange, 1 inch (2.5 cm) apart, on prepared baking sheets. Bake in top and bottom thirds of 375°F (190°C) oven, rotating and switching pans halfway through, until firm to the touch, 9 to 10 minutes. Let cool on pans on racks for 1 minute. Transfer to racks; let cool. **(Make-ahead: Layer between waxed paper in airtight container and store at room temperature for up to 1 week or freeze for up to 2 weeks.)**

Makes about 44 cookies. | PER COOKIE: about 44 cal, 1 g pro, 2 g total fat (1 g sat. fat), 6 g carb, 26 g fibre, 7 mg chol, 43 mg sodium. % RDI: 1% iron, 1% vit A.

Butter Pecan Toonies

Store shortbread dough in convenient logs ready to slice and bake anytime – you can even make the rounds sugar-free or gluten-free, if desired.

1 cup	butter, softened	250 mL	2 cups	all-purpose flour	500 mL
½ cup	icing sugar	125 mL	1½ cups	finely chopped pecans	375 mL
½ tsp	vanilla	2 mL	1	egg white, beaten	1

↜ Line 2 rimless baking sheets with parchment paper or grease; set aside.

↜ In bowl, beat together butter, icing sugar and vanilla until fluffy. Stir in flour in 2 additions to make soft dough. Stir in ½ cup (125 mL) of the pecans. Divide into quarters; shape each into 8-inch (20 cm) log.

↜ Spread remaining pecans on waxed paper. Brush each log with egg white; roll in pecans. Wrap each in waxed paper and refrigerate until firm, about 2 hours. **(Make-ahead: Refrigerate in airtight container for up to 3 days or freeze for up to 3 weeks.)**

↜ Cut rolls into generous ¼-inch (5 mm) thick slices. Arrange, 1 inch (2.5 cm) apart, on prepared baking sheets. Bake in top and bottom thirds of 325°F (160°C) oven, rotating and switching pans halfway through, until firm and just beginning to turn golden, about 16 minutes. Transfer to racks; let cool. **(Make-ahead: Layer between waxed paper in airtight container and store for up to 1 week or freeze for up to 2 weeks.)**

Makes about 80 cookies. | PER COOKIE: about 50 cal, 1 g pro, 4 g total fat (2 g sat. fat), 3 g carb, trace fibre, 7 mg chol, 24 mg sodium. % RDI: 1% iron, 2% vit A, 3% folate.

VARIATIONS

Gluten-Free Butter Pecan Toonies: Replace flour with gluten-free baking mix, available in the health food aisles of supermarkets, or bulk or health food stores.

Sugar-Free Butter Pecan Toonies: Replace icing sugar with Splenda No-Calorie Sweetener and 2 tbsp (25 mL) cornstarch.

Sesame Asiago Crisps

More savoury cracker than cookie, these crisps fit stylishly into the predinner hour as companions to a glass of wine or a cocktail.

½ cup	unsalted butter, softened	125 mL		1 cup	all-purpose flour	250 mL
				¼ cup	cornmeal	50 mL
1 tsp	each Dijon mustard and sesame oil	5 mL		Pinch	cayenne pepper	Pinch
				1	egg white	1
1 cup	shredded Asiago cheese	250 mL		⅓ cup	sesame seeds	75 mL

✤ Line 2 rimless baking sheets with parchment paper or leave ungreased; set aside.

✤ In large bowl, beat together butter, mustard and oil until smooth; stir in cheese. In small bowl, whisk together flour, cornmeal and cayenne; stir into butter mixture in 2 additions until smooth. Divide in half; form each into 6-inch (15 cm) long log.

✤ In small bowl, beat egg white until frothy. Spread sesame seeds evenly on each of 2 pieces of waxed paper. Roll logs, 1 at a time, in egg white, then in seeds. Wrap tightly in waxed paper; chill until firm, about 1 hour. **(Make-ahead: Refrigerate in airtight container for up to 3 days or freeze for up to 2 weeks.)**

✤ Cut into generous ¼-inch (5 mm) thick slices; arrange, 1 inch (2.5 cm) apart, on prepared baking sheets. Bake in top and bottom thirds of 325°F (160°C) oven, rotating and switching pans halfway through, until lightly browned on bottom, about 15 minutes. Let cool on pans on racks for 3 minutes. Transfer to racks; let cool.

Makes about 36 crisps. | PER CRISP: about 60 cal, 2 g pro, 4 g total fat (2 g sat. fat), 4 g carb, trace fibre, 9 mg chol, 36 mg sodium. % RDI: 3% calcium, 2% iron, 3% vit A, 5% folate.

Molasses Spice Cookies

For a sparkly finish, press the tops of the cookies into additional turbinado sugar, a coarse light brown sugar, before baking.

ITTY-BITTY TO SATISFYING

❯ The diameter of these dough logs provides one bite per cookie. To double the number of bites, roll logs to 2 inches (5 cm) in diameter and add about 2 minutes to baking time.

⅓ cup	butter, softened	75 mL	1 tsp	baking soda	5 mL
½ cup	packed brown sugar	125 mL	½ tsp	each ground ginger and cinnamon	2 mL
1	egg yolk	1	¼ tsp	ground allspice	1 mL
2 tbsp	fancy molasses	25 mL	¼ tsp	salt	1 mL
½ tsp	vanilla	2 mL	¼ cup	turbinado sugar	50 mL
1¼ cups	all-purpose flour	300 mL			

↜ Line 2 rimless baking sheets with parchment paper or leave ungreased; set aside.

↜ In large bowl, beat butter with brown sugar until fluffy; beat in egg yolk, molasses and vanilla. In separate bowl, whisk together flour, baking soda, ginger, cinnamon, allspice and salt. Stir into butter mixture in 2 additions.

↜ Divide dough into thirds. Place each on large piece of waxed paper; using paper as support, roll each into 1-inch (2.5 cm) diameter log. Wrap and refrigerate until firm, about 2 hours. **(Make-ahead: Refrigerate in airtight container for up to 3 days or freeze for up to 3 weeks.)**

↜ Sprinkle turbinado sugar on large piece of waxed paper; unwrap logs and roll in sugar. Cut into ¼-inch (5 mm) thick slices; place, about 2 inches (5 cm) apart, on prepared baking sheets. Freeze until firm, about 15 minutes.

↜ Bake in top and bottom thirds of 350°F (180°C) oven, rotating and switching pans halfway through, until bottoms are darkened, about 10 minutes. Let cool on pans on racks for 2 minutes. Transfer to racks; let cool. **(Make-ahead: Layer between waxed paper in airtight container and store at room temperature for up to 1 week or freeze for up to 1 month.)**

Makes about 60 cookies. | PER COOKIE: about 32 cal, trace pro, 1 g total fat (1 g sat. fat), 5 g carb, trace fibre, 6 mg chol, 39 mg sodium. % RDI: 1% iron, 1% vit A, 3% folate.

Sugar Cookies

Cream of tartar makes these sugar cookies crisp, while the icing sugar keeps them tender and makes the dough easy to work with.

1 cup	butter, softened	250 mL	1 tsp	each baking soda and cream of tartar	5 mL
1½ cups	icing sugar	375 mL	Pinch	salt	Pinch
1	egg	1			
1½ tsp	vanilla	7 mL		Royal Icing and Royal Icing Paint (recipes, page 67), optional	
2¾ cups	all-purpose flour	675 mL			

EMBELLISHING
SUGAR COOKIES

❧ Line 2 rimless baking sheets with parchment paper or grease; set aside.

❧ In large bowl, beat butter with icing sugar until fluffy; beat in egg and vanilla. In separate bowl, whisk together flour, baking soda, cream of tartar and salt. Stir into butter mixture in 3 additions. Divide in half; flatten into discs. Wrap individually and refrigerate until firm, about 1 hour. **(Make-ahead: Refrigerate for up to 1 day.)**

❧ Dust each disc with flour. Between waxed paper, roll out to scant ¼-inch (5 mm) thickness. Using 3-inch (8 cm) cookie cutter, cut out shapes. Place, 1 inch (2.5 cm) apart, on prepared baking sheets; freeze just until firm, about 15 minutes.

❧ Bake, 1 sheet at a time, in centre of 375°F (190°C) oven until firm and golden on edges, about 8 minutes. Transfer to racks; let cool. **(Make-ahead: Layer between waxed paper in airtight container and store at room temperature for up to 1 week or freeze for up to 1 month.)**

❧ Decorate with Royal Icing and Royal Icing Paint, if desired.

Makes about 36 cookies. | PER COOKIE: about 128 cal, 1 g pro, 5 g total fat (3 g sat. fat), 19 g carb, trace fibre, 19 mg chol, 74 mg sodium. % RDI: 5% iron, 5% vit A, 9% folate.

Spoon Royal Icing (recipe, page 67) into piping bag fitted with fine tip; pipe outline along edge of Sugar Cookies. Let dry.

Scoop about ½ tsp (2 mL) Royal Icing Paint (recipe, page 67) onto centre of each cookie. Using offset spatula, spread to cover, adding more if necessary. Let dry before piping on any more designs. If decorating with candy or sprinkles, add while icing is still wet.

VARIATIONS

Cardamom Spice Sugar Cookies: Add 1 tsp (5 mL) ground cardamom and ½ tsp (2 mL) cinnamon to dry ingredients.

Eggnog Sugar Cookies: Substitute rum extract for the vanilla, if desired. Add 2 tsp (10 mL) grated nutmeg to dry ingredients.

Hint-of-Cinnamon Sugar Cookies: Add ¼ tsp (1 mL) cinnamon to dry ingredients.

Lemon Sugar Cookies: Omit vanilla; add 2 tsp (10 mL) grated lemon rind and ½ tsp (2 mL) lemon extract to egg mixture.

Cocoa Sugar Cookies

Bake and decorate these as single cookies or turn them into jam-filled sandwiches as in the variation that follows.

SMOOTH ROLLING

❯ To keep the dark colour of this chocolate dough, roll discs between waxed paper and dip cookie cutters into cocoa powder, not flour, as you cut out shapes.

¾ cup	butter, softened	175 mL	2¼ cups	all-purpose flour	550 mL
1 cup	granulated sugar	250 mL	⅓ cup	cocoa powder	75 mL
1	egg	1	½ tsp	baking powder	2 mL
1 tsp	vanilla	5 mL	Pinch	salt	Pinch

❧ Line 2 rimless baking sheets with parchment paper or grease; set aside.

❧ In large bowl, beat butter with sugar until fluffy; beat in egg and vanilla. In separate bowl, whisk together flour, cocoa, baking powder and salt until no streaks remain; stir into butter mixture in 2 additions to make smooth dough. Divide dough in half and flatten into discs; wrap each and refrigerate until firm, about 1 hour. **(Make-ahead: Refrigerate for up to 1 day.)**

❧ On lightly floured surface, roll out each disc to ¼-inch (5 mm) thickness. Using floured 2-inch (5 cm) round fluted cutter, cut into rounds. Place, 1 inch (2.5 cm) apart, on prepared baking sheets. Refrigerate until firm, about 30 minutes.

❧ Bake in top and bottom thirds of 350°F (180°C) oven, rotating and switching pans halfway through, until edges begin to darken, about 12 minutes. Transfer to racks; let cool. **(Make-ahead: Layer between waxed paper in airtight container and store at room temperature for up to 1 week or freeze for up to 1 month.)**

Makes about 48 cookies. | PER COOKIE: about 66 cal, 1 g pro, 3 g total fat (2 g sat. fat), 9 g carb, trace fibre, 13 mg chol, 34 mg sodium. % RDI: 3% iron, 3% vit A, 6% folate.

VARIATION

Cocoa Raspberry Sandwich Cookies: Using piping tip or mini-cutter, cut ½-inch (1 cm) hole in centre of 24 of the cookies before baking. Spread about ½ tsp (2 mL) raspberry jam over remaining baked whole cookies; top each with cutout cookie. Makes 24 cookies.

Top to bottom: Apricot Hazelnut
Sandwich Cookies (page 52), Cocoa
Raspberry Sandwich Cookies (opposite)
and Chocolate Hazelnut Star of David
Sandwich Cookies (page 52)

Hazelnut Thins

These thin, crisp cookies are also delightful with other nuts and can be cut into a variety of shapes. Leave them whole for singles or cut a hole in half of them before baking for sandwich cookies.

¾ cup	butter, softened	175 mL	2½ cups	all-purpose flour	625 mL
¾ cup	packed brown sugar	175 mL	½ cup	finely chopped skinned toasted hazelnuts	125 mL
1	egg	1	Pinch	salt	Pinch
1 tsp	vanilla	5 mL			

❧ Line 2 rimless baking sheets with parchment paper or grease; set aside.

❧ In large bowl, beat butter with brown sugar until fluffy; beat in egg and vanilla. In separate bowl, whisk together flour, chopped hazelnuts and salt; stir into butter mixture in 2 additions to make smooth dough. Divide dough in half and flatten into discs; wrap each and refrigerate until firm, about 1 hour. **(Make-ahead: Refrigerate for up to 1 day.)**

❧ Between waxed paper, roll out each disc to ⅛-inch (3 mm) thickness; freeze until firm, about 30 minutes. Using floured 2-inch (5 cm) cutter, cut out shapes. Arrange, 1 inch (2.5 cm) apart, on prepared baking sheets. Refrigerate until firm, 30 minutes.

❧ Bake in top and bottom thirds of 350°F (180°C) oven, rotating and switching pans halfway through, until edges are golden, 12 minutes. Transfer to racks; let cool. **(Make-ahead: Layer between waxed paper in airtight container and store at room temperature for up to 1 week or freeze for up to 1 month.)**

Makes about 70 cookies. | PER COOKIE: about 49 cal, 1 g pro, 3 g total fat (1 g sat. fat), 6 g carb, trace fibre, 9 mg chol, 28 mg sodium. % RDI: 2% iron, 2% vit A, 5% folate.

VARIATIONS

Chocolate Hazelnut Star of David Sandwich Cookies: Cut Hazelnut Thins with triangular cutter; cut smaller triangle in centre of 35 of the unbaked cookies. Spread about ½ tsp (2 mL) hazelnut spread (Nutella) over remaining baked whole cookies; top each with cutout cookie, arranging triangles to form six-pointed star. Sprinkle with icing sugar. Makes 35 cookies.

Apricot Hazelnut Sandwich Cookies: Follow recipe for Chocolate Hazelnut Star of David Sandwich Cookies but use flower cutter. Substitute apricot jam for hazelnut spread. Omit icing sugar. Makes 35 cookies.

Apricot Almond Rugalahs

These spirals are a roll-and-slice version of rugalahs, with all the fixings of jam, nuts and white chocolate.

1	pkg (8 oz/250 g) cream cheese, softened	1	3 oz	white chocolate, finely chopped	90 g
1 cup	butter, softened	250 mL	¼ cup	granulated sugar	50 mL
2 tbsp	granulated sugar	25 mL	¼ cup	packed brown sugar	50 mL
2 cups	all-purpose flour	500 mL	½ cup	apricot jam	125 mL
FILLING:					
1 cup	finely chopped almonds	250 mL			

↜ Line 2 rimless baking sheets with parchment paper or grease; set aside.

↜ In large bowl, beat cream cheese with butter until fluffy; beat in sugar. Stir in flour in 2 additions to make soft dough. Form into rectangle; cut into quarters. Wrap each and refrigerate until firm, about 30 minutes. **(Make-ahead: Refrigerate for up to 1 day.)**

↜ FILLING: In small bowl, combine almonds, white chocolate and granulated and brown sugars; set aside.

↜ On lightly floured surface, roll out each quarter of dough into 12- x 8-inch (30 x 20 cm) rectangle; if necessary, chop any large pieces in apricot jam. Spread each rectangle of dough with 2 tbsp (25 mL) of the jam; sprinkle with one-quarter of the nut mixture. Starting at long side, tightly roll up into logs. Wrap and refrigerate until firm, about 1 hour. **(Make-ahead: Refrigerate in airtight container for up to 3 days or freeze for up to 3 weeks.)**

↜ Cut each log into ½-inch (1 cm) wide slices. Arrange, ½ inch (1 cm) apart, on prepared baking sheets. Bake, 1 sheet at a time, in centre of 350°F (180°C) oven until golden, 20 minutes. Transfer to racks; let cool. **(Make-ahead: Layer between waxed paper in airtight container and store at room temperature for up to 5 days or freeze for up to 3 weeks.)**

Makes about 80 cookies. | PER COOKIE: about 68 cal, 1 g pro, 5 g total fat (2 g sat. fat), 6 g carb, trace fibre, 11 mg chol, 35 mg sodium. % RDI: 1% calcium, 2% iron, 3% vit A, 4% folate.

A TREAT FOR THE COOK

❯ Cookies that are rolled around a jam filling then cut will always lose a little of the filling on the baking sheet. Once people realize how delicious these caramelized blobs are, be warned. You will have company as the cookies emerge from the oven. Just let them cool before indulging.

Maple Leaf Sandwich Cookies

This is what a real maple cookie should taste like. O Canada!

SHAPE SHIFTING

❯ What? No maple leaf cookie cutter? These cookies are just as deliciously maple-flavoured cut into rounds or other shapes. Some purist cookie lovers find them equally desirable without the maple butter filling.

1 cup	butter, softened	250 mL
1 cup	firmly packed brown sugar	250 mL
¼ cup	maple syrup	50 mL
1	egg	1
1 tsp	maple extract	5 mL
3¼ cups	all-purpose flour	800 mL

½ tsp	baking powder	2 mL
½ tsp	salt	2 mL
MAPLE BUTTER FILLING:		
¼ cup	butter, softened	50 mL
2 cups	icing sugar	500 mL
2 tbsp	whipping cream	25 mL
2 tsp	maple extract	10 mL

❧ Line 2 rimless baking sheets with parchment paper or grease; set aside.

❧ In large bowl, beat butter with brown sugar until fluffy; beat in maple syrup, egg and maple extract. In separate bowl, whisk together flour, baking powder and salt; stir into butter mixture in 2 additions to make smooth dough. Divide dough in half and flatten into discs; wrap each and refrigerate until firm, about 1 hour. (Make-ahead: Refrigerate for up to 1 day.)

❧ Between waxed paper, roll out each disc to generous ⅛-inch (3 mm) thickness. Using 2-inch (5 cm) maple leaf cutters, cut out cookies. Decorate half by scoring leaf pattern in surface. Arrange, 1 inch (2.5 cm) apart, on prepared baking sheets.

❧ Bake in top and bottom thirds of 350°F (180°C) oven, rotating and switching pans halfway through, until golden on bottoms and edges are darkened, 10 to 12 minutes. Transfer to racks; let cool.

❧ **MAPLE BUTTER FILLING:** In small bowl, beat butter until fluffy; beat in icing sugar, cream and maple extract until smooth. Spread 1 tsp (5 mL) over bottoms of undecorated cookies; sandwich with remaining cookies, bottom side down. (Make-ahead: Layer between waxed paper in airtight container and store at room temperature for up to 3 days or freeze for up to 2 weeks.)

Makes about 48 cookies. | PER COOKIE: about 115 cal, 1 g pro, 5 g total fat (3 g sat. fat), 16 g carb, trace fibre, 20 mg chol, 79 mg sodium. % RDI: 1% calcium, 4% iron, 5% vit A, 8% folate.

Empire Cookies

These cookies are best made a day ahead so the jam and shiny almond glaze have time to mellow and soften the cookie.

½ cup	unsalted butter, softened	125 mL
½ cup	granulated sugar	125 mL
1	egg	1
1 tsp	almond extract or vanilla	5 mL
2 cups	all-purpose flour	500 mL
1 tsp	baking powder	5 mL

⅓ cup	raspberry jam	75 mL
ICING:		
1 cup	icing sugar	250 mL
¼ tsp	almond extract or vanilla	1 mL
1 tbsp	hot water (approx)	15 mL
6	candied cherries, quartered	6

SWITCH THE GARNISH

❯ The Empire does not require that its cookies be garnished with candied cherries. Try icing and slivered or sliced almonds to complement the almond flavouring in the dough, or silver dragées to add a certain touch of class.

❧ Set out 2 rimless baking sheets; leave ungreased.

❧ In large bowl, beat butter with sugar until fluffy; beat in egg and almond extract. In separate bowl, whisk flour with baking powder; stir into butter mixture in 2 additions to make smooth dough.

❧ On lightly floured surface, roll out dough to scant ⅛-inch (3 mm) thickness. Using 1½- to 1¾-inch (4 to 4.5 cm) round cookie cutter, cut out shapes. Place, about 2 inches (5 cm) apart, on prepared baking sheets.

❧ Bake, 1 sheet at a time, in centre of 350°F (180°C) oven until edges are golden, about 10 minutes. Transfer to racks; let cool. **(Make-ahead: Layer between waxed paper in airtight container and store at room temperature for up to 3 days or freeze for up to 1 month.)**

❧ Spread bottoms of half of the cookies with jam; sandwich with remaining cookies, bottom side down.

❧ **ICING:** In small bowl, combine icing sugar, almond extract and enough of the hot water to make thin icing; spread over tops of cookies. Top each with cherry piece. Let stand until icing is dry, about 3 hours. **(Make-ahead: Layer between waxed paper in airtight container and store at room temperature for up to 3 days or freeze for up to 2 weeks.)**

Makes about 24 cookies. | PER COOKIE: about 126 cal, 1 g pro, 4 g total fat (3 g sat. fat), 21 g carb, trace fibre, 18 mg chol, 17 mg sodium. % RDI: 1% calcium, 4% iron, 4% vit A, 11% folate.

Basler Brunsli

This traditional Swiss cookie from the city of Basel is a lovely combination of bittersweet chocolate and spices, plus it is gluten- and dairy-free.

8 oz	bittersweet chocolate, chopped	250 g	¼ cup	instant dissolving (fruit/berry) sugar	50 mL
⅓ cup	cocoa powder	75 mL	3 cups	ground almonds	750 mL
2 tsp	cinnamon	10 mL	3 tbsp	kirsch or brandy	50 mL
¼ tsp	ground cloves	1 mL	¼ cup	granulated sugar	50 mL
2	egg whites	2	2 tbsp	coarse sugar	25 mL

❧ Line 2 rimless baking sheets with parchment paper or grease; set aside.

❧ In food processor, pulse together chocolate, cocoa powder, cinnamon and cloves until finely ground. Set aside.

❧ In large bowl, beat egg whites until foamy; beat in instant dissolving sugar, 1 tbsp (15 mL) at a time, until stiff peaks form. Fold in chocolate mixture, almonds and kirsch just until combined. Divide dough in half and shape into discs; wrap each and refrigerate until firm, about 30 minutes.

❧ Sprinkle work surface with half of the granulated sugar. Working with 1 piece of dough at a time, turn 2 or 3 times to coat with sugar. Roll out to scant ½-inch (1 cm) thickness. Using 2-inch (5 cm) heart-shaped cookie cutter, cut into hearts. Place on waxed paper; sprinkle with coarse sugar. Let dry for 1 hour.

❧ Arrange cutouts, about 1 inch (2.5 cm) apart, on prepared baking sheets. Bake, 1 sheet at a time, in centre of 325°F (160°C) oven just until firm, about 20 minutes. Transfer to racks; let cool. **(Make-ahead: Layer between waxed paper in airtight container and store at room temperature for up to 4 days or freeze for up to 1 month.)**

Makes about 45 cookies. | PER COOKIE: about 74 cal, 2 g pro, 5 g total fat (1 g sat. fat), 6 g carb, 1 g fibre, 0 mg chol, 3 mg sodium. % RDI: 2% calcium, 4% iron, 1% folate.

SUPERFINE SUGAR

❯ With the finest crystal size of all types of granulated sugar, superfine sugar goes by various names in Canada: bar, berry, caster, extra fine, fruit, instant dissolving and ultrafine. This sugar is often packaged in boxes and sold alongside bags of regular granulated sugar. You can make your own in a pinch: whirl granulated sugar in food processor until granules are smaller, finer and almost powdery. Let the dust settle before removing the lid.

Whipped Shortbread Toonies

Just a little mouthful of shortbread satisfies and impresses with the simplicity of good butter, vanilla, sugar and flour.

1 cup	unsalted butter, softened	250 mL
½ cup	instant dissolving (fruit/berry) sugar	125 mL

Pinch	salt	Pinch
½ tsp	vanilla	2 mL
½ cup	rice flour	125 mL
1¾ cups	all-purpose flour	425 mL

❧ Line 2 rimless baking sheets with parchment paper or leave ungreased; set aside.

❧ In large bowl, beat together butter, sugar and salt until fluffy and almost white. Stir in vanilla, then rice flour. Stir in all-purpose flour in 3 additions. Form into 2 flat rectangles.

❧ Between waxed paper, roll out rectangles to generous ¼-inch (5 mm) thickness. Cut out 1½-inch (4 cm) circles; place, 1 inch (2.5 cm) apart, on prepared pans, rerolling scraps and chilling dough between cutting. Refrigerate until firm, about 30 minutes. **(Make-ahead: Layer between waxed paper in airtight container and freeze for up to 1 month. Thaw on prepared baking sheets before baking.)**

❧ Bake in top and bottom thirds of 275°F (140°C) oven, rotating and switching pans halfway through, until bottoms are light golden, about 40 minutes. Let cool for 2 minutes on pans on racks. Transfer to racks; let cool. **(Make-ahead: Layer between waxed paper in airtight containers and store at room temperature for up to 5 days or freeze for up to 2 weeks.)**

Makes about 90 cookies. | PER COOKIE: about 34 cal, trace pro, 2 g total fat (1 g sat. fat), 4 g carb, trace fibre, 6 mg chol, 0 mg sodium. % RDI: 1% iron, 2% vit A, 1% folate.

VARIATIONS

Cardamom Shortbread: Use packed brown sugar instead of the instant dissolving and add 1½ tsp (7 mL) ground cardamom along with the rice flour. No cardamom? Use cinnamon.

Chippy Shortbread: Stir in ¾ cup (175 mL) small chips of your choice, such as chocolate or peanut butter.

Glazed Shortbread: Mix ¾ cup (175 mL) icing sugar with 2 tbsp (25 mL) liquid (such as water, milk, strained lemon or orange juice, tea or coffee); brush over hot cookies.

Lavender Shortbread: Mix in 2 tsp (10 mL) lightly crushed lavender along with rice flour.

Lemon Poppy Seed Shortbread: Stir in 1 tbsp (15 mL) poppy seeds and 1 tsp (5 mL) grated lemon rind along with rice flour.

Nutty Shortbread: Stir in ⅔ cup (150 mL) finely chopped Brazil nuts, macadamia nuts, walnut halves, pecans, toasted skinned hazelnuts or salted roasted peanuts. Dip cookies into or drizzle with melted bittersweet chocolate, if desired.

Sesame Seed Shortbread: Stir in ½ cup (125 mL) white sesame seeds along with rice flour.

Shortbread Stars, Bars, Trees, Bells, Candy Canes or Snowflakes: Choose desired shape. Yield will be affected by size of cutter.

Tea Shortbread: Mix 1 tsp (5 mL) crushed herbal tea, such as mango or passion fruit, or Earl Grey or green tea into dough along with rice flour.

Ginger Spice Shorties

Choose any shape you like for these cookies, which have the tender, melt-in-your-mouth qualities of shortbread and the sensual, come-hither allure of gingerbread.

1 cup	unsalted butter, softened	250 mL	¼ cup	rice flour	50 mL
			½ tsp	ground ginger	2 mL
⅓ cup	instant dissolving (fruit/berry) sugar	75 mL	¼ tsp	each cinnamon and salt	1 mL
2 tbsp	fancy molasses	25 mL	Pinch	ground cloves	Pinch
1¾ cups	all-purpose flour	425 mL	2 tbsp	granulated sugar	25 mL

❧ Line 2 rimless baking sheets with parchment paper or leave ungreased; set aside.

❧ In bowl, beat together butter, instant dissolving sugar and molasses until fluffy. In separate bowl, whisk together all-purpose and rice flours, ginger, cinnamon, salt and cloves; stir into butter mixture in 2 additions until smooth.

❧ Divide in half; press into discs. Between waxed paper, roll out 1 disc at a time to ¼-inch (5 mm) thickness. Using 2-inch (5 cm) cutter, cut out shapes. Arrange, 1 inch (2.5 cm) apart, on prepared baking sheets; chill until firm, about 20 minutes. Sprinkle with granulated sugar.

❧ Bake, 1 sheet at a time, in centre of 325°F (160°C) oven until darker on bottoms, 10 to 12 minutes. Let cool on pans on racks until firm, about 3 minutes. Transfer to racks; let cool. (Make-ahead: Layer between waxed paper in airtight container and store at room temperature for up to 5 days or freeze for up to 1 month.)

Makes about 47 cookies. | PER COOKIE: about 65 cal, 1 g pro, 4 g total fat (2 g sat. fat), 7 g carb, trace fibre, 10 mg chol, 13 mg sodium. % RDI: 2% iron, 4% vit A, 5% folate.

Rich Chocolate Shortbread

Compared with chocolate shortbread that's made with cocoa powder, this melted chocolate version is, bite-for-bite, denser and more chocolaty.

6 oz	semisweet chocolate, chopped	175 g	1 tsp	vanilla	5 mL
			Pinch	salt	Pinch
1 cup	butter, softened	250 mL	2¼ cups	all-purpose flour	550 mL
¼ cup	granulated sugar (approx)	50 mL	¼ cup	cornstarch	50 mL

❧ Line 2 rimless baking sheets with parchment paper or leave ungreased; set aside.

❧ In heatproof bowl set over saucepan of hot (not boiling) water, melt chocolate, stirring occasionally. Remove from heat; let cool.

❧ In bowl, beat butter until fluffy; beat in chocolate until smooth. Beat in 2 tbsp (25 mL) of the sugar, vanilla and salt. Stir in flour in 3 additions; stir in cornstarch to make firm, smooth dough.

❧ On waxed paper, press dough into 10- x 9-inch (25 x 23 cm) rectangle; trim edges. Refrigerate until chilled, about 30 minutes. Using floured knife, cut into 2- x 1-inch (5 x 2.5 cm) bars. Using spatula, place cookies, 1 inch (2.5 cm) apart, on prepared baking sheets. Prick each cookie with fork. Refrigerate until firm, about 2 hours. (Make-ahead: Layer between waxed paper in airtight container and freeze for up to 1 month. Add a few minutes to baking time.)

❧ Bake, 1 sheet at a time, in centre of 325°F (160°C) oven until firm, about 20 minutes. Let cool on pans on racks for 2 minutes. Spread remaining sugar in pie plate; gently press cookies into sugar to coat all sides, adding more sugar if necessary. Transfer to racks; let cool. (Make-ahead: Layer between waxed paper in airtight container and store at room temperature for up to 1 week or freeze for up to 1 month.)

Makes about 45 cookies. | PER COOKIE: about 84 cal, 1 g pro, 5 g total fat (3 g sat. fat), 9 g carb, 0 g fibre, 11 mg chol, 42 mg sodium. % RDI: 3% iron, 4% vit A, 3% folate.

Brown Sugar Shortbread Fingers

Brown sugar adds a caramel flavour to these buttery shortbread cookies.

1¼ cups	unsalted butter, softened	300 mL		2¾ cups	all-purpose flour	675 mL
				¼ cup	cornstarch	50 mL
⅔ cup	packed brown sugar	150 mL		¼ tsp	salt	1 mL
1 tsp	vanilla	5 mL				

~ Line 2 rimless baking sheets with parchment paper or leave ungreased; set aside.

~ In large bowl, beat together butter, brown sugar and vanilla until fluffy. In separate bowl, whisk together flour, cornstarch and salt; stir into butter mixture in 2 additions. Knead gently to make smooth dough. Divide in half; shape into rectangles. Wrap and refrigerate until chilled, about 30 minutes.

~ On lightly floured surface or between waxed paper, roll out dough to generous ¼-inch (5 mm) thickness. Cut into 1- x 2½-inch (2.5 x 6 cm) fingers, rerolling scraps. Prick each shortbread twice with fork. Place, 2 inches (5 cm) apart, on prepared baking sheets. Refrigerate for 30 minutes or freeze for 15 minutes until firm.

~ Bake, 1 sheet at a time, in centre of 300°F (150°C) oven until slightly darker on bottoms, about 20 minutes. Let cool on pans on racks until firm, about 3 minutes. Transfer to racks; let cool. (Make-ahead: Layer between waxed paper in airtight container and store at room temperature for up to 1 week or freeze for up to 1 month.)

Makes about 42 cookies. | PER COOKIE: about 94 cal, 1 g pro, 6 g total fat (3 g sat. fat), 10 g carb, trace fibre, 15 mg chol, 16 mg sodium. % RDI: 1% calcium, 4% iron, 5% vit A, 8% folate.

VARIATION

Brown Sugar Shortbread Thistles: Spray 3½-inch (9 cm) traditional Scottish thistle mould lightly with cooking spray or grease with unsalted butter; dust with flour. Tap out loose flour. Press 3 tbsp (50 mL) dough at a time into mould, smoothing top. Tap mould smartly on prepared baking sheet to release moulded dough. Turn thistle-design-side up. Repeat with remaining dough, spacing cookies 2 inches (5 cm) apart. Chill until firm, about 1 hour. Bake as directed.

Hamantaschen

Hamantaschen (also called Haman's Ears) are filled triangular cookies baked especially for Purim, a joyous Jewish festival. Children don costumes and deliver gifts of food, such as these cookies, to family and friends. The cookies are delicious, so even if you aren't celebrating Purim, make some to share.

SHAPING HAMANTASCHEN

Cup your hand to hold the filled round of dough. Pinch firmly to seal the edges, but not so forcefully that the edges are unevenly thick.

1 cup	unsalted butter, softened	250 mL
2 cups	granulated sugar	500 mL
2 tsp	grated orange rind	10 mL
2	eggs	2
3¾ cups	all-purpose flour	925 mL
2 tsp	baking powder	10 mL
½ tsp	salt	2 mL

POPPY SEED FILLING:

1 cup	poppy seeds	250 mL
1 cup	milk	250 mL
¼ cup	hot water	50 mL
½ cup	granulated sugar	125 mL
¼ cup	finely chopped raisins	50 mL
2 tbsp	liquid honey	25 mL
1 tbsp	grated orange rind	15 mL
¼ tsp	cinnamon	1 mL
Pinch	salt	Pinch

EGG WASH:

1	egg	1

➤ Line 2 rimless baking sheets with parchment paper; set aside.

➤ **POPPY SEED FILLING:** In clean coffee grinder, grind poppy seeds. In saucepan, bring milk and water to boil; stir in poppy seeds, sugar, raisins, honey, orange rind, cinnamon and salt. Return to boil; reduce heat to medium and simmer, stirring often, until dry and stiff, about 18 minutes. Let cool.

➤ In large bowl, beat together butter, sugar and orange rind until fluffy; beat in eggs, 1 at a time. In separate bowl, whisk together flour, baking powder and salt; stir into butter mixture in 2 additions to make smooth dough. Divide dough into thirds; form each into disc. Wrap each and refrigerate until firm, about 1 hour.

➤ Between waxed paper, roll out dough to generous ⅛-inch (3 mm) thickness. Using 3-inch (8 cm) round cookie cutter, cut out rounds.

➤ **EGG WASH:** Beat egg with 1 tbsp (15 mL) water; lightly brush over edges of rounds. Place heaping 1 tsp (5 mL) filling onto centre of each.

➤ Fold up 3 sides to make 3 corners; pinch corners to seal and leave pea-size opening in centre. Place, 2 inches (5 cm) apart, on prepared baking sheets. Refrigerate until firm, about 30 minutes.

➤ Brush with egg wash. Bake, 1 sheet at a time, in centre of 350°F (180°C) oven until golden, 15 to 20 minutes. Transfer to racks; let cool. (Make-ahead: Layer between waxed paper in airtight container; store at room temperature for up to 2 days or freeze for up to 1 month.)

Makes about 50 cookies. | PER COOKIE: about 130 cal, 2 g pro, 5 g total fat (3 g sat. fat), 19 g carb, 1 g fibre, 21 mg chol, 42 mg sodium. % RDI: 5% calcium, 5% iron, 4% vit A, 10% folate.

VARIATIONS

Apricot Filling: In saucepan, soak 1½ cups (375 mL) finely chopped dried apricots in 1½ cups (375 mL) hot water for 20 minutes. Bring to boil; cover and simmer over low heat until softened and almost no water remains, 30 minutes. Stir in 2 tbsp (25 mL) liquid honey; 2 tsp (10 mL) grated orange rind; and 4 tsp (20 mL) orange juice; cook, stirring constantly, for 5 minutes. Refrigerate filling until cold. In food processor, pulse until almost smooth.

Prune Filling: In food processor, finely chop 2 cups (500 mL) pitted prunes; 1 cup (250 mL) raisins; ½ cup (125 mL) walnuts; 2 tbsp (25 mL) granulated sugar; 1 tsp (5 mL) grated lemon rind; 2 tbsp (25 mL) lemon juice; and 1 tbsp (15 mL) water until thick and stiff, 1 minute.

Snowflake Forest Wreath

The coarse white sugar that frosts this wreath is available at cake-decorating stores and some bulk food outlets. The crystals of regular granulated sugar are just not sparkly enough. There's enough dough left over after making the dinner-plate-size wreath to make some cookies for tree ornaments, gift tags or place cards (see page 67), or keep in mind that snowflakes look pretty standing among seasonal greenery on a mantel.

	Gingerbread Dough (recipe, page 66)		Small candies or dragées
⅓ cup	coarse white sugar (approx)	75 mL	Wide (1 inch/2.5 cm) ribbon
	Royal Icing (recipe, page 67)		

Use fingertips to press the coarse sugar into the dough, keeping sugar away from the edges of the cutouts.

❧ Set out 12-inch (30 cm) pizza pan; leave ungreased. Line 2 rimless baking sheets with parchment paper or grease; set aside. Set out 1 additional rimless baking sheet.

❧ With compass on parchment or waxed paper, draw 2 concentric circles, the outer one 11 inches (28 cm) in diameter, the inner one 5 inches (12 cm) in diameter. Cut out along traced lines. Cut outside edge into shallow wavy curves.

❧ Between 20-inch (50 cm) lengths of parchment paper, roll out large disc of dough into 12-inch (30 cm) circle. Slide paper and dough onto additional rimless baking sheet; freeze until firm, about 15 minutes. Slide dough back onto work surface; peel off top paper.

❧ Centre pattern on dough; with tip of knife, cut out wreath. Peel scraps from edge and centre; set aside. Cut bottom paper to extend ¼ inch (5 mm) beyond edge of dough; slide paper and dough onto pizza pan. Freeze until firm, about 15 minutes.

❧ Using 1¾- and 1½-inch (4.5 and 4 cm) diameter snowflake cookie cutters, cut out about 6 snowflakes randomly from top half of wreath, leaving at least ¾ inch (2 cm) between snowflakes and edge of wreath.

❧ Using 1¾-inch (4.5 cm) Christmas tree cookie cutter, cut out 5 trees randomly from bottom half of wreath, leaving at least 1 inch (2.5 cm) from nearest snowflake and at least ¾ inch (2 cm) between trees and edge of wreath. Transfer snowflakes and trees to prepared baking sheet; set aside in freezer.

❧ Using mini star-shaped cookie cutter or ¼-inch (5 mm) piping tip, cut hole for hanging about ½ inch (1 cm) from top edge. Freeze wreath until firm, about 15 minutes.

❧ Being careful sugar does not go into cutouts, sprinkle wreath with 2 tbsp (25 mL) of the sugar. Lightly press sugar into dough. Bake in centre of 325°F (160°C) oven until slightly darker, 20 to 30 minutes. Let cool on pan on rack.

❧ Meanwhile, between 12-inch (30 cm) lengths of parchment paper, roll out small disc of dough to scant ¼-inch (5 mm) thickness. Using 2¾-inch (7 cm) snowflake cookie cutter, cut out 2 large snowflakes. Using tree cookie cutter, cut out 3 trees. ▷

With one hand gripping the pastry bag and the other hand guiding the tip, outline edges of cutouts.

❧ Using smaller cutter, cut out 3 snowflakes. Peel away scraps. Press all scraps together; wrap and reserve in refrigerator to make more cookies (see Gingerbread Cookie Decorations, opposite). Slide cutouts and paper onto additional rimless baking sheet; freeze for 15 minutes. Transfer snowflakes and trees to second prepared baking sheet.

❧ Bake, 1 sheet at a time, in centre of 325°F (160°C) oven until slightly darker, 15 to 20 minutes. Let cool on pan on rack. **(Make-ahead: Layer between waxed paper in airtight container and store at room temperature for up to 1 week or freeze for up to 1 month.)**

❧ In small bowl, whisk ¾ cup (175 mL) Royal Icing with 1 to 2 tbsp (15 to 25 mL) water until just thin enough to brush. Using paintbrush, brush icing over snowflakes and trees. Sprinkle some of the snowflakes with remaining sugar. To cover edges only of snowflakes, paint edge and press into sugar. Let dry, about 20 minutes.

❧ Using small pastry bag fitted with small plain tip (or small plastic bag with tiny corner snipped off), pipe some of the undiluted Royal Icing in zigzags or lines on trees to simulate branches. Decorate as desired with candies. Let dry, about 20 minutes.

❧ Pipe icing outline around cutouts in wreath to define shape. Let dry, about 20 minutes.

❧ Arrange trees over bottom half of wreath among and slightly overlapping tree cutouts. Arrange snowflakes over remainder of wreath singly or in groups of 2, slightly overlapping snowflake cutouts. Glue cookies to wreath with Royal Icing. Let dry for 24 hours.

❧ Thread ribbon through hole at top of wreath; tie firmly. Add bow, if desired. Hang away from heat or moisture for up to 2 weeks.

Makes 1 wreath and enough left over for Gingerbread Cookie Decorations.

Gingerbread Dough

½ cup	butter, softened	125 mL	3 cups	all-purpose flour	750 mL
½ cup	granulated sugar	125 mL	1 tsp	ground ginger	5 mL
1	egg	1	½ tsp	salt	2 mL
¼ cup	fancy molasses	50 mL	½ tsp	each ground cloves and cinnamon	2 mL
¼ cup	cooking or blackstrap molasses	50 mL	¼ tsp	baking soda	1 mL

❧ In large bowl, beat butter with sugar until fluffy; beat in egg. Beat in fancy and cooking molasses.

↬ In separate bowl, whisk together flour, ginger, salt, cloves, cinnamon and baking soda; stir into molasses mixture in 3 additions, mixing well and blending with hands, if necessary.

↬ Divide into thirds. Form 1 of the thirds into small flat disc; form remaining dough into large flat disc. Wrap each and refrigerate until firm, about 2 hours. **(Make-ahead: Refrigerate for up to 1 week or overwrap in heavy-duty foil and freeze for up to 2 weeks.)**

Makes 1 batch, enough for 1 Snowflake Forest Wreath and Gingerbread Cookie Decorations.

Royal Icing

Meringue powder is available at bulk or cake decorating stores.

3 tbsp	meringue powder	50 mL
3²⁄₃ cups	icing sugar	900 mL

↬ In bowl, beat meringue powder with ⅓ cup (75 mL) water until foamy, about 2 minutes. Add sugar; beat until stiff, about 6 minutes. Cover with damp cloth to prevent drying out.

Makes about 1½ cups (375 mL).

Gingerbread Cookie Decorations

↬ Roll out gingerbread dough scraps as directed. Using 2¾-inch (7 cm) snowflake and/or tree cookie cutter, cut out desired shapes. Or use other holiday cutters. Gingerbread girls and boys, candy canes and stars are always fun.

↬ For tree ornaments, use straw to cut out hole at top of cookie cutout. Freeze and bake as directed. Using Royal Icing, decorate cookies; add candies while icing is still wet. Thread ribbon through holes to hang on tree.

↬ For gift cards or place cards, freeze and bake as directed. Using Royal Icing, pipe desired names onto cookies.

ROYAL ICING PAINT

❯ To make icing you can use to paint on Sugar Cookies (recipe, page 49) or Gingerbread Cookie Decorations (recipe, left), thin Royal Icing with cold water. Start with about 1 tbsp (15 mL) water per cup (250 mL) Royal Icing, adding more until icing is brushable.

Stilton and Walnut Biscuits

These flaky biscuits feature the addictive taste combination of Stilton cheese and walnuts. They are simply perfect bites with a glass of champagne or port. If you like, you can decorate each one with a piece of a walnut half before baking.

½ cup	butter, softened	125 mL	½ cup	finely chopped walnut halves	125 mL
2 cups	crumbled Stilton cheese (8 oz/250 g)	500 mL	¼ tsp	each salt and pepper	1 mL
4	egg yolks	4	Pinch	each nutmeg and cayenne pepper	Pinch
1⅔ cups	all-purpose flour	400 mL			

⮑ Line 2 rimless baking sheets with parchment paper or grease; set aside.

⮑ In bowl, beat butter with cheese until fairly smooth; beat in egg yolks. In separate bowl, whisk together flour, walnuts, salt, pepper, nutmeg and cayenne; add to cheese mixture, ⅓ cup (75 mL) at a time, mixing to form ragged dough. Form into 2 discs; wrap each and refrigerate for 30 minutes.

⮑ Working with half of the dough at a time, roll out dough on lightly floured surface to ⅛-inch (3 mm) thickness. With 1½-inch (4 cm) round cookie cutter, cut out circles; place circles, 1 inch (2.5 cm) apart, on prepared baking sheets. Refrigerate for 15 minutes.

⮑ Bake in top and bottom thirds of 400°F (200°C) oven, rotating and switching pans halfway through, until biscuits are lightly browned, about 10 minutes. Serve warm or let cool on racks and serve at room temperature. **(Make-ahead: Layer between waxed paper in airtight container and store at room temperature for up to 2 days or freeze for up to 1 month. Reheat frozen in 375°F/190°C oven for 5 minutes.)**

Makes about 72 biscuits. | PER BISCUIT: about 47 cal, 1 g pro, 3 g total fat (2 g sat. fat), 2 g carb, trace fibre, 20 mg chol, 57 mg sodium. % RDI: 1% calcium, 1% iron, 26% vit A, 4% folate.

Walnut Oatcakes

Walnut-spiked oatcakes make a crisp foundation for your favourite blue cheese, especially when paired with honeyed figs (recipe, right).

2 cups	large-flake rolled oats	500 mL	1 tsp	baking powder	5 mL
½ cup	chopped walnut halves	125 mL	½ tsp	salt	2 mL
1 cup	all-purpose flour	250 mL	½ cup	cold butter, cubed	125 mL
2 tbsp	packed brown sugar	25 mL	¾ cup	buttermilk	175 mL

❧ Line 2 rimless baking sheets with parchment paper or grease; set aside.

❧ In food processor, pulse oats with walnuts until powdery yet with some small pieces; transfer to bowl. Whisk in flour, brown sugar, baking powder and salt. Using pastry blender, cut in butter until crumbly; stir in buttermilk to form stiff, smooth dough. Form into disc; wrap and refrigerate for 30 minutes. **(Make-ahead: Refrigerate for up to 1 day.)**

❧ On floured surface, roll out dough to scant ¼-inch (5 mm) thickness. Using 2-inch (5 cm) round cookie cutter, cut out rounds. Place, 1 inch (2.5 cm) apart, on prepared pans.

❧ Bake in top and bottom thirds of 350°F (180°C) oven, rotating and switching pans halfway through, until edges are crisp and golden, about 28 minutes. Let cool on pans on racks for 5 minutes. Transfer to racks; let cool. **(Make-ahead: Layer between waxed paper in airtight container and store at room temperature for up to 2 days or freeze for up to 1 month.)**

Makes about 40 pieces. | PER PIECE: about 64 cal, 1 g pro, 4 g total fat (2 g sat. fat), 7 g carb, 1 g fibre, 7 mg chol, 64 mg sodium. % RDI: 1% calcium, 3% iron, 2% vit A, 3% folate.

HONEYED FIGS

❯ Trim and chop 15 dried figs. In saucepan, combine figs, 1½ cups (375 mL) orange juice; and ⅓ cup (75 mL) liquid honey; simmer over low heat until tender, about 30 minutes. Uncover and simmer until liquid is syrupy, about 8 minutes. Store in airtight container in refrigerator for up to 2 weeks.

Toffee Cookie Brittle

Once this sheet of baked cookie dough, chunky with pieces of chocolate-covered toffee bars, is broken into pieces like brittle, it will disappear like magic – so be sure you help yourself to a few pieces first! For more-uniform pieces, cut the dough into large triangles just after you take the brittle out of the oven.

1¼ cups	butter, softened	300 mL	3 cups	all-purpose flour	750 mL
1½ cups	granulated sugar	375 mL	1 cup	chocolate chips	250 mL
1½ tsp	vanilla	7 mL	6	bars (each 39 g) milk-chocolate-covered toffee, chopped	6
½ tsp	salt	2 mL			

➤ Set out 17- x 11-inch (45 x 28 cm) rimmed baking sheet; leave ungreased.

➤ In large bowl, beat butter with sugar until fluffy; beat in vanilla and salt. Stir in flour, 1 cup (250 mL) at a time. Stir in chocolate chips and chopped chocolate bars.

➤ Gently squeeze handfuls of dough just until mixture holds together; pat evenly into baking sheet. Bake in centre of 325°F (160°C) oven until just firm to the touch, about 30 minutes. Let cool in pan on rack; break into pieces.

Makes about 72 pieces. | PER PIECE: about 93 cal, 1 g pro, 5 g total fat (3 g sat. fat), 12 g carb, trace fibre, 10 mg chol, 49 mg sodium. % RDI: 1% calcium, 2% iron, 3% vit A, 5% folate.

VARIATIONS

Chocolate Nougat Cookie Brittle: Replace chocolate chips and chocolate-covered toffee bars with coarsely chopped milk-chocolate nougat bars, such as Toblerone.

Hazelnut Cookie Brittle: Replace chocolate-covered toffee bars with 1½ cups (375 mL) coarsely chopped skinned toasted hazelnuts or toasted walnut halves.

Almond Orange Squares

There's a strong pull of orange and almond here, but the flavours meld and mellow, making these squares a delicious item for your repertoire – and coffee break.

3	eggs	3	2¼ cups	ground almonds	550 mL
3	egg yolks	3	2¼ cups	icing sugar	550 mL
1 cup	butter, melted and cooled	250 mL	1 cup	all-purpose flour	250 mL
2 tbsp	grated orange rind	25 mL	**TOPPING:**		
2 tsp	almond extract	10 mL	¾ cup	sliced almonds	175 mL
			1 tbsp	icing sugar	15 mL

~ Line 13- x 9-inch (3.5 L) metal cake pan with parchment paper or grease; set aside.

~ In large bowl, beat together eggs, egg yolks, butter, orange rind and almond extract. In separate bowl, whisk together almonds, sugar and flour; stir into egg mixture until thoroughly mixed. Scrape into prepared pan; smooth top.

~ **TOPPING:** Sprinkle with sliced almonds; press gently. Bake in centre of 325°F (160°C) oven until golden and slightly puffed, 40 to 45 minutes. Let cool in pan on rack. **(Make-ahead: Remove from pan; wrap and store at room temperature or up to 1 day or overwrap in heavy-duty foil and freeze for up to 1 month.)** Cut into squares. Dust with icing sugar.

Makes 40 squares. | PER SQUARE: about 126 cal, 2 g pro, 9 g total fat (3 g sat. fat), 10 g carb, 1 g fibre, 44 mg chol, 53 mg sodium. % RDI: 2% calcium, 4% iron, 6% vit A, 5% folate.

HOW TO LINE A PAN

● Place cake pan on parchment paper. Cut paper 3 inches (8 cm) larger on each side.

● To hold paper steady in pan, sprinkle a little water in the pan before fitting with paper.

● At each corner, make 3-inch (8 cm) long diagonal cut toward centre. Place in pan, creasing fold all around bottom inside edge.

● At each corner, tuck one piece of paper behind the other.

● There is enough paper overhang to act as handles when lifting the whole batch out of the pan and onto a cutting board for cutting into bars or squares.

Brazil Nut Crunch Bars

Any sliced nut, notably unblanched or blanched almonds or hazelnuts, works as the topping for this delightfully buttery bar.

½ cup	instant dissolving (fruit/berry) sugar	125 mL		2 tbsp	cornstarch or rice flour	25 mL
¼ cup	sliced Brazil nuts	50 mL		¼ tsp	each baking powder and salt	1 mL
¾ cup	unsalted butter, softened	175 mL		**NUT TOPPING:**		
1 tsp	vanilla	5 mL		¾ cup	sliced Brazil nuts	175 mL
1¼ cups	all-purpose flour	300 mL		2 tbsp	granulated sugar	25 mL
				1 tbsp	butter, melted	15 mL

〜 Line 9-inch (2.5 L) square metal cake pan with parchment paper or grease; set aside.

〜 In food processor, grind half of the sugar with the nuts. Pour into large bowl; beat in butter, remaining sugar and vanilla.

〜 In separate bowl, whisk together flour, cornstarch, baking powder and salt. Stir into butter mixture in 2 additions until smooth. Press into prepared pan; set aside.

〜 NUT TOPPING: In bowl, toss together nuts, sugar and butter; press over base. Bake in centre of 325°F (160°C) oven until slightly darkened, about 35 minutes. Let cool on rack. **(Make-ahead: Remove from pan; wrap and store at room temperature for 1 day or overwrap in heavy-duty foil and freeze for up to 2 weeks.)** Cut into bars.

Makes 24 bars. | PER BAR: about 126 cal, 1 g pro, 9 g total fat (5 g sat. fat), 11 g carb, trace fibre, 17 mg chol, 32 mg sodium. % RDI: 1% calcium, 3% iron, 6% vit A, 6% folate.

Back to the '50s Dream Bars

In the more than half-century since their creation, untallied pans of dream bars featuring candied fruit, nuts, shortbread and butter icing have emerged from Canadian kitchens. Named, no doubt, in reference to sweet dreams, these bars are quite sweet.

¾ cup	butter, softened	175 mL		1 cup	chopped walnut halves, toasted	250 mL
½ cup	granulated sugar	125 mL		1 cup	candied cherries, quartered	250 mL
¼ tsp	salt	1 mL				
2 cups	all-purpose flour	500 mL		½ cup	chopped pitted dates	125 mL
FILLING:				**ICING:**		
2	eggs	2		½ cup	butter, softened	125 mL
1½ cups	packed brown sugar	375 mL		2 tbsp	milk	25 mL
½ tsp	almond extract	2 mL		½ tsp	vanilla	2 mL
2 tbsp	all-purpose flour	25 mL		2 cups	icing sugar	500 mL
½ tsp	baking powder	2 mL				

❧ Line 13- x 9-inch (3.5 L) metal cake pan with parchment paper or grease; set aside.

❧ In bowl, beat together butter, sugar and salt until fluffy; stir in flour. Press into prepared pan. Bake in centre of 350°F (180°C) oven until golden, about 20 minutes. Let cool in pan on rack.

❧ **FILLING:** In bowl, whisk together eggs, brown sugar and almond extract; stir in flour and baking powder until smooth. Stir in walnuts, cherries and dates. Spread over base. Bake in centre of 350°F (180°C) oven until firm to the touch, about 20 minutes. Let cool in pan on rack.

❧ **ICING:** In bowl, beat together butter, milk and vanilla until creamy; beat in half of the icing sugar. Beat in remaining sugar until fluffy; spread over filling. Refrigerate until cold, about 1 hour. **(Make-ahead: Remove from pan; wrap and store at room temperature for up to 5 days or overwrap in heavy-duty foil and freeze for up to 2 weeks.)** Cut into bars.

Makes 40 bars. | PER BAR: about 181 cal, 2 g pro, 8 g total fat (4 g sat. fat), 27 g carb, 1 g fibre, 25 mg chol, 83 mg sodium. % RDI: 2% calcium, 4% iron, 6% vit A, 2% vit C, 5% folate.

Black Currant Almond Bars

Raspberry, lingonberry and blackberry jams are other flavourful choices to spread over the shortbread base.

½ cup	granulated sugar	125 mL	⅓ cup	all-purpose flour	75 mL
½ cup	marzipan	125 mL	⅔ cup	slivered almonds	150 mL
⅓ cup	butter, softened	75 mL	BASE:		
2	eggs	2	1 cup	all-purpose flour	250 mL
½ tsp	vanilla	2 mL	¼ cup	icing sugar	50 mL
¼ tsp	almond extract	1 mL	½ cup	cold butter, cubed	125 mL
Pinch	salt	Pinch	½ cup	black currant jam	125 mL

❧ Line 9-inch (2.5 L) square metal cake pan with parchment paper or grease; set aside.

❧ BASE: In large bowl, whisk flour with sugar; with pastry blender, cut in butter until mixture is moist and crumbly. Press firmly into prepared pan. Bake in centre of 350°F (180°C) oven until light golden, about 15 minutes. Let cool; spread with jam.

❧ In food processor, whirl together sugar, marzipan and butter until smooth. Pulse in eggs, vanilla, almond extract and salt. Add flour; pulse just until combined. Spread over jam; sprinkle with almonds.

❧ Bake in centre of 350°F (180°C) oven until set and light golden, about 30 minutes. Let cool in pan on rack. (Make-ahead: Remove from pan; wrap and refrigerate for up to 1 week or overwrap in heavy-duty foil and freeze for up to 1 month.) Cut into bars.

Makes 24 bars. | PER BAR: about 185 cal, 3 g pro, 11 g total fat (4 g sat. fat), 19 g carb, 1 g fibre, 36 mg chol, 75 mg sodium. % RDI: 2% calcium, 5% iron, 7% vit A, 2% vit C, 7% folate.

Iced Maple Walnut Bars

Look for walnut halves from California. They have none of the rancidity often found in already chopped walnuts.

			BASE:		
½ cup	butter, softened	125 mL	⅔ cup	butter, softened	150 mL
2 tbsp	maple syrup	25 mL	⅓ cup	packed brown sugar	75 mL
¾ tsp	maple extract	4 mL	Pinch	salt	Pinch
½ tsp	vanilla	2 mL	1⅓ cups	all-purpose flour	325 mL
2 cups	icing sugar	500 mL	½ cup	finely chopped walnut halves	125 mL
40	walnut halves	40			

❧ Line 13- x 9-inch (3.5 L) metal cake pan with parchment paper or grease; set aside.

❧ BASE: In bowl, beat together butter, sugar and salt until fluffy; stir in flour and walnuts. Press into prepared pan; with fork, prick at 1-inch (2.5 cm) intervals all over. Bake in centre of 350°F (180°C) oven until golden, 15 minutes. Let cool in pan on rack.

❧ In bowl, beat together butter, maple syrup and extract, and vanilla until creamy; beat in icing sugar in 2 additions. Spread icing over base.

❧ Press walnuts, in 8 rows of 5, into icing. Refrigerate until firm, about 1 hour. (Make-ahead: Remove from pan; wrap and refrigerate for up to 5 days or overwrap in heavy-duty foil and freeze for up to 1 month.) Cut into bars.

Makes 40 bars. | PER BAR: about 118 cal, 21 g pro, 8 g total fat (4 g sat. fat), 12 g carb, trace fibre, 14 mg chol, 39 mg sodium. % RDI: 1% calcium, 2% iron, 5% vit A, 5% folate.

Lemon Cheesecake Bars

A middle cream cheese layer makes these a change – for the better – from the usual lemon squares.

SMOOTH, EVEN FILLINGS

Hold an offset or rubber spatula as parallel to the surface as possible as you spread the filling evenly over the base.

4	eggs	4
1¼ cups	granulated sugar	300 mL
2 tbsp	finely grated lemon rind	25 mL
½ cup	lemon juice	125 mL
¼ cup	all-purpose flour	50 mL
1 tsp	baking powder	5 mL
1 tbsp	icing sugar	15 mL

CHEESECAKE LAYER:		
1	pkg (8 oz/250 g) cream cheese, softened	1
¼ cup	granulated sugar	50 mL
1	egg	1
BASE:		
30	lemon social tea cookies	30
½ cup	butter, melted	125 mL

CUT NEAT BARS AND SQUARES

❯ Let bars cool completely before cutting.

● Lift uncut bars out of pan using parchment paper liner as handles.

● Place on cutting board.

● With long knife, trim off edges to neaten up.

● A ruler is helpful so all pieces are the same size.

● For 13- x 9-inch (3.5 L) metal cake pan, cut crosswise into quarters. Cut each quarter in half lengthwise, then cut crosswise into fifths to make 10 squares.

● Keep a wet, wrung-out cloth handy to wipe knife clean between cuts.

Line 13- x 9-inch (3.5 L) metal cake pan with parchment paper or grease; set aside.

BASE: In food processor, whirl cookies to make 2 cups (500 mL) crumbs; pulse in butter until moistened. Press into prepared pan. Bake in centre of 325°F (160°C) oven until firm, about 12 minutes. Let cool in pan on rack.

CHEESECAKE LAYER: In bowl, beat cream cheese with sugar until smooth; beat in egg. Spread over base; set aside.

In bowl, beat eggs with sugar until thickened. Beat in lemon rind and juice, flour and baking powder until smooth; pour over cheesecake layer. Bake in centre of 325°F (160°C) oven until edges are set and lightly browned, about 35 minutes. Let cool in pan on rack. **(Make-ahead: Remove from pan; wrap and refrigerate for up to 5 days or overwrap in heavy-duty foil and freeze for up to 1 month.)** Cut into bars; dust with icing sugar.

Makes 60 bars. | PER BAR: about 71 cal, 1 g pro, 4 g total fat (2 g sat. fat), 9 g carb, 0 g fibre, 24 mg chol, 33 mg sodium. % RDI: 1% calcium, 1% iron, 4% vit A, 2% vit C, 2% folate.

Nanaimo Bars

While Nanaimo bars have only been on dainty trays and in coffee shops for a little more than a half-century, these creamy, chocolaty confections do reflect two long-standing Canadian characteristics: we love to bake, and we love sweets. Do buy the best chocolate and cocoa available, and the freshest eggs and butter.

1 cup	graham cracker crumbs	250 mL
½ cup	sweetened flaked or shredded coconut	125 mL
⅓ cup	finely chopped walnut halves	75 mL
¼ cup	cocoa powder	50 mL
¼ cup	granulated sugar	50 mL
⅓ cup	butter, melted	75 mL
1	egg, lightly beaten	1

FILLING:

¼ cup	butter	50 mL
2 tbsp	custard powder	25 mL
½ tsp	vanilla	2 mL
2 cups	icing sugar	500 mL
2 tbsp	milk (approx)	25 mL

TOPPING:

4 oz	semisweet chocolate, chopped	125 g
1 tbsp	butter	15 mL

➤ Line 9-inch (2.5 L) square metal cake pan with parchment paper or grease; set aside.

➤ In bowl, stir together graham crumbs, coconut, walnuts, cocoa powder and sugar; drizzle butter and egg over top. Stir until combined. Press into prepared pan. Bake in centre of 350°F (180°C) oven until firm, about 10 minutes. Let cool in pan on rack.

➤ **FILLING:** In bowl, beat together butter, custard powder and vanilla. Beat in icing sugar alternately with milk until smooth, adding up to 1 tsp (5 mL) more milk if filling is too thick to spread. Spread over base; refrigerate until cold and firm, about 1 hour.

➤ **TOPPING:** In heatproof bowl over saucepan of hot (not boiling) water, melt chocolate with butter. Spread evenly over filling; refrigerate until almost set, about 30 minutes. With tip of knife, score into bars; refrigerate until chocolate is set, about 1 hour. **(Make-ahead: Remove from pan; wrap and refrigerate for up to 4 days or overwrap in heavy-duty foil and freeze for up to 2 weeks.)** Cut into bars.

Makes 30 bars. | PER BAR: about 128 cal, 1 g pro, 7 g total fat (4 g sat. fat), 17 g carb, 1 g fibre, 17 mg chol, 58 mg sodium. % RDI: 1% calcium, 3% iron, 4% vit A, 3% folate.

VARIATION

Grand Marnier Nanaimo Bars: In the filling, replace milk with Grand Marnier or other orange-flavoured liqueur and add 1 tbsp (15 mL) grated orange rind.

Irresistible Turtle Bars

Chocolate, caramel and pecans stack up for a decadent take on the popular candy. Trust us – it's hard to stop at one, but you must.

¾ cup	butter, softened	175 mL	½ cup	packed brown sugar	125 mL
½ cup	granulated sugar	125 mL	½ cup	corn syrup	125 mL
1¾ cups	all-purpose flour	425 mL	2 tbsp	whipping cream	25 mL
½ cup	cocoa powder	125 mL	1 cup	chopped pecans, toasted	250 mL
FILLING:					
⅔ cup	butter	150 mL	2 oz	semisweet chocolate, melted	60 g

↜ Line 13- x 9-inch (3.5 L) metal cake pan with parchment paper or grease; set aside.

↜ In bowl, beat butter with sugar until fluffy. Sift flour and cocoa over top; stir until combined. Press into prepared pan. Bake in centre of 350°F (180°C) oven until firm, about 15 minutes. Let cool in pan on rack.

↜ **FILLING:** In saucepan, bring butter, sugar, corn syrup and cream to boil, stirring. Boil, without stirring, until thickened, about 1 minute. Remove from heat; stir in pecans. Spread over crust.

↜ Bake in centre of 350°F (180°C) oven until bubbly and edges are light golden, about 20 minutes. Let cool in pan on rack.

↜ Drizzle with melted chocolate. Let stand until chocolate is set. **(Make-ahead: Remove from pan; wrap and refrigerate for up to 4 days or overwrap in heavy-duty foil and freeze for up to 1 month.)** Cut into bars.

Makes 40 bars. | PER BAR: about 140 cal, 1 g pro, 9 g total fat (5 g sat. fat), 14 g carb, 1 g fibre, 19 mg chol, 73 mg sodium. % RDI: 1% calcium, 4% iron, 6% vit A, 6% folate.

VARIATION

Irresistible Black Forest Bars: Omit filling. Spread cooled base with ¾ cup (175 mL) sour cherry jam. Whisk together ½ cup (125 mL) all-purpose flour, ⅓ cup (75 mL) granulated sugar and 2 tbsp (25 mL) cocoa powder. Cut in ⅓ cup (75 mL) cold butter until crumbly. Sprinkle over jam. Bake in centre of 350°F (180°C) oven until firm to the touch, about 30 minutes. Let cool in pan on rack. Dust with 1 tbsp (15 mL) icing sugar.

Blueberry Oatmeal Squares

A perfect summer recipe – not complicated but fresh and appealing with blueberries.

2½ cups	large-flake rolled oats	625 mL
1¼ cups	all-purpose flour	300 mL
1 cup	packed brown sugar	250 mL
1 tbsp	grated orange rind	15 mL
¼ tsp	salt	1 mL
1 cup	cold butter, cubed	250 mL

BLUEBERRY FILLING:

3 cups	fresh blueberries	750 mL
½ cup	granulated sugar	125 mL
⅓ cup	orange juice	75 mL
4 tsp	cornstarch	20 mL

❧ Line 8-inch (2 L) square metal cake pan with parchment paper or grease; set aside.

❧ BLUEBERRY FILLING: In saucepan, bring blueberries, sugar and orange juice to boil; reduce heat and simmer until tender, about 10 minutes. Whisk cornstarch with 2 tbsp (25 mL) water; whisk into blueberries and boil, stirring, until thickened, about 1 minute. Place plastic wrap directly on surface; refrigerate until cold, about 1 hour.

❧ In large bowl, whisk together oats, flour, brown sugar, orange rind and salt; with pastry blender, cut in butter until crumbly. Press half into prepared pan; spread with blueberry filling. Sprinkle with remaining oat mixture, pressing lightly.

❧ Bake in centre of 350°F (180°C) oven until light golden, about 45 minutes. Let cool in pan on rack. **(Make-ahead: Remove from pan; wrap and refrigerate for up to 2 days or overwrap in heavy-duty foil and freeze for up to 2 weeks.)** Cut into squares.

Makes 24 squares. | PER SQUARE: about 193 cal, 2 g pro, 8 g total fat (5 g sat. fat), 28 g carb, 2 g fibre, 20 mg chol, 84 mg sodium. % RDI: 2% calcium, 7% iron, 7% vit A, 5% vit C, 8% folate.

VARIATIONS

Lunch Box Date Squares: Omit blueberry filling. In saucepan, combine 1 pkg (375 g) pitted dates, chopped; 2 cups (500 mL) water; ¾ cup (175 mL) granulated sugar; 1 tsp (5 mL) grated lemon rind; and ¼ cup (50 mL) lemon juice. Bring to boil; reduce heat and simmer gently, stirring often, until filling is thick enough to mound firmly on spoon, about 15 minutes. Let cool.

Mincemeat Pear Oatmeal Squares: Omit blueberry filling. In saucepan, combine 1½ cups (375 mL) mincemeat; 2 pears, peeled, cored and chopped; and 1 tbsp (15 mL) rum extract or rum. Bring to boil; reduce heat and simmer gently, stirring often, until filling is thick enough to mound firmly on spoon, 15 to 20 minutes. Let cool.

Cheddar Apple Bars

Carried in their baking pan or packed in a cookie tin, these fruity oat bars make a welcome summer or fall cottage dessert or lunch box treat any time of the year. Golden Delicious or Crispin apples are perfect for this spin on the apple-Cheddar duo.

4	apples	4	1 cup	all-purpose flour	250 mL
⅓ cup	granulated sugar	75 mL	⅔ cup	packed brown sugar	150 mL
2 tbsp	lemon juice	25 mL	¼ tsp	salt	1 mL
½ tsp	cinnamon	2 mL	¾ cup	butter, melted	175 mL
CHEDDAR CRUST AND CRUMBLE:			1 cup	shredded extra-old Cheddar cheese	250 mL
1½ cups	large-flake rolled oats	375 mL			

❧ Line 9-inch (2.5 L) square metal cake pan with parchment paper or grease; set aside.

❧ **CHEDDAR CRUST AND CRUMBLE:** In bowl, whisk together oats, flour, brown sugar and salt. With fork, stir in butter until mixture clumps and is crumbly. Add cheese, tossing to mix. Press all but 1 cup (250 mL) evenly into prepared pan. Bake in centre of 350°F (180°C) oven until edges are golden, about 15 minutes. Let cool.

❧ Meanwhile, peel, core and cut apples into ½-inch (1 cm) thick slices. In skillet or shallow saucepan, bring apples, sugar, lemon juice and cinnamon to boil, adding up to ¼ cup (50 mL) water if apples stick to pan. Reduce heat and simmer, stirring occasionally, until tender-crisp, about 5 minutes.

❧ Spread apple mixture over base; sprinkle with remaining oat mixture. Bake in centre of 350°F (180°C) oven until golden, about 30 minutes. Let cool in pan on rack. **(Make-ahead: Remove from pan; wrap and refrigerate for up to 3 days or overwrap in heavy-duty foil and freeze for up to 2 weeks.)** Cut into squares.

Makes 20 squares. | PER SQUARE: about 189 cal, 3 g pro, 9 g total fat (6 g sat. fat), 24 g carb, 1 g fibre, 28 mg chol, 138 mg sodium. % RDI: 5% calcium, 6% iron, 8% vit A, 2% vit C, 5% folate.

Oatmeal Energy Bars

Everyone needs a little energy to get through the day. Chewy and nutty, these lunch box bars will satisfy any sweet cravings as well as deliver a delicious pick-me-up.

⅔ cup	butter, softened	150 mL		½ tsp	baking soda	2 mL
1 cup	packed brown sugar	250 mL		¼ tsp	salt	1 mL
1	egg	1		½ cup	chopped dried apricots	125 mL
1 tsp	vanilla	5 mL		½ cup	slivered almonds	125 mL
1½ cups	large-flake rolled oats	375 mL		½ cup	dried cranberries	125 mL
1 cup	all-purpose flour	250 mL		½ cup	sweetened shredded or flaked coconut	125 mL
½ tsp	baking powder	2 mL				

❧ Line 13- x 9-inch (3.5 L) metal cake pan with parchment paper or grease; set aside.

❧ In large bowl, beat butter with brown sugar until fluffy; beat in egg and vanilla. In separate bowl, whisk together oats, flour, baking powder, baking soda and salt; stir in apricots, almonds, cranberries and coconut. Stir into butter mixture. Spread evenly in prepared pan.

❧ Bake in centre of 350°F (180°C) oven for 30 minutes. Let cool in pan on rack for 10 minutes. Cut into bars; let cool. (**Make-ahead: Layer between waxed paper in airtight container and store at room temperature for up to 1 week.**)

Makes 12 bars. | PER BAR: about 319 cal, 5 g pro, 15 g total fat (8 g sat. fat), 43 g carb, 3 g fibre, 48 mg chol, 237 mg sodium. % RDI: 4% calcium, 14% iron, 14% vit A, 2% vit C, 10% folate.

Tropical Fruit Bars

There's a nice hint of rum in these chewy bars packed with fruit, coconut and nuts.

1	can (300 mL) sweetened condensed milk	1
3 tbsp	rum	50 mL
2 tbsp	all-purpose flour	25 mL
1½ cups	coarsely chopped macadamia nuts or cashews	375 mL
1 cup	each sweetened flaked or shredded coconut and chopped dried mango	250 mL

BASE:

1½ cups	graham cracker crumbs	375 mL
½ cup	each sweetened flaked or shredded coconut and packed brown sugar	125 mL
½ cup	butter, melted	125 mL

RUM BUTTER ICING:

½ cup	butter, softened	125 mL
1 tbsp	each milk and rum	15 mL
2 cups	icing sugar	500 mL

❧ Line 13- x 9-inch (3.5 L) metal cake pan with parchment paper or grease; set aside.

❧ BASE: In bowl, combine graham cracker crumbs, coconut and brown sugar; stir in butter until moistened. Press into prepared pan. Bake in centre of 325°F (160°C) oven until firm, about 15 minutes. Let cool in pan on rack.

❧ In large bowl, mix together condensed milk, rum and flour; stir in nuts, coconut and mango. Spread over base. Bake in centre of 325°F (160°C) oven until golden and set, about 35 minutes. Let cool.

❧ RUM BUTTER ICING: In large bowl, beat together butter, milk and rum until creamy; beat in sugar in 2 additions until fluffy. Spread over filling. Refrigerate until firm, about 1 hour. (Make-ahead: Remove from pan; wrap and refrigerate for up to 1 week or overwrap in heavy-duty foil and freeze for up to 1 month.) Cut into bars.

Makes 40 bars. | PER BAR: about 182 cal, 2 g pro, 11 g total fat (5 g sat. fat), 21 g carb, 1 g fibre, 18 mg chol, 93 mg sodium. % RDI: 3% calcium, 3% iron, 6% vit A, 3% vit C, 3% folate.

VARIATION

Not-Quite-Tropical Fruit Bars: Substitute dried apricots for the dried mango.

White Chocolate Blondie Bars

Sour cherries add a tart bite to these decidedly sweet bars.

6 oz	white chocolate, chopped	175 g	1¼ cups	all-purpose flour	300 mL
⅓ cup	butter	75 mL	Pinch	salt	Pinch
¾ cup	granulated sugar	175 mL	½ cup	halved dried sour cherries	125 mL
2	eggs	2			
2 tsp	vanilla	10 mL	2 oz	white chocolate, melted	60 g

❧ Line 9-inch (2.5 L) square metal cake pan with parchment paper or grease; set aside.

❧ In saucepan, melt chopped white chocolate with butter over low heat. Remove from heat; whisk in sugar. Whisk in eggs, 1 at a time, whisking well after each; stir in vanilla. Stir in flour, salt and cherries. Scrape into prepared pan; smooth top.

❧ Bake in centre of 325°F (160°C) oven until cake tester inserted in centre comes out clean, about 35 minutes. Let cool in pan on rack. Drizzle with melted white chocolate. Refrigerate until cold, about 3 hours. (**Make-ahead: Remove from pan; wrap and refrigerate for up to 4 days or overwrap in heavy-duty foil and freeze for up to 2 weeks.**) Cut into bars.

Makes 24 bars. | PER BAR: about 138 cal, 2 g pro, 6 g total fat (4 g sat. fat), 19 g carb, trace fibre, 23 mg chol, 33 mg sodium. % RDI: 3% calcium, 3% iron, 3% vit A, 7% folate.

Peanut Butter Brownies

Because peanut butter makes the batter and icing stiff, an offset spatula is the best utensil to use for spreading.

6 oz	bittersweet chocolate, chopped	175 g	1 cup	chopped unsalted peanuts	250 mL
4 oz	unsweetened chocolate, chopped	125 g	Pinch	salt	Pinch
⅓ cup	butter	75 mL	**ICING:**		
⅓ cup	natural peanut butter, at room temperature	75 mL	⅓ cup	butter, softened	75 mL
2 cups	granulated sugar	500 mL	¼ cup	natural peanut butter, at room temperature	50 mL
1 tsp	vanilla	5 mL	½ tsp	vanilla	2 mL
4	eggs	4	2 cups	icing sugar	500 mL
1⅔ cups	all-purpose flour	400 mL	1 tbsp	milk	15 mL
			3 oz	bittersweet chocolate, melted	90 g

❧ Line 13- x 9-inch (3.5 L) metal cake pan with parchment paper or grease; set aside.

❧ In large saucepan, melt together bittersweet and unsweetened chocolates, butter and peanut butter over medium-low heat, stirring occasionally; let cool for 10 minutes. Whisk in sugar and vanilla. Whisk in eggs, 1 at a time. Stir in flour, peanuts and salt. Spread in prepared pan.

❧ Bake in centre of 350°F (180°C) oven until cake tester inserted in centre comes out with just a few moist crumbs clinging, about 25 minutes. Let cool in pan on rack.

❧ **ICING:** In bowl, beat together butter, peanut butter and vanilla until creamy. Beat in icing sugar in 2 additions; beat in milk. Spread over brownies. Drizzle with chocolate. Refrigerate until firm, about 1 hour. **(Make-ahead: Remove from pan; wrap and refrigerate for up to 5 days or overwrap in heavy-duty foil and freeze for up to 1 month.)** Cut into bars.

Makes 60 bars. | PER BAR: about 139 cal, 3 g pro, 7 g total fat (3 g sat. fat), 17 g carb, 1 g fibre, 18 mg chol, 20 mg sodium. % RDI: 1% calcium, 4% iron, 2% vit A, 5% folate.

Super Chocolate Chunk Fudge Brownies

These brownies are so chocolaty and full of bittersweet and white chocolate chunks that there is no need for icing. For super indulgers, go for Silk-Topped Fudge Brownies (see variation, below).

¾ cup	granulated sugar	175 mL	1 tsp	vanilla	5 mL
⅓ cup	butter	75 mL	¾ cup	all-purpose flour	175 mL
8 oz	bittersweet chocolate, chopped	250 g	¼ tsp	each baking soda and salt	1 mL
2	eggs	2	4 oz	white chocolate, chopped	125 g

- Line 9-inch (2.5 L) square metal cake pan with parchment paper or grease; set aside.
- In saucepan over medium-high heat, bring sugar, butter and 2 tbsp (25 mL) water to boil, stirring occasionally. Remove from heat; stir in half of the bittersweet chocolate until melted. Let cool for 10 minutes. Whisk in eggs, 1 at a time, then vanilla.
- In separate bowl, whisk together flour, baking soda and salt; stir into chocolate mixture. Stir in remaining bittersweet chocolate and white chocolate. Scrape into prepared pan; smooth top.
- Bake in centre of 325°F (160°C) oven until cake tester inserted in centre comes out with a few moist crumbs clinging, about 30 minutes. Let cool in pan on rack. (Make-ahead: Remove from pan; wrap and store at room temperature for up to 3 days or overwrap in heavy-duty foil and freeze for up to 2 weeks.) Cut into squares.

Makes 24 squares. | PER SQUARE: about 146 cal, 2 g pro, 8 g total fat (5 g sat. fat), 17 g carb, 1 g fibre, 23 mg chol, 44 mg sodium. % RDI: 2% calcium, 5% iron, 3% vit A, 5% folate.

VARIATIONS

Silk-Topped Fudge Brownies: Place 3 oz (90 g) bittersweet chocolate, chopped, in heatproof bowl. In saucepan, heat ⅓ cup (75 mL) whipping cream with 1 tbsp (15 mL) corn syrup until boiling; pour over chocolate and whisk until smooth. Let stand for 3 minutes. Spread over cooled brownies.

Super Chocolate Walnut Fudge Brownies: Reduce bittersweet chocolate to 4 oz (125 g). Replace chopped bittersweet and white chocolate in batter with 1 cup (250 mL) chopped walnut halves.

Raspberry Marble Brownies

Certain fruits, raspberries being one of them, have a real affinity with chocolate. Take these to a party and you'll get definitely get requests for the recipe.

4 oz	unsweetened chocolate, chopped	125 g
½ cup	butter, cubed	125 mL
1 cup	raspberries, fresh or thawed frozen	250 mL
3	eggs	3
1¼ cups	granulated sugar	300 mL
½ tsp	vanilla	2 mL
¾ cup	all-purpose flour	175 mL

CREAM CHEESE FILLING:

¾ cup	cream cheese, softened	175 mL
½ cup	butter, softened	125 mL
½ cup	granulated sugar	125 mL
2	eggs	2
1 tsp	vanilla	5 mL
2 tbsp	all-purpose flour	25 mL

➥ Line 9-inch (2.5 L) square metal cake pan with parchment paper or grease; set aside.

➥ CREAM CHEESE FILLING: In bowl, beat cream cheese with butter until blended; beat in sugar. Beat in eggs, 1 at a time, then vanilla. Stir in flour. Set aside.

➥ In bowl over saucepan of hot (not boiling) water, melt chocolate with butter; let cool.

➥ Press raspberries through fine sieve to remove seeds. Set purée aside.

➥ In separate bowl, beat eggs with sugar until pale and thickened, about 5 minutes. Beat in vanilla and raspberry purée. Stir in flour and chocolate mixture.

➥ Scrape three-quarters of the chocolate batter into prepared pan. Spread cream cheese filling over top. Dollop with remaining batter; swirl with tip of knife to create marble effect.

➥ Bake in centre of 350°F (180°C) oven until cake tester inserted in centre comes out with a few moist crumbs clinging, about 35 minutes. Let cool in pan on rack. **(Make-ahead: Remove from pan. Wrap and refrigerate for up to 5 days or overwrap in heavy-duty foil and freeze for up to 1 month.)** Cut into squares.

Makes 16 large squares. | PER SQUARE: about 312 cal, 4 g pro, 21 g total fat (12 g sat. fat), 30 g carb, 2 g fibre, 106 mg chol, 170 mg sodium. % RDI: 3% calcium, 8% iron, 18% vit A, 2% vit C, 9% folate.

Chapter 2

Cakes

When life calls for a celebration, there will be a cake. Luckily, in our modern kitchens with reliable ingredients, electric mixers and good ovens, beautiful cakes worthy of special occasions are well within a home baker's reach.

Three kinds of cake inhabit this chapter, organized by the method by which they're made. We start with cakes based on beating (or creaming) butter with sugar and alternately adding dry and wet ingredients. These cakes rely on fast-acting baking powder and baking soda for their leavening. The second kind of cake, foam-based, relies on beaten egg whites, yolks or whole eggs to lighten and raise the batter. The third type is cheesecake. While called a cake and served like one, cheesecake uses a different, more custard-like technique. And what would a cake chapter be without a delectable few of these creamy creations?

Temperature: The Key to Success

> A successful cake starts out with room-temperature ingredients. This is especially true of milk, eggs and butter. Ideally, measure and set them out two hours before you need them.

However, if the inspiration or need to bake a cake arises unexpectedly, or if you've forgotten, there are quick ways to remedy the situation. Cube cold, hard butter or shred it on the largest holes of a box grater. Spread over the bottom of a mixing bowl and let soften for about 20 minutes. Avoid the temptation to heat the butter, as all too often it will melt and not incorporate enough air into the batter for the cake to rise successfully. Set cold eggs in a bowl with enough warm water to cover for 10 minutes. Warm cold milk to room temperature in the microwave. Meanwhile, prepare the pans, measure out the dry and any other wet ingredients, adjust the oven racks and preheat the oven.

If a cake requires separated eggs, it is easier to separate them while they're still cold, then let the yolks and whites come to room temperature in separate bowls set in a shallow pan or sink of barely warm water.

Cake Tips and Techniques

> Beating or creaming the butter with the sugar incorporates air into the mixture. Use an electric mixer on high to beat the butter with the sugar until very fluffy and lightened in colour to a very pale yellow, like cream.

> Beating in the eggs one at a time and beating well after each ensures that the eggs are emulsified in the batter. Scrape down the side of the bowl often.

> Add the dry ingredients in three stages, the liquid in two, using a wooden spoon or a mixer on low speed to prevent the elasticity, or gluten, in the flour from developing. Scrape down the side of the bowl frequently.

> Fill prepared cake pans half to two-thirds full. Measure the batter or use a kitchen scale to ensure that filled pans are of equal weight, which will produce layers of equal height.

> Before baking, tap pans lightly on counter to remove air bubbles in batter.

> Rely on more than one test for doneness. A cake tester or skewer inserted into the centre of the cake will come out clean, the cake will have shrunk away from the side of the pan, and the centre of the cake will be firm to a light touch.

> A layer cake should be cooled for about 10 minutes, longer for a larger cake, in the pan before turning it out onto a rack to finish cooling. This wait gives the cake's delicate structure time to firm up.

EQUIPMENT
FOR CAKES

- Bundt pans: 9-inch (2.5 L) and 10-inch (3 L)

- Tube pan: 10-inch (4 L)

- Straight-sided shiny metal cake pans: 8-inch (2 L) square, 9-inch (2.5 L) square and 13- x 9-inch (3.5 L)

- Springform pans: 8-inch (2 L), 9-inch (2.5 L), 9½-inch (2.75 L) and 10-inch (3 L)

- Shiny metal loaf pans: 5¾- x 3¼-inch (625 mL), 8- x 4-inch (1.5 L) and 9- x 5-inch (2 L)

- Shiny metal rimmed baking sheet (jelly roll pan): 15- x 10-inch (40 x 25 cm)

- Muffin or tart pans, with cups about 2¾ inches (7 cm) in diameter and ⅓- to ½-cup (75 to 125 mL) capacity

- Mini cheesecake pan, with twelve 4-oz (125 mL) cups

- Cake tester or metal skewer

- Stand mixer with paddle and whisk attachments

- Cake dome

- Kitchen scale

- Paper muffin/cupcake liners

- Plastic squeeze bottle for sauces

- Cake-decorating turntable (the ultimate for icing cakes; invest in one if you're really into cake decorating)

Foolproof Layer Cake Assembly

❯ Trim layers so they are even. Save the scraps for later to fill in holes or for snacks.

❯ Brushing crumbs off layers helps keep icing clean. Repeat after cutting or trimming layers and stacking them with filling.

❯ To cut a layer in half horizontally, hold a ruler against the side to find the halfway point; mark in 6 places around the layer with toothpicks. Using toothpicks as a guide, cut layers in half with a long serrated knife (don't press; let the blade do the work). A gentle sawing motion is recommended.

❯ Dollop a bit of the icing in the centre of the cake plate to anchor the first layer. Using one hand and a spatula, lift one layer, cut side up, onto the plate.

❯ Slip four strips of waxed paper under the edge of the cake to keep the plate clean. Slide them out after the cake is iced.

❯ Spread icing with even strokes using a metal spatula or palette knife. Bring firm fillings, such as jam, just to edge and softer fillings, such as buttercream or whipped cream, to about ¼ inch (5 mm) from edge to allow them to spread when layers are stacked.

❯ Stack layers and filling, saving one bottom half for top. Adjust where necessary with extra icing or cake trimmings to make cake even. Scrape off any excess fillings. Refrigerate for 30 minutes to firm up before icing.

❯ The secret to a beautifully iced cake is the masking, or crumb coat. Use just enough of the icing to thinly coat: sides first, then top, anchoring any stray crumbs. Let the icing harden for 30 minutes in the refrigerator before adding the final coat.

❯ Hold a long palette knife or spatula flat against side of cake, touching from bottom to top, and make long, sweeping strokes to ensure an even final coat. Decorate with swirls or lines as desired.

Foam Cake Tips and Techniques

❯ Use a perfectly clean metal or glass bowl for beating egg whites. Even a smear of grease or a speck of egg yolk mixed into the whites will prevent them from reaching firm, glossy, high peaks, which are the secret to beautiful angel food and chiffon cakes.

❯ Beat egg whites at high speed until soft peaks that droop form.

❯ To egg whites, add sugar, about 1 tbsp (15 mL) at a time, while continuing to beat until stiff, opaque white peaks form. These unwavering peaks will stand up straight when the beaters are lifted out of the whites.

❯ To fold in dry ingredients, sprinkle them evenly over surface. Use a rubber spatula to cut down through the dry ingredients into the egg whites, then skim along the bottom of the bowl, bringing up some of the whites as the spatula comes up along the side of the bowl. Without lifting the spatula from the batter, cut down through the batter again. Rotate the bowl, continuing to cut and lift until there are no longer any streaks of dry ingredients.

❯ Once the batter is in the pan, eliminate air pockets by running a spatula through the batter.

❯ If your tube pan does not have legs that allow air circulation around the baked and cooling cake, set the cake pan upside down over a large bottle or inverted large funnel.

Black Forest Mousse Cake

This is a downright decadent cake: layers of chocolate cake and tart red Morello or Montmorency cherries are crowned with whipped cream and chocolate curls. Our version of the splendid German cake goes one step further with a luscious chocolate mousse filling. You can find sour cherries preserved in a light syrup in jars at delis and supermarkets.

PREP PANS

Do this step before you start the cake. For layer and casual slab cakes made with beaten butter and sugar, start by brushing butter, preferable unsalted, around inside side of pan. (Some bakers grease the whole inside of pan to anchor the paper.)

Trace around bottom of cake pan on parchment paper.

Cut out shape, turn over and press onto bottom of pan. For most cakes, waxed paper works, too.

1	jar (28 oz/796 mL) sour cherries	1
⅔ cup	granulated sugar	150 mL
1 tbsp	brandy or kirsch	15 mL
2½ cups	whipping cream	625 mL
1 tsp	vanilla	5 mL
Half	batch Chocolate Shavings (recipe, page 337)	Half

CHOCOLATE MOUSSE:

6 oz	semisweet chocolate, chopped	175 g
2 cups	whipping cream	500 mL
2 tbsp	brandy or kirsch	25 mL

CHOCOLATE CAKE:

1 cup	butter, softened	250 mL
1½ cups	granulated sugar	375 mL
2	eggs	2
1 tsp	vanilla	5 mL
2 cups	all-purpose flour	500 mL
½ cup	cocoa powder	125 mL
1 tsp	each baking powder and baking soda	5 mL
¼ tsp	salt	1 mL
1½ cups	buttermilk	375 mL

∾ Grease sides of two 8-inch (2 L) springform pans or two 8-inch (1.2 L) round metal cake pans; line bottoms with parchment or waxed paper. Line rimmed baking sheet with waxed paper. Set all pans aside.

∾ CHOCOLATE CAKE: In large bowl, beat butter with sugar until light and fluffy; beat in eggs, 1 at a time, beating well after each. Beat in vanilla.

∾ In separate bowl, sift together flour, cocoa, baking powder, baking soda and salt; sift again. With wooden spoon, stir into butter mixture alternately with buttermilk, making 3 additions of dry ingredients and 2 of buttermilk. Scrape into prepared springform pans; smooth tops.

∾ Bake in centre of 350°F (180°C) oven until cake tester inserted in centre comes out clean, about 35 minutes. Let cool in pans on racks for 10 minutes. Turn out onto racks; peel off paper. Invert; let cool. (Make-ahead: Wrap in plastic wrap and refrigerate for up to 1 day or overwrap in heavy-duty foil and freeze for up to 2 weeks.)

∾ Meanwhile, in sieve over bowl, drain cherries, pressing lightly; reserve ⅓ cup (75 mL) of the juice for cake (save remainder for drinks). In small saucepan, bring ⅓ cup (75 mL) of the sugar and reserved juice to boil; boil until reduced to ½ cup (125 mL), about 5 minutes. Let cool; stir in brandy. (Make-ahead: Refrigerate cherries and syrup separately in airtight containers for up to 2 days; reheat syrup to continue.)

⌁CHOCOLATE MOUSSE: Place chocolate in large heatproof bowl. In saucepan, bring cream and brandy just to boil; pour over chocolate, whisking until melted and smooth. Refrigerate until thickened and chilled, about 1 hour. Beat until soft peaks form. Cover and set mousse aside. (Make-ahead: Refrigerate in airtight container for up to 2 days.)

⌁Brush loose crumbs from cake layers. Cut each layer in half horizontally; place, cut side up, on waxed paper. Brush each cut side with 2 tbsp (25 mL) of the cherry syrup; let stand for 5 minutes.

⌁Meanwhile, in large bowl, whip together cream, remaining sugar and vanilla. Transfer one-quarter to large piping bag fitted with ¾-inch (2 cm) star tip.

⌁Place 1 cake layer, cut side up, on flat cake plate; slide 4 strips of waxed paper between cake and plate. Spread with 1 cup (250 mL) of the mousse. Arrange ¾ cup (175 mL) of the cherries over top. Repeat to make second and third layers; top with remaining layer, cut side down. Spread reserved whipped cream over top and side. Pipe rosettes on top; decorate with remaining cherries. Using toothpick or tongs, press Chocolate Shavings to side of cake. Remove paper strips. (Make-ahead: Cover loosely with plastic wrap and refrigerate for up to 1 day.)

Makes 16 servings. | PER SERVING: about 625 cal, 6 g pro, 41 g total fat (25 g sat. fat), 63 g carb, 3 g fibre, 146 mg chol, 301 mg sodium. % RDI: 9% calcium, 15% iron, 38% vit A, 2% vit C, 15% folate.

KEEPING CAKES FRESH
> Cover with a cake dome or insert toothpicks in unobtrusive spots on top and side of cake. Drape plastic wrap over cake.

....

VARIATIONS

The Canadian Living Chocolate Layer Cake: Make Chocolate Cake as above, omitting all other ingredients. Assemble layers and ice as directed, using Creamy Chocolate Icing.

⌁CREAMY CHOCOLATE ICING: In bowl, beat 1½ cups (375 mL) butter, softened, until fluffy; gradually beat in ½ cup (125 mL) whipping cream. Beat in 1 tbsp (15 mL) vanilla. Beat in 3 cups (750 mL) icing sugar, 1 cup (250 mL) at a time. Add 6 oz (175 g) unsweetened chocolate, melted and cooled; beat until fluffy.

Chocolate Cupcakes: Spoon Chocolate Cake batter into paper-lined or greased muffin cups. Bake until cake tester inserted in centre comes out clean, about 20 minutes. Transfer to racks; let cool. Spread tops with half-batch of Creamy Chocolate Icing or your favourite icing. Makes 18 cupcakes.

Chocolate Raspberry Curl Cake

Take note, chocolate lovers and cake bakers (even novices), this party-size curl-coated cake is surprisingly straightforward to make. A hint of raspberry complements the bittersweet chocolate, and fresh raspberries make a stylish garnish (see photo, opposite).

1½ cups	butter, softened	375 mL		2 cups	sour cream	500 mL
2¼ cups	granulated sugar	550 mL			Short Round Chocolate Curls (recipe, page 336)	
3	eggs	3		**FILLING AND ICING:**		
¼ cup	thawed raspberry cocktail concentrate	50 mL		1 lb	bittersweet or semisweet chocolate, chopped	500 g
2 tsp	vanilla	10 mL		2⅓ cups	sour cream	575 mL
3 cups	all-purpose flour	750 mL		¼ cup	granulated sugar	50 mL
¾ cup	cocoa powder	175 mL		1 tsp	vanilla	5 mL
1½ tsp	each baking powder and baking soda	7 mL		⅓ cup	seedless raspberry jam	75 mL
½ tsp	salt	2 mL				

❧ Grease sides of three 9-inch (1.5 L) round metal cake pans; line bottoms with parchment or waxed paper. Set aside.

❧ In large bowl, beat butter with sugar until light and fluffy; beat in eggs, 1 at a time, beating well after each. Beat in raspberry concentrate and vanilla.

❧ In separate bowl, sift together flour, cocoa, baking powder, baking soda and salt; sift again. With wooden spoon, stir into butter mixture alternately with sour cream, making 3 additions of dry ingredients and 2 of sour cream. Scrape into prepared pans; smooth tops.

❧ Bake in centre of 350°F (180°C) oven until cake tester inserted in centre comes out clean, 30 to 35 minutes. Let cool in pans on racks for 10 minutes. Turn out onto racks; peel off paper. Invert; let cool. **(Make-ahead: Wrap in plastic wrap and refrigerate for up to 1 day or overwrap in heavy-duty foil and freeze for up to 2 weeks.)**

❧**FILLING AND ICING:** In large heatproof bowl over saucepan of hot (not boiling) water, melt chocolate, stirring occasionally. Remove from heat. Whisk in half of the sour cream; whisk in remaining sour cream until smooth. Whisk in sugar and vanilla.

❧ Trim cake layers flat if necessary. Brush loose crumbs from layers. Place 1 layer on flat cake plate, bottom side down; slide 4 strips of waxed paper between cake and plate. Spread with ⅓ cup (75 mL) of the icing. Spread jam over bottoms of remaining 2 layers. Place 1 layer, jam side down, over icing.

❧ Spread ⅓ cup (75 mL) of the remaining icing on top of second layer; top with third layer, jam side down. Brush off any loose crumbs. Spread about one-third of the remaining icing over side and top of cake to mask. Refrigerate until firm, about 30 minutes. Spread with remaining icing.

✒ Using toothpick to lift chocolate curls, gently press against side of cake. Remove paper strips. Refrigerate for 30 minutes. **(Make-ahead: Cover loosely and refrigerate for up to 1 day. Let come to room temperature before serving.)**

Makes 16 servings. | PER SERVING: about 798 cal, 12 g pro, 59 g total fat (35 g sat. fat), 76 g carb, 11 g fibre, 114 mg chol, 431 mg sodium. % RDI: 13% calcium, 40% iron, 25% vit A, 2% vit C, 21% folate.

German Chocolate Cake

Named not after its country of origin but after Samuel German, who created Baker's German's Sweet Chocolate, this confection – four layers of cake sandwiched together with a super rich pecan-and-coconut filling – is one special cake. The chocolate ganache icing is not traditional but cuts nicely through the cake's sweetness and adds a certain polish to its presentation.

4 oz	bittersweet chocolate, chopped	125 g	1½ cups	sweetened shredded or flaked coconut	375 mL
½ cup	water	125 mL	1 cup	granulated sugar	250 mL
1 cup	butter, softened	250 mL	1 cup	evaporated milk	250 mL
1½ cups	granulated sugar	375 mL	3	egg yolks	3
4	eggs	4	⅓ cup	butter	75 mL
2 tsp	vanilla	10 mL	1 tsp	vanilla	5 mL
2 cups	all-purpose flour	500 mL	**GANACHE ICING:**		
1 tsp	each baking powder and baking soda	5 mL	8 oz	bittersweet chocolate, chopped	250 g
½ tsp	salt	2 mL	3 tbsp	butter	50 mL
1 cup	sour cream	250 mL	2 tbsp	corn syrup	25 mL
FILLING:			1 cup	whipping cream	250 mL
1½ cups	chopped pecans	375 mL			

❧ Grease sides of two 9-inch (1.5 L) or 8-inch (1.2 L) round cake pans; line bottoms with parchment or waxed paper. Set out 2 rimmed baking sheets. Set all pans aside.

❧ In heatproof bowl set over saucepan of hot (not boiling) water, melt chocolate with water, stirring until smooth; let cool to room temperature, about 30 minutes.

❧ In large bowl, beat butter with sugar until light and fluffy. Beat in eggs, 1 at a time, beating well after each. Mix in vanilla and chocolate mixture.

❧ In separate bowl, whisk together flour, baking powder, baking soda and salt. With wooden spoon, stir into butter mixture alternately with sour cream, making 3 additions of dry ingredients and 2 of sour cream. Scrape into prepared cake pans; smooth tops.

❧ Bake in centre of 350°F (180°C) oven until cake tester inserted in centre comes out clean, about 35 minutes. Let cool in pans on racks for 10 minutes. Turn out onto racks; peel off paper. Invert; let cool. **(Make-ahead: Wrap in plastic wrap and store at room temperature for up to 1 day or overwrap in heavy-duty foil and freeze for up to 1 month.)**

❧ **FILLING:** Arrange pecans and coconut separately on baking sheets. Toast in 350°F (180°C) oven, stirring once, until coconut is golden and pecans are darkened, 6 to 7 minutes for coconut, 8 to 9 minutes for pecans. Transfer to large bowl; let cool.

↜ Meanwhile, in saucepan, whisk together sugar, milk and egg yolks; cook, stirring, over medium heat until mixture is thick enough to coat spoon thickly, about 5 minutes. Stir in butter and vanilla; remove from heat. Add to pecan mixture; stir until butter is melted. Refrigerate until cold and thickened enough to spread without running, about 2 hours. **(Make-ahead: Cover and refrigerate for up to 1 day.)**

↜ GANACHE ICING: Place chocolate, butter and corn syrup in heatproof bowl. In saucepan, bring cream just to boil; pour over chocolate, whisking until melted and smooth. Let cool to almost room temperature.

↜ Brush loose crumbs from cake layers. Cut each layer in half horizontally. Place 1 cake layer, cut side up, on flat cake plate; slide 4 strips of waxed paper between cake and plate. Spread with one-third of the filling, spreading right to edge. Repeat to make second and third layers; top with remaining layer, cut side down.

↜ Brush off any loose crumbs. Spread about one-third of the icing over top and side of cake to mask. Refrigerate until firm, about 30 minutes.

↜ Meanwhile, stir icing occasionally to keep spreadable. Spread remaining icing (it should be room temperature and slightly thickened) smoothly over cake. Remove paper strips. Refrigerate until firm, about 1 hour. **(Make-ahead: Cover and refrigerate for up to 1 day.)**

Make 16 servings. | PER SERVING: about 690 cal, 9 g pro, 46 g total fat (25 g sat. fat), 65 g carb, 4 g fibre, 157 mg chol, 366 mg sodium. % RDI: 10% calcium, 17% iron, 26% vit A, 3% vit C, 22% folate.

CUTTING CAKES

❯ There is an art to cutting a cake or cheesecake so that each piece is neat, with no gummy ridges or smears of icing.

● Start by planning out the cuts. For layer and Bundt cakes, it is easiest to simply cut out wedges, sized appropriately for your crowd.

● The only equipment you need is a knife with a long blade, a tall pitcher of hot water and a clean tea towel.

● Let knife blade stand in hot water until hot, then wipe dry. Immediately cut decisively through the icing and cake or cheesecake. Avoid sawing back and forth.

● Wipe the blade clean between every cut and rewarm the knife every two or three cuts or as needed.

● For a birthday cake, bring the cake to the birthday girl or boy to make the first symbolic cut and wish, then whisk the cake back into the kitchen, where the pitcher of hot water and an increasingly messy towel will not detract from the festive table.

● For angel food, chiffon and sponge cakes, we recommend a serrated knife.

Maple Crunch Layer Cake

Candied maple walnuts add a pleasing crunch to this towering treat of a dessert.

1 cup	butter, softened	250 mL
1 cup	granulated sugar	250 mL
2	eggs	2
2 tsp	maple extract	10 mL
2½ cups	all-purpose flour	625 mL
1 tsp	each baking powder and baking soda	5 mL
½ tsp	ground ginger	2 mL
¼ tsp	salt	1 mL
¾ cup	each buttermilk and maple syrup	175 mL

CANDIED WALNUTS:

2 tbsp	each maple syrup and butter	25 mL
¼ tsp	salt	1 mL
2¼ cups	walnut halves	550 mL

MAPLE BUTTER ICING:

1¼ cups	butter, softened	300 mL
6 cups	icing sugar	1.5 L
⅔ cup	whipping cream	150 mL
⅓ cup	maple syrup	75 mL
1 tsp	maple extract	5 mL

STORING CAKE LAYERS

> It's very handy to make layers a day or two before assembling a cake, or to freeze them for up to 2 weeks. For short storage at room temperature, layer between waxed paper in large airtight containers or wrap in plastic wrap. To freeze, layers will be safe from freezer burn beneath two layers of protection. Choose from quality vapour-proof plastic wrap, heavy-duty foil, freezer bags and rigid airtight containers.

◞ Grease sides of two 9-inch (1.5 L) round metal cake pans; line bottoms with parchment or waxed paper. Line small rimmed baking sheet with foil. Set all pans aside.

◞ In large bowl, beat butter with sugar until light and fluffy; beat in eggs, 1 at a time, beating well after each. Beat in maple extract.

◞ In separate bowl, whisk flour, baking powder and soda, ginger and salt. Stir into butter mixture alternately with buttermilk and maple syrup, making 3 additions of dry ingredients and 2 of wet. Scrape into pans; smooth. Bake in centre of 350°F (180°C) oven until cake tester comes out clean, 30 minutes. Let cool in pans for 10 minutes. Turn out onto racks; peel off paper. Invert; let cool. **(Make-ahead: Wrap and store at room temperature for up to 1 day or overwrap in heavy-duty foil and freeze for up to 2 weeks.)**

◞ **CANDIED WALNUTS:** In bowl, microwave maple syrup, butter, 2 tbsp (25 mL) water and salt at high until butter is melted, 30 seconds; whisk. Add walnuts; toss to coat. Spread on baking sheet. Bake in 325°F (160°C) oven, turning once, until golden, about 20 minutes. Let cool. Reserve 12 walnuts for garnish; finely chop remainder. Set aside.

◞ **MAPLE BUTTER ICING:** In bowl, beat butter until light; gradually beat in sugar and cream, making 3 additions of sugar and 2 of cream. Beat in maple syrup and maple extract. **(Make-ahead: Cover and refrigerate for up to 3 days; let soften and beat to use.)**

◞ Trim layers flat if necessary; brush off crumbs. Cut each in half horizontally. Place 1 layer, cut side up, on cake plate; slide 4 strips of waxed paper under edge. Spread with scant 1 cup (250 mL) of the icing; sprinkle with one-third of the chopped walnuts. Repeat layers twice. Top with remaining layer, cut side down. Brush off loose crumbs.

◞ Spread scant 1 cup (250 mL) icing over top and side of cake to mask. Refrigerate until firm, 30 minutes. Spread with remaining icing. Remove paper strips. **(Make-ahead: Cover loosely and refrigerate for up to 2 days. Let come to room temperature before serving.)** Press reserved walnuts onto cake just before serving.

Makes 12 to 16 servings. | PER EACH OF 16 SERVINGS: about 714 cal, 6 g pro, 41 g total fat (20 g sat. fat), 85 g carb, 2 g fibre, 123 mg chol, 466 mg sodium. % RDI: 72% calcium, 2% iron, 303% vit A, 58% folate.

Golden Layer Cake

This buttery golden cake features raspberry jam and buttercream fillings and a sleek all-over buttercream covering. Four layers tall, it has celebration written all over it. For the buttercream, a stand mixer will give the smoothest, most satiny results.

1 cup	butter, softened	250 mL
1⅔ cups	granulated sugar	400 mL
4	eggs	4
1 tsp	vanilla	5 mL
3 cups	all-purpose flour	750 mL
1 tbsp	baking powder	15 mL
½ tsp	baking soda	2 mL
¼ tsp	salt	1 mL
1¼ cups	buttermilk	300 mL

VANILLA BUTTERCREAM ICING:

2⅔ cups	unsalted butter, softened	650 mL
6	egg whites	6
1¼ cups	granulated sugar	300 mL
2 tsp	vanilla	10 mL

FILLING:

¾ cup	seedless raspberry jam	175 mL

❧ Grease sides of two 9-inch (1.5 L) round metal cake pans; line bottoms with parchment or waxed paper. Set aside.

❧ In large bowl, beat butter with sugar until light and fluffy. Beat in eggs, 1 at a time, beating well after each; beat in vanilla.

❧ In separate bowl, whisk together flour, baking powder, baking soda and salt; stir into butter mixture alternately with buttermilk, making 3 additions of dry ingredients and 2 of buttermilk. Scrape into prepared pans; smooth tops.

❧ Bake in centre of 350°F (180°C) oven until cake tester inserted in centre comes out clean, 30 to 35 minutes. Let cool in pans on racks for 10 minutes. Turn out onto racks; peel off paper. Let cool. **(Make-ahead: Wrap in plastic wrap and store at room temperature for up to 1 day or overwrap in heavy-duty foil and freeze for up to 1 month.)**

❧ **VANILLA BUTTERCREAM ICING:** In large bowl, beat butter until fluffy. Set aside.

❧ In large heatproof bowl, whisk egg whites with sugar. Place over saucepan of simmering water; cook, whisking often, until opaque and candy thermometer registers 110°F (43°C) or finger can remain in mixture for no longer than 10 seconds, about 1 minute. Remove from heat. In stand mixer, beat until cool, about 10 minutes.

❧ Beat in butter, 2 tbsp (25 mL) at a time, until satiny (initially mixture will curdle). Beat in vanilla.

❧ **FILLING:** Trim tops of cakes to level if necessary. Brush loose crumbs from layers. Cut each layer in half horizontally. Place 1 layer, cut side up, on flat cake plate; slide 4 strips of waxed paper between cake and plate. Spread cut side with ¼ cup (50 mL) of the raspberry jam, almost to edge. Spread cut side of second layer with ¾ cup (175 mL) of the buttercream; place, buttercream side down, over jam-topped layer. Spread top with ¼ cup (50 mL) of the raspberry jam; spread ¾ cup (175 mL) of the buttercream over cut side of third layer. Place, buttercream side down, over second layer. Repeat layers once. Scrape off any excess fillings.

🍂 Brush off any loose crumbs. Spread 1 cup (250 mL) of the buttercream over top and side of cake to mask; refrigerate until firm, about 30 minutes. Spread with remaining buttercream; refrigerate until firm, about 30 minutes. Remove paper strips. (Make-ahead: Cover loosely and refrigerate for up to 8 hours. Let stand at room temperature for 30 minutes before serving.)

Makes 16 servings. | PER SERVING: about 677 cal, 7 g pro, 44 g total fat (27 g sat. fat), 66 g carb, 1 g fibre, 160 mg chol, 274 mg sodium. % RDI: 7% calcium, 10% iron, 39% vit A, 3% vit C, 28% folate.

VARIATIONS

Happy Birthday Layer Cake with Chocolate Buttercream Icing: Bake cake as directed. Add 4 oz (125 g) bittersweet chocolate, melted and cooled, before adding vanilla to Vanilla Buttercream Icing. Reduce vanilla to 1½ tsp (7 mL). Assemble cake as directed, omitting jam, if desired.

Golden Cupcakes: Spoon batter into 24 paper-lined or greased muffin cups. Bake until cake tester inserted in centre comes out clean, about 20 minutes. Transfer to racks; let cool. Ice with your favourite icing. Makes 24 cupcakes.

THE SILKIEST BUTTERCREAM

● We have found that the butter beats in better if it first comes to room temperature. Once it has, beat it for a few minutes to lighten before incorporating into buttercream.

● As the egg whites and sugar warm up over the simmering water, they turn from translucent to nearly opaque. Check that the mixture has reached 110°F (43°C) with an instant-read thermometer or by holding your finger in the mixture. If you can hold it for exactly 10 seconds, it is ready for the second stage, beating until cool. This takes about 10 minutes, preferably using a stand mixer with a whisk attachment. It is possible with a hand mixer but takes more effort.

● The texture should be firm but easily spreadable.

Walnut Mocha Torte

Try as we may, we can't think of any other word than *majestic* to describe this tall European-inspired torte. Real buttercream glistens between the layers of sponge cake, with chocolate and coffee marrying to make every crumb of this cake a must-eat.

THE BEST PANS FOR LAYER CAKES

❯ Look for cake pans with sides that are at a 90-degree angle to the base. Avoid pans with angled sides, as they create an uneven stack of layers that need to be trimmed. If you do have them, use the scraps that result from the trimming to level low spots on the cake, or cube and sprinkle over ice cream. Or have an ahead-of-time cake tasting. The baker has to be sure it tastes good!

1 tsp	instant coffee or espresso granules	5 mL
1 tsp	vanilla	5 mL
8	eggs, separated	8
1 cup	granulated sugar	250 mL
1 tsp	grated lemon rind	5 mL
2½ cups	ground walnut halves	625 mL
¼ cup	each all-purpose flour and dry bread crumbs	50 mL

SUGAR SYRUP:

¼ cup	granulated sugar	50 mL
¼ cup	water	50 mL
1 tbsp	coffee-flavoured liqueur or cold extra-strong coffee	15 mL

MOCHA BUTTERCREAM:

2¼ cups	unsalted butter, softened	550 mL
4 tsp	instant coffee granules	20 mL
1½ tsp	vanilla	7 mL
5	egg whites	5
1 cup	granulated sugar	250 mL
1½ oz	bittersweet chocolate, melted	45 g

GARNISH:

16	chocolate-covered coffee beans	16
½ cup	coarsely chopped toasted walnut halves	125 mL

❧ Line bottoms and sides of two 9-inch (1.5 L) round cake pans with parchment paper tall enough to come 1 inch (2.5 cm) above sides; set aside.

❧ In small bowl, dissolve coffee in vanilla; set aside.

❧ In large bowl, beat egg yolks with ½ cup (125 mL) of the sugar until light; beat in coffee mixture and lemon rind. In separate bowl and using clean beaters, beat egg whites until foamy; beat in remaining sugar, 2 tbsp (25 mL) at a time, until stiff peaks form. In another bowl, whisk together walnuts, flour and bread crumbs; fold into egg yolk mixture alternately with egg whites, making 3 additions of walnut mixture and 2 of egg whites. Scrape into prepared pans; smooth tops.

❧ Bake in centre of 325°F (160°C) oven until cake tester inserted in centre comes out clean, 35 to 40 minutes. Let cool in pans on rack.

❧ SUGAR SYRUP: In small saucepan, bring sugar and water to boil over medium-high heat, stirring until sugar is dissolved; boil until clear, about 1 minute. Stir in liqueur; let cool. (Make-ahead: Set aside in airtight container for up to 1 day.)

❧**MOCHA BUTTERCREAM:** In large bowl, beat butter until fluffy. In small bowl, dissolve coffee granules in vanilla. Set both aside.

❧In large heatproof bowl, whisk egg whites with sugar. Place over saucepan of simmering water; cook, whisking often, until opaque and candy thermometer registers 110°F (43°C) or finger can remain in mixture for no longer than 10 seconds, about 1 minute. Remove from heat. In stand mixer, beat until cool, about 10 minutes.

❧Beat in butter, 2 tbsp (25 mL) at a time, until satiny (initially mixture will curdle). Beat in coffee mixture. Transfer 1¾ cups (425 mL) to separate bowl; beat in melted chocolate until smooth.

❧Brush loose crumbs from cake layers. Cut each layer in half horizontally. Place 1 cake layer, cut side up, on flat cake plate; slide 4 strips of waxed paper between cake and plate. Brush with syrup, then spread with about ¾ cup (175 mL) of the plain coffee buttercream. Repeat to make second and third layer; top with remaining layer, cut side down. Brush off any loose crumbs.

❧Spread thin layer of coffee buttercream over top and side to mask (using some of the chocolate buttercream if no more coffee buttercream remains). Refrigerate until firm, about 30 minutes.

❧Transfer about ⅓ cup (75 mL) of the chocolate buttercream to piping bag fitted with star tip. Spread remaining chocolate buttercream over top and side of cake. Pipe 16 small rosettes on top around edge.

❧**GARNISH:** Top each rosette with coffee bean. Press nuts in ½-inch (1 cm) border around bottom edge of cake. Refrigerate until set, about 30 minutes. **(Make-ahead: Cover loosely and refrigerate for up to 1 day. Remove from refrigerator 30 minutes before serving.)**

Makes 16 servings. | PER SERVING: about 527 cal, 8 g pro, 42 g total fat (20 g sat. fat), 36 g carb, 2 g fibre, 162 mg chol, 64 mg sodium. % RDI: 4% calcium, 9% iron, 26% vit A, 16% folate.

Dulce de Leche Cream Cake

Imagine layers of almond-scented cake, whipped cream and the Latin American caramel sauce called *dulce de leche* served on individual plates. A sensational dessert!

FRUITY SHORTCAKES

❯ This quick-to-make, freezeable cake is a versatile foundation for shortcakes like the strawberry-topped variation below. For variety, try sliced peaches or nectarines, blueberries or raspberries – or a mix of these fruits – once strawberry season is over.

½ cup	butter, softened	125 mL		¼ tsp	each baking soda and salt	1 mL
1 cup	granulated sugar	250 mL		⅔ cup	milk	150 mL
2	eggs	2		1½ cups	whipping cream	375 mL
½ tsp	almond extract	2 mL			Dulce de Leche (recipe, page 325)	
1½ cups	all-purpose flour	375 mL		¾ cup	sliced almonds, toasted	175 mL
1½ tsp	baking powder	7 mL				

❧ Grease sides of 8-inch (2 L) square metal cake pan; line bottom with parchment or waxed paper; set aside.

❧ In large bowl, beat butter with sugar until light and fluffy; beat in eggs, 1 at a time, beating well after each. Beat in almond extract.

❧ In separate bowl, whisk together flour, baking powder, baking soda and salt; stir into butter mixture alternately with milk, making 3 additions of dry ingredients and 2 of milk. Scrape into prepared pan; smooth top.

❧ Bake in centre of 350°F (180°C) oven until cake tester inserted in centre comes out clean, about 40 minutes. Let cool in pan on rack. **(Make-ahead: Cover and store at room temperature for up to 1 day.)** Remove from pan; peel off paper.

❧ Cut cake in half horizontally; without separating layers, cut into 9 pieces. In bowl, whip cream; fold in ¼ cup (50 mL) Dulce de Leche.

❧ Spoon 1 tbsp (15 mL) Dulce de Leche onto centre of each serving plate; top with bottom slice of cake. Top with 1 tbsp (15 mL) Dulce de Leche and 2 tbsp (25 mL) of the whipped cream mixture. Cover with top slice of cake; top with 1 tbsp (15 mL) each Dulce de Leche and whipped cream mixture. Sprinkle with almonds.

Makes 9 servings. | PER SERVING: about 644 cal, 15 g pro, 32 g total fat (18 g sat. fat), 77 g carb, 2 g fibre, 131 mg chol, 445 mg sodium. % RDI: 35% calcium, 12% iron, 32% vit A, 12% vit C, 27% folate.

VARIATION

Orange White Chocolate Strawberry Shortcake: Bake cake as directed; omit filling and topping. Cut cake in half horizontally. Spread cut side of bottom with 4 oz (125 g) semisweet chocolate, melted. Spread Orange White Chocolate Curd (recipe, page 335) over chocolate; refrigerate until firm, about 30 minutes. Top with remaining cake, cut side down. Whip 1 cup (250 mL) whipping cream. Cut cake into 9 pieces. Top each serving with whipped cream and Macerated Strawberry Sauce (recipe, page 321).

Cookies and Cream Celebration Cake

This big citrus-scented layer cake and creamy icing are good basics to use time and time again.

1½ cups	butter, softened	375 mL	½ tsp	salt	2 mL	
2¼ cups	granulated sugar	550 mL	2¼ cups	milk	550 mL	
3	eggs	3	24	Sugar Cookies (recipe, page 49)	24	
2 tsp	each grated lemon and orange rind	10 mL				
4 tsp	lemon juice	20 mL	**CREAMY ALMOND BUTTER ICING:**			
1½ tsp	vanilla	7 mL	1½ cups	butter, softened	375 mL	
3¾ cups	all-purpose flour	925 mL	7½ cups	icing sugar	1.875 L	
1½ tsp	baking powder	7 mL	1 cup	whipping cream	250 mL	
1½ tsp	baking soda	7 mL	¾ tsp	almond extract	4 mL	

CHANGE UP THE COOKIES

❯ When making the cookies that dress up this cake, choose a cookie cutter that suits the occasion: doves and rings for an engagement party or wedding shower, baby carriages and umbrellas for a baby shower, hearts and cupids for Valentine's Day and so on.

❧ Line bottoms and sides of one 6-inch (1.25 L) and one 9-inch (2.5 L) springform pan with parchment paper; set aside.

❧ CAKE: In large bowl, beat butter with sugar until light and fluffy; beat in eggs, 1 at a time, beating well after each. Beat in lemon and orange rinds, lemon juice and vanilla.

❧ In separate bowl, whisk together flour, baking powder, baking soda and salt; stir into butter mixture alternately with milk, making 3 additions of dry ingredients and 2 of milk. Scrape 2¼ cups (550 mL) into small prepared pan; scrape remaining batter into large prepared pan. Smooth tops. Bake in centre of 350°F (180°C) oven until cake tester inserted in centre comes out clean, about 50 minutes for small cake and 1 hour for large. Let cool in pans on racks for 10 minutes. Turn out onto racks; peel off paper. Invert; let cool. **(Make-ahead: Wrap separately in plastic wrap; store at room temperature for up to 1 day. Or overwrap in heavy-duty foil and freeze for up to 2 weeks.)**

❧ CREAMY ALMOND BUTTER ICING: In bowl, beat butter until light. Beat in sugar and whipping cream, making 3 additions of sugar and 2 of cream. Beat in extract.

❧ Trim tops of cakes to level. Cut each in half horizontally. Brush off crumbs. Place l large layer, cut side up, on cake board, stand or tray; slide 4 strips of waxed paper under edge. Spread top with 1 cup (250 mL) of the icing. Top with second large layer, cut side down; spread scant 1 cup (250 mL) of the icing over top and side to mask.

❧ Place 1 small layer, cut side up, on waxed paper–lined baking sheet; spread top with ⅓ cup (75 mL) of the icing. Top with second small layer, cut side down; spread ⅓ cup (75 mL) of the icing over top and side to mask. Chill each until firm, 30 minutes.

❧ Spread remaining icing over top and sides of both cakes. Using palette knife dipped in hot water and wiped dry, smooth icing. Chill until firm, about 1 hour.

❧ Centre small cake on large cake. Decorate with Sugar Cookies. **(Make-ahead: Cover loosely; refrigerate for up to 1 day. Let stand at room temperature for 45 minutes before serving.)**

Makes 24 servings. | PER SERVING: about 650 cal, 5 g pro, 31 g total fat (19 g sat. fat), 89 g carb, 1 g fibre, 126 mg chol, 438 mg sodium. % RDI: 5% calcium, 11% iron, 31% vit A, 2% vit C, 18% folate.

Orange Sour Cream Bundt Cake

This velvety-textured cake hails from the kitchen of veteran cake baker Malcah Sufrin. You can serve it with the syrup or an orange glaze (recipe, left), as we have in our photo. Either way, add orange sections and blueberries to each serving if you like.

ORANGE GLAZE

In bowl, mix ¾ cup (175 mL) icing sugar with 4 tsp (20 mL) orange juice, adding a little more juice if necessary to make pourable. Slowly pour over cooled cake. Let stand until glaze is dry, about 1 hour.

1 cup	butter, softened	250 mL	½ tsp	salt	2 mL
1¼ cups	granulated sugar	300 mL	1½ cups	sour cream	375 mL
4	eggs, separated	4	SYRUP:		
1 tbsp	finely grated orange rind	15 mL	½ cup	granulated sugar	125 mL
1 tsp	vanilla	5 mL	½ cup	orange juice	125 mL
2 cups	all-purpose flour	500 mL	⅓ cup	orange-flavoured liqueur	75 mL
1½ tsp	each baking powder and baking soda	7 mL			

Grease 9-inch (2.5 L) fancy or classic Bundt or tube pan; dust with flour. Set aside.

In large bowl, beat butter with 1 cup (250 mL) of the sugar until light and fluffy; beat in egg yolks, 1 at a time, beating well after each. Beat in orange rind and vanilla.

In separate bowl, whisk together flour, baking powder, baking soda and salt; stir into butter mixture alternately with sour cream, making 3 additions of dry ingredients and 2 of sour cream. In separate bowl and with clean beaters, beat egg whites until frothy; beat in remaining sugar, 1 tbsp (15 mL) at a time, until stiff peaks form. Fold one-third into batter; fold in remainder. Scrape into prepared pan; smooth top.

Bake in centre of 325°F (160°C) oven until cake tester inserted in centre comes out clean, about 1 hour. Let cool in pan on rack for 20 minutes. Turn out onto rack.

SYRUP: Meanwhile, in small saucepan, bring sugar, orange juice and liqueur to boil over medium heat; reduce heat to low and simmer until reduced to ¾ cup (175 mL), about 7 minutes. Let cool for 5 minutes. Brush half over warm cake. Let cool. **(Make-ahead: Wrap in plastic wrap; store at room temperature for up to 1 day or overwrap in heavy-duty-foil and freeze for up to 1 month.)** Serve with remaining syrup.

TURNING OUT A BUNDT CAKE

Let a large cake, like a Bundt cake, cool in pan on rack for 20 minutes. With knife, gently loosen cake around edge and centre. Place rack over pan. Grasp bottom of pan and, holding rack firmly to top, turn cake over. Lift pan off. If pan sticks, turn cake and rack back over and, with thin flexible plastic blade, loosen cake where it is stuck. The pan should slide off when it's turned over.

Makes 16 servings. | PER SERVING: about 314 cal, 4 g pro, 16 g total fat (10 g sat. fat), 38 g carb, 1 g fibre, 86 mg chol, 325 mg sodium. % RDI: 4% calcium, 6% iron, 14% vit A, 7% vit C, 19% folate.

Hot Fudge Banana Bundt Cake

Some of the hot fudge sauce is swirled into the batter, and the rest is left to bathe each slice of the cake.

RELEASING AIR BUBBLES

Tap pan lightly on counter to remove any air bubbles and to ensure that the batter has filled all the pan's decorative crevices.

1 cup	unsalted butter, softened	250 mL
1¾ cups	granulated sugar	425 mL
6	eggs	6
3 cups	all-purpose flour	750 mL
1½ tsp	baking powder	7 mL
¾ tsp	baking soda	4 mL
¾ tsp	salt	4 mL
1½ cups	mashed bananas (about 5 small)	375 mL
1½ tsp	vinegar	7 mL

HOT FUDGE SAUCE:

1½ cups	whipping cream	375 mL
1¼ cups	granulated sugar	300 mL
4 oz	unsweetened chocolate, coarsely chopped	125 g
2 oz	bittersweet chocolate, coarsely chopped	60 g
2 tbsp	butter	25 mL
2 tbsp	corn syrup	25 mL
½ tsp	vanilla	2 mL

↬ Grease 10-inch (3 L) Bundt pan; dust with flour. Set aside.

↬ **HOT FUDGE SAUCE:** In heavy saucepan, combine cream, sugar, unsweetened and bittersweet chocolates, butter and corn syrup; heat over low heat, whisking constantly, until sugar is dissolved and butter and chocolates are melted. Whisking constantly, boil over medium-high heat until sauce is reduced to 2½ cups (625 mL), about 8 minutes. Let cool until room temperature but still pourable. **(Make-ahead: Refrigerate in airtight container for up to 1 week; reheat gently.)** Stir in vanilla.

↬ In bowl, beat butter with sugar until light and fluffy. Beat in eggs, 1 at a time, beating well after each.

↬ In separate bowl, whisk together flour, baking powder, baking soda and salt. In another bowl, stir bananas with vinegar. Using wooden spoon, stir dry ingredients into butter mixture alternately with banana mixture, making 3 additions of dry ingredients and 2 of wet.

↬ Scrape one-quarter of the batter into prepared pan; drizzle with ¼ cup (50 mL) of the fudge sauce, keeping sauce ½ inch (1 cm) from side of pan. Repeat twice. Top with remaining batter. Run thin knife or skewer through batter to create swirls.

↬ Bake in centre of 350°F (180°C) oven until cake tester inserted in centre of cake comes out clean, about 1 hour. Let cool in pan on rack for 30 minutes. Turn out onto rack; let cool. **(Make-ahead: Wrap in plastic wrap and store at room temperature for up to 2 days or overwrap in heavy-duty foil and freeze for up to 2 weeks.)** Serve in thick slices with remaining slightly warm sauce.

Makes 12 servings. | PER SERVING: about 704 cal, 9 g pro, 38 g total fat (23 g sat. fat), 88 g carb, 4 g fibre, 192 mg chol, 320 mg sodium. % RDI: 6% calcium, 19% iron, 31% vit A, 3% vit C, 21% folate.

Three-Ginger Gingerbread with Lemon Sauce

Calling all ginger lovers! This three-ginger cake is great hot with the lemon sauce or at room temperature with whipped cream. The secret to turning out a perfect cake is to grease and flour the pan thoroughly (see tips, right).

3 cups	all-purpose flour	750 mL
1 tbsp	cinnamon	15 mL
2 tsp	baking soda	10 mL
1½ tsp	ground cloves	7 mL
1 tsp	ground ginger	5 mL
¾ tsp	salt	4 mL
1½ cups	granulated sugar	375 mL
1 cup	each vegetable oil and fancy molasses	250 mL
2	eggs	2

1 tbsp	minced gingerroot	15 mL
½ cup	chopped crystallized ginger	125 mL
LEMON SAUCE:		
½ cup	granulated sugar	125 mL
2 tbsp	cornstarch	25 mL
Pinch	salt	Pinch
1	egg yolk	1
3 tbsp	lemon juice	50 mL
2 tbsp	butter	25 mL

❧ Grease 10-inch (3 L) Bundt pan; dust with flour. Set aside.

❧ In large bowl, whisk together flour, cinnamon, baking soda, cloves, ground ginger and salt. In separate bowl, whisk together sugar, oil, molasses, eggs, gingerroot and ½ cup (125 mL) water; stir in flour mixture, 1 cup (250 mL) at a time, and crystallized ginger. Scrape into prepared pan; smooth top.

❧ Bake in centre of 350°F (180°C) oven until cake tester inserted in centre of cake comes out clean, about 1 hour. Let cool in pan on rack for 30 minutes. Turn out onto rack; let cool. (**Make-ahead: Wrap in plastic wrap and store at room temperature for up to 1 day or overwrap in heavy-duty foil and freeze for up to 2 weeks.**)

❧ **LEMON SAUCE:** In saucepan, whisk together sugar, cornstarch and salt; whisk in 1 cup (250 mL) water. Bring to boil, stirring, over medium-high heat; boil until clear and thickened, about 1 minute. Remove from heat. In small bowl, beat egg yolk. Whisk in one-quarter of the hot mixture; whisk back into pan. Add lemon juice and butter; stir until melted. Pour into heatproof pitcher and serve with warm cake.

Makes 12 servings. | PER SERVING: about 545 cal, 5 g pro, 22 g total fat (3 g sat. fat), 85 g carb, 1 g fibre, 59 mg chol, 381 mg sodium. % RDI: 8% calcium, 34% iron, 4% vit A, 8% vit C, 18% folate.

PREPARING BUNDT PANS

Liberally brush inside of pan with very soft butter, preferably unsalted, or vegetable oil, making sure to coat all crevices.

Sprinkle a couple of generous tablespoonfuls of all-purpose flour into pan. Rotate and tilt pan, tapping to coat the inside of the pan evenly.

Turn pan over and tap out excess flour.

Glazed Chocolate Marble Cake

White and dark chocolate batters swirl together in this ganache-glazed cake.

GREASING FANCY PANS

❯ Nordic Ware, the manufacturer of fancy shaped nonstick Bundt pans, recommends avoiding commercial vegetable spray, which, over time, can pit the finish on the inside of the pan.

2 oz	unsweetened chocolate, chopped	60 g
3 oz	white chocolate, chopped	90 g
⅔ cup	butter, softened	150 mL
1½ cups	granulated sugar	375 mL
3	eggs	3
2 tsp	vanilla	10 mL
2¼ cups	all-purpose flour	550 mL
1 tsp	baking powder	5 mL

1 tsp	baking soda	5 mL
½ tsp	salt	2 mL
1 cup	buttermilk	250 mL

GANACHE:

2 oz	bittersweet chocolate, chopped	60 g
¼ cup	whipping cream	50 mL

GARNISH:

White Chocolate Shards
(recipe, page 337)

❧ Grease 9-inch (2.5 L) fancy or classic Bundt or tube pan; dust with flour. Set aside.

❧ In heatproof bowl over saucepan of hot (not boiling) water, melt unsweetened chocolate, stirring occasionally; repeat with white chocolate in separate bowl. Let both cool to room temperature.

❧ In large bowl, beat butter with sugar until light and fluffy; beat in eggs, 1 at a time, beating well after each. Beat in vanilla. Scrape half of the batter into separate bowl; stir in unsweetened chocolate. Stir white chocolate into remaining batter.

❧ In separate bowl, whisk together flour, baking powder, baking soda and salt. Stir half into dark chocolate mixture alternately with half of the buttermilk, making 2 additions of dry ingredients and 1 of buttermilk. Repeat with white chocolate batter and remaining dry ingredients and buttermilk. Drop spoonfuls of dark and white batters into prepared pan. With tip of knife, swirl to marble.

❧ Bake in centre of 325°F (160°C) oven until cake tester inserted in centre of cake comes out clean, about 55 minutes. Let cool in pan on rack for 20 minutes. Turn out cake onto rack; let cool. **(Make-ahead: Wrap in plastic wrap and store at room temperature for up to 1 day or overwrap in heavy-duty foil and freeze for up to 1 month.)**

❧ GANACHE: Place bittersweet chocolate in heatproof bowl. In saucepan, bring cream just to boil over medium heat; pour over chocolate. Stir until chocolate is melted and smooth. Let stand for 10 minutes; brush over cake.

❧ GARNISH: Sprinkle white chocolate shards on cake. Let stand until ganache is set, about 40 minutes. **(Make-ahead: Cover cake with cake dome or place in large airtight container; store at room temperature for up to 1 day.)**

Makes 16 servings. | PER SERVING: about 304 cal, 5 g pro, 15 g total fat (9 g sat. fat), 39 g carb, 1 g fibre, 64 mg chol, 275 mg sodium. % RDI: 5% calcium, 9% iron, 10% vit A, 12% folate.

Custard-Topped Berry Kuchen

Any cake tagged with the German word *kuchen* is bound to be tender and moist. The creamy berry topping, sort of a baked custard, is traditional yet feels new and interesting.

½ cup	butter, softened	125 mL		½ cup	sour cream	125 mL
¾ cup	granulated sugar	175 mL		2 cups	raspberries	500 mL
2	eggs	2		1 cup	blackberries or blueberries	250 mL
½ tsp	each grated lemon rind and vanilla	2 mL		1 tbsp	icing sugar	15 mL
1½ cups	all-purpose flour	375 mL		TOPPING:		
1½ tsp	baking powder	7 mL		2	egg yolks	2
½ tsp	baking soda	2 mL		½ cup	sour cream	125 mL
¼ tsp	each salt and grated nutmeg	1 mL		2 tbsp	granulated sugar	25 mL

ᴖ Line bottom and side of 9-inch (2.5 L) springform pan with parchment paper; set aside.

ᴖ In large bowl, beat butter with sugar until light and fluffy; beat in eggs, 1 at a time, beating well after each. Beat in lemon rind and vanilla.

ᴖ In separate bowl, whisk together flour, baking powder, baking soda, salt and nutmeg; stir into butter mixture alternately with sour cream, making 3 additions of dry ingredients and 2 of sour cream.

ᴖ Sprinkle ⅔ cup (150 mL) of the raspberries and ⅓ cup (75 mL) of the blackberries in prepared pan. Scrape batter over top; smooth top. Scatter remaining berries over batter. Bake in centre of 350°F (180°C) oven until cake tester inserted in centre comes out clean, about 1 hour.

ᴖ **TOPPING:** Meanwhile, in small bowl, stir together egg yolks, sour cream and sugar; pour evenly over hot cake. Bake until set, about 10 minutes. Let cool in pan on rack for 20 minutes. Remove side of pan; let cool for 10 minutes to serve warm, or completely to serve at room temperature. **(Make-ahead: Let cool completely. Wrap in plastic wrap and refrigerate for up to 1 day.)** Dust with icing sugar.

Makes 8 servings. | PER SERVING: about 379 cal, 6 g pro, 19 g total fat (11 g sat. fat), 48 g carb, 3 g fibre, 139 mg chol, 319 mg sodium. % RDI: 8% calcium, 12% iron, 18% vit A, 15% vit C, 32% folate.

Plum Sour Cream Kuchen

This light, plum-topped cake is a superb fall dessert and comes from celebrated baker Dufflet Rosenberg, dubbed the Queen of Cake by her many fans and customers.

4	large plums (about 1 lb/500 g)	4	1 tsp	vanilla	5 mL
2 tbsp	packed brown sugar	25 mL	2¼ cups	all-purpose flour	550 mL
½ tsp	cinnamon	2 mL	1½ tsp	baking powder	7 mL
½ cup	unsalted butter, softened	125 mL	½ tsp	baking soda	2 mL
			¼ tsp	salt	1 mL
1½ cups	granulated sugar	375 mL	1½ cups	sour cream	375 mL
3	eggs	3	⅓ cup	vegetable oil	75 mL
1 tbsp	grated orange rind	15 mL	¾ cup	apricot jam	175 mL

❧ Grease 10-inch (3 L) springform pan; dust with flour. Set aside.

❧ Pit plums and cut into ¼-inch (5 mm) thick slices. In bowl, toss together plums, brown sugar and cinnamon; set aside.

❧ In large bowl, beat butter with granulated sugar until fluffy. Beat in eggs, 1 at a time, beating well after each. Beat in orange rind and vanilla.

❧ In separate bowl, whisk together flour, baking powder, baking soda and salt. In separate bowl, stir sour cream with oil. Stir dry ingredients into butter mixture alternately with sour cream mixture, making 3 additions of dry ingredients and 2 of wet. Scrape into prepared pan; smooth top. Arrange plums in 2 concentric circles on top, leaving about ½ inch (1 cm) between circles.

❧ Bake in centre of 350°F (180°C) oven until cake tester inserted in centre comes out clean, about 1 hour and 20 minutes. Let cool in pan on rack for 20 minutes. Remove side of pan. (Make-ahead: Let cool completely. Cover with plastic wrap and store at room temperature for up to 1 day or overwrap in heavy-duty foil and freeze for up to 2 weeks.)

❧ Transfer cake to flat cake plate. In small saucepan or microwaveable bowl, melt jam; strain and brush over top of cake. Serve slightly warm or at room temperature.

Makes 12 servings. | PER SERVING: about 443 cal, 5 g pro, 19 g total fat (8 g sat. fat), 64 g carb, 2 g fibre, 79 mg chol, 167 mg sodium. % RDI: 6% calcium, 11% iron, 14% vit A, 5% vit C, 20% folate.

Glazed Lemon Cake

Serve with berries and/or vanilla ice cream, or whipped cream and a dollop of Lemon Curd (recipe, page 335) for lemon lovers.

1 cup	butter, softened	250 mL	½ tsp	salt	2 mL
2 cups	granulated sugar	500 mL	1¼ cups	milk	300 mL
4	eggs	4	**TOPPING:**		
2 tbsp	grated lemon rind	25 mL	1½ cups	icing sugar	375 mL
1 tsp	vanilla	5 mL	2 tsp	grated lemon rind	10 mL
3 cups	all-purpose flour	750 mL	¼ cup	lemon juice	50 mL
1 tbsp	baking powder	15 mL			

❧ Grease 13- x 9-inch (3.5 L) metal cake pan; set aside.

❧ In large bowl, beat butter with sugar until light and fluffy; beat in eggs, 1 at a time, beating well after each. Beat in lemon rind and vanilla.

❧ In separate bowl, whisk together flour, baking powder and salt. Using wooden spoon, stir into butter mixture alternately with milk, making 3 additions of dry ingredients and 2 of milk. Scrape into prepared pan; smooth top.

❧ Bake in centre of 350°F (180°C) oven until cake tester inserted in centre comes out clean, 35 to 40 minutes. Place pan on rack.

❧ **TOPPING:** In bowl, whisk together icing sugar, lemon rind and juice. With skewer, poke holes, at 1-inch (2.5 cm) intervals, all over top of cake. Spoon sugar mixture evenly over top, smoothing with back of spoon. Let cool. **(Make-ahead: Cover lightly and store at room temperature for up to 12 hours.)**

Makes 12 to 16 servings. | PER EACH OF 16 SERVINGS: about 352 cal, 5 g pro, 13 g total fat (8 g sat. fat), 54 carb, 1 g fibre, 86 mg chol, 263 mg sodium. % RDI: 5% calcium, 9% iron, 14% vit A, 5% vit C, 14% folate.

ZESTING AND JUICING CITRUS FRUIT

❯ Citrus juice and grated zest add heady aromas and flavours to baking. Fresh is always best.

● Choose firm fruit. Firmness is an indication of freshness and gives a zester or grater better contact with the peel.

● Scrub fruit with a stiff vegetable brush in hot soapy water; rinse well and dry before grating.

● For finely grated rind, use a fine Microplane rasp or the rough, small-holed side of a box grater, turning the fruit often to avoid grating into the bitter white pith.

● For coarser shreds, use a zester to strip off outermost coloured part of rind.

● For strips you can use to infuse a liquid with flavour or as a garnish, use a paring knife or vegetable peeler to pare off thin, shallow strips of the peel.

● To juice, let fruit come to room temperature naturally or heat for 10 seconds in the microwave or in a bowl of warm water. Roll fruit firmly on cutting board to crush pulp. Cut in half crosswise and press, turning, on a reamer (a.k.a. citrus juicer) to extract as much juice as possible.

Applesauce Spice Cake with Fudge Icing

The icing on this old-fashioned cake sets quickly to a fudgelike consistency, so act fast and spread it while still warm.

¾ cup	butter, softened	175 mL
1½ cups	packed brown sugar	375 mL
3	eggs	3
1 tsp	vanilla	5 mL
3 cups	all-purpose flour	750 mL
2¼ tsp	baking powder	11 mL
1 tsp	salt	5 mL
¾ tsp	baking soda	4 mL
¾ tsp	cinnamon	4 mL
½ tsp	ground ginger	2 mL
¼ tsp	each ground allspice and nutmeg	1 mL

1½ cups	unsweetened applesauce	375 mL
⅓ cup	buttermilk	75 mL
ICING:		
⅓ cup	butter	75 mL
⅔ cup	packed brown sugar	150 mL
2 tbsp	corn syrup	25 mL
2 tbsp	milk	25 mL
½ tsp	vanilla	2 mL
1½ cups	icing sugar	375 mL

THE ROLE OF CORN SYRUP

❯ Corn syrup serves several purposes. In Silky Bittersweet Chocolate Sauce (recipe, page 323), it adds thickness and gloss. Here in the Fudge Icing, it helps prevent the icing from becoming granular. In cakes or muffins, corn syrup, like honey and sugar, attracts moisture and keeps products fresh.

❧ Grease sides of 13- x 9-inch (3.5 L) metal cake pan; line bottom with parchment paper. Set aside.

❧ In large bowl, beat butter with brown sugar until light and fluffy; beat in eggs, 1 at a time, beating well after each. Beat in vanilla.

❧ In separate bowl, whisk together flour, baking powder, salt, baking soda, cinnamon, ginger, allspice and nutmeg. Stir into butter mixture alternately with applesauce and buttermilk, making 3 additions of dry ingredients and 2 of wet. Scrape into prepared pan; smooth top.

❧ Bake in centre of 350°F (180°C) oven until cake tester inserted in centre comes out clean, about 35 minutes. Let cool in pan on rack. Turn out onto rack; peel off paper. **(Make-ahead: Wrap and store at room temperature for up to 2 days or overwrap in heavy-duty foil and freeze for up to 2 weeks.)**

❧ **ICING:** In saucepan, melt butter over medium heat. Add brown sugar and corn syrup; bring to boil, stirring constantly. Boil just until blended, about 1 minute. Remove from heat.

❧ Using wooden spoon, stir in milk and vanilla; beat in icing sugar until icing is smooth and spreadable. Let cool for 1 minute. Spread over top of cake just to edge, letting icing flow over slightly.

Makes 12 servings. | PER SERVING: about 508 cal, 5 g pro, 18 g total fat (11 g sat. fat), 83 g carb, 1 g fibre, 99 mg chol, 527 mg sodium. % RDI: 8% calcium, 18% iron, 18% vit A, 3% vit C, 32% folate.

Rhubarb Crumble Cake

If you're using frozen rhubarb for this year-round snacking cake, don't thaw it first.

1 cup	all-purpose flour	250 mL	⅔ cup	granulated sugar	150 mL
¼ cup	granulated sugar	50 mL	⅓ cup	butter, softened	75 mL
¼ cup	packed brown sugar	50 mL	2	eggs	2
½ tsp	cinnamon	2 mL	1 tsp	vanilla	5 mL
⅓ cup	butter, softened	75 mL	1½ cups	all-purpose flour	375 mL
CAKE:			1 tsp	baking powder	5 mL
3 cups	fresh or frozen rhubarb, cut in ½-inch (1 cm) pieces	750 mL	½ tsp	baking soda	2 mL
			¼ tsp	salt	1 mL
			½ cup	sour cream	125 mL

❧ Grease 9-inch (2.5 L) square metal cake pan; set aside.

❧ In bowl, whisk together flour, granulated and brown sugars and cinnamon. With fork, cut in butter, mashing to form clumps. Set crumble topping aside.

❧ CAKE: In bowl, toss rhubarb with 2 tbsp (25 mL) of the sugar; set aside.

❧ In large bowl, beat butter with remaining sugar until light and fluffy; beat in eggs, 1 at a time, beating well after each. Beat in vanilla.

❧ In separate bowl, whisk together flour, baking powder, baking soda and salt; stir into butter mixture alternately with sour cream, making 3 additions of dry ingredients and 2 of sour cream to make thick smooth batter. Scrape into prepared pan; smooth top.

❧ Sprinkle with half of the crumble mixture. Cover with rhubarb. Sprinkle with remaining crumble. Bake in centre of 350°F (180°C) oven until cake tester inserted in centre comes out clean, about 1¼ hours. Let cool in pan on rack. (**Make-ahead: Wrap and store at room temperature for up to 1 day. Or remove from pan and overwrap in heavy-duty foil; freeze in airtight container for up to 2 weeks.**)

Makes 12 servings. | PER SERVING: about 296 cal, 4 g pro, 13 g total fat (8 g sat. fat), 42 g carb, 1 g fibre, 62 mg chol, 216 mg sodium. % RDI: 6% calcium, 11% iron, 11% vit A, 3% vit C, 27% folate.

Layered Apple Cake

Layers of grated apple and buttery almond crumbs intermingle to form this very apple-flavoured, dense cake. This cake stays right in the pan to take to a party or to serve to family or guests at home. Use apples such as Spartan, Jonagold or Ambrosia.

3 cups	all-purpose flour	750 mL
1¼ cups	granulated sugar	300 mL
1 cup	ground almonds	250 mL
1 tsp	baking powder	5 mL
1 tsp	cinnamon	5 mL
¼ tsp	salt	1 mL
1½ cups	cold unsalted butter, cubed	375 mL
2	eggs, lightly beaten	2

6 cups	grated peeled apples (about 9)	1.5 L
½ tsp	grated lemon rind	2 mL
2 tbsp	lemon juice	25 mL
GLAZE:		
1 cup	icing sugar	250 mL
2 tbsp	lemon juice	25 mL
¼ tsp	almond extract	1 mL

❧ Grease 13- x 9-inch (3.5 L) metal cake pan; set aside.

❧ In bowl, whisk together flour, ½ cup (125 mL) of the sugar, the almonds, baking powder, cinnamon and salt. Using pastry blender, cut in butter until crumbly. Drizzle eggs over top; stir with fork until mixture resembles coarse crumbs.

❧ In separate bowl, toss together apples, remaining sugar and lemon rind and juice.

❧ Sprinkle one-third of the crumbs into prepared pan; top with half of the apple mixture. Repeat layers. Top with remaining crumbs.

❧ Bake in centre of 325°F (160°C) oven until golden and cake tester inserted in centre comes out clean, 75 to 85 minutes. Let cool completely in pan on rack.

❧ GLAZE: In bowl, stir together icing sugar, lemon juice and almond extract; drizzle over cake. (**Make-ahead: Wrap and store at room temperature for up to 1 day.**)

Makes 12 servings. | PER SERVING: about 519 cal, 6 g pro, 28 g total fat (15 g sat. fat), 64 g carb, 3 g fibre, 98 mg chol, 85 mg sodium. % RDI: 4% calcium, 13% iron, 23% vit A, 7% vit C, 18% folate.

Coconut Cupcakes

Snow-topped cupcakes with a tangy cream cheese icing and coconut are easy to make – and freeze well, too. Keep them in mind for bake sales and birthday parties.

VARY THE CITRUS

❯ This fine cupcake batter and icing are equally delicious using finely grated orange rind and juice instead of lemon.

½ cup	butter, softened	125 mL
1 cup	granulated sugar	250 mL
2	eggs	2
1½ cups	all-purpose flour	375 mL
½ cup	sweetened shredded or flaked coconut	125 mL
4 tsp	grated lemon rind	20 mL
1 tsp	baking powder	5 mL
¼ tsp	salt	1 mL
½ cup	milk	125 mL

LEMON CREAM CHEESE ICING:

2 tbsp	cream cheese, softened	25 mL
1 tbsp	butter, softened	15 mL
½ tsp	grated lemon rind	2 mL
1½ tsp	lemon juice	7 mL
1 cup	icing sugar	250 mL
½ cup	sweetened shredded or flaked coconut	125 mL
	Shredded lemon rind, optional	

↜ Line 12 muffin cups with paper liners or grease; set aside.

↜ In large bowl, beat butter with sugar until light and fluffy; beat in eggs, 1 at a time, beating well after each.

↜ In separate bowl, whisk together flour, coconut, lemon rind, baking powder and salt; stir into butter mixture alternately with milk, making 3 additions of dry ingredients and 2 of milk. Spoon into prepared muffin cups.

↜ Bake in centre of 350°F (180°C) oven until cake tester inserted in centre comes out clean, about 20 minutes. Transfer to rack; let cool. **(Make-ahead: Store in single layer in airtight container for up to 1 day or wrap each in plastic wrap and freeze in airtight container for up to 2 weeks.)**

↜ **LEMON CREAM CHEESE ICING:** In bowl, beat cream cheese with butter until fluffy; beat in grated lemon rind and juice. Beat in icing sugar until fluffy. Spread over each cupcake; dip icing into coconut. Top with shredded lemon rind (if using). **(Make-ahead: Refrigerate in single layer in airtight container for up to 1 day.)**

Makes 12 cupcakes. | PER CUPCAKE: about 302 cal, 3 g pro, 13 g total fat (9 g sat. fat), 43 g carb, 1 g fibre, 57 mg chol, 177 mg sodium. % RDI: 3% calcium, 7% iron, 10% vit A, 2% vit C, 17% folate.

Queen Elizabeth Cake

While this cake is fit for a queen, especially one with a sweet tooth, it did not originate in either of the Queen Elizabeths' royal households. Naming a particularly delicious cake after a member of the Royal Family is a long-established Canadian tradition, each generation of bakers updating names with current royals. In older cookbooks you'll find Prince Albert, Queen Victoria, the Prince of Wales and King Edward gracing the cake chapters.

1 cup	boiling water	250 mL	1 tsp	cinnamon	5 mL
½ cup	each raisins and chopped pitted dates	125 mL	½ tsp	each baking powder, salt and nutmeg	2 mL
½ cup	butter, softened	125 mL	BROILED COCONUT TOPPING:		
1 cup	packed brown sugar	250 mL	¼ cup	butter, softened	50 mL
1	egg	1	½ cup	packed brown sugar	125 mL
1 tsp	vanilla	5 mL	3 tbsp	10% cream	50 mL
1½ cups	all-purpose flour	375 mL	¾ cup	unsweetened desiccated coconut	175 mL
1 tsp	baking soda	5 mL			

➳ Grease 9-inch (2.5 L) square metal cake pan; set aside.

➳ In heatproof bowl, combine water, raisins and dates; let cool, about 30 minutes.

➳ In large bowl, beat butter with brown sugar until light and fluffy. Beat in egg, then vanilla. In separate bowl, whisk together flour, baking soda, cinnamon, baking powder, salt and nutmeg. Stir into butter mixture alternately with date mixture, making 3 additions of dry ingredients and 2 of wet.

➳ Scrape into prepared pan, pushing batter slightly higher at edges. Bake in centre of 350°F (180°C) oven until cake tester inserted in centre comes out clean, 35 to 40 minutes. Remove cake from oven; let stand in pan on rack. Move oven rack to top third of oven; set to broil.

➳ BROILED COCONUT TOPPING: Meanwhile, in bowl, mash butter with brown sugar until smooth. Mix in cream, in 3 additions, then coconut. Spread icing over hot cake; broil, watching carefully to prevent topping from burning (the sugar caramelizes very quickly), until topping bubbles and browns, 1 to 2 minutes. Let cool in pan on rack. (Make-ahead: Wrap and store at room temperature for up to 1 day.)

Makes 12 servings. | PER SERVING: about 349 cal, 3 g pro, 16 g total fat (11 g sat. fat), 51 g carb, 2 g fibre, 47 mg chol, 318 mg sodium. % RDI: 5% calcium, 13% iron, 11% vit A, 16% folate.

VARIATION

Queen Elizabeth Cake II: While the topping is exactly the same, this second moist, less-sweet snacking cake features rolled oats.

➳ In bowl, combine 1½ cups (375 mL) boiling water with 1 cup (250 mL) large-flake rolled oats; let cool. Meanwhile, beat ½ cup (125 mL) butter, softened, with 1½ cups (375 mL) packed brown sugar until fluffy. Beat in 2 eggs, then 1 tsp (5 mL) vanilla. In separate bowl, whisk together 1¾ cups (425 mL) all-purpose flour; 1 tsp (5 mL) each cinnamon and baking soda; and ½ tsp (2 mL) each baking powder, salt and nutmeg. Stir into butter mixture alternately with oat mixture, making 3 additions of dry ingredients and 2 of wet. Bake and top as directed.

Molten Chocolate Cakes

Each of these mini-cakes has a truffle in the middle, which melts as the cake bakes, ready to flow at the first stab of a spoon. These rich cakes are meant to be shared.

¾ cup	butter, softened	175 mL		1 cup	all-purpose flour	250 mL
1 cup	granulated sugar (approx)	250 mL		TRUFFLE:		
12 oz	bittersweet chocolate, chopped	375 g		4 oz	bittersweet chocolate, chopped	125 g
4	eggs	4		⅓ cup	whipping cream	75 mL
4	egg yolks	4		2 tbsp	Irish cream liqueur (or 1 tsp/5 mL vanilla)	25 mL
1 tbsp	vanilla	15 mL				

❧ Grease eight ¾-cup (175 mL) custard cups or ramekins with no more than 1 tbsp (15 mL) of the butter. Line bottoms with parchment paper; sprinkle scant 1 tsp (5 mL) of the sugar inside each. Line small rimmed baking sheet with waxed paper. Set cups and baking sheet aside.

❧ TRUFFLE: Place chocolate in heatproof bowl. In small saucepan, heat cream over medium heat until steaming. Pour over chocolate; whisk until melted and smooth. Whisk in liqueur; refrigerate until firm, about 1 hour. Scoop into 8 mounds onto prepared baking sheet. Roll into balls. Cover and freeze until firm, about 4 hours. **(Make-ahead: Freeze in airtight container for up to 1 week.)**

❧ In heatproof bowl over saucepan of hot (not boiling) water, melt chocolate with remaining butter. Let cool to room temperature.

❧ In large bowl, beat together eggs, egg yolks and remaining sugar until thickened, about 5 minutes. Fold in chocolate mixture and vanilla. Stir in flour. Spoon half into prepared cups; place frozen truffle in centre of each. Spoon remaining batter over top. **(Make-ahead: Cover and refrigerate for up to 1 day.)**

❧ Bake on rimmed baking sheet in centre of 350°F (180°C) oven until centres are sunken, soft and shiny, about 22 minutes. Let cool for 2 minutes. With knife, gently loosen edges. Unmould onto plates; peel off paper. Serve immediately.

Makes 8 servings. | PER SERVING: about 737 cal, 11 g pro, 48 g total fat (28 g sat. fat), 67 g carb, 7 g fibre, 254 mg chol, 165 mg sodium. % RDI: 6% calcium, 27% iron, 26% vit A, 26% folate.

Chocolate Torte with Pecans

This single-layer torte is dense and divine. Serve with a dollop of whipped cream or an oval of fancy ice cream, such as pistachio.

6 oz	bittersweet chocolate, chopped	175 g
2 oz	milk chocolate, chopped	60 g
⅔ cup	whipping cream	150 mL
¼ cup	unsalted butter	50 mL
3	eggs	3

⅓ cup	packed brown sugar	75 mL
3 tbsp	all-purpose flour	50 mL
1 tbsp	bourbon, coffee-flavoured liqueur or strong coffee	15 mL
1 cup	coarsely chopped pecans	250 mL

❧ Grease 8-inch (2 L) springform pan; set aside.

❧ In heatproof bowl over saucepan of hot (not boiling) water, melt together bittersweet and milk chocolates, cream and butter, stirring occasionally, until smooth.

❧ In large bowl, whisk together eggs, sugar, flour and bourbon; scrape in chocolate mixture, stirring just until combined. Fold in nuts. Scrape into prepared pan; smooth top.

❧ Bake in centre of 275°F (140°C) oven until centre is firm to the touch, about 1 hour. Let cool in pan on rack for 15 minutes. Turn out onto flat cake plate; let cool.

(Make-ahead: Cover and refrigerate for up to 2 days.)

Makes 12 to 14 servings. | PER EACH OF 14 SERVINGS: about 252 cal, 4 g pro, 29 g total fat (9 g sat. fat), 17 g carb, 2 g fibre, 64 mg chol, 23 mg sodium. % RDI: 4% calcium, 7% iron, 8% vit A, 5% folate.

LIQUEUR SUBSTITUTIONS

❯ While the taste will not be exactly the same, these substitutions will provide some of the spirit's flavour and volume in baking.

AMARETTO: For each tbsp (15 mL), substitute ⅛ tsp (0.5 mL) almond extract, making up the rest of the volume with water.

BOURBON: For each tbsp (15 mL), substitute 1 tsp (5 mL) vanilla and 2 tsp (10 mL) water.

BRANDY OR RUM: For each tbsp (15 mL), substitute ½ tsp (2 mL) brandy or rum extract, making up the rest of the volume with water.

COFFEE-FLAVOURED LIQUEUR: Replace with an equal amount of strong coffee, such as espresso. You can replace up to one-quarter of the strong coffee with vanilla.

KIRSCH: Replace with an equal amount of cherry juice or concentrated cherry juice.

ORANGE-FLAVOURED LIQUEUR: Replace with an equal amount of thawed unsweetened orange juice concentrate.

Sour Cream Pound Cake

This rich and buttery pound cake is a classic to have in your baking repertoire. Dress it up with macerated berries or peaches, crème fraîche or whipped cream, or enjoy it unadorned, savouring every nibble. Or up the ante and make the rum-drenched variation (sorry, there's no substitute for the rum except brandy or orange-flavoured liqueur) – it's a delight with fresh pineapple or mango.

1 cup	unsalted butter, softened	250 mL	2¼ cups	all-purpose flour	550 mL
1 cup	granulated sugar	250 mL	1½ tsp	baking powder	7 mL
4	eggs	4	½ tsp	salt	2 mL
2 tsp	vanilla	10 mL	½ cup	sour cream	125 mL

❧ Line 9- x 5-inch (2 L) loaf pan with double layer of parchment paper or grease; set aside.

❧ In large bowl, beat butter until light and fluffy; beat in sugar until combined. Beat in eggs, 1 at a time, beating well after each; beat in vanilla.

❧ In separate bowl, whisk together flour, baking powder and salt; stir into butter mixture alternately with sour cream, making 3 additions of dry ingredients and 2 of sour cream. Scrape into pan; smooth top.

❧ Bake in centre of 325°F (160°C) oven until cake tester inserted in centre comes out clean, about 1¼ hours. Let cool in pan on rack for 20 minutes. Transfer to rack; let cool. **(Make-ahead: Wrap in plastic wrap and store at room temperature for up to 1 day or overwrap in heavy-duty foil and freeze for up to 2 weeks.)**

Makes 1 loaf, 16 slices. | PER SLICE: about 244 cal, 4 g pro, 14 g total fat (8 g sat. fat), 27 g carb, 1 g fibre, 80 mg chol, 120 mg sodium. % RDI: 3% calcium, 7% iron, 13% vit A, 20% folate.

VARIATION

Rum-Drenched Pound Cake: Bake cake as directed. Meanwhile, in saucepan over medium-high heat, bring ½ cup (125 mL) granulated sugar, ¼ cup (50 mL) water and 2 tbsp (25 mL) corn syrup to boil, stirring. Boil for 1 minute. Remove from heat; stir in ⅓ cup (75 mL) rum. Let cool for 5 minutes.

❧ Let cake cool in pan on rack for 10 minutes. Using skewer, poke about 15 holes evenly over top of cake. Brush half of the syrup over top of cake; let stand for 5 minutes. Brush remaining syrup over cake; let stand for 30 minutes. Transfer to rack; let cool. **(Make-ahead: Wrap in plastic wrap and store at room temperature for up to 3 days or overwrap in heavy-duty foil and freeze for up to 2 weeks.)**

Cherry Pecan Pound Cake

Dust this teatime cake with icing sugar or, for a glaze, whisk ½ cup (125 mL) icing sugar with reserved kirsch or 4 tsp (20 mL) lemon juice and pour over cooled cake.

½ cup	dried sour cherries	125 mL
2 tbsp	kirsch or water	25 mL
½ cup	unsalted butter, softened	125 mL
½ cup	cream cheese, softened	125 mL
1 cup	granulated sugar	250 mL
2	eggs	2
½ tsp	vanilla	2 mL
1½ cups	sifted cake-and-pastry flour	375 mL
½ cup	chopped pecan halves	125 mL
1 tsp	grated lemon rind	5 mL
¼ tsp	each baking powder and baking soda	1 mL
¼ tsp	salt	1 mL

❧ Line 8- x 4-inch (1.5 L) loaf pan with double layer of parchment paper or grease; set aside.

❧ In small bowl, soak cherries in kirsch for 15 minutes; drain, reserving kirsch for glaze, if desired (see above), and pat dry.

❧ In large bowl, beat butter with cream cheese until creamy; beat in sugar until light and fluffy. Beat in eggs, 1 at a time, beating well after each; beat in vanilla.

❧ In separate bowl, whisk together flour, pecans, lemon rind, baking powder, baking soda and salt. Stir into butter mixture in 3 additions. Stir in cherries. Scrape into prepared pan; smooth top.

❧ Bake in centre of 325°F (160°C) oven until cake tester inserted in centre comes out clean, 55 to 65 minutes. Let cool in pan on rack for 20 minutes. Transfer to rack; let cool. **(Make-ahead: Wrap and store at room temperature for up to 2 days. Or overwrap in heavy-duty foil; freeze for up to 2 weeks.)**

Makes 1 loaf, 8 slices. | PER SLICE: about 429 cal, 5 g pro, 23 g total fat (11 g sat. fat), 52 g carb, 2 g fibre, 93 mg chol, 183 mg sodium. % RDI: 5% calcium, 15% iron, 19% vit A, 15% folate.

LINING LOAF PANS

❯ Pound cakes, and even some quick bread loaves, have very thick batters, and the length of time required to bake them through can result in too-dark crusts. In the Test Kitchen, we've found that lining the loaf pan with a double layer of parchment paper helps keep the crusts light-coloured. Wrestling parchment paper into pans can be tiresome but, trust us, it's worth the bother. To anchor the first layer firmly in place, some bakers like to grease the inside of the pan, or drop a splat of batter or a dribble of water on the bottom of the pan.

Very Chocolate Loaf

Serve as a polished dessert with an oval of mascarpone and raspberries, either whole or in luscious Raspberry Sauce (recipe, page 320).

(recipe, page 320)

CHOCOLATE UPGRADE

❯ Chocolate chips are certainly handy, but for a magnificent chocolate pound cake like this one, why not splurge on good bittersweet chocolate and chop it to about the size of large chips?

½ cup	butter, softened	125 mL
1¼ cups	packed brown sugar	300 mL
2	eggs	2
2 tsp	vanilla	10 mL
1¾ cups	all-purpose flour	425 mL
¾ cup	cocoa powder	175 mL

1 tsp	baking powder	5 mL
½ tsp	each baking soda and salt	2 mL
1 cup	sour cream	250 mL
¾ cup	chocolate chips	175 mL
¼ cup	chopped pecan halves	50 mL

❧ Line 9- x 5-inch (2 L) loaf pan with double layer of parchment paper or grease; set aside.

❧ In large bowl, beat butter with brown sugar until light and fluffy; beat in eggs, 1 at a time, beating well after each. Beat in vanilla.

❧ In separate bowl, sift together flour, cocoa, baking powder, baking soda and salt until no longer streaky; stir half into butter mixture. Stir in sour cream; stir in remaining dry ingredients. Fold in chocolate chips and pecans. Scrape into prepared pan; smooth top.

❧ Bake in centre of 350°F (180°C) oven until cake tester inserted in centre comes out clean, about 70 minutes. Let cool in pan on rack for 20 minutes. Transfer to rack; let cool. **(Make-ahead: Wrap in plastic wrap and store at room temperature for up to 3 days or overwrap in heavy-duty foil and freeze for up to 1 month.)**

Makes 1 loaf, 12 slices. | PER SLICE: about 345 cal, 5 g pro, 16 g total fat (9 g sat. fat), 47 g carb, 3 g fibre, 63 mg chol, 273 mg sodium. % RDI: 6% calcium, 19% iron, 11% vit A, 22% folate.

VARIATION

Chocolate Toffee Loaf: This is an over-the-top loaf, studded with toffee and chocolate. Completely irresistible!

❧ Replace chocolate chips with ½ cup (125 mL) each chopped chocolate-covered toffee bars (such as Skor, about two 34 g bars) and chopped bittersweet chocolate. Fold half each of the bittersweet chocolate and chopped toffee bars into batter along with pecans. Scrape into prepared pan; smooth top. Sprinkle remaining bittersweet chocolate and chopped toffee bars over top. Bake as directed.

Dundee Cake

The Scottish city of Dundee is famous throughout the British Isles for this easy-to-make fruitcake and is known worldwide for its Seville orange marmalade. Unlike other dense, fruit-laden Christmas cakes, Dundee Cake has more cake and is notable for its pattern of blanched almonds on top.

1 cup	butter, softened	250 mL
1⅓ cups	packed brown sugar	325 mL
1 tbsp	each grated orange and lemon rind	15 mL
4	eggs	4
2 cups	all-purpose flour	500 mL
1 tsp	baking powder	5 mL
1 cup	sultana raisins	250 mL
1 cup	dried currants	250 mL
1 cup	chopped candied cherries or mixed fruit	250 mL
1 cup	whole blanched almonds	250 mL
2 tbsp	corn syrup	25 mL
½ cup	dark rum or brandy	125 mL

FOR LONGER STORAGE

❯ At the 2-week mark, unwrap foil and plastic wrap; brush cheesecloth with an additional ¼ cup (50 mL) rum. Rewrap cake, then overwrap in heavy-duty foil and freeze for up to 6 months.

❧ Line bottom and side of 8-inch (2 L) springform pan with double layer of parchment paper; set aside.

❧ In large bowl, beat together butter, brown sugar, and orange and lemon rinds until light and fluffy. Beat in eggs, 1 at a time, beating well after each.

❧ In separate bowl, whisk flour with baking powder; stir in raisins, currants and cherries until separated and well coated. Stir into butter mixture, 1 cup (250 mL) at a time, until well combined. Spoon into prepared pan; smooth top.

❧ Starting at edge, arrange almonds, rounded ends out and with sides touching, in tight concentric circles over batter. Gently press almonds into batter.

❧ Set shallow pan on bottom rack of 300°F (150°C) oven; pour in enough very hot water to come halfway up sides of pan. Bake cake on centre rack until deep golden and cake tester inserted in centre comes out clean, 2 to 2½ hours. Let cool in pan on rack for 20 minutes. Transfer to rack; brush with corn syrup. Let cool.

❧ Soak 24- x 15-inch (60 x 38 cm) piece of cheesecloth in half of the rum; wrap around cake. Wrap in plastic wrap, then foil; refrigerate for 1 week. Unwrap and brush with remaining rum; rewrap and refrigerate for 1 week.

Makes 20 servings. | PER SERVING: about 317 cal, 5 g pro, 14 g total fat (6 g sat. fat), 46 g carb, 2 g fibre, 62 mg chol, 105 mg sodium. % RDI: 5% calcium, 12% iron, 9% vit A, 3% vit C, 15% folate.

VARIATIONS

Apricot Dundee Cake: Substitute 1 cup (250 mL) chopped dried apricots for the candied cherries.

Canadian Dundee Cake: Substitute 1 cup (250 mL) dried cranberries or sour cherries for the candied cherries.

Dark and Delicious Christmas Cake

In spite of anti-fruitcake propaganda, there are plenty of people who appreciate a slice of the really good stuff. What's nice about this recipe is that it makes a 13- x 9-inch (33 x 23 cm) cake that bakes quickly and divides into 6 neat little logs for your friends to share and enjoy. If you like, top with almond paste and icing (see recipe, left) before cutting into logs.

ALMOND PASTE AND ICING

> Dressing up fruitcake is as easy as 1,2,3.

✒ Beat ½ cup (125 mL) butter, softened, until fluffy. Beat in 2½ cups (625 mL) icing sugar, ¼ cup (50 mL) whipping cream and 1 tsp (5 mL) vanilla.

✒ Brush 2 tbsp (25 mL) corn syrup over cake top.

✒ Dust icing sugar on counter; roll out 1½ lb (750 g) almond paste into 13- x 9-inch (33 x 23 cm) rectangle.

✒ Press onto top of cake. Spread with icing.

✒ Cover loosely with plastic wrap and enclose in airtight container. Refrigerate for 1 day to firm up.

✒ Cut into bars.

2 cups	dried currants	500 mL	½ tsp	baking soda	2 mL
2 cups	candied mixed peel	500 mL	¼ tsp	each ground allspice, cinnamon and nutmeg	1 mL
1½ cups	coarsely chopped candied pineapple	375 mL	Pinch	salt	Pinch
1½ cups	red candied cherries, halved	375 mL	¾ cup	butter, softened	175 mL
1½ cups	seeded raisins (Muscat or Lexia)	375 mL	1 cup	packed brown sugar	250 mL
1 cup	brandy or rum	250 mL	⅓ cup	strawberry jam	75 mL
2 cups	all-purpose flour	500 mL	2 tbsp	fancy molasses	25 mL
2 tsp	baking powder	10 mL	5	eggs	5
			1½ cups	chopped walnut halves	375 mL

✒ Line bottom and sides of 13- x 9-inch (3.5 L) metal cake pan with double layer of parchment paper; set aside.

✒ In large bowl, combine currants, mixed peel, pineapple, cherries, raisins and ¾ cup (175 mL) of the brandy; cover and let stand for 1 day, stirring occasionally.

✒ In separate bowl, whisk together flour, baking powder, baking soda, allspice, cinnamon, nutmeg and salt; remove ½ cup (125 mL) and toss with fruit mixture.

✒ In another large bowl, beat together butter, brown sugar, jam and molasses until fluffy; beat in eggs, 1 at a time, beating well after each. Stir in remaining flour mixture all at once just until incorporated. Add fruit mixture and walnuts; stir to combine. Scrape into prepared pan; smooth top.

✒ Set shallow pan on bottom rack of 300°F (150°C) oven; pour in enough very hot water to come halfway up sides of pan. Bake cake on centre rack for 1 hour. Lay foil loosely over cake; bake until cake tester inserted in centre comes out clean but a little sticky, 45 to 60 minutes. Let cool in pan on rack.

✒ Remove cake from pan; peel off paper. Soak double-thickness 16-inch (40 cm) square of cheesecloth in remaining brandy; wrap around cake. Wrap in plastic wrap, then foil. Refrigerate for 1 month. **(Make-ahead: Refrigerate for up to 3 months.)** Cut crosswise into 6 bars.

Makes 6 small cakes, 14 slices each. | PER SLICE: about 113 cal, 1 g pro, 3 g total fat (1 g sat. fat), 20 g carb, 1 g fibre, 16 mg chol, 40 mg sodium. % RDI: 2% calcium, 4% iron, 2% vit A, 7% vit C, 4% folate.

Red Grapefruit Chiffon Cake

To get the highest, lightest cake, be sure to use a regular – not nonstick – tube pan. Serve with ruby red grapefruit segments.

2¼ cups	sifted cake-and-pastry flour	550 mL
1½ cups	granulated sugar	375 mL
1 tbsp	baking powder	15 mL
½ tsp	salt	2 mL
6	egg yolks	6
2 tbsp	grated grapefruit rind	25 mL
¾ cup	strained red grapefruit juice	175 mL

½ cup	vegetable oil	125 mL
8	egg whites	8
¼ tsp	cream of tartar	1 mL
ICING:		
4 cups	icing sugar	1 L
⅓ cup	red grapefruit juice (approx)	75 mL

꙰ Set out 10-inch (4 L) tube pan.

꙰ Into large bowl, sift together flour, ¾ cup (175 mL) of the sugar, baking powder and salt. In separate bowl, whisk together egg yolks, grapefruit rind and juice, and oil; pour over flour mixture and whisk just until smooth. Set aside.

꙰ In another large bowl, beat egg whites until foamy; beat in cream of tartar until soft peaks form. Beat in remaining sugar, 2 tbsp (25 mL) at a time, until stiff peaks form; fold one-quarter into batter. Fold in remaining whites. Scrape into tube pan. Run spatula through batter to eliminate any large air bubbles; smooth top.

꙰ Bake in bottom third of 350°F (180°C) oven until cake springs back when lightly touched, about 40 minutes. Turn pan upside down and let hang on legs attached to pan or on inverted large funnel or bottle until cooled.

꙰ Run long palette knife around centre and side of pan. (Make-ahead: Invert into large plastic wrap–lined airtight container; fold plastic wrap over cake. Cover and store at room temperature for up to 2 days or freeze for up to 2 weeks.) Turn out, bottom side up, onto flat cake plate.

꙰ ICING: In bowl, whisk icing sugar with grapefruit juice, adding up to 1 tbsp (15 mL) more juice, 1 tsp (5 mL) at a time, if too thick to spoon. Spoon over top of cake, letting excess run down sides.

Makes 12 servings. | PER SERVING: about 459 cal, 5 g pro, 12 g total fat (2 g sat. fat), 84 g carb, trace fibre, 102 mg chol, 210 mg sodium. % RDI: 5% calcium, 14% iron, 5% vit A, 15% vit C, 17% folate.

SECTIONING CITRUS FRUIT

❯ To section oranges and grapefruits, first slice off bottom (blossom end) and top (stem end) of fruit, cutting just beyond the membranes. Stand fruit on one flat end. Cut off the peel in strips, cutting just beyond the membrane. Working over a bowl and holding fruit in palm, cut between membranes to release sections. Once all sections have been cut out, squeeze membranes to release remaining juice.

Chocolate Chip Angel Food Cake

Beating the egg whites with a stand mixer gives great height to this cake. An electric hand mixer still gives a pillowy texture, but the cake will not be as high.

1¼ cups	sifted cake-and-pastry flour	300 mL	½ cup	mini or regular chocolate chips	125 mL
1½ cups	granulated sugar	375 mL	**GLAZE:**		
1½ cups	egg whites (about 11)	375 mL	2 oz	bittersweet chocolate, coarsely chopped	60 g
1 tbsp	lemon juice	15 mL	⅓ cup	whipping cream	75 mL
1 tsp	cream of tartar	5 mL	1 tsp	corn syrup	5 mL
½ tsp	salt	2 mL			
2 tsp	vanilla	10 mL			

➤ Set out 10-inch (4 L) tube pan.

➤ Into bowl, sift flour with ¾ cup (175 mL) of the sugar; sift again into separate bowl. Set aside.

➤ In large bowl, beat egg whites until foamy. Add lemon juice, cream of tartar and salt; beat until soft peaks form. Beat in remaining sugar, 2 tbsp (25 mL) at a time, until stiff glossy peaks form. Sift flour mixture over top, one-quarter at a time, gently folding in each addition until blended. Fold in vanilla and chocolate chips. Scrape into tube pan. Run spatula through batter to eliminate any large air bubbles; smooth top.

➤ Bake in centre of 350°F (180°C) oven until cake springs back when lightly touched, 45 to 50 minutes. Turn pan upside down and let hang on legs attached to pan or on inverted large funnel or bottle until cooled, about 3 hours. Run long palette knife around centre and side of pan, pressing blade against pan, to loosen cake. Turn out, bottom side up, onto flat cake plate. (**Make-ahead: Wrap in plastic wrap and store at room temperature for up to 2 days or overwrap in heavy-duty foil and freeze for up to 1 month.**)

➤ GLAZE: In bowl over saucepan of hot (not boiling) water, melt chocolate. Stir in cream and corn syrup until smooth. Spread over top of cake. (**Make-ahead: Cover and refrigerate for up to 1 day.**)

Makes 12 servings. | PER SERVING: about 239 cal, 5 g pro, 7 g total fat (4 g sat. fat), 41 g carb, 1 g fibre, 9 mg chol, 148 mg sodium. % RDI: 1% calcium, 10% iron, 2% vit A, 7% folate.

VARIATIONS

Chocolate Chocolate Chip Angel Food Cake: Replace ¼ cup (50 mL) of the flour with cocoa powder.

Classic Angel Food Cake: Omit chocolate chips. If desired, omit glaze and serve cake with whipped cream and fruit, or just fruit.

Sunshine Cake

Sunshine cake is angel food cake made with whole eggs. With its light, moist texture, golden colour and citrus flavour, it makes an ideal Easter dessert or, using kosher-for-Passover ingredients, an equally anticipated Passover dessert (see variation, opposite).

PREVENT OVERBROWNING

❯ If the cake is golden before the 40-minute mark, loosely shield the surface with foil to keep the crust from getting too dark.

2	egg yolks	2
7	eggs, separated	7
1½ cups	granulated sugar	375 mL
1⅔ cups	sifted cake-and-pastry flour	400 mL
3 tbsp	grated orange rind	50 mL
¼ cup	orange juice	50 mL
1 tsp	vanilla	5 mL
½ tsp	salt	2 mL
2 cups	halved strawberries	500 mL
1½ cups	raspberries	375 mL
½ cup	slivered peeled mango	125 mL

CITRUS CURD:

2	eggs	2
1 cup	granulated sugar	250 mL
3 tbsp	grated orange rind	50 mL
½ cup	orange juice	125 mL
½ cup	lemon juice	125 mL
1 tbsp	cornstarch	15 mL
¼ cup	butter	50 mL

↜ Set out 10-inch (4 L) tube pan (not nonstick).

↜ In large bowl, beat together all 9 of the egg yolks, half of the sugar, the flour, orange rind and juice, and vanilla until blended. Set aside.

↜ In separate large bowl and using clean beaters, beat egg whites with salt until soft peaks form. Beat in remaining sugar, 2 tbsp (25 mL) at a time, until stiff peaks form.

↜ With spatula, gently fold one-third of the egg whites into yolk mixture; fold in remaining whites just until no streaks remain. Scrape into prepared pan; smooth top. Bake in centre of 350°F (180°C) oven until top springs back when lightly touched, about 50 minutes.

↜ Turn pan upside down and let hang on legs attached to pan or on inverted large funnel or bottle until cooled, about 3 hours. Run long palette knife around centre and side of pan, pressing blade against pan, to loosen cake. Turn out, bottom side up, onto flat cake plate. **(Make-ahead: Wrap in plastic wrap and store at room temperature for up to 1 day or overwrap in heavy-duty foil and freeze for up to 2 weeks.)**

↜ CITRUS CURD: In saucepan, whisk together eggs, sugar, orange rind, orange and lemon juices, and cornstarch. Bring to boil over medium-high heat; boil, stirring, for 1 minute. Remove from heat; whisk in butter. Strain through fine sieve into bowl. Place plastic wrap directly on surface; refrigerate until cold, about 2 hours. **(Make-ahead: Refrigerate for up to 2 days.)**

↜ Spread ⅓ cup (75 mL) of the citrus curd over top of cake; top with strawberries, raspberries and mango. Serve with remaining curd.

Makes 12 servings. | PER SERVING: about 351 cal, 7 g pro, 9 g total fat (4 g sat. fat), 63 g carb, 2 g fibre, 184 mg chol, 171 mg sodium. % RDI: 4% calcium, 14% iron, 13% vit A, 60% vit C, 25% folate.

VARIATION

Passover Sunshine Cake: Omit 2 egg yolks; increase whole eggs to 9. Substitute ¾ cup (175 mL) matzo cake meal (preferably Manischewitz brand) and ¼ cup (50 mL) potato flour for the cake-and-pastry flour. Replace vanilla with vanillin sugar. In Citrus Curd, replace cornstarch with potato flour and butter with pareve margarine.

White Chocolate Strawberry Roll

This not-too-sweet ricotta filling provides a pleasant backdrop to summer-ripe berries. Be sure to use good-quality white chocolate made with cocoa butter.

NO TO NONSTICK

❯ Do not use a nonstick rimmed baking sheet, also known as a jelly roll pan; the batter needs something to stick to as it climbs up the sides of the pan while baking. There's no worry about getting the cake out of the pan – running a table knife around the inside edge will easily dislodge it.

¼ cup	granulated sugar	50 mL
¼ cup	water	50 mL
JELLY ROLL CAKE:		
3	egg whites	3
¼ tsp	cream of tartar	1 mL
¾ cup	granulated sugar	175 mL
6	egg yolks	6
1 tsp	vanilla	5 mL
½ cup	all-purpose flour	125 mL
¼ tsp	salt	1 mL

3 tbsp	icing sugar	50 mL
2 cups	sliced strawberries	500 mL
WHITE CHOCOLATE ORANGE RICOTTA FILLING:		
6 oz	white chocolate, chopped	175 g
2 cups	extra-smooth ricotta cheese	500 mL
⅓ cup	orange-flavoured liqueur or orange juice	75 mL
½ cup	whipping cream	125 mL

✎ Line bottom of 15- x 10-inch (40 x 25 cm) rimmed baking sheet with parchment paper; set aside.

✎ **JELLY ROLL CAKE:** In bowl, beat egg whites with cream of tartar until soft peaks form; beat in ¼ cup (50 mL) of the sugar, 1 tbsp (15 mL) at a time, until stiff peaks form.

✎ In large bowl, beat egg yolks with remaining sugar until pale and thickened and mixture falls in ribbons when beaters are lifted, about 3 minutes; beat in vanilla. In separate bowl, whisk flour with salt. Fold egg white mixture into yolk mixture alternately with dry ingredients, making 3 additions of egg whites and 2 of dry ingredients. Spread evenly on prepared baking sheet; smooth top.

✎ Bake in centre of 375°F (190°C) oven until top springs back when lightly touched, 12 to 15 minutes. Set aside 2 tsp (10 mL) of the icing sugar; dust clean tea towel with remaining sugar. Using knife, loosen edges of cake; invert onto towel. Remove pan; peel off paper. Trim long edges. Starting at 1 short edge, immediately roll up with towel. Let cool on rack. **(Make-ahead: Place rolled cake in airtight container and store at room temperature for up to 1 day. Or unroll cake and reroll between sheets of waxed paper; overwrap in heavy-duty foil and freeze for up to 2 weeks.)**

✎ In small saucepan, bring granulated sugar and water to boil, stirring. Let syrup cool.

✎ **WHITE CHOCOLATE ORANGE RICOTTA FILLING:** In heatproof bowl over saucepan of hot (not boiling) water, melt white chocolate. Meanwhile, in separate bowl, mix ricotta to loosen; whisk in liqueur. Whisk one-quarter of the ricotta mixture into white chocolate. Stir into remaining ricotta mixture until combined. Whip cream; fold into ricotta mixture.

⤴ Unroll cake. Brush with syrup; spread with filling. Sprinkle with strawberries. Using towel as support, roll up cake without towel. Place, seam side down, on flat rectangular serving plate. Dust with reserved icing sugar.

Makes 12 servings. | PER SERVING: about 342 cal, 9 g pro, 17 g total fat (10 g sat. fat), 37 carb, 1 g fibre, 144 mg chol, 119 mg sodium. % RDI: 13% calcium, 6% iron, 14% vit A, 23% vit C, 9% folate.

VARIATIONS

White Chocolate and Cream Roll: Prepare cake and syrup as directed. Omit ricotta and liqueur in filling. Increase whipping cream to 1½ cups (375 mL). In large bowl, melt white chocolate with ¼ cup (50 mL) of the cream; let cool to room temperature. Whip remaining cream; whisk one-quarter into white chocolate mixture. Fold in remaining whipped cream. Refrigerate for 1 hour or until stiff. Assemble as directed.

Lemon Jelly Roll: Prepare cake as directed. Substitute Lemon Curd (recipe, page 335) for Chocolate Orange Ricotta Filling. Assemble as directed. Dust top generously with icing sugar before serving.

HOW TO MAKE A CAKE ROLL

This method works for all jelly rolls. For our photos, we used the Lemon Jelly Roll, left.

● The sugar liberally dusted over the tea towel prevents the cake from sticking to the towel as it's rolled up. Use a gentle touch to peel off the paper.

● Fold the towel over the end of the cake and begin to roll just tight enough to give the cake shape, but without squeezing.

● Unroll the cake, removing the towel. Spread with filling (here, Lemon Curd; recipe, page 335) and reroll, again with a firm enough touch to keep the cake rolled but without squishing out the filling.

● To dust any dessert with icing sugar, hold a fine sieve over top. Add icing sugar and tap the sieve gently, moving it over the dessert as you tap to give the top a fine, even dusting.

Raspberry Lemon Cream Cake

While almost all of the cakes created in the Test Kitchen can be made with a hand mixer, for this stunning berry cake a stand mixer will deliver higher, lighter results. You can also make the cake with fresh wild or cultivated blueberries, or ripe blackberries.

MAKING IT TO THE RIBBON STAGE

It can take up to 10 minutes of beating for the sugar and eggs – or, in some cases, just egg yolks – to thicken enough to fall in ribbons.

3 cups	raspberries	750 mL
1 tbsp	icing sugar	15 mL
CAKE:		
6	eggs	6
1 cup	granulated sugar	250 mL
1 tbsp	grated lemon rind	15 mL
1 tsp	vanilla	5 mL
1 cup	all-purpose flour	250 mL
½ tsp	baking powder	2 mL
Pinch	salt	Pinch

⅓ cup	butter, melted	75 mL
LEMON CREAM:		
1	pkg (7 g) unflavoured gelatin	1
3	eggs	3
2	egg yolks	2
1¼ cups	granulated sugar	300 mL
1 tbsp	grated lemon rind	15 mL
⅔ cup	lemon juice	150 mL
1⅓ cups	whipping cream	325 mL

↜ Grease side of 10-inch (3 L) springform pan; line bottom with parchment or waxed paper. Set aside.

↜ **CAKE:** Set eggs in bowl of warm (100°F/40°C) water for 5 minutes.

↜ In electric stand mixer on medium-high speed, beat eggs until foamy. Gradually beat in sugar until pale yellow and batter falls in ribbons when beaters are lifted, about 10 minutes. Fold in lemon rind and vanilla.

↜ Sift together flour, baking powder and salt; sift one-third over egg mixture and fold in. Repeat twice. Transfer one-quarter of the batter to bowl; fold in butter. Fold back into remaining batter. Scrape into prepared pan.

↜ Bake in centre of 325°F (160°C) oven until cake springs back when lightly touched in centre, 45 to 50 minutes. Let cool in pan on rack for 10 minutes. Remove side of pan; let cool on base on rack. **(Make-ahead: Remove base and peel off paper; wrap in plastic wrap. Store for up to 1 day or overwrap in heavy-duty foil and freeze for up to 2 weeks.)** Wash pan.

↜ **LEMON CREAM:** In small bowl, sprinkle gelatin over 3 tbsp (50 mL) water; set aside.

↜ In heatproof bowl, whisk together eggs, egg yolks, sugar, and lemon rind and juice. Place over saucepan of simmering water; cook, stirring frequently, until translucent and thick enough to softly mound on spoon, about 20 minutes.

↜ Strain into large bowl. Add gelatin mixture, stirring until melted. Place plastic wrap directly on surface; refrigerate, stirring every 10 minutes, until cool and mixture mounds smartly on spoon, about 1 hour.

↜ In bowl, whip cream; fold one-third into lemon mixture. Fold in remaining cream. Fold in 2⅓ cups (575 mL) of the raspberries; set aside.

↜ Line bottom and side of same pan with parchment or waxed paper. Cut cake horizontally into thirds. Place top cake layer, cut side up, in pan; spread with half of the lemon cream. Top with middle cake layer, remaining lemon cream, then remaining cake layer, cut side down. Cover and refrigerate until set, about 4 hours. **(Make-ahead: Refrigerate for up to 1 day.)**

⌁ Remove side of pan. Dust top with icing sugar. Arrange remaining raspberries around top edge.

Makes 12 servings. | PER SERVING: about 404 cal, 8 g pro, 19 g total fat (11 g sat. fat), 52 g carb, 3 g fibre, 221 mg chol, 107 mg sodium. % RDI: 5% calcium, 9% iron, 21% vit A, 25% vit C, 25% folate.

Chestnut Cream Cake

This light sponge cake is the perfect base for the subtle nut-flavoured cream filling. Look for cans of sweetened chestnut spread or chestnut cream in gourmet stores or the baking aisles of grocery stores. Chocolate hazelnut spread, such as Nutella, is an often-easier-to-locate substitute.

2	eggs	2
3	eggs, separated	3
¾ cup	granulated sugar	175 mL
¼ cup	butter, softened	50 mL
½ tsp	vanilla	2 mL
Pinch	salt	Pinch
¾ cup	all-purpose flour	175 mL

CHESTNUT CREAM FILLING:

2 cups	whipping cream	500 mL
3 tbsp	cognac or brandy	50 mL
¾ cup	sweetened chestnut spread	175 mL
½ oz	bittersweet chocolate, finely grated	15 g

❧ Grease side of 9-inch (2.5 L) springform pan; line bottom with parchment or waxed paper. Set aside.

❧ In large bowl, beat eggs with egg yolks just until blended; beat in half of the sugar until light and fluffy, about 2 minutes. Beat in butter, vanilla and salt. Set aside.

❧ In separate bowl and using clean beaters, beat egg whites until foamy. Beat in remaining sugar, 1 tbsp (15 mL) at a time, until soft peaks form. Fold into yolk mixture alternately with flour, making 2 additions of each. Scrape into prepared pan; smooth top.

❧ Bake in centre of 350°F (180°C) oven until cake springs back when lightly touched in centre, 30 to 40 minutes. Let cool in pan on rack. Run knife around edge; remove pan side. Turn out onto rack; peel off paper. Invert; let cool. **(Make-ahead: Wrap in plastic wrap and store in airtight container at room temperature for up to 2 days or overwrap in heavy-duty foil and freeze for up to 2 weeks. Thaw.)**

❧ **CHESTNUT CREAM FILLING:** In large bowl, whip cream with cognac. Fold in ¼ cup (50 mL) of the chestnut spread and half of the chocolate.

❧ Cut cake horizontally into thirds. Place bottom layer, cut side up, on flat cake plate; slide 4 strips of waxed paper between cake and plate. Spread ¼ cup (50 mL) of the remaining chestnut spread evenly over layer. Using piping bag fitted with star tip or spatula, pipe or spread one-third of the chestnut cream filling over chestnut spread. Repeat layers once. Top with remaining layer, cut side up.

❧ Pipe or spread remaining cream filling over cake. Refrigerate until firm, about 1 hour. **(Make-ahead: Cover loosely; refrigerate for up to 1 day.)** Sprinkle with remaining chocolate.

Makes 10 to 12 servings. | PER EACH OF 12 SERVINGS: about 323 cal, 4 g pro, 21 g total fat (12 g sat. fat), 30 g carb, 1 g fibre, 139 mg chol, 69 mg sodium. % RDI: 4% calcium, 6% iron, 21% vit A, 3% vit C, 14% folate.

New York Cheesecake

Topped with stunning, glossy strawberries, this cheesecake is a show-stopper. You can omit the strawberries and top with Mango Sauce (recipe, page 321) or Fancy Cranberry Sauce Topping (recipe, page 329) for delicious variety.

1½ cups	chocolate wafer crumbs	375 mL
¼ cup	butter, melted	50 mL

NEW YORK CHEESECAKE:

3	pkg (each 8 oz/250 g) cream cheese, softened	3
¾ cup	granulated sugar	175 mL
4	eggs	4
1 tbsp	each lemon juice and vanilla	15 mL

Pinch	salt	Pinch
1 cup	sour cream	250 mL

GLAZED STRAWBERRY TOPPING:

6 cups	strawberries	1.5 L
1 tsp	unflavoured gelatin	5 mL
⅓ cup	seedless raspberry jam	75 mL
1 tsp	orange-flavoured liqueur (optional)	5 mL

↜ Grease bottom of 9-inch (2.5 L) springform pan; line side with parchment paper. Centre pan on large square of heavy-duty foil; bring foil up and press to side of pan. Set aside.

↜ In bowl, stir crumbs with butter until moistened; press onto bottom of prepared pan. Bake in centre of 350°F (180°C) oven until firm to the touch, about 10 minutes. Let cool in pan on rack.

↜ **NEW YORK CHEESECAKE:** Meanwhile, in large bowl, beat cream cheese until smooth; beat in sugar until smooth. Beat in eggs, 1 at a time. Beat in lemon juice, vanilla and salt; beat in sour cream just until blended. Pour over crust.

↜ Set pan in larger shallow pan; pour in enough hot water to come 1 inch (2.5 cm) up side of springform pan. Bake in centre of 325°F (160°C) oven until shine disappears and edge is set but centre is still jiggly, about 1¼ hours. Turn off oven; let stand in oven for 1 hour.

↜ Transfer springform pan to rack and remove foil; let cool. Cover and refrigerate until firm, about 4 hours. **(Make-ahead: Refrigerate for up to 2 days or overwrap in heavy-duty foil and freeze for up to 2 weeks.)**

↜ **GLAZED STRAWBERRY TOPPING:** Cut tops off strawberries; place, cut side down, in concentric circles on top of cheesecake. In small bowl, sprinkle gelatin over 1 tbsp (15 mL) water; let stand for 5 minutes to soften. In saucepan, stir together softened gelatin, jam, and liqueur, if using; heat over low heat, stirring, until melted and smooth, 2 minutes. Brush over strawberries. Refrigerate until set, about 30 minutes. **(Make-ahead: Refrigerate for up to 6 hours.)**

Makes 16 to 20 servings. | PER EACH OF 20 SERVINGS: about 280 cal, 5 g pro, 19 g total fat (11 g sat. fat), 23 g carb, 1 g fibre, 90 mg chol, 202 mg sodium. % RDI: 5% calcium, 8% iron, 19% vit A, 48% vit C, 13% folate.

MAKING SPRINGFORM PANS LEAKPROOF

To make sure your cheesecake doesn't crack, bake it in a water bath, or *bain marie*. To keep water from getting in and making the crust soggy, the bottom and side of the springform pan must be foil-wrapped. Regular foil is too narrow and will leak even if 2 pieces are folded together. Wider, stronger heavy-duty foil is a must.

Two-Tone Mocha Cheesecake

Chocolate and coffee are a heavenly match made right in your kitchen, and when they are combined in this rich, creamy-smooth layered cheesecake, each mouthful is divine. If you like, decorate the cake with Piped Chocolate Garnishes (recipe, page 338).

MAKING A FIRM BASE

The flat bottom of a glass makes a great tool to press crumbs evenly and firmly into pan, especially around the edge.

1½ cups	chocolate wafer crumbs	375 mL
3 tbsp	butter, melted	50 mL
1 tsp	instant coffee granules or instant espresso powder	5 mL
FILLING:		
8 oz	milk chocolate, chopped	250 g
4 oz	bittersweet chocolate, chopped	125 g

3	pkg (each 8 oz/250 g) cream cheese, softened	3
¾ cup	granulated sugar	175 mL
3	eggs	3
1 cup	whipping cream	250 mL
3 tbsp	coffee-flavoured liqueur	50 mL

ELIMINATING AIR BUBBLES

❯ To prevent air bubbles from permeating your cheesecakes, beat in the eggs just long enough to incorporate them – no more. Keep in mind that a cheesecake is a custard, not a cake. Then, just before putting it into the water bath, hold the pan about 1 inch (2.5 cm) above the counter and let it drop gently.

❧ Grease bottom of 9½-inch (2.75 L) springform pan; line side with parchment paper. Centre pan on large square of heavy-duty foil; bring foil up and press to side of pan. Set aside.

❧ In bowl, stir together crumbs, butter and coffee granules until evenly moistened. Press onto bottom and ½ inch (1 cm) up side of prepared pan. Bake in centre of 325°F (160°C) oven until firm to the touch, about 10 minutes. Let cool.

❧ FILLING: Meanwhile, in heatproof bowl over saucepan of hot (not boiling) water, melt milk chocolate, stirring occasionally; repeat with bittersweet chocolate in separate bowl. Let both cool to room temperature.

❧ In large bowl, beat cream cheese until smooth; beat in sugar. Beat in eggs, 1 at a time. Beat in cream, coffee liqueur and milk chocolate just until blended.

❧ Transfer one-third of the batter to separate bowl; whisk in bittersweet chocolate. Scrape bittersweet chocolate batter over prepared crust; smooth top. Spoon remaining batter over top; smooth top.

❧ Set springform pan in larger shallow pan; pour in enough hot water to come 1 inch (2.5 cm) up side of springform pan. Bake in centre of 325°F (160°C) oven until set around edge but centre is still jiggly, about 1 hour. Turn off oven; let stand in oven for 1 hour.

❧ Transfer springform pan to rack and remove foil; let cool. Cover and refrigerate until chilled, about 4 hours. **(Make-ahead: Refrigerate for up to 3 days or overwrap in heavy-duty foil and freeze for up to 2 weeks.)**

Makes 12 servings. | PER SERVING: about 592 cal, 10 g pro, 46 g total fat (27 g sat. fat), 41 g carb, 2 g fibre, 160 mg chol, 336 mg sodium. % RDI: 11% calcium, 17% iron, 40% vit A, 8% folate.

Ricotta Honey Cheesecake

Greek thyme honey, traditionally used in this cheesecake, adds an intriguing herbal flavour. Closer to home, try wildflower, berry or melon honey. Even mild clover is excellent.

1½ cups	all-purpose flour	375 mL		4	eggs	4
½ cup	cold butter, cubed	125 mL		¼ cup	whipping cream	50 mL
2 tbsp	granulated sugar	25 mL		3 tbsp	all-purpose flour	50 mL
¼ tsp	salt	1 mL		1 tbsp	finely grated lemon rind	15 mL
RICOTTA HONEY FILLING:				2 tbsp	lemon juice	25 mL
2 cups	ricotta cheese	500 mL		**GARNISH:**		
½ cup	liquid honey	125 mL		¼ cup	liquid honey	50 mL
¼ cup	granulated sugar	50 mL		¾ tsp	ground cinnamon	4 mL

SCRAPING DOWN THE BOWL

❯ When beating butter with sugar, or batter for cakes and cheesecakes, it's important to scrape down the side of the bowl often to ensure that the ingredients are evenly blended.

❧ Set out 9-inch (2.5 L) springform pan.

❧ In food processor, pulse together flour, butter, sugar and salt until mixture resembles rolled oats. Add 3 tbsp (50 mL) cold water; pulse just until clumped together. Press onto bottom and 2 inches (5 cm) up side of springform pan; prick all over with fork. Refrigerate for 30 minutes.

❧ Line pastry with foil; fill with pie weights or dried beans. Bake in bottom third of 375°F (190°C) oven for 15 minutes. Remove weights and foil; bake until golden, about 20 minutes. Let cool in pan on rack.

❧ **RICOTTA HONEY FILLING:** Meanwhile, in food processor, whirl ricotta until smooth. Add honey and sugar; whirl until smooth. Blend in eggs, 1 at a time. Blend in cream, flour and lemon rind and juice; scrape into crust. Bake in centre of 325°F (160°C) oven until golden and set around edge but centre is still jiggly, about 50 minutes.

❧ Transfer to rack and loosen side of pan; let cool for 1 hour. Refrigerate until cold, about 4 hours. Remove from pan and place on flat cake plate. **(Make-ahead: Cover and refrigerate for up to 2 days.)**

❧ **GARNISH:** Cut cheesecake into wedges. Drizzle with honey; dust with cinnamon.

Makes 10 to 12 servings. | PER EACH OF 12 SERVINGS: about 333 cal, 9 g pro, 17 g total fat (10 g sat. fat), 39 g carb, 1 g fibre, 113 mg chol, 184 mg sodium. % RDI: 10% calcium, 9% iron, 16% vit A, 3% vit C, 16% folate.

Lemon Shimmer Cheesecake

While chocolate has become the No. 1 flavour for desserts, lemon is a very popular choice in the Test Kitchen and for our readers. For a pretty touch, garnish with Syrup Poached Lemon Rind (recipe, page 333) and sugared blueberries (recipe, page 330), as in our photo.

23	lemon social tea cookies	23	2	eggs	2
⅓ cup	butter, melted	75 mL	1¾ cups	sour cream	425 mL
FILLING:			**LEMON TOPPING:**		
2	pkg (each 8 oz/250 g) cream cheese, softened	2	2	eggs	2
			2	egg yolks	2
½ cup	granulated sugar	125 mL	⅔ cup	granulated sugar	150 mL
½ cup	frozen lemonade concentrate, thawed	125 mL	1 tbsp	grated lemon rind	15 mL
1 tbsp	grated lemon rind	15 mL	½ cup	lemon juice	125 mL

❧ Grease bottom of 9-inch (2.5 L) springform pan; line side with parchment paper. Centre pan on large square of heavy-duty foil; bring foil up and press to side of pan. Set aside.

❧ LEMON TOPPING: In heatproof bowl over saucepan of simmering water, whisk together eggs, egg yolks, sugar and lemon rind and juice; cook, stirring, until thick enough to mound on spoon, about 10 minutes. Place plastic wrap directly on surface; refrigerate until cold, about 1 hour. (Make-ahead: Refrigerate for up to 1 day.)

❧ In food processor, crush cookies to make 1½ cups (375 mL) coarse crumbs; pulse in butter until moistened. Press onto bottom of prepared pan; bake in centre of 325°F (160°F) oven until firm to the touch, about 12 minutes. Let cool.

❧ FILLING: In bowl, beat cream cheese with sugar; beat in lemonade concentrate and lemon rind. Beat in eggs, 1 at a time. Beat in ¾ cup (175 mL) of the sour cream. Scrape over baked crust; smooth top. Set pan in larger shallow pan; pour in enough hot water to come 1 inch (2.5 cm) up side of springform pan. Bake in centre of 325°F (160°C) oven until edge is set but centre is still jiggly, about 1 hour. Remove pan from water bath; let cool on rack for 5 minutes.

❧ In bowl, whisk remaining sour cream until smooth; spread over cake. Return to water bath; bake until top is set, about 5 minutes. Turn off oven; let stand in oven for 1 hour. Transfer springform pan to rack and remove foil; let cool for 5 minutes. Run knife between edge of cake and paper; let cool.

❧ Whisk lemon topping until smooth; spread over cake. Refrigerate until firm, about 4 hours. (Make-ahead: Cover with plastic wrap and refrigerate for up to 3 days.)

Makes 12 to 16 servings. | PER EACH OF 16 SERVINGS: about 324 cal, 6 g pro, 21 g total fat (12 g sat. fat), 29 g carb, trace fibre, 128 mg chol, 159 mg sodium. % RDI: 6% calcium, 5% iron, 22% vit A, 10% vit C, 8% folate.

Camembert Cheesecakes

Garnished with frizzled prosciutto, these mini-cheesecakes are a delicious first course for a dinner party any time of year. Serve with Roasted Red Pepper Coulis (recipe, opposite) or on a bed of lightly dressed frisée or watercress.

1	pkg (8 oz/250 g) cream cheese, softened	1
4 oz	Camembert cheese, diced	125 g
1	egg	1
1 tsp	minced fresh rosemary	5 mL
¼ tsp	pepper	1 mL
⅔ cup	sour cream	150 mL

CRUST:

¼ cup	toasted unblanched almonds or walnut halves	50 mL
¼ cup	butter, softened	50 mL
½ cup	all-purpose flour	125 mL
½ tsp	minced fresh rosemary	2 mL
¼ tsp	salt	1 mL

GARNISH:

4	thin slices prosciutto	4
½ tsp	vegetable oil	2 mL

☙ **CRUST:** In food processor, finely grind almonds. In bowl, beat butter until fluffy; stir in almonds, flour, rosemary and salt. Press onto bottoms of twelve 4-oz (125 mL) mini cheesecake cups. Bake in centre of 350°F (180°C) oven until firm to the touch, about 10 minutes. Let cool on rack.

☙ In large bowl, beat cream cheese with Camembert until almost smooth. Beat in egg, rosemary and pepper; beat in sour cream. Spoon over bases. Bake in centre of 325°F (160°C) oven until puffed but centres are still slightly jiggly, about 12 minutes. Run hot knife around edge of each cheesecake. Let cool on rack. Cover and refrigerate until set, about 2 hours. **(Make-ahead: Refrigerate for up to 2 days.)**

☙ **GARNISH:** Slice prosciutto crosswise into thin strips. In large skillet, heat oil over medium-high heat; fry prosciutto, stirring, until crisp, about 3 minutes. **(Make-ahead: Cover and refrigerate for up to 1 day.)** Garnish each cheesecake with prosciutto.

Makes 12 pieces. | PER PIECE: about 204 cal, 7 g pro, 17 g total fat (10 g sat. fat), 6 g carb, trace fibre, 64 mg chol, 317 mg sodium. % RDI: 7% calcium, 5% iron, 16% vit A, 10% folate.

VARIATION

Camembert Cheesecake Squares: Instead of cheesecake cups, press crust into parchment paper–lined 8-inch (2 L) square metal cake pan. Scrape in filling; bake as directed, adding 2 to 3 minutes to baking time. Let cool on rack. Refrigerate until cold and firm. Using paper, transfer to cutting board; pull paper on sides down. Cut into squares, wiping knife clean between cuts. Garnish with prosciutto.

Roasted Red Pepper Coulis

Use a squeeze bottle to drizzle this zesty sauce alongside Camembert Cheesecakes
(recipe, opposite).

1 cup	chopped roasted red peppers	250 mL	2 tbsp	red wine vinegar	25 mL
¼ cup	extra-virgin olive oil	50 mL	¼ tsp	salt	1 mL
			Pinch	cayenne pepper	Pinch

In blender, combine red peppers, oil, vinegar, salt and cayenne pepper. Blend until smooth; press through fine sieve.

Makes 1 cup (250 mL). | PER 1 TBSP (15 mL): about 33 cal, trace pro, 3 g total fat (trace sat. fat), 1 g carb, 0 g fibre, 0 mg chol, 63 mg sodium. % RDI: 1% iron, 4% vit A, 33% vit C, 1% folate.

Meringue Nests with Strawberries and Lemon Sherry Syllabub

Syllabub is a thick, frothy English dessert that was popular during the Victorian era. This version is adapted from recipe No. 1486 in Isabella Beeton's *Book of Household Management,* originally published in the mid-1800s. It combines deliciously with the first strawberries of the season and another still-popular Victorian favourite, crisp meringues.

1 cup	sliced strawberries	250 mL		**LEMON SHERRY SYLLABUB:**		
	Mint leaves			¾ cup	whipping cream	175 mL
MERINGUE NESTS:				4 tsp	granulated sugar	20 mL
3	egg whites	3		4 tsp	sherry or Madeira	20 mL
Pinch	cream of tartar	Pinch		1 tsp	finely grated lemon rind	5 mL
¾ cup	granulated sugar	175 mL		1½ tsp	lemon juice	7 mL

❧ Line large rimless baking sheet with silicone baking mat or parchment paper; set aside.

❧ **MERINGUE NESTS:** In bowl, beat egg whites until foamy; beat in cream of tartar until soft peaks form. Beat in sugar, 2 tbsp (25 mL) at a time, until stiff glossy peaks form.

❧ Using piping bag fitted with star tip, pipe meringue into eight 3-inch (8 cm) circles on prepared baking sheet; pipe to fill in centre of each circle. Along edge of each circle, pipe second circle to form raised edge for nest. (Alternatively, spoon meringue into rounds; with back of spoon, form each round into nest.)

❧ Bake in centre of 200°F (100°C) oven until dry and crisp, about 2 hours. Turn off oven; let stand in oven for 1 hour. Transfer to rack; let cool. **(Make-ahead: Store in airtight container at room temperature for up to 3 days.)**

❧ **LEMON SHERRY SYLLABUB:** In bowl, whip cream with sugar. Fold in sherry and lemon rind and juice. **(Make-ahead: Cover and refrigerate for up to 6 hours.)** Spoon syllabub into meringue nests; top with sliced strawberries. Garnish with mint leaves.

Makes 8 servings. | PER SERVING: about 168 cal, 2 g pro, 8 g total fat (5 g sat. fat), 23 g carb, trace fibre, 29 mg chol, 28 mg sodium. % RDI: 2% calcium, 1% iron, 9% vit A, 18% vit C, 2% folate.

Lemon Dacquoise

Syrup-poached lemon rind is a lovely garnish for this crowd-pleasing meringue dessert.

	Syrup-Poached Lemon Rind (recipe, page 333)	

MERINGUE:

2¼ cups	sliced almonds	550 mL
1½ cups	granulated sugar	375 mL
2 tbsp	cornstarch	25 mL
9	egg whites	9

½ tsp	almond extract	2 mL

LEMON CREAM:

2 cups	whipping cream	500 mL
¾ cup	icing sugar	175 mL
2 tbsp	lemon juice	25 mL
1 tbsp	grated lemon rind	15 mL

WARM, HUMID WEATHER WARNING

❯ Choose a dry, cool day to make meringue-based desserts such as Meringue Nests (recipe, opposite) or dacquoises. On a sultry day, the meringue will start to bead and disintegrate.

❧ Line 2 large rimmed baking sheets with parchment paper. Using 8-inch (20 cm) round cake pan as guide, draw 2 circles on each paper; turn papers over and set aside.

❧ MERINGUE: Spread almonds on separate rimmed baking sheet; bake in 350°F (180°C) oven until golden, about 8 minutes. Let cool.

❧ In food processor, grind 1½ cups (375 mL) of the almonds, ½ cup (125 mL) of the sugar and cornstarch until powdery.

❧ In large bowl, beat egg whites until soft peaks form. Beat in remaining sugar, 1 tbsp (15 mL) at a time, until stiff glossy peaks form. Beat in almond extract. Sprinkle with half of the ground almond mixture; fold into egg whites. Fold in remaining ground almond mixture.

❧ Divide among circles on sheets, spreading evenly to fill. Bake in top and bottom thirds of 275°F (140°C) oven, rotating and switching pans halfway through, until firm to the touch, 65 to 75 minutes.

❧ While hot and using serrated knife and same cake pan as guide, trim to even circles if edges are ragged. Slide metal spatula under meringues to loosen; transfer to rack and let cool. (Make-ahead: Store in airtight container at room temperature for up to 1 week.)

❧ LEMON CREAM: In bowl, whip together cream, icing sugar and lemon juice; stir in lemon rind. Set aside 2 cups (500 mL) for icing.

❧ Place 1 meringue layer on flat cake plate; slide 4 strips of waxed paper between meringue and plate. Spread with one-third of the remaining lemon cream. Repeat layers twice; top with remaining meringue. Spread reserved lemon cream over top and side. Press remaining almonds onto side of cake. Refrigerate for 1 hour. (Make-ahead: Cover and refrigerate for up to 8 hours.) Remove paper strips.

❧ Garnish top with Syrup-Poached Lemon Rind. Slice with serrated knife, wiping knife clean between cuts.

Makes 12 servings. | PER SERVING: about 387 cal, 8 g pro, 24 g total fat (9 g sat. fat), 39 g carb, 2 g fibre, 51 mg chol, 59 mg sodium. % RDI: 7% calcium, 6% iron, 15% vit A, 5% vit C, 4% folate.

Chapter 3

Pies & Pastries

A beautiful pie is the crowning glory of home baking. Pastry is more of a challenge than the cookies, cakes or even breads contained in this book, as it requires judgment and an appreciation of texture and moisture. Having had your hands on pastry a few times before counts when manipulating a fragile sheet of pastry into a nicely fluted crust.

While pastry takes a bit more to master, we know from experience with our readers that everyone is up to the challenge. This is definitely the case with the various pastries in this chapter – they are easy to work with and stand up to handling. There are also pat-in and crumb-crust options so even the most fledgling of bakers can succeed. Pastry goes global, too: there's phyllo from the Eastern Mediterranean plus savoury Latin American empanadas and South Asian samosas. For the advanced baker, there is puff and choux pastry to tackle.

Choosing the best fillings to include was hard. In The Canadian Living Test Kitchen, we have so many favourites, both sweet and savoury, all tucked under, over or into a variety of pastries. But choose we did, and we encourage you to discover your favourites as you become an expert with a rolling pin. Making pastry, like learning to drive or dance the tango, opens many doors and is practical and fun; in other words, it's worth mastering.

Mastering Pie Pastry

❯ Seeing is believing, and seeing the steps to a perfect pie will make you believe you can turn out one as lovely as our Prizewinning Apple Pie (recipe, page 161).

❯ Chill Your Ingredients

Keep butter and liquids cold. Before measuring out dry ingredients, fill a glass with water and ice cubes so water's ready to measure out and add when the time comes. Refrigerate fat until the last minute.

❯ Cutting in Butter or Lard

The purpose of cutting the butter or lard into the dry ingredients is not to blend them into a smooth mixture but rather to coat small bits of fat with flour. When high heat hits the pastry, these pockets of fat melt, creating steam that separates the dry ingredients into flaky layers. We recommend you cut in butter or lard until most of it is the size of long-grain rice with some bigger, green-pea-size pieces.

❯ Adding the Liquid

Drizzle in the liquid, about 1 tbsp (15 mL) at a time, tossing the wet and dry ingredients together and moving the drizzles around the bowl so they fall on the driest places. A fork is ideal for this stage. Add a little more ice water if needed to moisten dry areas.

Whether you're mixing by hand or pulsing ingredients together in the food processor, the mixture should end up looking ragged but will hold together when pressed. Stop right here – do not let the mixture form a ball or your pastry will toughen.

❯ Gathering Up the Pastry

On a lightly floured work surface, press the ragged dough together firmly into 1 or 2 smooth discs, depending on amount. Wrap and chill for about 30 minutes to relax the gluten and firm up the butter. If the dough is too hard to roll when it comes out of the refrigerator, let it rest for a few minutes at room temperature.

❯ Rolling Out the Pastry

On a lightly floured work surface or on a floured pastry cloth and using a rolling pin (stockinette-covered if you have one), roll out the pastry using a light touch. Think of the pastry as a clock; rolling from the middle out to the edge, roll to 12 o'clock, then 3 o'clock, then 6 o'clock, then 9 o'clock. Keep the rolling pin and counter lightly dusted with flour to prevent sticking. Repeat this pattern until pastry is the proper thickness. Or give the pastry a quarter-turn every few rolls. Lift the rolling pin as you near the edge to keep the pastry uniform. Aim for an even, generous ⅛-inch (3 mm) or scant ¼-inch (5 mm) thickness.

- Wooden rolling pin: 12 to 15 inches (30 to 38 cm) long

- Canvas rolling mat for pastry and stockinette rolling pin cover (recommended if you're a beginner or have never had any luck with rolling out pastry)

- Dough scraper

- Pastry blender

- Glass pie plates: one each 9-inch (23 cm) regular and deep-dish, and 10-inch (25 cm)

- Tart pans with removable bottoms: 9-inch (23 cm), 10-inch (25 cm) and 11-inch (28 cm)

- Muffin or tart pans, with cups about 2¾ inches (7 cm) in diameter and ⅓- to ½-cup (75 to 125 mL) capacity

- Miniature muffin or tart pans, with cups about 1¾ inches (4.5 cm) in diameter and 2-tbsp (25 mL) capacity

- Pizza pans: 12-inch (30 cm) and 14-inch (35 cm)

- Straight-sided shiny metal cake pan: 9-inch (2.5 L) square

- Heatproof ramekins or baking cups, with 1-cup (250 mL) capacity

- Small decorative cookie cutters

- Pie weights or dried beans

Single-Crust Pie

❯ Position the pie plate on the counter just beyond the rolled-out dough. Place the rolling pin at the top of the dough; roll it toward you, rolling the dough loosely around the pin. Use your fingers to keep the dough loosely rolled as you lift the pin up and gently unroll the dough over the pie plate. Dust your hands with flour and shift the pastry around if necessary to centre. Without stretching, ease the pastry down into the pie plate and press gently onto the inside.

❯ Trim the pastry, leaving a ½-inch (1 cm) overhang beyond the rim of the pie plate. If you like a thicker crust, increase overhang to ¾ inch (2 cm) or even 1 inch (2.5 cm).

❯ To crimp edge: Fold overhang under, leaving it flat on rim of pie plate. Press together with a fork all the way around rim.

❯ To flute edge: Fold overhang under, then tilt both layers up like a collar. Place index finger and thumb of one hand, ½ inch (1 cm) apart, outside rim of pie plate to support turned-up pastry. Using index finger of other hand, press pastry, without squeezing and thinning, into space between finger and thumb. Repeat around rim of pie plate to make attractive scalloped edge.

❯ Fill and bake as directed. To bake blind, see recipe and tips on page 173.

Double-Crust Pie

❯ Prepare filling before rolling out pastry.

❯ Follow first step for single-crust pie. Trim dough even with rim of pie plate.

❯ Brush pastry on rim with egg wash (see page 159).

❯ Arrange filling in pie shell, making sure pastry along rim is clear of filling.

❯ Roll out top pastry. Position the filled pie plate just beyond the rolled-out dough and roll pastry loosely around the rolling pin. Lift and roll pastry over filling.

❯ Trim excess pastry at edge of pie plate, leaving ¾-inch (2 cm) overhang.

❯ Gently lift bottom pastry rim and fold overhang underneath, gently pressing the two layers together.

❯ Tilt sealed pastry edge up like a collar.

❯ To flute edge: Place index finger and thumb of one hand, ½ inch (1 cm) apart, outside rim of pie plate to support turned-up pastry. Using index finger of other hand, press pastry, without squeezing and thinning, into space between finger and thumb. Repeat around rim of pie plate to make attractive scalloped edge.

❯ Brush pastry with egg wash.

❯ If desired, from pastry scraps, cut out decorative shapes and place on top of pie. Brush cutouts with egg wash.

❯ Sprinkle with coarse sugar, then cut steam vents near the centre of the top pastry.

❯ Bake pies in bottom third of oven, where the heat from the lower source will ensure that the bottom crust bakes through.

Double-Crust Sour Cream Pastry

A fear of pastry lives on in some cooks, but fear not – both this and the Double-Crust Perfect Pastry, below, are easy to handle, roll out nicely and bake up flaky, golden and tender.

2½ cups	all-purpose flour	625 mL	½ cup	cold lard, cubed	125 mL
½ tsp	salt	2 mL	¼ cup	ice water (approx)	50 mL
½ cup	cold butter, cubed	125 mL	3 tbsp	sour cream	50 mL

❧ In large bowl, whisk flour with salt. Using pastry blender, cut in butter and lard until in fine crumbs with a few larger pieces.

❧ In liquid measure, whisk water with sour cream. Drizzle over flour mixture, tossing briskly with fork and adding a little more water if necessary, until ragged dough forms.

❧ Divide in half; press into 2 discs. Wrap; refrigerate until chilled, 30 minutes. **(Make-ahead: Refrigerate for up to 3 days or freeze in airtight container for up to 1 month.)**

Makes enough for 1 double-crust 9-inch (23 cm) pie.

....

VARIATION

Single-Crust Sour Cream Pastry: Halve ingredients, using 4 tsp (20 mL) sour cream. Press into 1 disc. Makes enough for 1 single-crust 9-inch (23 cm) pie.

Double-Crust Perfect Pastry

Perfect for all kinds of pies, and perfectly easy to make, this pastry also has a convenient food processor variation.

3 cups	all-purpose flour	750 mL	1	egg	1
1 tsp	salt	5 mL	2 tsp	vinegar	10 mL
½ cup	each cold butter and lard, cubed	125 mL		Ice water	

❧ In large bowl, whisk flour with salt. Using pastry blender, cut in butter and lard until in coarse crumbs with a few larger pieces.

❧ In liquid measuring cup, beat egg with vinegar; add enough ice water to make ⅔ cup (150 mL). Drizzle over flour mixture, tossing with fork until ragged dough forms.

❧ Divide in half; press into 2 discs. Wrap; refrigerate until chilled, 30 minutes. **(Make-ahead: Refrigerate for up to 3 days or freeze in airtight container for up to 1 month.)**

Makes enough for 1 double-crust 9-inch (23 cm) pie.

VARIATIONS

Single-Crust Perfect Pastry: Halve flour, salt, butter and lard. Whisk dry ingredients together and cut in butter and lard as directed. In liquid measuring cup, beat 1 egg yolk with 1 tsp (5 mL) vinegar; pour in enough ice water to make ⅓ cup (75 mL). Mix as directed. Press dough into 1 disc. Makes enough for 1 single-crust 9-inch (23 cm) pie.

Food Processor Perfect Pastry: Follow recipe for either Double-Crust or Single-Crust Perfect Pastry. In food processor, blend flour with salt. Pulse in butter and lard until in fine crumbs with a few larger pieces. Remove lid; pour egg mixture all over flour mixture; pulse just until dough begins to clump together. Do not let dough form ball. Press into 2 discs for double-crust pie or 1 disc for single-crust pie.

Winter Fruit Pie

Plan ahead for this pie by buying the pears a few days before baking. Let them ripen at room temperature until they give when you touch them gently.

	Double-Crust Sour Cream Pastry (recipe, opposite)				
1	egg yolk	1	1 cup	fresh or frozen cranberries	250 mL
1 tsp	coarse sugar	5 mL	1 cup	granulated sugar	250 mL
FILLING:			¼ cup	all-purpose flour	50 mL
3 cups	diced peeled pears	750 mL	1 tsp	grated orange rind	5 mL
3 cups	frozen cut rhubarb	750 mL	2 tsp	orange juice	10 mL

↝ Set out 9-inch (23 cm) pie plate.

↝ FILLING: In large bowl, toss together pears, rhubarb, cranberries, sugar, flour and orange rind and juice.

↝ On lightly floured surface, roll out half of the pastry to generous ⅛-inch (3 mm) thickness; fit into pie plate. Trim to leave ½-inch (1 cm) overhang; fold overhang under and flute edge. Scrape in filling.

↝ Roll out remaining pastry to generous ⅛-inch (3 mm) thickness. Using 2-inch (5 cm) star-shaped cutter, cut out 24 stars (or cut out other shapes, such as hearts, to suit the occasion). Arrange over filling, overlapping as necessary. Whisk egg yolk with 1 tbsp (15 mL) water; brush over stars. Sprinkle with coarse sugar.

↝ Bake in bottom third of 425°F (220°C) oven for 15 minutes. Reduce heat to 350°F (180°C); bake until bottom is golden, filling is bubbly and pears are soft, 1¼ to 1½ hours. Let cool on rack. **(Make-ahead: Set aside at room temperature for up to 8 hours.)**

Makes 8 servings. | PER SERVING: about 427 cal, 4 g pro, 18 g total fat (9 g sat. fat), 63 g carb, 4 g fibre, 56 mg chol, 160 mg sodium. % RDI: 11% calcium, 13% iron, 9% vit A, 10% vit C, 33% folate.

EGG WASH

❯ It seals, glazes and gives a professional-looking finish to pastry, biscuits or scones, breads and certain cookies. Egg wash is easy to make: just whisk egg or egg yolk with 1 tbsp (15 mL) cold water or milk. If you don't use it all up at once, cover and refrigerate for up to 1 day. Add any leftovers to scrambled eggs.

Prizewinning Apple Pie

On Thanksgiving weekend The Village at Blue Mountain, Ont., fills with the fragrance of freshly baked apple pies. For this Quintessential Apple Pie Contest, bakers from this apple-growing region that rings Georgian Bay carry their pies – double crust, single crust, lattice top, streusel and more – to the judging tables. Baking enthusiast Brenda Hall of Collingwood, Ont., took first prize with this pie, which she called "Grandma Thompson's," a classic double-crust pie that's not too sweet but full and juicy with freshly harvested local McIntosh apples. For a fall pie, reroll the pastry scraps and cut out maple leaves to arrange over the top crust, as we have in our photo.

	Double-Crust Sour Cream Pastry (recipe, page 158)				
1	egg yolk	1	¾ cup	granulated sugar	175 mL
2 tbsp	coarse sugar	25 mL	2 tbsp	cornstarch	25 mL
FILLING:			1 tsp	cinnamon	5 mL
8	apples (such as McIntosh or Northern Spy), about 3 lb (1.5 kg)	8	Pinch	each nutmeg and salt	Pinch
			2 tbsp	butter, softened	25 mL

Set out 9-inch (23 cm) pie plate.

FILLING: Peel and core apples; cut into ¼-inch (5 mm) thick slices to make 8 cups (2 L). Place in large bowl. In small bowl, toss together sugar, cornstarch, cinnamon, nutmeg and salt; add to apples and toss until coated.

On lightly floured surface, roll out half of the pastry to generous ⅛-inch (3 mm) thickness; fit into pie plate. Trim to rim of pie plate. Scrape in filling; dot with butter.

Roll out remaining pastry. Whisk egg yolk with 1 tbsp (15 mL) water; brush some of this egg wash over pastry on rim. Fit pastry over filling; trim to leave ¾-inch (2 cm) overhang. Fold upper layer of pastry under pastry on rim; flute to seal. Brush some of the remaining egg wash lightly over pastry. Cut steam vents in top; sprinkle with coarse sugar.

Bake in bottom third of 450°F (230°C) oven for 10 minutes. Reduce heat to 350°F (180°C); bake until bottom is deep golden, apples are tender and filling is bubbly and thickened, about 65 minutes. Let cool on rack. **(Make-ahead: Set aside at room temperature for up to 8 hours.)**

Makes 8 servings. | PER SERVING: about 489 cal, 4 g pro, 25 g total fat (13 g sat. fat), 65 g carb, 3 g fibre, 70 mg chol, 208 mg sodium. % RDI: 2% calcium, 13% iron, 13% vit A, 7% vit C, 31% folate.

MOST-WANTED APPLE PIE

> Every fall The Canadian Living Test Kitchen gets requests for an apple pie we published years ago. It's essentially this recipe, but uses brown sugar instead of granulated and adds ¼ cup (50 mL) raisins or dried cranberries to the filling.

Deep Skillet Apple and Walnut Pie

This rustic deep-dish pie's dramatic presentation – right in the skillet – is intriguing.

2½ cups	all-purpose flour	625 mL
2 tbsp	granulated sugar	25 mL
¼ tsp	salt	1 mL
¾ cup	cold butter, cubed	175 mL
¾ cup	ice water	175 mL
FILLING:		
8	apples (about 3 lb/1.5 kg)	8
¾ cup	packed brown sugar	175 mL
3 tbsp	all-purpose flour	50 mL

1 tbsp	lemon juice	15 mL
1 tsp	cinnamon	5 mL
CRUMBLE TOPPING:		
2 tbsp	butter, softened	25 mL
2 tbsp	packed brown sugar	25 mL
2 tbsp	all-purpose flour	25 mL
¼ cup	chopped walnut halves	50 mL
2 tbsp	milk	25 mL
1 tbsp	granulated sugar	15 mL

❧ Set out 10-inch (25 cm) cast-iron skillet or deep 10-inch (25 cm) pie plate.

❧ In bowl, whisk together flour, sugar and salt. Using pastry blender, cut in butter until in fine crumbs with a few larger pieces. Sprinkle ice water over dry ingredients; toss with fork just until dough comes together. Press into disc. Wrap; refrigerate until chilled, about 30 minutes. **(Make-ahead: Refrigerate for up to 3 days or overwrap in heavy-duty foil and freeze for up to 2 weeks.)**

❧ FILLING: Peel, core and cut apples into ½-inch (1 cm) thick wedges. In bowl, toss together apples, brown sugar, flour, lemon juice and cinnamon; set aside.

❧ On lightly floured surface, roll out pastry into 17-inch (43 cm) round. Fit into skillet, letting excess hang over. Spoon in filling; fold pastry over filling, making rough folds and leaving centre uncovered. Bake in centre of 350°F (180°C) oven for 1 hour.

❧ CRUMBLE TOPPING: In bowl and using fork, blend butter, brown sugar and flour; stir in walnuts. Crumble over filling in centre of pie. Brush exposed pastry with milk; sprinkle with granulated sugar. Bake until pastry is golden and filling is tender and bubbly, about 30 minutes. Let cool on rack. **(Make-ahead: Set aside at room temperature for up to 4 hours.)**

Makes 8 to 10 servings. | PER EACH OF 10 SERVINGS: about 438 cal, 5 g pro, 19 g total fat (10 g sat. fat), 65 g carb, 4 g fibre, 51 mg chol, 232 mg sodium. % RDI: 4% calcium, 16% iron, 16% vit A, 5% vit C, 22% folate.

Apple and Cherry Pie

You have probably noticed apple pies with a top crust domed way above the filling. You can avoid this if you precook the apples; that way, the filling and pastry cook through at the same time without a gap. This recipe shows you how.

	Double-Crust Sour Cream Pastry (recipe, page 158)		8	apples (such as Northern Spy or Jonagold), about 3 lb (1.5 kg)	8
1	egg yolk	1	½ cup	granulated sugar	125 mL
2 tbsp	coarse sugar	25 mL	1 tbsp	lemon juice	15 mL
FILLING:			¼ tsp	cinnamon	1 mL
¼ cup	brandy, kirsch or water	50 mL	2 tbsp	unsalted butter	25 mL
⅔ cup	dried sour cherries	150 mL	2 tbsp	all-purpose flour	25 mL

❧ Set out 9-inch (23 cm) pie plate.

❧ FILLING: In measuring cup, microwave brandy at high until steaming, about 20 seconds. Mix in cherries; let stand for 30 minutes.

❧ Meanwhile, peel and core apples; cut into ¼-inch (5 mm) thick slices to make 8 cups (2 L). Place in bowl. Add sugar, lemon juice and cinnamon; toss until coated.

❧ In large skillet, melt half of the butter over medium heat; cook half of the apples, turning slices gently, until slightly tender and glazed, about 5 minutes. Transfer to large shallow bowl.

❧ Heat remaining butter in pan; cook remaining apples, turning slices gently, for 4 minutes. Add cherries and any remaining brandy; cook, stirring, until almost no liquid remains, about 1 minute. Add to bowl; toss gently and let cool to room temperature, about 20 minutes. Sprinkle with flour; toss gently to combine.

❧ On lightly floured surface, roll out half of the pastry to generous ⅛-inch (3 mm) thickness; fit into pie plate. Trim to rim of pie plate. Scrape in filling.

❧ Roll out remaining pastry. Whisk egg yolk with 1 tbsp (15 mL) water; brush some of this egg wash over pastry on rim. Fit pastry over filling; trim to leave ¾-inch (2 cm) overhang. Fold upper layer of pastry under pastry on rim; flute to seal. Cut out decorative shapes from leftover pastry. Brush some of the egg wash over pastry. Arrange cutouts on top; brush lightly with some of the remaining egg wash. Cut steam vents in top; sprinkle with coarse sugar.

❧ Bake in bottom third of 425°F (220°C) oven for 15 minutes. Reduce heat to 350°F (180°C); bake until bottom is deep golden and filling is bubbly, about 50 minutes. Let cool on rack. (Make-ahead: Set aside at room temperature for up to 8 hours.)

Makes 8 servings. | PER SERVING: about 552 cal, 6 g pro, 26 g total fat (13 g sat. fat), 75 g carb, 4 g fibre, 90 mg chol, 332 mg sodium. % RDI: 5% calcium, 17% iron, 16% vit A, 7% vit C, 42% folate.

Tangy Rhubarb Lattice Pie

Lattice tops look complicated and time-consuming to assemble. But with our easy-to-follow photos and steps, even a beginner baker will be weaving like a pro. Serve this pie the same day it's made if you want a standing ovation.

PREVENTING OVEN SPILLS

❯ Rhubarb pie is notorious for running over and spilling onto the oven. There are two ways of preventing this. The first is to place a foil-lined baking sheet under the pie to catch any drips. The second is to use the folded-up pastry rim technique illustrated opposite. This vertical rim acts like a dam, forcing the bubbling juices back into the pie.

	Double-Crust Perfect Pastry (recipe, page 158)	
1	egg yolk	1
½ tsp	granulated sugar	2 mL
FILLING:		
5 cups	chopped rhubarb	1.25 L

1 cup	granulated sugar	250 mL
⅓ cup	all-purpose flour	75 mL
1 tsp	grated orange rind	5 mL
Pinch	grated nutmeg	Pinch

↜ Set out 9-inch (23 cm) pie plate.

↜ **FILLING:** In large bowl, toss together rhubarb, sugar, flour, orange rind and nutmeg; set aside.

↜ Divide pastry into 2 discs, one slightly smaller than the other. On floured surface, roll out smaller pastry disc to generous ⅛-inch (3 mm) thickness; fit into pie plate. Trim to leave ½-inch (1 cm) overhang. Scrape in filling.

↜ Roll out remaining pastry; cut into fourteen 1-inch (2.5 cm) wide strips. Arrange half over filling, leaving scant ¼-inch (5 mm) space between strips.

↜ Fold back every other strip slightly past centre. Place strip across centre of pie perpendicular to first strips.

↜ Unfold strips. Working on same side, fold back strips that were not folded back first time. Place another perpendicular strip on top, leaving scant ¼-inch (5 mm) space between strips. Unfold strips. Repeat on same side with two more strips. Repeat with remaining strips on opposite side. Trim strips to edge of pie plate.

↜ Whisk egg yolk with 1 tbsp (15 mL) water; brush some of this egg wash over pastry overhang. Fold overhang up and over strips; flute edge. Brush edge and strips with remaining egg wash; sprinkle with sugar.

↜ Place foil-lined rimmed baking sheet on lowest rack of 425°F (220°C) oven. Place pie on rack above baking sheet in bottom third of oven; bake for 20 minutes. Reduce heat to 350°F (180°C); bake until golden and filling is bubbly, about 70 minutes. Let cool on rack.

Makes 8 servings. | PER SERVING: about 489 cal, 7 g pro, 23 g total fat (11 g sat. fat), 64 g carb, 3 g fibre, 88 mg chol, 365 mg sodium. % RDI: 7% calcium, 18% iron, 12% vit A, 8% vit C, 30% folate.

MASTERING A BEAUTIFUL LATTICE TOP

Step 2 in the quest to master pastry is weaving a lattice top. It looks tricky but is really simple.

● Start with rolled-out pastry. Cut neatly into fourteen 1-inch (2.5 cm) wide strips, using a ruler as guide.

● Lay half of the strips over the filling and bottom pastry overhang, arranging the longest in the middle and shorter ones toward the edge.

● Starting in the centre, fold back every other strip. Keep the folds loose so the pastry doesn't crack.

● Lay long strip perpendicular to first strips. Unfold strips over the perpendicular strip.

● Working on the same side, fold back alternating strips. Insert strip perpendicular to the folded-back strips. Continue alternately folding and unfolding strips, inserting increasingly shorter strips. Repeat for the other side.

● Scissors are handy for trimming the strips.

● A coat of egg wash ensures a good seal on the overhang and a gloss on the finished pastry.

The Complete Canadian Living Baking Book **165**

Rhubarb Sour Cream Pie

This Waterloo County, Ont., heritage pie features a custard filling and crumbly topping.

TIME CHECK

❯ Check pie 10 minutes after reducing temperature; cover loosely with foil if topping is darker than light golden.

	Single-Crust Perfect Pastry, (recipe, page 159)	
FILLING:		
4 cups	chopped rhubarb	1 L
1	egg	1
1½ cups	granulated sugar	375 mL

1 cup	sour cream	250 mL
⅓ cup	all-purpose flour	75 mL
TOPPING:		
½ cup	all-purpose flour	125 mL
½ cup	packed brown sugar	125 mL
¼ cup	butter, melted	50 mL

❧ Set out 9-inch (23 cm) pie plate.

❧ On lightly floured surface, roll out pastry to generous ⅛-inch (3 mm) thickness; fit into pie plate. Trim to leave ½-inch (1 cm) overhang; fold overhang under and flute edge.

❧ **FILLING:** Arrange rhubarb evenly in pie shell. In bowl, whisk together egg, sugar, sour cream and flour until smooth. Scrape over fruit.

❧ **TOPPING:** In small bowl, mix flour with sugar. Drizzle in butter; mix with fork until crumbly. Sprinkle over filling.

❧ Bake in bottom third of 450°F (230°C) oven for 15 minutes. Reduce heat to 350°F (180°C); bake until edge is puffed, filling is set but slightly jiggly and topping is golden, about 40 minutes. Let cool on rack. **(Make-ahead: Set aside at room temperature for up to 4 hours.)**

Makes 8 servings. | PER SERVING: about 515 cal, 5 g pro, 21 g total fat (12 g sat. fat), 77 g carb, 2 g fibre, 69 mg chol, 165 mg sodium. % RDI: 10% calcium, 13% iron, 14% vit A, 8% vit C, 32% folate.

Peaches and Cream Pie

Golden pastry holding a creamy sliced-peach filling and a crumbly topping deliciously shows off the best of the summer fruit harvest season. The sooner you eat this pie after it cools, the better.

	Single-Crust Perfect Pastry (recipe, page 159)		5 cups	thickly sliced peeled peaches (about 5 large)	1.25 L
½ cup	granulated sugar	125 mL	**TOPPING:**		
¼ cup	all-purpose flour	50 mL	½ cup	all-purpose flour	125 mL
¾ cup	sour cream or Balkan-style yogurt	175 mL	½ cup	packed brown sugar	125 mL
			¼ cup	cold butter, cubed	50 mL
Dash	almond extract	Dash	⅓ cup	slivered almonds	75 mL

❧ Set out 9-inch (23 cm) pie plate.

❧ On lightly floured surface, roll out pastry to generous ⅛-inch (3 mm) thickness; fit into pie plate. Trim to leave ½-inch (1 cm) overhang; fold overhang under and flute edge.

❧ In large bowl, whisk sugar with flour; whisk in sour cream and almond extract. Add peaches; stir just until coated. Scrape into pie shell; set aside.

❧ TOPPING: In bowl, stir flour with brown sugar; using pastry blender, cut in butter until crumbly. Mix in almonds; sprinkle over filling.

❧ Bake in bottom third of 425°F (220°C) oven for 15 minutes. Reduce heat to 350°F (180°C); bake until pastry and topping are golden and filling starts to bubble around edge, about 35 minutes. Let cool on rack. **(Make-ahead: Set aside at room temperature for up to 4 hours.)**

Makes 8 servings. | PER SERVING: about 513 cal, 6 g pro, 28 g total fat (13 g sat. fat), 62 g carb, 4 g fibre, 68 mg chol, 213 mg sodium. % RDI: 6% calcium, 16% iron, 16% vit A, 12% vit C, 34% folate.

Maple Butter Tarts

The country is divided. No, not just about the Oilers versus the Habs, or the Leafs duelling with the Sens. It's about how you line up when it comes to butter tarts – gooey or custardy? This recipe sides with the custardy, and instead of making bakers choose between nuts or raisins and currants, we've included them all.

	Single-Crust Sour Cream Pastry (recipe, page 158)			2	eggs	2
MAPLE SYRUP FILLING:				1 tbsp	cider vinegar	15 mL
				½ tsp	salt	2 mL
¾ cup	packed brown sugar	175 mL		½ cup	chopped walnut halves	125 mL
½ cup	maple syrup (No. 1 medium grade)	125 mL		¼ cup	dried currants	50 mL
⅓ cup	butter, melted	75 mL		¼ cup	golden raisins	50 mL

↜ Set out muffin or tart pan with twelve 2¾- x 1¼-inch (7 x 3 cm) cups.

↜ On lightly floured surface, roll out pastry to generous ⅛-inch (3 mm) thickness. Using 4-inch (10 cm) round cutter, cut out 12 circles, rerolling scraps. Fit into muffin cups; refrigerate for 30 minutes.

↜ **MAPLE SYRUP FILLING:** Meanwhile, in bowl, whisk together brown sugar, maple syrup, butter, eggs, cider vinegar and salt. Divide walnuts, currants and raisins evenly among pastry shells. Spoon scant ¼ cup (50 mL) filling into each shell.

↜ Bake in centre of 350°F (180°C) oven until filling is set and pastry is golden, 20 to 25 minutes. Run thin knife blade around edges to release tarts. Let cool in pan on rack for 20 minutes. Transfer to rack; let cool. **(Make-ahead: Store in single layer in airtight container at room temperature for up to 1 day.)**

Makes 12 tarts. | PER TART: about 283 cal, 3 g pro, 15 g total fat (7 g sat. fat), 35 g carb, 1 g fibre, 55 mg chol, 204 mg sodium. % RDI: 4% calcium, 9% iron, 8% vit A, 13% folate.

VARIATIONS

Maple Chocolate Butter Tarts: Replace currants and raisins with ½ cup (125 mL) chopped bittersweet chocolate or semisweet chocolate chips.

Maple Pecan Butter Tarts: Omit currants. Replace walnuts with ½ cup (125 mL) broken pecan halves.

Honey Pecan Pumpkin Tarts

You can serve these glossy tarts with a spoonful of honey-sweetened whipped cream.

	Single-Crust Sour Cream Pastry (recipe, page 158)	

PUMPKIN FILLING:

¾ cup	canned pumpkin purée	175 mL
⅓ cup	evaporated milk	75 mL
⅓ cup	liquid honey	75 mL
2	eggs	2
1 tbsp	all-purpose flour	15 mL
1 tsp	vanilla	5 mL
¾ tsp	cinnamon	4 mL
¼ tsp	each ground ginger, nutmeg, cloves and salt	1 mL

PECAN TOPPING:

⅓ cup	finely chopped pecans	75 mL
¼ cup	packed brown sugar	50 mL
2 tsp	butter, melted	10 mL

❧ Set out muffin pan with twelve 2¾- x 1¼-inch (7 x 3 cm) cups.

❧ On lightly floured surface, roll out pastry to generous ⅛-inch (3 mm) thickness. Using 4-inch (10 cm) round cutter, cut out 12 circles, rerolling scraps. Press gently into bottoms and up sides of cups, to within ⅛ inch (3 mm) of top; prick with fork. Refrigerate for 30 minutes.

❧ Cut squares of foil to fit cups. Line shells with foil squares; fill with pie weights or dried beans. Bake in bottom third of 400°F (200°C) oven until edges are light golden, about 15 minutes. Remove weights and foil; let cool in pan on rack.

❧ PECAN TOPPING: In bowl, combine pecans, brown sugar and butter until evenly mixed; set aside.

❧ PUMPKIN FILLING: In bowl, whisk together pumpkin, milk, honey, eggs, flour, vanilla, cinnamon, ginger, nutmeg, cloves and salt. Spoon scant ¼ cup (50 mL) into each cup. Sprinkle with pecan topping.

❧ Bake in bottom third of 350°F (180°C) oven until filling is set and pastry is golden, about 30 minutes. Let cool in pan on rack for 5 minutes. Transfer to rack; let cool. **(Make-ahead: Refrigerate in single layer in airtight container for up to 1 day.)**

Makes 12 tarts. | PER TART: about 199 cal, 3 g pro, 11 g total fat (5 g sat. fat), 24 g carb, 1 g fibre, 45 mg chol, 135 mg sodium. % RDI: 4% calcium, 8% iron, 35% vit A, 2% vit C, 14% folate.

PRIZE PIE PUMPKINS

❯ Got a post-Halloween hankering for pumpkin pie? Don't try to recycle Jack. Large lantern pumpkins tend to be stringy and flavourless, not to mention candle-singed. Early in October, look for pumpkins labelled "pie pumpkins," such as Small Sugar or Spooky. Smaller, sweeter and with denser flesh, they give the best taste and texture. A 4-lb (2 kg) pumpkin will yield about 4 cups (1 L) cooked purée, enough for two pies or about 36 tarts.

HOMEMADE PUMPKIN PURÉE

❧ Halve and seed pumpkin; cut into wedges. Place, flesh side up, in roasting pan; pour in enough water to come 1 inch (2.5 cm) up side of pan. Roast in 400°F (200°C) oven until tender, 30 to 60 minutes. Let cool; scrape flesh from skin. Purée in food processor; press through sieve. You can freeze the purée for up to 2 months in an airtight container.

Easy Fresh Fruit Pies

It's as simple as, well, pie to put together one of these fantastic home-style desserts. Use whatever fruit you have on hand – or have a craving for – and serve with ice cream.

Double-Crust Sour Cream Pastry (recipe, page 158)		2 tbsp	milk or cream (or 1 egg yolk mixed with 1 tbsp/15 mL water)	25 mL
Fruit filling (see Variations, below)		1 tbsp	coarse sugar	15 mL

❧ Set out 9-inch (23 cm) pie plate.

❧ On lightly floured surface, roll out a little more than half of the pastry to generous ⅛-inch (3 mm) thickness; fit into pie plate. Trim to rim of pie plate. Scrape in filling.

❧ Roll out remaining pastry. Lightly brush milk over pastry on rim. Fit pastry over filling; trim to leave ¾-inch (2 cm) overhang. Fold top layer of pastry under pastry at rim; flute to seal. Brush remaining milk over pastry. Cut steam vents in top; sprinkle with coarse sugar.

❧ Bake in bottom third of 425°F (220°C) oven for 15 minutes. Reduce heat to 350°F (180°C); bake until bottom is golden and filling is bubbly, 60 to 75 minutes. Let cool on rack. **(Make-ahead: Set aside at room temperature for up to 8 hours.)**

Makes 8 servings. | PER SERVING (USING APPLE BERRY FILLING): about 448 cal, 4 g pro, 21 g total fat (11 g sat. fat), 62 g carb, 3 g fibre, 37 mg chol, 195 mg sodium. % RDI: 3% calcium, 13% iron, 9% vit A, 17% vit C, 35% folate.

VARIATIONS

Apple Berry: In large bowl, combine 6 cups (1.5 L) sliced peeled apples, 1 cup (250 mL) blackberries or raspberries, ¾ cup (175 mL) granulated sugar, 3 tbsp (50 mL) all-purpose flour and 1 tbsp (15 mL) lemon juice.

Blueberry: In large bowl, combine 5 cups (1.25 L) fresh or frozen wild blueberries, ¾ cup (175 mL) granulated sugar and ¼ cup (50 mL) all-purpose flour.

Peach or Nectarine: In large bowl, combine 5 cups (1.25 L) sliced peeled peaches or nectarines, ¾ cup (175 mL) granulated sugar, ¼ cup (50 mL) all-purpose flour, 2 tbsp (25 mL) chopped candied ginger (optional), and 1 tbsp (15 mL) lemon juice.

Raspberry: In large bowl, combine 4 cups (1 L) raspberries, 1 cup (250 mL) granulated sugar, 3 tbsp (50 mL) all-purpose flour and 1 tbsp (15 mL) lemon juice.

Raspberry Nectarine: In large bowl, combine 5 cups (1.25 L) sliced nectarines, 1½ cups (375 mL) raspberries, ¾ cup (175 mL) granulated sugar, ¼ cup (50 mL) all-purpose flour and 1 tbsp (15 mL) lemon juice.

Saskatoon Berry: In large bowl, combine 5 cups (1.25 L) saskatoon berries, ¾ cup (175 mL) granulated sugar, ¼ cup (50 mL) all-purpose flour, ½ tsp (2 mL) grated lemon rind, 1 tbsp (15 mL) lemon juice and ½ tsp (2 mL) cinnamon.

FROZEN SOUR CHERRY PIE FILLING

❧ Defrost 8 cups (2 L) frozen sweetened sour cherries, reserving ¾ cup (175 mL) juice. In saucepan, heat half of the reserved juice over medium heat until steaming. Meanwhile, in small bowl, whisk ¾ cup (175 mL) sugar with ¼ cup (50 mL) cornstarch; whisk in remaining juice until smooth. Whisk into pan; cook, whisking, until boiling and thickened, 6 to 8 minutes. Add cherries; remove from heat. Stir in 2 tsp (10 mL) lemon juice and 1 tsp (5 mL) vanilla. Let cool. Use as filling for Easy Fresh Fruit Pies.

THE PERFECT GOLDEN CRUST

❯ Check these fruit pies after 40 minutes of baking at 350°F (180°C). If the pastry is darker than light golden, cover lightly with foil.

Creamy Lemon Meringue Pie

While not the traditional lemon meringue pie, this filling, more like Key lime pie filling, is less likely to split – but it's just as lemony as the original.

	Single-Crust Sour Cream Pastry (recipe, page 158)			**MERINGUE:**		
4	egg yolks	4		1 tbsp	cornstarch	15 mL
1 tbsp	finely grated lemon rind	15 mL		4	egg whites (at room temperature)	4
1	can (300 mL) sweetened condensed milk	1		¼ tsp	cream of tartar	1 mL
½ cup	lemon juice	125 mL		⅓ cup	instant dissolving (fruit/berry) sugar	75 mL

• Set out 9-inch (23 cm) pie plate.

• On lightly floured surface, roll out pastry to generous ⅛-inch (3 mm) thickness; fit into pie plate. Trim to leave ½-inch (1 cm) overhang; fold overhang under and flute edge.

• Prick pastry at 1-inch (2.5 cm) intervals all over; line with foil and fill with pie weights or dried beans. Bake in bottom third of 400°F (200°C) oven for 15 minutes. Remove weights and foil. Bake until golden, about 10 minutes. Let cool on rack. **(Make-ahead: Set aside at room temperature for up to 1 day.)**

• In bowl, beat egg yolks with lemon rind until light, about 2 minutes. Beat in condensed milk and lemon juice. Pour into pie shell; smooth top. Bake in centre of 325°F (160°C) oven for 7 minutes.

• **MERINGUE:** Meanwhile, in small microwaveable bowl, whisk cornstarch with ⅓ cup (75 mL) cold water. Microwave at high, stirring twice, until thickened, about 40 seconds. Cover with plastic wrap and keep warm.

• In bowl, beat egg whites with cream of tartar until soft peaks form. Beat in sugar, 1 tbsp (15 mL) at a time, until stiff peaks form. Beat in cornstarch mixture, 1 tbsp (15 mL) at a time, until incorporated.

• Starting at edge and using spatula, spread meringue around outside of hot filling, sealing it to crust. Spread over remaining filling, making peaks with back of spoon. Bake in centre of 350°F (180°C) oven until peaks are golden, about 20 minutes. Let cool on rack until set, about 3 hours.

Makes 8 servings. | PER SERVING: about 419 cal, 9 g pro, 20 g total fat (10 g sat. fat), 52 g carb, 1 g fibre, 141 mg chol, 207 mg sodium. % RDI: 15% calcium, 9% iron, 14% vit A, 15% vit C, 28% folate.

Divine French Lemon Tart

There's no better way to showcase the puckery tart flavour of lemon than in a French-style tart, with its tender, buttery crust and a filling that is baked just enough to set. Serve a flourish of fresh berries alongside.

1 cup	all-purpose flour	250 mL
2 tbsp	granulated sugar	25 mL
½ cup	cold butter, cubed	125 mL
1	egg yolk	1
2 tbsp	water	25 mL

LEMON FILLING:

5	eggs	5
3	egg yolks	3

1 cup	granulated sugar	250 mL
¾ cup	lemon juice	175 mL
2 tbsp	cold butter, cubed	25 mL

TOPPING:

3 tbsp	apple jelly, melted	50 mL
	Assorted fruit (such as Cape gooseberries, blackberries and raspberries) or icing sugar	

BAKING BLIND

Lining an unfilled pie shell with foil, then pie weights before baking prevents the pastry from blistering and shrinking. This step, often combined with pricking the pie shell, is called baking blind. This procedure is used when pastry, which requires high heat, is paired with a filling that requires moderate heat, such as a curd or custard. It's also used when a pie shell is to be filled with an already-cooked filling. In either case, the foil and pie weights are removed when the pastry is partially baked. The crust is then either fully baked, or filled and baked, depending on the recipe.

❧ Set out 9-inch (23 cm) tart pan with removable bottom.

❧ In bowl, whisk flour with sugar. Using pastry blender, cut in butter until in fine crumbs with a few larger pieces. Whisk egg yolk with water; drizzle over flour mixture, tossing with fork until dough clumps.

❧ Turn out onto floured work surface; press into disc. Roll out into 11-inch (28 cm) circle; fit into tart pan. Trim to leave 1-inch (2.5 cm) overhang; fold inside and press pastry together. Refrigerate for 30 minutes. **(Make-ahead: Cover and refrigerate for up to 1 day.)**

❧ With fork, prick bottom at ½-inch (1 cm) intervals all over. Line with foil; fill with pie weights or dried beans. Bake in bottom third of 400°F (200°C) oven until edge starts to turn golden, 15 to 20 minutes. Remove weights and foil; bake until evenly golden, about 10 minutes. Let cool on rack.

❧ **LEMON FILLING:** In top of double-boiler or large heatproof bowl over saucepan of simmering water, whisk together eggs, egg yolks, sugar and lemon juice; cook, stirring often, until translucent and thick enough to mound on spoon, 15 to 20 minutes.

❧ Strain through fine sieve into bowl; stir in butter. Place plastic wrap directly on surface; refrigerate until cold, about 2 hours. **(Make-ahead: Refrigerate for up to 1 day.)**

❧ Spoon lemon filling into pie shell; smooth top. Bake in bottom third of 325°F (160°C) oven until filling loses some shine and forms thin skin, about 12 minutes. Let cool on rack. Refrigerate until cold, about 2 hours.

❧ **TOPPING:** Spoon jelly evenly over filling, spreading to cover. Refrigerate until set, about 30 minutes. **(Make-ahead: Cover with large inverted bowl; refrigerate for up to 8 hours.)** Garnish with fruit or, using tart pan bottom to shield rest of tart, dust top edge of crust and narrow border of filling with icing sugar.

Makes 8 to 10 servings. | PER EACH OF 10 SERVINGS (WITHOUT FRUIT): about 314 cal, 6 g pro, 16 g total fat (9 g sat. fat), 37 g carb, trace fibre, 213 mg chol, 157 mg sodium. % RDI: 3% calcium, 9% iron, 18% vit A, 5% vit C, 19% folate.

Blueberry Frangipane Tart

This tart is so pretty that guests will find it hard to believe it's homemade. The combination of fresh blueberries and almonds is delicious, with the berries adding a decidedly Canadian touch to a French pastry shop classic.

PATTING IN PASTRY

❯ To make sure that pat-in pastry is evenly thick, loosely divide the crumbs into quarters. Pat each quarter into one-quarter of the tart tin. Dip your fingers in flour as necessary to keep them from sticking as you press the pastry evenly over bottom and up side of tart pan or pie plate.

1½ cups	fresh wild or cultivated blueberries	375 mL
⅓ cup	seedless raspberry jam or red currant jelly, melted	75 mL
⅓ cup	sliced almonds	75 mL
1 tbsp	icing sugar	15 mL
PAT-IN SWEET PASTRY:		
1½ cups	all-purpose flour	375 mL
2 tbsp	granulated sugar	25 mL
4 tsp	cornstarch	20 mL

Pinch	salt	Pinch
¾ cup	cold unsalted butter, cubed	175 mL
FRANGIPANE FILLING:		
⅔ cup	whole unblanched or blanched almonds	150 mL
¼ cup	granulated sugar	50 mL
2 tbsp	all-purpose flour	25 mL
2 tbsp	butter, softened	25 mL
1	egg	1
¼ tsp	almond extract	1 mL

🍂 Set out 9-inch (23 cm) tart pan with removable bottom.

🍂 **PAT-IN SWEET PASTRY:** In large bowl, whisk together flour, sugar, cornstarch and salt. Using pastry blender, cut in butter until mixture clumps together. With floured hands, press evenly over bottom and up side of tart pan. Cover and refrigerate until chilled, about 1 hour.

🍂 With fork, prick pastry at 1-inch (2.5 cm) intervals all over; bake in bottom third of 350°F (180°C) oven until just starting to turn golden, about 20 minutes. Let cool on rack. **(Make-ahead: Set aside at room temperature for up to 1 day.)**

🍂 **FRANGIPANE FILLING:** In food processor, finely chop almonds. Add sugar and flour; pulse to combine. Add butter, egg and almond extract; pulse until smooth, about 30 seconds. **(Make-ahead: Refrigerate in airtight container for up to 1 day. Bring to room temperature.)** Spread evenly in tart shell.

🍂 Sprinkle blueberries evenly over filling. Bake in bottom third of 375°F (190°C) oven for 25 minutes. Remove from oven. Brush top with ¼ cup (50 mL) of the jam; sprinkle almonds around edge. Bake until cake tester inserted in centre comes out clean and almonds are golden, 10 to 15 minutes. Let cool on rack. **(Make-ahead: Set aside at room temperature for up to 3 hours.)**

🍂 Remelt remaining jam; brush over blueberries. Dust almonds with icing sugar.

Makes 8 servings. | PER SERVING: about 468 cal, 7 g pro, 29 g total fat (14 g sat. fat), 47 g carb, 3 g fibre, 77 mg chol, 38 mg sodium. % RDI: 5% calcium, 14% iron, 19% vit A, 7% vit C, 30% folate.

Glazed Strawberry Tart

You can bake the tart shell, make the pastry cream filling and prep the berries a few hours ahead. Do the assembly as close to serving time as possible.

1 oz	bittersweet chocolate, melted	30 g
4 cups	halved small strawberries	1 L
2 tbsp	strawberry or red currant jelly	25 mL
PASTRY:		
1 cup	all-purpose flour	250 mL
2 tbsp	granulated sugar	25 mL
½ cup	cold butter, cubed	125 mL
1	egg yolk	1

2 tbsp	water	25 mL
1½ tsp	lemon juice	7 mL
PASTRY CREAM FILLING:		
1	egg	1
¼ cup	granulated sugar	50 mL
2 tbsp	all-purpose flour	25 mL
1 tsp	cornstarch	5 mL
1 cup	milk	250 mL
2 tsp	butter	10 mL
1 tsp	vanilla	5 mL

THE QUICK CHILL

❯ When cooling the pastry cream for this lovely tart, use the trick pastry chefs use: set the bowl of hot pastry cream in a large bowl of ice water. The ice water and frequent stirring chill the cream faster than using the fridge.

❧ Set out 9-inch (23 cm) tart pan with removable bottom.

❧ PASTRY: In bowl, whisk flour with sugar. Using pastry blender, cut in butter until in fine crumbs with a few larger pieces. Whisk together egg yolk, water and lemon juice; drizzle over flour, tossing with fork until dough clumps.

❧ Turn out onto floured work surface; press into disc. Roll out into 11-inch (28 cm) circle; fit into tart pan. Trim to leave 1-inch (2.5 cm) overhang; fold inside and press pastry together. Refrigerate for 30 minutes. **(Make-ahead: Cover; refrigerate for up to 1 day.)**

❧ With fork, prick bottom at ½-inch (1 cm) intervals all over. Line with foil; fill with pie weights or dried beans. Bake in bottom third of 400°F (200°C) oven until top edge is light golden, about 20 minutes. Remove weights and foil; bake until crisp and evenly golden, about 15 minutes. Let cool on rack.

❧ PASTRY CREAM FILLING: In bowl, whisk together egg, sugar, flour and cornstarch. In heavy saucepan, heat milk until bubbles form around edge; slowly whisk into egg mixture. Return to saucepan.

❧ Cook, whisking, over medium-low heat until thick enough to mound on spoon, 5 to 8 minutes. Remove from heat; stir in butter and vanilla. Scrape into bowl; place plastic wrap directly on surface. Refrigerate until firm and cold, about 3 hours. (Or, for faster results, see The Quick Chill, right.)

❧ Meanwhile, spread melted chocolate over bottom and up side of tart shell; let stand until set, about 30 minutes.

❧ Spoon pastry cream into tart shell; smooth top. Starting from outside edge, arrange strawberries in concentric circles on top. Melt jelly; brush over fruit. Refrigerate until set, about 15 minutes. **(Make-ahead: Refrigerate for up to 1 hour.)**

Makes 8 servings. | PER SERVING: about 272 cal, 5 g pro, 14 g total fat (8 g sat. fat), 34 g carb, 3 g fibre, 74 mg chol, 98 mg sodium. % RDI: 6% calcium, 10% iron, 12% vit A, 82% vit C, 27% folate.

Peach Galette with Almond Buttermilk Crust

While this free-form pie is from an old country tradition, the use of fresh in-season peaches sets it firmly within the scope of contemporary food trends.

The pastry will fall naturally into folds over the filling. This gives the galette its characteristic rough-hewn look.

1¾ cups	all-purpose flour	425 mL		½ cup	granulated sugar	125 mL
¾ cup	ground almonds	175 mL		½ cup	all-purpose flour	125 mL
2 tbsp	granulated sugar	25 mL		2 tbsp	peach- or almond-flavoured liqueur or orange juice	25 mL
½ tsp	salt	2 mL				
¾ cup	cold unsalted butter, cubed	175 mL		¼ cup	dry bread crumbs	50 mL
				1 tbsp	butter, softened	15 mL
½ cup	buttermilk (approx)	125 mL		**GLAZE:**		
FILLING:				1	egg yolk	1
7 cups	sliced peeled peaches (about 8)	1.75 L		2 tbsp	granulated sugar	25 mL

❧ Set out 20- x 15-inch (50 x 38 cm) piece of parchment paper and 12-inch (30 cm) pizza pan or large rimless baking sheet.

❧ In bowl, whisk together flour, almonds, sugar and salt; using pastry blender, cut in butter until in large crumbs. Drizzle with buttermilk, tossing with fork until ragged dough forms, adding up to 1 tbsp (15 mL) more buttermilk if necessary. Press into disc. Wrap; refrigerate until chilled, about 30 minutes. (Make-ahead: Refrigerate for up to 3 days. Or place in airtight container and freeze for up to 1 month; let thaw at room temperature before rolling out.)

❧ FILLING: In large bowl, toss together peaches, sugar, flour and liqueur; set aside.

❧ Sprinkle parchment paper lightly with flour. Using floured rolling pin, roll out pastry on paper into 14-inch (35 cm) circle, leaving edge ragged. Slide paper onto pizza pan. Trim paper, leaving 1-inch (2.5 cm) border.

❧ Sprinkle pastry with bread crumbs, leaving 4-inch (10 cm) border uncovered. Spoon filling over crumbs; dot with butter. Lift pastry up over filling to form 10-inch (25 cm) circle, letting pastry fall naturally into folds around edge and leaving centre uncovered.

❧ GLAZE: Beat yolk with 1 tbsp (15 mL) water; brush over pastry. Sprinkle with sugar.

❧ Bake in bottom third of 425°F (220°C) oven for 10 minutes. Reduce heat to 350°F (180°C); bake until peaches are tender, filling is bubbly and crust is golden, about 50 minutes. Let cool on pan on rack for 30 minutes. (Make-ahead: Set aside at room temperature for up to 8 hours.)

Makes 8 servings. | PER SERVING: about 511 cal, 8 g pro, 25 g total fat (13 g sat. fat), 66 g carb, 5 g fibre, 76 mg chol, 199 mg sodium. % RDI: 6% calcium, 19% iron, 23% vit A, 17% vit C, 40% folate.

Sugar Pie

Tarte au sucre is a typical Quebec recipe you will find on the menu at L'Échaudé in Quebec City. Slim wedges, attractively garnished with fresh fruit and a swish of crème anglaise, intrigue visitors and satisfy locals who cherish memories of their mothers' and grandmothers' versions.

1¾ cups	all-purpose flour	425 mL	**FILLING:**		
¼ cup	granulated sugar	50 mL	1 cup	packed brown sugar	250 mL
Pinch	salt	Pinch	2 tbsp	all-purpose flour	25 mL
½ cup	cold unsalted butter, cubed	125 mL	1	egg	1
			1	egg yolk	1
1	egg yolk	1	1 cup	whipping cream	250 mL
⅓ cup	milk	75 mL			

❧ Set out 11-inch (28 cm) tart pan with removable bottom.

❧ In large bowl, whisk together flour, sugar and salt. Using pastry blender, cut in butter until crumbly. Mix egg yolk with milk; drizzle over crumbs, tossing with fork to make loose shaggy dough. Press into disc. Wrap and refrigerate for 1 hour. **(Make-ahead: Refrigerate for up to 1 day.)** Let dough soften at room temperature for about 20 minutes before rolling out.

❧ On lightly floured surface, roll out dough into 12-inch (30 cm) circle; fit into tart pan, pressing to side and folding any excess pastry inside and pressing together. Refrigerate for 30 minutes. **(Make-ahead: Cover and refrigerate for up to 12 hours.)**

❧ With fork, prick bottom at ½-inch (1 cm) intervals all over. Line with foil; fill with pie weights or dried beans. Bake in bottom third of 375°F (190°C) oven until light golden and firm, about 15 minutes. Remove foil and weights; let cool on rack.

❧ FILLING: In large bowl and using fingertips, blend brown sugar with flour. Add egg and egg yolk; whisk until smooth. Meanwhile, in small saucepan, bring whipping cream to boil; whisk into egg mixture until blended. Pour through sieve into pastry. Bake in centre of 350°F (180°C) oven until centre is just firm, about 30 minutes. Let cool in pan on rack. **(Make-ahead: Set aside at room temperature for up to 4 hours.)**

Makes 12 servings. | PER SERVING: about 315 cal, 4 g pro, 17 g total fat (10 g sat. fat), 37 g carb, 1 g fibre, 138 mg chol, 22 mg sodium. % RDI: 4% calcium, 11% iron, 18% vit A, 13% folate.

Caramel Almond Tart

With a pat-in pastry and stir-together filling, this tart is easy and quick to prepare but still a dazzler of a dessert. Look for sliced almonds with the skins on for a two-tone effect. For a special treat, add a splash of almond liqueur to the whipped cream topping.

1½ cups	all-purpose flour	375 mL
¼ cup	icing sugar	50 mL
¼ tsp	salt	1 mL
Pinch	each cinnamon and nutmeg	Pinch
½ cup	cold butter, cubed	125 mL
1	egg yolk	1
1 tbsp	water	15 mL

FILLING:

¾ cup	packed brown sugar	175 mL
¼ cup	corn syrup	50 mL
2 tbsp	butter	25 mL
1½ cups	sliced almonds	375 mL
⅓ cup	whipping cream	75 mL

TOPPING:

½ cup	whipping cream	125 mL

❧ Set out 9-inch (23 cm) tart pan with removable bottom. Line rimmed baking sheet with foil; set aside.

❧ In food processor or bowl, pulse or whisk together flour, icing sugar, salt, cinnamon and nutmeg. Pulse or cut in butter until in fine crumbs with a few larger pieces. Whisk egg yolk with water; drizzle over flour mixture. Pulse or toss with fork just until dough clumps together; press evenly over bottom and up side of tart pan. Refrigerate for 30 minutes.

❧ Line tart shell with foil; fill with pie weights or dried beans. Bake in bottom third of 375°F (190°C) oven until light golden, about 25 minutes. Remove foil and weights. Let cool on rack.

❧ FILLING: In saucepan over medium heat, melt together sugar, corn syrup and butter, stirring often; simmer for 1 minute. Add almonds and cream; simmer for 1 minute, stirring often. Pour into tart shell.

❧ Bake on prepared baking sheet in centre of 350°F (180°C) oven until bubbly and golden, about 25 minutes. Let cool in pan on rack, loosening edge of pastry while still warm if caramel bubbled over. **(Make-ahead: Set aside at room temperature for up to 1 day.)**

❧ TOPPING: In bowl, whip cream. Spoon or pipe border along edge of tart.

Makes 8 servings. | PER SERVING: about 526 cal, 7 g pro, 33 g total fat (15 g sat. fat), 54 g carb, 3 g fibre, 95 mg chol, 210 mg sodium. % RDI: 8% calcium, 16% iron, 22% vit A, 26% folate.

Chocolate Ricotta Tart

Ricotta cheese is the base of the dense, not-too-sweet filling in this Italian-inspired tart.

1	egg yolk	1

CHOCOLATE PASTRY:

1¼ cups	all-purpose flour	300 mL
¼ cup	cocoa powder	50 mL
2 tbsp	granulated sugar	25 mL
½ tsp	salt	2 mL
¼ cup	cold butter, cubed	50 mL
¼ cup	cold lard, cubed	50 mL
1	egg yolk	1
1 tsp	vinegar	5 mL
	Ice water	

FILLING:

½ cup	whole hazelnuts	125 mL
2	egg yolks	2
½ cup	granulated sugar	125 mL
1	tub (475 g) ricotta cheese, softened	1
1 oz	semisweet or bittersweet chocolate, finely chopped	30 g
1 tbsp	grated orange rind	15 mL
1 tsp	vanilla	5 mL

❧ Set out 9-inch (23 cm) tart pan with removable bottom.

❧ **CHOCOLATE PASTRY:** In large bowl, sift together flour, cocoa, sugar and salt. Using pastry blender, cut in butter and lard until in fine crumbs with a few larger pieces.

❧ In liquid measuring cup, whisk egg yolk with vinegar. Add enough ice water to make ⅓ cup (75 mL). Drizzle over flour mixture, stirring briskly with fork until dough holds together. Press into disc. Wrap; refrigerate until chilled, about 30 minutes. **(Make-ahead: Refrigerate for up to 3 days.)**

❧ On lightly floured surface, roll out three-quarters of the pastry to generous ⅛-inch (3 mm) thickness; fit into tart pan. Trim off excess and press together with remaining pastry. Press into disc; wrap in plastic wrap and refrigerate until chilled, 30 minutes.

❧ **FILLING:** Toast hazelnuts on rimmed baking sheet in 350°F (180°C) oven until fragrant, about 8 minutes. Place in clean tea towel; rub briskly to remove as much of the skins as possible. Let cool; coarsely chop. In bowl, beat egg yolks with sugar until pale and thickened. Add ricotta; beat until smooth. Stir in hazelnuts, chocolate, orange rind and vanilla. Scrape into tart shell; smooth top.

❧ On lightly floured surface, roll out reserved pastry. Using fluted pastry wheel or knife, cut into eight ¾-inch (2 cm) wide strips, rerolling scraps. Brush pastry rim with water. Weave strips over filling, ½ inch (1 cm) apart, to make lattice top (see Mastering a Beautiful Lattice Top, page 165); press ends firmly to rim. Trim pastry at rim; press to seal. Whisk egg yolk with 1 tbsp (15 mL) water; brush over lattice.

❧ Bake in bottom third of 425°F (220°C) oven for 15 minutes. Reduce heat to 350°F (180°C); bake until filling is firm, about 30 minutes. Let cool on rack. **(Make-ahead: Cover and refrigerate for up to 8 hours. Let stand at room temperature for 30 minutes before serving.)**

Makes 8 servings. | PER SERVING: about 456 cal, 12 g pro, 30 g total fat (12 g sat. fat), 38 g carb, 2 g fibre, 147 mg chol, 257 mg sodium. % RDI: 15% calcium, 16% iron, 17% vit A, 2% vit C, 22% folate.

Sweet Cherry Custard Tart

Sweet cherries are so wonderful – it's hard to get past just eating them out of hand. But you can with this French tart. It is worth the effort and highlights the cherries in a chic new way.

1 cup	all-purpose flour	250 mL	2	eggs, beaten	2
½ cup	butter, softened	125 mL	½ cup	whipping cream	125 mL
1	egg yolk	1	¼ cup	all-purpose flour	50 mL
1 tbsp	granulated sugar	15 mL	¼ cup	granulated sugar	50 mL
Pinch	salt	Pinch	1 tbsp	grated lemon rind	15 mL
FILLING:			1 tbsp	vanilla	15 mL
2 cups	pitted sweet cherries	500 mL	Pinch	salt	Pinch

❧ Set out 9-inch (23 cm) tart pan with removable bottom and rimmed baking sheet.

❧ Place flour in bowl; make well in centre. Add butter, egg yolk, sugar and salt; mix with fork until egg mixture is smooth. Gradually stir in flour to make dough that holds together. Press into disc; wrap and refrigerate for 1 hour. Between waxed paper, roll out pastry into 11-inch (28 cm) circle. Peel off top paper; invert pastry and fit into pan. Trim to leave 1-inch (2.5 cm) overhang; fold inside and press pastry together.

❧ FILLING: Spread cherries over pastry. Whisk together eggs, cream, flour, sugar, lemon rind, vanilla and salt; pour over cherries. Bake on baking sheet in bottom third of 375°F (190°C) oven until golden and tip of knife inserted into custard comes out clean, about 45 minutes. Let cool on rack. (Make-ahead: Set aside at room temperature for up to 1 hour.)

Makes 12 servings. | PER SERVING: about 207 cal, 3 g pro, 13 g total fat (7 g sat. fat), 20 g carb, 1 g fibre, 88 mg chol, 93 mg sodium. % RDI: 2% calcium, 6% iron, 13% vit A, 3% vit C, 4% folate.

Spiced Pecan Bourbon Tart

A twist on classic pecan pie, this tart is lip-smackingly good with or without the bourbon. If you yearn for a more traditional pecan pie, omit the spices. And don't deprive yourself of a dollop of whipped cream on top.

3	eggs	3
1 cup	packed brown sugar	250 mL
½ cup	corn syrup	125 mL
¼ cup	bourbon or rye whisky	50 mL
2 tbsp	butter, melted	25 mL
½ tsp	cinnamon	2 mL
¼ tsp	each nutmeg, ground cloves and ground allspice	1 mL
1½ cups	pecan halves	375 mL

PAT-IN PASTRY:

1¼ cups	all-purpose flour	300 mL
2 tbsp	granulated sugar	25 mL
¼ tsp	salt	1 mL
⅓ cup	cold butter, cubed	75 mL
2 tbsp	cold water	25 mL
1 tsp	vinegar	5 mL

GLAZE:

2 tbsp	corn syrup, warmed	25 mL

❧ Set out 9-inch (23 cm) tart pan with removable bottom.

❧ PAT-IN PASTRY: In food processor, pulse together flour, sugar and salt. Add butter; using on-off motion, pulse until in fine crumbs. Add water and vinegar; pulse 2 or 3 times or until blended but still crumbly. With floured hands, squeeze together small handfuls of dough until mixture holds together; by handfuls, press firmly and evenly over bottom and up side of tart pan. Refrigerate for 15 minutes. **(Make-ahead: Cover and refrigerate for up to 1 day.)**

❧ In bowl, whisk together eggs, brown sugar, corn syrup, bourbon, butter, cinnamon, nutmeg, cloves and allspice; stir in pecans. Scrape filling into prepared tart shell.

❧ Bake in bottom third of 375°F (190°C) oven until pastry is golden and filling is just firm to the touch, about 45 minutes.

❧ GLAZE: Brush filling with corn syrup; let cool. **(Make-ahead: Cover loosely and set aside at room temperature for up to 1 day.)** Cut with serrated knife.

Makes 12 servings. | PER SERVING: about 347 cal, 4 g pro, 18 g total fat (6 g sat. fat), 46 g carb, 1 g fibre, 65 mg chol, 161 mg sodium. % RDI: 3% calcium, 10% iron, 9% vit A, 12% folate.

VARIATION

Spiced Pecan Tart: Omit bourbon. Decrease brown sugar to ¾ cup (175 mL) and increase corn syrup in filling to ¾ cup (175 mL).

Retro Banana Cream Pie

Everything old is new again, and banana cream pie is no exception. But paint the bottom crust with chocolate and garnish the top with chocolate shavings and you get an updated, irresistible look – and taste.

PASTRY CREAM

It takes about 5 to 7 minutes for the cornstarch in the pastry cream to thicken the milk enough for it to mound on a spoon. The pastry cream will further thicken as it chills. Cover the surface with plastic wrap to prevent a skin from forming on top.

1½ cups	graham wafer crumbs	375 mL	2 tbsp	butter	25 mL
⅓ cup	butter, melted	75 mL	1 tsp	vanilla	5 mL
2 oz	semisweet chocolate, melted	60 g	2	small ripe bananas, sliced	2

PASTRY CREAM FILLING:			GARNISH:		
4	egg yolks	4	1 cup	whipping cream	250 mL
3 cups	milk	750 mL	2 tbsp	grated semisweet chocolate (½ oz/15 g)	25 mL
½ cup	granulated sugar	125 mL			
⅓ cup	cornstarch	75 mL			

❧ Set out 9-inch (23 cm) pie plate.

❧ **PASTRY CREAM FILLING:** In large bowl, whisk together egg yolks, ½ cup (125 mL) of the milk, sugar and cornstarch; set aside.

❧ In heavy saucepan, heat remaining milk over medium heat until bubbles form around edge; gradually whisk into yolk mixture. Return to pan and cook at bare simmer over medium-low heat, stirring, until thick enough to mound on spoon, about 5 minutes. Stir in butter and vanilla; scrape into bowl. Place plastic wrap directly on surface; refrigerate just until cooled, about 2 hours. (Or try The Quick Chill; see page 175.)

❧ Meanwhile, in bowl, stir graham wafer crumbs with butter until moistened; press onto bottom and up side of pie plate. Refrigerate until firm, about 30 minutes.

❧ Drizzle melted chocolate over bottom of crust; spread evenly with offset spatula or back of spoon. Refrigerate until set, about 10 minutes. Without stirring custard, spoon half over chocolate. Arrange banana slices over top, overlapping slightly. Top with remaining custard. Place plastic wrap directly on surface; refrigerate until cold, about 2 hours. **(Make-ahead: Refrigerate for up to 12 hours.)**

❧ **GARNISH:** In bowl, whip cream. Using piping bag or spatula, pipe into rosettes or spread to cover top. Sprinkle with grated chocolate. **(Make-ahead: Insert 6 toothpicks into pie; drape plastic wrap loosely over top and refrigerate for up to 4 hours.)**

Makes 8 to 10 servings. | PER EACH OF 10 SERVINGS: about 393 cal, 6 g pro, 24 g total fat (14 g sat. fat), 40 g carb, 1 g fibre, 144 mg chol, 234 mg sodium. % RDI: 11% calcium, 9% iron, 24% vit A, 3% vit C, 14% folate.

Mint Chocolate Chip Ice-Cream Pie

Cool, easy to make and still a crowd-pleaser, this pie has summer fun written all over it.

2 cups	chocolate wafer crumbs	500 mL
⅓ cup	butter, melted	75 mL
⅓ cup	chocolate sauce	75 mL
4 cups	mint chocolate chip ice cream, softened	1 L

¾ cup	whipping cream	175 mL
1 tbsp	granulated sugar	15 mL
2 tsp	chocolate sprinkles	10 mL

❧ Set out 9-inch (23 cm) pie plate.

❧ In bowl, stir chocolate wafer crumbs with butter until moistened; press over bottom and up side of pie plate. Bake in centre of 325°F (160°C) oven until firm to the touch, about 12 minutes. Let cool on rack. Spread with chocolate sauce.

❧ In bowl and using wooden spoon, beat ice cream until smooth; spread over chocolate. Cover with plastic wrap; freeze until firm, about 1 hour.

❧ In separate bowl, whip cream with sugar; spread over ice cream. Freeze until set, about 1 hour. Garnish with chocolate sprinkles. **(Make-ahead: Cover with plastic wrap then heavy-duty foil; freeze for up to 1 day.)**

Makes 12 servings. | PER SERVING: about 302 cal, 4 g pro, 19 g total fat (11 g sat. fat), 32 g carb, 1 g fibre, 50 mg chol, 213 mg sodium. % RDI: 7% calcium, 8% iron, 15% vit A, 7% folate.

VARIATIONS

Raspberry, Dulce de Leche, Strawberry or Butterscotch Ice-Cream Pies: Have fun with your favourite ice cream, using the recipe for the crust and whipped cream above.

ICE-CREAM PIE KNOW-HOW

❯ Avoid low-fat ice creams, which tend to become icy when softened and refrozen.

❯ If ice cream is too hard, transfer to refrigerator and let stand for 30 minutes or until soft enough to scoop and measure.

❯ To cut slices easily and neatly, transfer the frozen pie to the refrigerator 30 minutes before serving. Dip knife into hot water, dry and cut pie into wedges.

Chocolate Lime Chiffon Pie

Citrus is a Florida specialty, and none is more characteristic of the Florida Keys than Key limes. Look in specialty greengrocers for these smaller limes or use larger, smoother Persian limes, which are widely available.

1 tbsp	unflavoured gelatin	15 mL
3	eggs	3
1	egg yolk	1
1 cup	granulated sugar	250 mL
⅔ cup	lime juice	150 mL
4 tsp	finely grated lime rind	20 mL
½ cup	pasteurized egg whites	125 mL

CRUST:

1½ cups	graham wafer crumbs	375 mL
½ cup	butter, melted	125 mL
2 tbsp	granulated sugar	25 mL
2 tbsp	cocoa powder	25 mL

GARNISH:

1 cup	whipping cream	250 mL
¼ cup	semisweet chocolate, coarsely grated (1 oz/30 g)	50 mL

↩ Set out 9-inch (23 cm) pie plate.

↩ **CRUST:** In bowl, stir together graham wafer crumbs, butter, sugar and cocoa until moistened; press evenly over bottom and up side of pie plate. Bake in centre of 350°F (180°C) oven until firm to the touch, about 10 minutes. Let cool on rack.

↩ In small bowl, sprinkle gelatin over ¼ cup (50 mL) water; set aside.

↩ In heatproof bowl over saucepan of simmering water, whisk together eggs, egg yolk, ¾ cup (175 mL) of the sugar and lime juice; cook, stirring frequently, until translucent and thick enough to mound on spoon, about 20 minutes. Remove from heat.

↩ Stir in gelatin mixture until melted. Press through sieve into large bowl; stir in grated lime rind. Place plastic wrap directly on surface; refrigerate, stirring occasionally, until slightly colder than room temperature and consistency of raw egg whites, about 30 minutes.

↩ In separate bowl, beat pasteurized egg whites until soft peaks form. Beat in remaining sugar, 1 tbsp (15 mL) at a time, until stiff glossy peaks form. Fold one-third into lime mixture; fold in remaining whites. Scrape into crust; smooth top. Refrigerate until set, about 2 hours. **(Make-ahead: Cover loosely with plastic wrap; refrigerate for up to 1 day.)**

↩ **GARNISH:** In bowl, whip cream; garnish each serving with spoonful. Sprinkle with chocolate.

Makes 8 to 10 servings. | PER EACH OF 10 SERVINGS: about 374 cal, 6 g pro, 22 g total fat (12 g sat. fat), 40 g carb, 1 g fibre, 136 mg chol, 242 mg sodium. % RDI: 4% calcium, 8% iron, 21% vit A, 7% vit C, 11% folate.

Peanut Butter Chocolate Tart

A small slice of this impressive and, yes, very rich dessert is totally satisfying. Treat it like a chocolate bar.

FROM TART RING TO SERVING PLATE

Place tart on upside-down bowl and ease outside ring down. Lift tart and hold just above and beside a flat serving platter. Slip a long, wide spatula between the base and pastry and slide tart onto serving platter.

2 cups	chocolate wafer crumbs	500 mL		1 tsp	vanilla	5 mL
⅓ cup	butter, melted	75 mL		½ cup	whipping cream	125 mL
FILLING:				**CHOCOLATE GLAZE:**		
1	pkg (8 oz/250 g) cream cheese, softened	1		5 oz	bittersweet chocolate, chopped	150 g
1 cup	icing sugar	250 mL		⅔ cup	whipping cream	150 mL
1 cup	smooth natural peanut butter	250 mL			Roasted peanuts, optional	

❧ Set out 10-inch (25 cm) tart pan with removable bottom.

❧ In bowl, stir chocolate wafer crumbs with butter until moistened; press over bottom and up side of tart pan. Bake in centre of 350°F (180°C) oven until firm to the touch, about 8 minutes. Let cool on rack.

❧ **FILLING:** In large bowl, beat together cream cheese, sugar, peanut butter and vanilla until smooth. In separate bowl, whip cream; fold one-quarter into filling. Fold in remaining cream. Spread over crust. Cover loosely and refrigerate until firm, about 2 hours.

❧ **CHOCOLATE GLAZE:** Place chocolate in heatproof bowl. In saucepan, heat cream just until boiling; pour over chocolate and whisk until smooth. Let cool for 3 minutes. Spread over filling. Refrigerate until set, about 1 hour. Garnish with peanuts, if using.

(Make-ahead: Cover and refrigerate for up to 2 days; let stand at room temperature for 15 minutes before serving.)

Makes 16 to 20 servings. | PER EACH OF 20 SERVINGS: about 304 cal, 6 g pro, 25 g total fat (12 g sat. fat), 19 g carb, 3 g fibre, 40 mg chol, 133 mg sodium. % RDI: 4% calcium, 11% iron, 12% vit A, 4% folate.

Quiche of Many Colours

Thinly sliced capocollo (spicy cured pork) from the deli counter adds colourful curls to the top of this spinach-and-red-pepper quiche. You can use chopped prosciutto or cooked ham instead.

	Single-Crust Perfect Pastry (recipe, page 159)			½ tsp	dried thyme	2 mL
FILLING:				¼ tsp	salt	1 mL
1	pkg (1 lb/500 g) fresh spinach	1		4	eggs	4
2 tbsp	butter	25 mL		½ cup	milk	125 mL
1	onion, finely chopped	1		½ cup	5% or 6% cream	125 mL
1	sweet red pepper, finely chopped	1		2 tbsp	Dijon mustard	25 mL
½ tsp	pepper	2 mL		¾ cup	crumbled feta cheese	175 mL
				8	thin slices capocollo, halved	8

➤ Set out 9-inch (23 cm) pie plate.

➤ On floured surface, roll out pastry to generous ⅛-inch (3 mm) thickness; fit into pie plate. Trim to leave ½-inch (1 cm) overhang; fold overhang under and flute edge. With fork, prick at 1-inch (2.5 cm) intervals all over. Refrigerate for 30 minutes.

➤ Line pie shell with foil; fill with pie weights or dried beans. Bake in bottom third of 400°F (200°C) oven until edge is light golden, about 20 minutes. Remove weights and foil; let cool on rack.

➤ **FILLING:** Meanwhile, trim off any coarse stems from spinach. Rinse spinach; shake off excess water. In large Dutch oven, cover and cook spinach, with just the water clinging to leaves, over medium heat until wilted, about 6 minutes. Drain in sieve; let cool. Squeeze out liquid; chop.

➤ In large skillet, melt butter over medium heat; fry onion, red pepper, pepper, thyme and salt, stirring occasionally, until softened, about 5 minutes.

➤ Add spinach; cook, stirring, until mixture is dry, about 4 minutes. Let cool slightly. In large bowl, whisk together eggs, milk and cream; add spinach mixture.

➤ Brush mustard over base of pastry shell. Sprinkle with ¼ cup (50 mL) of the feta; pour in egg mixture. Arrange 2 pieces capocollo on each of the 8 servings. Sprinkle remaining feta between capocollo.

➤ Bake in centre of 375°F (190°C) oven until knife inserted in centre comes out clean, 40 to 45 minutes. Let cool on rack for 10 minutes. (Make-ahead: Let cool for 30 minutes. Refrigerate until cold. Cover and refrigerate for up to 1 day. Or overwrap in heavy-duty foil and freeze for up to 2 weeks. Thaw in refrigerator; reheat in 350°F/180°C oven for about 20 minutes.)

Makes 8 servings. | PER SERVING: about 361 cal, 12 g pro, 24 g total fat (12 g sat. fat), 25 g carb, 2 g fibre, 171 mg chol, 664 mg sodium. % RDI: 19% calcium, 26% iron, 72% vit A, 50% vit C, 66% folate.

Swiss Cheese Tartlets

In Switzerland, these feature local cheese. Aged Cheddar or other firm cheeses make nice, albeit not Swiss, tarts. Contributing Food Editor Andrew Chase is responsible for introducing these tarlets – his Swiss-born mother's – to our readers.

½ cup	cold butter, cubed	125 mL		1	onion, chopped	1
1 tbsp	cold lard or butter, cubed	15 mL		2	eggs	2
				1⅓ cups	18% cream	325 mL
1⅔ cups	all-purpose flour	400 mL		¼ tsp	salt	1 mL
1	egg yolk	1		Pinch	each pepper and nutmeg	Pinch
¼ cup	ice water	50 mL				
FILLING:				1½ cups	each shredded Gruyère and Emmenthal cheese (each 6 oz/175 g)	375 mL
1 tbsp	butter	15 mL				

❧ Grease 24 muffin cups; set aside.

❧ In bowl and using pastry blender, cut butter and lard into flour until in coarse crumbs. Drizzle egg yolk and water over flour mixture, tossing briskly with fork just until pastry holds together. Form into ball. Wrap and refrigerate for 1 hour. **(Make-ahead: Refrigerate for up to 5 days or freeze in airtight container for up to 2 weeks. Let come to cool room temperature.)**

❧ Divide pastry in half. On lightly floured surface, roll out each half to generous ⅛-inch (3 mm) thickness. Using 3-inch (8 cm) round cookie cutter, cut out 12 circles from each half. Fit into prepared muffin cups, pressing to make sure pastry reaches top. Refrigerate for 30 minutes.

❧ **FILLING:** In skillet, melt butter over medium heat; fry onion until lightly browned, 10 to 12 minutes. Set aside. In bowl, beat together eggs, cream, salt, pepper and nutmeg until combined but not frothy.

❧ Spoon about 1 tsp (5 mL) onion into each tart shell; spoon Gruyère and Emmenthal cheeses loosely into each, mounding in centre. Pour in egg mixture to top of pastry.

❧ Bake in bottom third of 400°F (200°C) oven until lightly browned, about 20 minutes. Serve warm. **(Make-ahead: Transfer to rack; let cool. Refrigerate in single layer in airtight container for up to 3 days; reheat on baking sheet in 400°F/200°C oven for 4 minutes.)**

Makes 24 pieces. | PER PIECE: about 165 cal, 6 g pro, 12 g total fat (7 g sat. fat), 8 g carb, trace fibre, 62 mg chol, 121 mg sodium. % RDI: 14% calcium, 4% iron, 11% vit A, 6% folate.

Christmas Eve Tourtière

This is just one of the half-dozen or more kinds of tourtière made every festive season in Quebec. It freezes well and is nicely complemented by fruity chili sauce, salsa or chutney.

	Double-Crust Perfect Pastry (recipe, page 158)		2	onions, finely chopped	2
			2	large cloves garlic, minced	2
1	egg yolk	1			
FILLING:			1 tsp	salt	5 mL
			½ tsp	pepper	2 mL
2 cups	cubed peeled potatoes	500 mL	¼ tsp	celery seed, crushed	1 mL
2 lb	lean ground pork (or half each pork and veal)	1 kg	¼ tsp	ground cloves	1 mL

ᴖ Set out 10-inch (25 cm) pie plate.

ᴖ **FILLING:** In small saucepan of boiling salted water, cover and cook potatoes until tender, about 15 minutes. Reserving 1½ cups (375 mL) of the cooking liquid, drain and return to pot. Mash potatoes until smooth; set aside.

ᴖ In large Dutch oven, sauté ground pork over medium-high heat until no longer pink, breaking up with fork. Drain off fat.

ᴖ Add onions, garlic, salt, pepper, celery seed and cloves to pan; sauté until onions are tender, about 10 minutes.

ᴖ Add reserved cooking liquid and bring to boil. Reduce heat and simmer, stirring occasionally, until spoon drawn across bottom of pan leaves space that fills in slowly, 20 to 25 minutes. Remove from heat; mix in mashed potatoes. Let cool.

ᴖ On lightly floured surface, roll out slightly more than half of the pastry to generous ⅛-inch (3 mm) thickness; fit into pie plate. Trim to rim of pie plate. Spoon in filling; brush water over pastry on rim.

ᴖ Roll out remaining pastry; fit over filling. Trim to leave ¾-inch (2 cm) overhang. Fold upper layer of pastry under pastry on rim; flute to seal.

ᴖ Roll out pastry scraps; cut out holiday shapes, such as stars. **(Make-ahead: Wrap tourtière in plastic wrap and layer pastry shapes between waxed paper in airtight container; refrigerate for up to 1 day. To freeze, overwrap tourtière in heavy-duty foil; freeze tourtière and container of pastry shapes for up to 2 weeks. Thaw in refrigerator, about 1 day.)** Cut ½-inch (1 cm) circle out of centre of pastry top. Mix egg yolk with 2 tsp (10 mL) water; lightly brush some of this egg wash over top. Place cutouts decoratively around steam hole; brush with some of the remaining egg wash.

ᴖ Bake in bottom third of 400°F (200°C) oven, shielding edge after 30 minutes with strips of foil to prevent overbrowning, until golden and steaming, 50 to 60 minutes.

Makes 8 to 10 servings. | PER EACH OF 10 SERVINGS: about 467 cal, 21 g pro, 28 g total fat (12 g sat. fat), 32 g carb, 2 g fibre, 124 mg chol, 652 mg sodium. % RDI: 3% calcium, 19% iron, 8% vit A, 5% vit C, 36% folate.

Cheddar and Onion Galette

This free-form pie is an impressive item on a weekend brunch or fireside supper menu. Side it with a crisp salad featuring a mix of greens and crunchy radishes.

	Single-Crust Perfect Pastry (recipe, page 159)	
1	egg yolk	1
FILLING:		
1 tbsp	each butter and vegetable oil	15 mL
6 cups	thinly sliced onions	1.5 L
1 tsp	granulated sugar	5 mL

½ tsp	salt	2 mL
¼ tsp	pepper	1 mL
1	egg yolk	1
1 cup	shredded extra-old Cheddar cheese	250 mL
½ cup	sour cream	125 mL
½ tsp	herbes de Provence or dried sage	2 mL

❧ Set out 20- x 15-inch (50 x 38 cm) piece of parchment paper and 12-inch (30 cm) pizza pan or rimless baking sheet.

❧ FILLING: In large skillet, heat butter and oil over medium-low heat; fry onions, sugar, salt and pepper, stirring occasionally, until very soft and light golden, about 30 minutes. Scrape into bowl; let cool.

❧ Add egg yolk, ¾ cup (175 mL) of the cheese, sour cream and herbes de Provence to onions; stir to combine. Set aside.

❧ Sprinkle flour on parchment paper; on paper and using floured rolling pin, roll out pastry into 15-inch (38 cm) circle, leaving edge ragged. Slide paper and pastry onto pizza pan; trim paper to leave 1-inch (2.5 cm) border. Spoon filling onto pastry, leaving 4-inch (10 cm) border uncovered. Sprinkle with remaining cheese. Fold up pastry border over filling, making evenly spaced pleats. **(Make-ahead: Cover and refrigerate for up to 8 hours.)**

❧ Whisk egg yolk with 1 tbsp (15 mL) water; brush over pastry. Bake in bottom third of 425°F (220°C) oven for 10 minutes. Reduce heat to 375°F (190°C); bake until crust is golden, about 30 minutes. Let cool on pan on rack for 10 minutes. **(Make-ahead: Let cool for 30 minutes; refrigerate until cold. Cover and refrigerate for up to 1 day. Reheat in 350°F/180°C oven for 20 minutes.)**

Makes 8 servings. | PER SERVING: about 357 cal, 11 g pro, 24 g total fat (12 g sat. fat), 24 g carb, 2 g fibre, 186 mg chol, 458 mg sodium. % RDI: 14% calcium, 12% iron, 18% vit A, 10% vit C, 36% folate.

Galette

Vegetable Samosas

Tasty spiced potato-filled pastries are best fresh, but for convenience sake, you can freeze them. Serve them warm with Fresh Coriander Chutney (recipe, left).

(recipe, left)

FILLING SAMOSAS

The cone shape is stable in your hand, and is easy to fill and seal.

2 cups	diced peeled potatoes	500 mL
½ cup	diced carrots	125 mL
3 tbsp	vegetable oil	50 mL
1 tsp	each fennel and cumin seeds	5 mL
1 tsp	brown or black mustard seeds	5 mL
½ tsp	ground turmeric	2 mL
½ tsp	each coriander and fenugreek seeds	2 mL
¼ tsp	cayenne pepper	1 mL
1	onion, chopped	1
2	cloves garlic, minced	2
1 tbsp	grated gingerroot	15 mL
½ tsp	salt	2 mL
½ cup	frozen peas	125 mL
3 tbsp	lemon juice	50 mL
2 tbsp	chopped fresh coriander	25 mL
	Vegetable oil for frying	

DOUGH:

2 cups	all-purpose flour	500 mL
1 tsp	cumin seeds (preferably black)	5 mL
½ tsp	salt	2 mL
½ cup	cold butter, cubed	125 mL
½ cup	milk	125 mL

FRESH CORIANDER CHUTNEY

❧ In food processor, purée together 4 cups (1 L) fresh coriander leaves; ¼ cup (50 mL) water; half hot green finger pepper, seeded; 4 tsp (20 mL) lemon juice; and ¼ tsp (1 mL) salt until smooth. *(Make-ahead: Refrigerate in airtight container for up to 4 hours.)* Makes ½ cup (125 mL).

❧ Set out wok, deep saucepan or deep-fryer.

❧ **DOUGH:** In food processor or bowl, combine flour, cumin seeds and salt; pulse or cut in butter with pastry blender until in fine crumbs. Pulse or stir in milk until dough begins to form ball; press into disc. Wrap; refrigerate for 30 minutes. **(Make-ahead: Refrigerate for up to 1 day.)**

❧ In saucepan of boiling salted water, cover and cook potatoes and carrots until tender, 10 minutes; drain. Meanwhile, in skillet, heat oil over medium heat; fry fennel, cumin and mustard seeds, turmeric, coriander and fenugreek seeds, and cayenne just until cumin seeds begin to pop, 1 minute. Add onion, garlic, ginger and salt; fry until softened, 3 minutes. Stir in potato mixture, peas, lemon juice and coriander; let cool.

❧ Cut dough into 12 pieces; form each into flat round. On floured surface, roll out each to 6-inch (15 cm) circle; cut in half. One piece at a time, moisten half of the cut edge with water. Form cone shape by overlapping cut edges by ¼ inch (5 mm); press together.

❧ Fill with rounded 1 tbsp (15 mL) potato mixture. Moisten top inside edges of pastry; press to seal. Trim any jagged edges; crimp with fork.

❧ In wok, heat oil to 350°F (180°C) or until 1-inch (2.5 cm) cube of white bread turns golden in 45 seconds. Fry samosas, in batches, until golden, 4 minutes. Transfer to paper towel–lined tray. Or bake in 425°F (220°C) oven for 15 minutes. **(Make-ahead: Let cool. Refrigerate in airtight container for up to 1 day. Or freeze on waxed paper–lined tray; transfer to airtight container and freeze for up to 2 weeks. Reheat in 350°F/180°C oven for 10 to 20 minutes.)**

Makes 24 pieces. | PER PIECE: about 133 cal, 2 g pro, 9 g total fat (3 g sat. fat), 12 g carb, 1 g fibre, 12 mg chol, 200 mg sodium. % RDI: 2% calcium, 6% iron, 11% vit A, 5% vit C, 8% folate.

Empanadas

Served all over Latin America, empanadas (filled pastries) have one thing in common: their aromatic street-food appeal. In this version, the pastry encases a traditional Chilean slow-simmered beef-and-olive filling. You can substitute chicken and chicken stock for the beef and beef stock. Serve with Fresh Salsa (recipe, right).

3 cups	all-purpose flour	750 mL	2 tbsp	vegetable oil	25 mL
¾ tsp	salt	4 mL	2	onions, chopped	2
3 tbsp	lard	50 mL	1 tbsp	paprika	15 mL
2	eggs	2	1 tsp	ground cumin	5 mL
¾ cup	milk	175 mL	1 cup	beef stock	250 mL
FILLING:			2 tsp	wine vinegar	10 mL
2 lb	boneless beef blade pot roast	1 kg	2	hard-cooked eggs	2
¾ tsp	each salt and pepper	4 mL	1 cup	halved pimiento-stuffed green olives	250 mL

CREATING THE DECORATIVE EDGE

Use a combination of techniques, pinching pleats and twisting at the same time.

❧ Grease rimless baking sheet; set aside.

❧ In bowl, whisk flour with salt. Using pastry blender, cut in lard until in very fine crumbs. In small bowl, whisk 1 of the eggs with milk; pour over flour mixture and stir until mixture clumps together. Scrape onto floured surface; knead to form soft dough. Wrap and refrigerate for 30 minutes. **(Make-ahead: Refrigerate for up to 2 days.)**

❧ FILLING: Trim beef. Cut into ½-inch (1 cm) chunks; sprinkle with salt and pepper. In Dutch oven, heat oil over medium-high heat; brown beef. Transfer to plate. Drain off fat; fry onions, paprika and cumin over medium heat until softened, 3 minutes. Add stock, ½ cup (125 mL) water and vinegar; scrape up brown bits from bottom of pan.

❧ Return beef and any accumulated juices to pan. Cover, reduce heat and simmer over low heat until tender, about 1 hour. Uncover and simmer over medium heat until liquid is reduced by two-thirds, about 20 minutes; let cool slightly. Transfer to food processor; pulse until shredded. Transfer to bowl; refrigerate until cold. Chop eggs; add to meat mixture along with olives.

❧ Divide dough into 12 pieces. On lightly floured surface, roll out each into 6-inch (15 cm) circle. Beat remaining egg; lightly brush some over edge of each circle.

❧ Spoon rounded ⅓ cup (75 mL) filling onto half of each circle; mound slightly. Fold other half over; press seam to seal. At ½-inch (1 cm) intervals, fold seam over, pinching and twisting to seal. **(Make-ahead: Refrigerate in single layer in airtight container for up to 4 hours or freeze for up to 1 month; thaw.)**

❧ Arrange on prepared baking sheet; brush lightly with beaten egg. Bake in centre of 375°F (190°C) oven until golden and crisp, about 25 minutes.

FRESH SALSA

❧ In small bowl, combine 2 cups (500 mL) diced tomatoes; ⅓ cup (75 mL) finely chopped red onion; ¼ cup (50 mL) chopped fresh coriander; 1 tbsp (15 mL) each minced jalapeño pepper and wine vinegar; and ¼ tsp (1 mL) salt. Makes 2 cups (500 mL).

Makes 12 pieces. | PER PIECE: about 324 cal, 22 g pro, 14 g total fat (4 g sat. fat), 27 g carb, 1 g fibre, 106 mg chol, 737 mg sodium. % RDI: 5% calcium, 27% iron, 7% vit A, 2% vit C, 25% folate.

Torta Verde

Italian *torta verde* is a novel pie filled with sautéed greens and made with dough so thin that you can see the filling through it. It's the kind of pie to serve at a friends-over pizza party or casual come-for-a-glass-of-wine get-together.

1⅓ cups	all-purpose flour	325 mL
½ cup	water	125 mL
3 tbsp	extra-virgin olive oil	50 mL
¾ tsp	salt	4 mL

FILLING:

1	head garlic	1
4 tsp	extra-virgin olive oil	20 mL
1	onion, sliced	1

1	sweet red pepper, sliced	1
2	pkg (each 284 g/10 oz) fresh spinach	2
1½ cups	shredded Fontina cheese	375 mL
½ cup	shredded Asiago cheese	125 mL
½ cup	packed fresh basil, torn	125 mL
½ tsp	each salt and pepper	2 mL
1	egg yolk	1

❧ Set out 14-inch (35 cm) pizza pan.

❧ In bowl and using wooden spoon, stir together flour, water, oil and salt until ragged dough forms. Turn out onto floured surface; knead until smooth and soft, about 5 minutes. Divide in half; form into balls. Place each in greased bowl, turning to grease all over. Cover and let rest for 1 hour. **(Make-ahead: Refrigerate for up to 1 day. Let come to room temperature.)**

❧ **FILLING:** Trim tip off garlic; place, cut side up, on square of foil. Drizzle with 1 tsp (5 mL) of the oil. Wrap and roast in 400°F (200°C) oven or toaster oven until golden and tender, about 45 minutes. Let cool.

❧ Meanwhile, in large skillet, heat remaining oil over medium-high heat; sauté onion and red pepper until tender and golden, about 6 minutes. Add spinach; sauté until wilted and no liquid remains, about 5 minutes. Transfer to large bowl; let cool.

❧ Squeeze roasted garlic into spinach. Add half each of the Fontina and Asiago cheeses, the basil, salt and pepper. **(Make-ahead: Refrigerate in airtight container for up to 1 day. Let come to room temperature.)**

❧ Whisk egg yolk with 1 tbsp (15 mL) water to make egg wash.

❧ On floured surface, roll out 1 ball of the dough into 14-inch (35 cm) circle; place on pizza pan. Spread with spinach mixture, leaving 1-inch (2.5 cm) border. Lightly brush border with some of the egg wash. Sprinkle remaining cheeses over spinach mixture.

❧ Roll out remaining dough into 14-inch (35 cm) circle. Cut ½-inch (1 cm) round hole in centre. Fit over filling, pressing out air bubbles. Working around edge, pinch and twist dough together (see photo, page 195). **(Make-ahead: Cover; refrigerate for up to 4 hours.)**

❧ Brush top with egg wash. Bake in bottom third of 425°F (220°C) oven for 15 minutes. Reduce heat to 400°F (200°C); bake until golden, about 10 minutes.

Makes 8 to 10 servings. | PER EACH OF 10 SERVINGS: about 233 cal, 10 g pro, 14 g total fat (5 g sat. fat), 18 g carb, 3 g fibre, 43 mg chol, 401 mg sodium. % RDI: 21% calcium, 22% iron, 56% vit A, 45% vit C, 49% folate.

Deep-Dish Chicken Pot Pie

Chicken pot pie is a crowd favourite. We've added some fennel to the mix of vegetables. It imparts a charming licorice flavour to the filling, but you can replace it with extra carrots and celery. While you can bake and reheat the pie, you're going to the trouble of making a homemade one, so enjoy it freshly baked, golden and bubbly.

	Single-Crust Perfect Pastry (recipe, page 159)	
1	egg yolk	1

FILLING:

2¼ cups	sodium-reduced chicken stock	550 mL
¾ cup	dry white wine	175 mL
2 lb	boneless skinless chicken breasts or thighs	1 kg
Half	small bulb fennel	Half

2	carrots, sliced	2
1	stalk celery, sliced	1
2 tbsp	vegetable oil	25 mL
1	onion, chopped	1
6	cloves garlic, sliced	6
½ tsp	each dried thyme and salt	2 mL
¼ tsp	pepper	1 mL
¼ cup	all-purpose flour	50 mL
1 tbsp	chopped fresh parsley	15 mL

❧ Set out deep 9- or 10-inch (23 or 25 cm) pie plate.

❧ FILLING: In large saucepan, bring stock and wine to boil. Add chicken; reduce heat, cover and simmer until juices run clear when chicken is pierced, about 12 minutes. Reserving stock mixture and using slotted spoon, transfer chicken to plate; let cool. Cut into bite-size pieces.

❧ Meanwhile, chop enough of the fennel fronds to make 2 tbsp (25 mL); set aside. Trim and thinly slice fennel lengthwise; add to stock mixture along with carrots and celery. Cover; simmer just until tender, 5 minutes. Reserving stock mixture, drain in colander.

❧ In clean saucepan, heat oil over medium heat; fry onion, garlic, thyme, salt and pepper, stirring occasionally, until onions are softened, about 5 minutes. Add flour; cook, stirring, for 1 minute. Whisk in reserved stock mixture; bring to boil, stirring. Reduce heat and simmer until thick enough to coat back of spoon, about 5 minutes. Add chicken, fennel mixture, fennel fronds and parsley. Scrape into pie plate; let cool.

❧ On lightly floured surface, roll out pastry to generous ⅛-inch (3 mm) thickness; trim to leave 1-inch (2.5 cm) overhang. Using small decorative cutter, cut out steam vent in centre. Brush rim of plate with water; cover with pastry and press overhang to dish. Cut out decorative shapes from leftover pastry. (Make-ahead: Cover and refrigerate pie and shapes separately for up to 1 day; add 15 minutes to baking time.)

❧ Mix egg yolk with 1 tbsp (15 mL) water; brush some of this egg wash over pastry. Arrange pastry cutouts on top; brush with egg wash. Bake in bottom third of 375°F (190°C) oven until hot and golden, about 45 minutes. Let stand for 10 minutes.

Makes 8 servings. | PER SERVING: about 380 cal, 30 g pro, 17 g total fat (6 g sat. fat), 24 g carb, 2 g fibre, 134 mg chol, 574 mg sodium. % RDI: 4% calcium, 16% iron, 53% vit A, 8% vit C, 30% folate.

Individual Roasted Vegetable Pot Pies

For a vegetarian dish, make the sour cream pastry with non-hydrogenated shortening (available at health food stores and some supermarkets) instead of lard.

	Double-Crust Sour Cream Pastry (recipe, page 158)		3 tbsp	extra-virgin olive oil	50 mL
1	egg yolk	1	2 tsp	herbes de Provence	10 mL
FILLING:			½ tsp	each salt and pepper	2 mL
3	small sweet potatoes (about 1 lb/500 g)	3	2 cups	frozen corn, thawed	500 mL
			2 tbsp	butter or vegetable oil	25 mL
2	onions	2	⅓ cup	all-purpose flour	75 mL
2	sweet red or yellow peppers	2	1¾ cups	water	425 mL
1	large bulb fennel	1	1½ cups	vegetable stock	375 mL
1	eggplant	1	1½ cups	frozen peas, thawed	375 mL
8	cloves garlic, peeled	8	2 tbsp	chopped fresh parsley	25 mL
			1½ tsp	lemon juice	7 mL

↜ Grease 2 rimmed baking sheets; set aside. Set out eight 1-cup (250 mL) baking dishes.

↜ FILLING: Peel sweet potatoes; cut into 1-inch (2.5 cm) chunks. Leaving root ends intact, cut onions into 1-inch (2.5 cm) thick wedges. Seed and core red peppers; cut into 1-inch (2.5 cm) wide strips. Trim off top of fennel; cut fennel into 1-inch (2.5 cm) chunks. Cut eggplant into 1-inch (2.5 cm) chunks.

↜ In large bowl, toss together sweet potatoes, onions, red peppers, fennel, eggplant, garlic, oil, herbes de Provence, salt and pepper. Arrange on prepared pans. Roast in top and bottom thirds of 400°F (200°C) oven for 30 minutes.

↜ Rotate and switch pans. Add corn to top pan. Roast until vegetables are tender and golden, about 30 minutes.

↜ Meanwhile, in saucepan, melt butter over medium heat; whisk in flour and cook, stirring, for 1 minute. Whisk in water and stock; cook, whisking, until boiling and thickened, about 15 minutes. Stir in peas, parsley and lemon juice.

↜ Divide vegetables among baking dishes; pour sauce over top. Let cool.

↜ On lightly floured surface, roll out pastry to generous ⅛-inch (3 mm) thickness. Cut out 8 circles large enough to fit tops of dishes and leave 1-inch (2.5 cm) overhang. With small decorative cutter, cut out steam vent in centre of each. Brush edge of each dish with water; place pastry over dish and press overhang to dish. (**Make-ahead: Cover and refrigerate for up to 1 day; add 15 minutes to baking time.**)

↜ Whisk egg yolk with 1 tbsp (15 mL) water; brush over pastry. Bake on rimmed baking sheet in centre of 375°F (190°C) oven until golden and bubbly, about 55 minutes. Let cool for 5 minutes.

Makes 8 servings. | PER SERVING: about 498 cal, 8 g pro, 27 g total fat (12 g sat. fat), 58 g carb, 8 g fibre, 64 mg chol, 560 mg sodium. % RDI: 7% calcium, 24% iron, 109% vit A, 110% vit C, 57% folate.

New Brunswick Potato Cake

Chefs Margret and Axel Begner of the Opera Bistro in Saint John, N.B., take full advantage of the variety of fine fresh vegetables, fruits and herbs grown locally. They certainly don't neglect their home province's humble potato in this signature dish.

5	Yukon Gold potatoes (about 1½ lb/750 g)	5
1	leek (white and light green parts only), diced	1
	Single-Crust Sour Cream Pastry (recipe, page 158)	

8 oz	soft goat cheese	250 g
½ tsp	each salt and pepper	2 mL
4	eggs	4
2 tbsp	chopped fresh rosemary	25 mL

❧ Line 9-inch (2.5 L) springform pan with parchment paper. Centre pan on 14-inch (35 cm) square of heavy-duty foil; bring foil up around side of pan, pressing to side. Set aside.

❧ Peel and thinly slice potatoes. In large pot of boiling salted water, cover and cook for 4 minutes. Add leek; cover and cook for 1 minute. Drain; let cool.

❧ On lightly floured surface, roll out pastry into 11-inch (28 cm) circle. Fit into prepared pan, pressing gently up side; trim edge neatly, if desired.

❧ Layer potatoes with leek in pastry shell. In bowl, beat together goat cheese, salt and pepper until fluffy. Beat in eggs, 1 at a time, until smooth. Pour slowly over potato mixture, shaking pan occasionally to let mixture seep around potato filling. Sprinkle with rosemary.

❧ Bake in centre of 375°F (190°C) oven until golden, about 1¼ hours. (Make-ahead: Let cool. Cover and refrigerate for up to 1 day. Reheat, covered, in 350°F/180°C oven for 1 hour.)

Makes 8 to 10 servings. | PER EACH OF 10 SERVINGS: about 350 cal, 10 g pro, 23 g total fat (11 g sat. fat), 27 g carb, 2 g fibre, 127 mg chol, 531 mg sodium. % RDI: 5% calcium, 14% iron, 14% vit A, 8% vit C, 28% folate.

Mushroom Crescents

This cream cheese pastry is easy to mix and roll out, and its tanginess is a subtle foil to the rich mushroom filling.

2 tbsp	butter	25 mL
1	small onion, chopped	1
3	cloves garlic, minced	3
¾ tsp	each dried thyme and sage	4 mL
½ tsp	pepper	2 mL
¼ tsp	salt	1 mL
1½ cups	finely chopped portobello mushrooms	375 mL
1½ cups	finely chopped button mushrooms	375 mL
⅓ cup	white wine or water	75 mL

PASTRY:

Half	pkg (8 oz/250 g pkg), cream cheese, softened	Half
⅓ cup	butter, softened	75 mL
1 cup	all-purpose flour	250 mL
1	egg, beaten	1

❧ Set out large rimless baking sheet.

❧ In large saucepan, melt butter over medium heat; fry onion, garlic, thyme, sage, pepper and salt, stirring occasionally, until onion is softened, about 3 minutes. Increase heat to medium-high. Add portobello and button mushrooms; fry, stirring occasionally, until browned, about 10 minutes. Stir in wine, scraping up brown bits from bottom of pan. Cook until liquid is evaporated, about 5 minutes. Let cool to room temperature. (Make-ahead: Refrigerate in airtight container for up to 1 day.)

❧ PASTRY: In large bowl, beat cream cheese with butter until fluffy. Stir in flour until dough begins to form; knead in bowl until smooth. Divide dough in half; flatten into 2 discs. Wrap; refrigerate until firm, at least 30 minutes. (Make-ahead: Refrigerate for up to 2 days.)

❧ On lightly floured surface, roll out each disc into 10-inch (25 cm) circle. With 2½-inch (6 cm) round cookie cutter, cut out circles, rerolling scraps. Working with 6 circles at a time, brush edges lightly with egg. Place 1 tsp (5 mL) of the filling in centre of each; fold dough over filling, pinching edges to seal. Place, 1 inch (2.5 cm) apart, on baking sheet. (Make-ahead: Layer between waxed paper in airtight container and freeze for up to 3 weeks; do not thaw.) Brush tops with remaining egg.

❧ Bake in centre of 400°F (200°C) oven until light golden, 12 to 15 minutes. Serve warm or at room temperature.

Makes about 40 pieces. | PER PIECE: about 45 cal, 1 g pro, 3 g total fat (2 g sat. fat), 3 g carb, trace fibre, 14 mg chol, 46 mg sodium. % RDI: 1% calcium, 2% iron, 4% vit A, 1% folate.

Quick Puff Pastry

Make your own puff pastry to use in any of the recipes that follow or buy the frozen butter puff pastry that is already rolled out into 10-inch (25 cm) squares.

1 cup	cold unsalted butter	250 mL	¾ tsp	salt	4 mL
1⅔ cups	all-purpose flour	400 mL	⅓ cup	cold water	75 mL

❧ Cut butter into ½-inch (1 cm) cubes; set aside ¾ cup (175 mL) in refrigerator. In food processor, pulse flour with salt. Sprinkle remaining butter over top; pulse until indistinguishable, about 10 seconds. Sprinkle with reserved butter; pulse 4 or 5 times to cut into pea-size pieces.

❧ Pour water evenly over mixture (not through feed tube). Pulse 6 to 8 times until mixture is loose and ragged (do not let form ball). Transfer to floured waxed paper; gather and press into rectangle. Dust with flour; top with waxed paper. Roll out into 15- x 12-inch (38 x 30 cm) rectangle.

❧ Remove top paper. Starting at long edge and using bottom paper to lift pastry, fold over one-third; fold opposite long edge over top, bringing flush with edge of first fold to make 15- x 4-inch (38 x 10 cm) rectangle. Starting from 1 short end, roll up firmly; flatten into 5-inch (12 cm) square. Cut in half; wrap and refrigerate until firm, about 1 hour. **(Make-ahead: Refrigerate for up to 5 days or freeze in airtight container for up to 2 weeks.)**

Makes 1 lb (500 g).

Roasted Heirloom Tomato Tart

The colour contrast of large red and small yellow tomatoes is striking. However, red tomatoes in differing sizes are also quite attractive.

8	red or striped heirloom plum tomatoes, about 1¼ lb (625 g)	8
1 cup	yellow teardrop or cherry tomatoes (about 10 oz/300 g), halved lengthwise	250 mL
2 tbsp	extra-virgin olive oil	25 mL
1	clove garlic, minced	1
½ tsp	salt	2 mL
¼ tsp	pepper	1 mL
Half	batch Quick Puff Pastry (recipe, page 201) or 1 sheet (from 450 g pkg) frozen butter puff pastry, thawed and cold	Half
1	egg, beaten	1
1 cup	shredded Gruyère cheese	250 mL
2 tsp	chopped fresh thyme or oregano (or ½ tsp/ 2 mL dried)	10 mL

ROLLING PUFF PASTRY

Keep steady, firm hands on the rolling pin to soften the cold pastry.

Roll all around to get a piece of pastry 10 inches (25 cm) square, applying a little more pressure on high spots and along any ragged edges to even them out. Trim the edges if desired.

➤ Line 2 rimmed baking sheets with parchment paper or leave ungreased; set aside.

➤ Cut red tomatoes crosswise into ½-inch (1 cm) thick slices. In bowl, gently toss together red and yellow tomatoes, oil, garlic, salt and pepper; spread on one of the prepared pans. Roast in 400°F (200°C) oven until slightly charred and shrivelled, about 30 minutes. Let cool. **(Make-ahead: Refrigerate in airtight container for up to 1 day.)**

➤ On lightly floured surface, roll out pastry into 10-inch (25 cm) square; transfer to second pan. Using fork, prick pastry at 1-inch (2.5 cm) intervals all over; refrigerate for 30 minutes.

➤ Bake pastry in centre of 400°F (200°C) oven until light golden and puffed, 12 to 15 minutes. Let cool slightly.

➤ Lightly brush pastry all over with some of the egg; sprinkle with cheese, leaving 1-inch (2.5 cm) border. Arrange red tomatoes in overlapping rows on cheese. Scatter yellow tomatoes over top; sprinkle with thyme.

➤ Bake until golden and puffed, 12 to 15 minutes. Let cool for 5 minutes; cut into squares. Serve warm or at room temperature. **(Make-ahead: Let cool. Cover and refrigerate for up to 1 day. Reheat in 350°F/180°C oven for 5 minutes.)**

Makes 6 to 9 servings. | PER EACH OF 9 SERVINGS: about 303 cal, 8 g pro, 20 g total fat (8 g sat. fat), 24 g carb, 3 g fibre, 54 mg chol, 346 mg sodium. % RDI: 13% calcium, 14% iron, 16% vit A, 20% vit C, 8% folate.

Almond Apple Tarts

Enjoy these glistening apple tarts warm from the oven. They can be assembled ahead of time and popped into the oven as you sit down to dinner.

	Quick Puff Pastry (recipe, page 201) or 1 pkg (450 g) frozen butter puff pastry, thawed and cold		½ cup	granulated sugar	125 mL
			½ tsp	cinnamon	2 mL
1	egg	1	3	apples (such as Golden Delicious or Cortland)	3
¾ cup	finely chopped toasted almonds	175 mL	⅓ cup	apple jelly, melted	75 mL

➥ Line 2 large rimmed baking sheets with parchment paper or leave ungreased; set aside.

➥ On floured surface, roll out half of the puff pastry into 10-inch (25 cm) square; cut into 4 squares. Place on prepared baking sheet. Repeat with remaining pastry. Whisk egg with 1 tbsp (15 mL) water; brush over pastry.

➥ In bowl, combine almonds, ⅓ cup (75 mL) of the sugar and cinnamon; evenly divide among squares.

➥ Peel and core apples; slice very thinly. Arrange about 10 apple slices in overlapping circle on top of each square. **(Make-ahead: Cover and refrigerate for up to 2 hours.)** Sprinkle with remaining sugar.

➥ Bake in top and bottom thirds of 425°F (220°C) oven, switching and rotating pans halfway through, until pastry is puffed and golden and apples are tender, about 20 minutes. Let cool for 10 minutes.

➥ Brush jelly over apples.

Makes 8 servings. | PER SERVING: about 475 cal, 6 g pro, 29 g total fat (15 g sat. fat), 51 g carb, 3 g fibre, 84 mg chol, 234 mg sodium. % RDI: 4% calcium, 13% iron, 21% vit A, 3% vit C, 27% folate.

Welly Bites

Inspired by Beef Wellington, the must-serve entrée of the 1960s, this mini make-ahead appetizer has fewer steps and ingredients. Serve it as a stand-up appetizer with a glass of Cabernet Sauvignon or with dressed greens as a plated first course.

3 tbsp	Dijon mustard	50 mL		Quick Puff Pastry (recipe, page 201) or 1 pkg (450 g) frozen butter puff pastry, thawed and cold	
1 tbsp	chopped fresh thyme (or 1 tsp/5 mL dried)	15 mL			
¼ tsp	each salt and pepper	1 mL			
12 oz	beef tenderloin premium oven roast, cut into 1-inch (2.5 cm) cubes	375 g	1	egg	1

❧ Line rimmed baking sheet with parchment paper or leave ungreased; set aside.

❧ In bowl, mix together mustard, thyme, salt and pepper; add beef, tossing to coat.

❧ On floured surface, roll out half of the puff pastry into 12-inch (30 cm) square; cut into 16 squares. Repeat with remaining pastry. Lay 1 piece mustard-coated beef in centre of each square. Brush edges with water. Bring up corners and pinch together in centre; pinch sides closed to make neat pouches. Transfer to prepared pan. Refrigerate for 30 minutes. **(Make-ahead: Cover and refrigerate for up to 12 hours.)**

❧ In small bowl, beat egg with 2 tsp (10 mL) water; brush over pastry. Bake in centre of 425°F (220°C) oven until golden and puffed, about 15 minutes. Serve warm.

Makes 32 pieces. | PER PIECE: about 95 cal, 3 g pro, 7 g total fat (4 g sat. fat), 5 g carb, trace fibre, 27 mg chol, 99 mg sodium. % RDI: 1% calcium, 5% iron, 6% vit A, 7% folate.

Baklawa

Baklawa, the flowerlike individual Lebanese version of the familiar layered baklava, contains pistachios, rose water and orange blossom water, all available at specialty and Middle Eastern food stores. Baklawa is typically served among a variety of sweets at Eid-ul-Fitr, a time of celebration that marks the end of Ramadan in the Islamic calendar.

EXOTIC PRESENTATION MADE EASY

The flower shape holds the filling neatly.

Though the baklawa are doused with syrup, they retain their crispness.

¾ cup	unsalted butter	175 mL
2 cups	each walnut halves and shelled pistachios	500 mL
½ cup	granulated sugar	125 mL
½ tsp	each ground cardamom and cinnamon	2 mL
2	egg whites	2
1 tsp	rose water	5 mL
16	sheets phyllo pastry	16

SYRUP:		
2 cups	granulated sugar	500 mL
1 cup	water	250 mL
1 tsp	lemon juice	5 mL
1 tsp	orange blossom water	5 mL
1 tsp	rose water	5 mL
GARNISH:		
3 tbsp	finely chopped pistachios	50 mL

❧ Grease two 9-inch (1.5 L) round metal cake pans; set aside.

❧ SYRUP: In saucepan, combine sugar with water. Bring to boil over medium heat, stirring until sugar is dissolved; reduce heat and simmer until syrupy, about 10 minutes. Add lemon juice, orange blossom water and rose water; let cool.

❧ Meanwhile, in small saucepan, melt butter over low heat until white milky liquid sinks to bottom. Skim off foam; pour clear melted clarified butter into bowl, leaving milky liquid in pan. Set aside.

❧ In food processor, pulse together walnuts, pistachios, sugar, cardamom and cinnamon until in coarse crumbs. In bowl, beat egg whites until stiff peaks form; fold in nut mixture and rose water. Set aside.

❧ Place 1 sheet of the phyllo on work surface, keeping remainder covered with damp towel to prevent drying out. Brush with butter; top with second sheet and brush with butter. Repeat to form stack of 8 sheets.

❧ Cut phyllo stack into 20 squares. Place heaping 1 tbsp (15 mL) filling in centre of each. Bring up corners of phyllo and gently squeeze sides. Place in prepared pan. Cover pan with plastic wrap to prevent drying out. Repeat with remaining phyllo and filling to fill second pan.

❧ Bake in centre of 350°F (180°C) oven until golden and crisp, about 45 minutes. Pour all but 2 tbsp (25 mL) of the syrup over top. Let cool on rack. (**Make-ahead: Cover; set aside at room temperature for up to 1 day.**) Warm reserved syrup; brush over filling and phyllo.

❧ GARNISH: Sprinkle filling with chopped pistachios.

Makes 40 pieces. | PER PIECE: about 186 cal, 3 g pro, 11 g total fat (3 g sat. fat), 21 g carb, 1 g fibre, 9 mg chol, 51 mg sodium. % RDI: 2% calcium, 6% iron, 4% vit A, 2% vit C, 8% folate.

Pistachio Wafers with Lemon Honey Mousse

This is the most unintimidating pastry recipe! All you have to do is butter, stack and cut phyllo pastry into rectangles and bake them pressed flat between parchment paper–lined baking sheets. The mousse, all pillowy and creamy, adds a totally different texture to these crisp wafers.

⅔ cup	shelled pistachios	150 mL	2	eggs	2
¼ cup	granulated sugar	50 mL	⅓ cup	lemon juice	75 mL
6	sheets phyllo pastry	6	¼ cup	liquid honey	50 mL
⅓ cup	butter, melted	75 mL	¼ cup	cold butter, cubed	50 mL
LEMON HONEY MOUSSE:			1 tbsp	grated lemon rind	15 mL
4	egg yolks	4	1½ cups	whipping cream	375 mL

LEFTOVER PHYLLO
❯ Whenever possible, use up a whole package. Rewrap any leftovers and refrigerate for up to 2 days. Use them to make items that don't require a lot of manipulation, such as these wafers.

❧ Line large rimless baking sheet with parchment paper. Cut second sheet of parchment paper same size as baking sheet. Set out second large rimless baking sheet. Set aside.

❧ In food processor, chop pistachios with sugar until crumbly. Remove 2 tbsp (25 mL) and set aside for garnish.

❧ Place 1 sheet of the phyllo on prepared pan, keeping remainder covered with damp towel to prevent drying out. Lightly brush with butter; sprinkle with generous 2 tbsp (25 mL) of the remaining pistachio mixture. Top with second sheet of phyllo; brush with butter. Repeat layers with remaining pistachios, phyllo and butter.

❧ Cut phyllo stack in half lengthwise; cut each half crosswise into 8 rectangles. Cover with parchment paper; set second baking sheet on top. Bake in centre of 375°F (190°C) oven for 10 minutes.

❧ Remove top baking sheet and paper; bake until wafers are golden, about 5 minutes. Let cool on pan on rack. **(Make-ahead: Layer between waxed paper in airtight container and store at room temperature for up to 1 week.)**

❧ **LEMON HONEY MOUSSE:** In heatproof bowl, whisk together egg yolks, eggs, lemon juice and honey. Place over saucepan of simmering water over low heat; cook, stirring constantly, until mixture is thick enough to mound on spoon, 10 minutes. Strain into large bowl. Add butter and lemon rind; stir until butter melts. Place plastic wrap directly on surface; refrigerate until cold, 2 hours. **(Make-ahead: Refrigerate for up to 2 days.)**

❧ In bowl, whip cream; fold one-third into lemon mixture. Fold in remaining whipped cream. Place 1 wafer on each of 8 plates; spoon ¼ cup (50 mL) mousse over top of each. Top with second wafer, then scant ¼ cup (50 mL) of the remaining mousse. Sprinkle with reserved pistachio mixture.

Makes 8 servings. | PER SERVING: about 486 cal, 8 g pro, 39 g total fat (20 g sat. fat), 30 g carb, 1 g fibre, 248 mg chol, 261 mg sodium. % RDI: 6% calcium, 11% iron, 37% vit A, 10% vit C, 19% folate.

Spinach Phyllo Slices

If you love to entertain, this is the recipe for you. The cheese and spinach phyllo rolls are quick to make and freeze beautifully for occasions when make-ahead recipes are a necessity. At party hour, bake the rolls from frozen, slice and serve.

THE 411 ON PHYLLO

❯ There are 18 to 20 sheets of pastry in each 1-lb (500 g) box of frozen phyllo. Let thaw in the refrigerator for up to 24 hours or at room temperature for about 3 hours before using. If outer sheets are ragged or brittle, discard them and use moister sheets further down in the stack. Otherwise, the filling may seep out during baking.

❯ Starting at one corner of the stack of phyllo, gently and slowly pull sheets apart. If two sheets will not separate, leave together and brush as usual with butter.

❯ When working with phyllo, always keep the reserved stack of sheets covered with a barely damp clean tea towel. Avoid letting anything wet touch the sheets or they will be impossible to separate.

9	sheets phyllo pastry	9
½ cup	butter, melted	125 mL

FILLING:

1 tbsp	vegetable oil	15 mL
1	onion, finely chopped	1
2	cloves garlic, minced	2
1	pkg (10 oz/300 g) frozen spinach, thawed	1
1 cup	grated Romano or Parmesan cheese	250 mL
1 cup	crumbled feta cheese	250 mL
1	egg, lightly beaten	1
¼ cup	diced roasted red pepper	50 mL
3 tbsp	chopped fresh dill (or 2 tsp/10 mL dried dillweed)	50 mL
½ tsp	pepper	2 mL
Pinch	nutmeg	Pinch

❧ Line large rimless baking sheet with parchment paper or leave ungreased; set aside.

❧ FILLING: In skillet, heat oil over medium heat; fry onion and garlic, stirring often, until softened, about 5 minutes. Scrape into bowl; let cool.

❧ Squeeze moisture from spinach; chop finely and add to bowl. Add Romano and feta cheeses, egg, red pepper, dill, pepper and nutmeg; stir to combine. Set aside.

❧ Place 1 sheet of the phyllo on work surface, keeping remainder covered with damp towel to prevent drying out. Lightly brush with butter. Top with 2 more phyllo sheets, brushing each with butter. Spoon about 1 cup (250 mL) of the filling along 1 long side, leaving 1-inch (2.5 cm) border on each end; fold ends over filling. Roll up to form log. Place on prepared pan. With sharp knife, score top through phyllo into 12 portions. Repeat with remaining phyllo and filling. **(Make-ahead: Cover with plastic wrap; refrigerate for up to 1 day. Or place wrapped rolls in airtight container and freeze for up to 2 weeks.)**

❧ Brush with butter. Bake in centre of 400°F (200°C) oven until golden, about 25 minutes, 30 minutes if frozen. With serrated knife, slice along score marks.

Makes 36 servings. | PER SERVING: about 69 cal, 2 g pro, 5 g total fat (3 g sat. fat), 4 g carb, trace fibre, 19 mg chol, 136 mg sodium. % RDI: 5% calcium, 3% iron, 8% vit A, 5% vit C, 6% folate.

Roast Garlic and Goat Cheese Strudel

This strudel slices neatly to serve as finger food or on a bed of dressed baby greens as a first course.

2	small heads garlic	2	2 tbsp	chopped fresh chives	25 mL
1 tsp	extra-virgin olive oil	5 mL	1 tsp	chopped fresh rosemary	5 mL
¾ cup	soft goat cheese (6 oz/175 g)	175 mL	¼ tsp	pepper	1 mL
			5	sheets phyllo pastry	5
¼ cup	chopped fresh basil or parsley	50 mL	¼ cup	butter, melted	50 mL

↜ Line rimless baking sheet with parchment paper or leave ungreased; set aside.

↜ Trim tips off garlic; place garlic, cut side up, on square of foil. Drizzle with oil. Wrap loosely and roast in 400°F (200°C) oven or toaster oven until golden and tender, about 45 minutes. Let cool. **(Make-ahead: Wrap and refrigerate for up to 1 day.)**

↜ Squeeze roasted garlic into bowl. Add goat cheese; mash until combined. Stir in basil, chives, rosemary and pepper; set aside.

↜ Place 1 sheet of the phyllo on work surface, keeping remainder covered with damp towel to prevent drying out. Brush lightly with butter. Top with second sheet of phyllo; brush with butter. Repeat with remaining phyllo and butter.

↜ Spoon goat cheese mixture along 1 long side, leaving 2-inch (5 cm) border on each end; fold ends over filling . Roll up to form long roll. Place on prepared pan. Brush all over with remaining butter. With sharp knife, score top diagonally through phyllo into 8 to 12 portions. **(Make-ahead: Cover with plastic wrap; refrigerate for up to 1 day.)**

↜ Bake in centre of 400°F (200°C) oven until golden, about 15 minutes. Let cool for 20 minutes. With serrated knife, slice along score marks. **(Make-ahead: Set aside at room temperature for up to 3 hours.)**

Makes 8 to 12 servings. | PER EACH OF 12 SERVINGS: about 116 cal, 4 g pro, 8 g total fat (5 g sat. fat), 8 g carb, trace fibre, 19 mg chol, 142 mg sodium. % RDI: 3% calcium, 6% iron, 8% vit A, 3% vit C, 5% folate.

RELEASING STEAM

❯ Use a serrated knife to cut slits, about 1 inch (2.5 cm) apart, into top of strudel (or any phyllo roll). These vents release steam that can build up and burst the strudel. These vents also make slicing the strudel neater.

Profiteroles

Surprisingly easy, this French classic will definitely impress. You can make just the choux pastry balls ahead, or make and fill them with ice cream up to three days before serving.

Seeing the texture of choux pastry before and after the eggs are added is a help when you make this classic the first time.

1 cup	water	250 mL
½ cup	butter	125 mL
Pinch	salt	Pinch
1¼ cups	all-purpose flour	300 mL
4	eggs, beaten	4
6 cups	vanilla ice cream	1.5 L
GLAZE:		
1	egg	1
1 tbsp	water	15 mL

CHOCOLATE SAUCE:		
6 oz	semisweet chocolate, chopped	175 g
¾ cup	whipping cream	175 mL
RASPBERRY COULIS:		
3 cups	thawed frozen raspberries	750 mL
3 tbsp	icing sugar	50 mL

❧ Line 2 large rimless baking sheets with parchment paper; set aside.

❧ In heavy saucepan, bring water, butter and salt just to boil; remove from heat. Add flour all at once; stir vigorously with wooden spoon until mixture comes away from side of pan in smooth ball.

❧ Reduce heat to medium-low; cook, stirring constantly, until coating begins to form on bottom of pan, 1 to 2 minutes. Transfer to large bowl; stir for 30 seconds to cool slightly.

❧ Make well in centre of dough. Using electric mixer, beat in eggs, one-quarter at a time, beating well after each. Beat until smooth, shiny and dough holds its shape in bowl.

❧ Spoon into pastry bag fitted with ½-inch (1 cm) plain tip, or use spoon; pipe or spoon twenty-four 2-inch (5 cm) wide by 1-inch (2.5 cm) high mounds onto prepared pans.

❧ **GLAZE:** Beat egg with water; lightly brush over mounds, flattening tips and making sure glaze doesn't drip onto paper, or pastry will not rise to its full height.

❧ Bake in top and bottom thirds of 425°F (220°C) oven for 20 minutes. Reduce heat to 375°F (190°C); switch and rotate pans. Bake until golden and crisp, about 15 minutes. Turn off oven; let stand in oven for 10 minutes to dry. Transfer to rack; let cool. **(Make-ahead: Store in airtight container for up to 1 day. Recrisp in 350°F/180°C oven for 5 minutes.)**

❧ **CHOCOLATE SAUCE:** Place chocolate in heatproof bowl. In saucepan, bring cream to boil; pour over chocolate. Whisk until melted and smooth.

❧ **RASPBERRY COULIS:** Press raspberries through fine sieve into bowl. Whisk in sugar. **(Make-ahead: Refrigerate chocolate sauce and coulis in separate airtight containers for up to 3 days. Rewarm chocolate sauce to liquefy.)**

❧ Cut profiteroles in half horizontally. Spoon ¼ cup (50 mL) ice cream into bottom half of each; replace top. **(Make-ahead: Wrap each in foil and freeze for up to 3 days.)** Drizzle coulis onto plates. Arrange 2 profiteroles on each plate; spoon chocolate sauce over top.

Makes 12 servings. | PER SERVING: about 419 cal, 8 g pro, 26 g total fat (15 g sat. fat), 39 g carb, 1 g fibre, 146 mg chol, 138 mg sodium. % RDI: 11% calcium, 11% iron, 22% vit A, 13% vit C, 23% folate.

Prosciutto and Cheddar Puffs

Cheese puffs, or *gougères,* are a French hors d'oeuvre traditionally made of choux pastry and Gruyère cheese. Caraway seeds, specks of prosciutto and aged Cheddar cheese make this a new version. For the fullest flavour and the highest, lightest puffs, use a well-aged cheese, such as three-year-old Cheddar.

1 cup	water	250 mL	1 cup	shredded extra-old Cheddar cheese	250 mL
½ cup	butter, cubed	125 mL	½ cup	finely diced prosciutto or crumbled cooked bacon	125 mL
¼ tsp	each salt and pepper	1 mL			
Pinch	cayenne pepper	Pinch			
1¼ cups	all-purpose flour	300 mL	1½ tsp	caraway seeds, optional	7 mL
4	eggs, beaten	4			

❧ Line 2 large rimless baking sheets with parchment paper; set aside.

❧ In heavy saucepan, bring water, butter, salt, pepper and cayenne pepper just to boil; remove from heat. Add flour all at once; stir vigorously with wooden spoon until mixture comes away from side of pan in smooth ball.

❧ Reduce heat to medium-low; cook, stirring constantly, until coating begins to form on bottom of pan, 1 to 2 minutes. Transfer to large bowl; stir for 30 seconds to cool slightly.

❧ Make well in centre of dough. Using electric mixer, beat in eggs, one-quarter at a time, beating well after each. Beat until smooth, shiny and dough holds its shape in bowl. Stir in cheese, prosciutto, and caraway seeds (if using).

❧ Drop by scant tablespoonfuls (15 mL), 2 inches (5 cm) apart, on prepared pans. Bake in top and bottom thirds of 425°F (220°C) oven, rotating and switching pans halfway through, until puffed and golden, about 20 minutes. (Make-ahead: Let cool on rack. Store in airtight container for up to 2 days. Reheat in 375°F/190°C oven until warm and crisp, about 5 minutes.)

Makes 45 pieces. | PER PIECE: about 50 cal, 2 g pro, 3 g total fat (2 g sat. fat), 3 g carb, trace fibre, 26 mg chol, 75 mg sodium. % RDI: 2% calcium, 1% iron, 3% vit A, 3% folate.

ANCHOR THE PAPER

❯ To prevent the parchment paper from moving on the baking sheet while piping, dab a bit of the pastry under each corner as glue.

CHANGE THE SHAPE

❯ You can also make finger-shaped puffs. Spoon dough into piping bag fitted with large plain tip; pipe 2½-inch (6 cm) long strips of dough onto baking sheets.

Chapter 4

Yeast Breads

Yeast is the most reliable of leaveners – and your friend in the kitchen. Give it some flour and moisture and, no matter what, there will be bread.

Just what kind of bread depends on a host of variables, from the flour you choose to the time you can devote to your project to the occasion. It could be a rustic country loaf, crusty and golden outside with an enjoyable chewiness and moist, firm crumb. Or a pan of buns to make into sandwiches or keep company with chili and stews. Or a flatbread, topped with herbs and olive oil or rolled out into a pizza base and topped with tomato sauce, grilled vegetables and stretchy cheese. You could make paper-thin crackers to underscore dips and spreads. And let's not forget the sweet side – yeast is also the key to a range of loaves and confections, rich with brown sugar and cinnamon, almonds, poppy seeds, chocolate or cranberries. All are breads. All are different. And all are satisfying.

From Flour to Finished Loaf

❯ There are a number of steps to making breads that you'll be proud of. Except for the kneading, they don't require much time – or effort.

❯ The Right Water Temperature

The water you combine with active dry yeast should be slightly warmer than lukewarm, about 110°F (45°C). To test, sprinkle a little on your wrist; it should register as slightly warm. For quick-rising (instant) dry yeast mixed with dry ingredients, water needs to be warmer to be effective, about 120°F to 130°F (50°C to 55°C). It should still feel comfortable to the touch, but use an instant-read thermometer to ensure it's at the correct temperature.

❯ Proofing Yeast

Testing the rising power of your yeast is an important first step in our bread baking recipes. In a bowl, combine warm water and a little sugar to nourish the yeast (but not enough to make the bread taste sweet). Sprinkle dry granular yeast over the surface, place the bowl in a warm spot and wait for 10 minutes – if frothy foam rises, that's the proof that your yeast is alive and raring to grow. If there are no bubbles or increase in volume, the water might have been too hot or the yeast too old. Check the expiry date on the package. If you've been treating yeast like a prized antique, begin again with a freshly purchased package that hasn't yet reached its best-before date.

❯ Flour: How Much Is Enough?

When you initially stir in flour, it's prudent to not add the entire amount called for in the recipe. Why? Flour varies slightly in dryness from season to season, and from brand to brand, and, alas, from the North American practice of measuring by volume instead of weight. Save out the remainder recommended in each recipe and use it to flour the counter before and during kneading.

❯ Kneading the Dough

● This step can take 8 to 10 minutes by hand, or 4 to 5 minutes in a heavy-duty stand mixer using the dough hook.

● The dough will start out rough and shaggy. Use some of the remaining flour to dust the counter and to sprinkle over the dough.

● Pull the far side of the dough up and fold it over toward you.

● Press dough, pushing it away from you in a rolling motion with the heels of your hands.

● Give the dough a quarter-turn before repeating the same motions. Set a rhythm that is both relaxing and vigorous.

● To keep the dough from sticking to the work surface, sprinkle lightly with some of the remaining flour. Resist the temptation to add generous sprinkles of flour early on, as this can result in dry bread. Instead, keep kneading, adding the lightest dusting of flour when absolutely necessary. As the dough becomes stretchier, it will absorb some of its own moisture and becomes less sticky.

● The goal is a smooth and elastic ball of dough that feels silky.

EQUIPMENT FOR YEAST BREADS

- Shiny metal rimless baking sheets
- Instant-read thermometer
- Shiny metal loaf pans: 8- x 4-inch (1.5 L) and 9- x 5-inch (2 L)
- Pizza pan: 14-inch (35 cm)
- Springform pan: 10-inch (3 L)
- Straight-sided shiny metal cake pan: 13- x 9-inch (3.5 L)
- Wooden rolling pin
- Pizza cutter
- Stand mixer with dough hook (optional)
- Bread machine (optional)

❯ The First Rise and Forced Fall

- With butter, grease a bowl large enough to hold double the quantity of dough. Add the dough, turn to grease all over. This film of fat prevents a skin from forming on the dough, which will make the bread streaky.

- The best cover for the bowl is plastic wrap, which holds in moisture.

- Set the bowl in a warm, draft-free spot. It usually takes between one and three hours for dough to double in bulk. Doughs that are rich in eggs and butter or other fat will take the longer time.

- To test whether dough has risen sufficiently, push two fingers into it. If the impression remains after you remove your fingers, move on to the next stage. If not, re-cover the bowl and check at 10-minute intervals until the dough passes the indent test.

- With closed fist, gently press down dough to remove air. Pull dough from side of bowl, turning over and forming a ball. This is called "punching down" the dough, but gentle pressure is better than a rough punch. Ideally, cover and let dough rest for 10 minutes before shaping.

❯ Shaping

- If at any time the dough becomes too elastic and resists rolling or shaping, cover and let rest for a few minutes before continuing.
- Depending on the recipe, shape dough into loaf, buns or free-form round or oval.
- To shape a sandwich-style loaf, gently pull dough into rectangle, one side as long as the loaf pan, the other slightly longer. Starting at narrow end, roll tightly to form cylinder. Pinch seam and ends firmly to seal. Place, seam side down, in greased pan.
- For free-form loaves, dust baking sheet with cornmeal or grease before shaping.

❯ The Second Rise

Cover the shaped dough with a clean tea towel and let rise in a warm spot away from drafts until doubled in bulk. This usually takes less time than the first rise.

❯ Glazing and Slashing

- For a shiny crust, beat 1 egg or egg yolk with 1 tbsp (15 mL) water, or use milk instead. With a gentle touch, brush over risen bread or rolls. Sprinkle with seeds, grains, herbs or salt as recipe directs or as you like.
- For an artisanal granary touch, omit the glaze and generously dust the surface of the loaf with the same flour used in the recipe.
- For a decorative top, use a very sharp blade to make ½-inch (1 cm) deep slashes in the surface of the dough, stopping the cuts 1 inch (2.5 cm) from the edge of the pan or the base of the loaf. For a loaf, this can be as simple as a single end-to-end slash or as complex as a crisscross pattern or a six-point crown.

> Baking

● Bake in centre of preheated oven; the temperature will vary depending on the recipe you're making.

● For rolls, the preferred method is one pan in the centre of the oven. However, you can bake two pans at the same time, placing one each on the racks just above and below the centre rack position. This method works reliably, especially when you switch and rotate the pans halfway through baking.

● To test for doneness, invert the bread onto a rack and tap the bottom gently. It should sound hollow. To guarantee doneness, you can use an instant-read thermometer. Insert it into the centre of the bread; the loaf is ready if the thermometer registers 200°F (93°C), or 215°F (101°C) for especially dense breads such as sourdough. Return underbaked bread to oven and check again in 5 to 10 minutes.

● For pizza, choose the lowest rack position.

> Cooling and Storing

● It is crucial to remove bread from the pan and transfer it to a rack as soon as it comes out of the oven. Otherwise, steam builds up between the bread and the pan, and the crust gets soggy.

● Always let bread cool completely before slicing, or before enclosing it in a paper or plastic bag to eat later. Make sure you eat it within a few days.

● For longer storage, freeze yeast breads. Enclose them within two airtight layers. This can be a combination of any of the following: quality plastic wrap, heavy-duty foil or airtight containers, including freezer bags. We recommend freezing bread for no longer than one month. Undo wrapping slightly to let moisture escape and thaw at room temperature.

Crusty Crown Loaf

This bread dough is incredibly versatile. Make it plain or the delicious seedy variation, or shape into sandwich or dinner rolls. The interior is beautifully tender and even, but the crust is crackled and crisp.

Pinch	granulated sugar	Pinch	4½ cups	all-purpose flour (approx)	1.125 L
¾ cup	warm water	175 mL	2 tsp	salt	10 mL
2½ tsp	active dry yeast	12 mL		Cornmeal	
¾ cup	warm milk	175 mL			
¼ cup	olive oil	50 mL			

DUSTING THE WORK SURFACE

❯ You don't have to get out more flour when you're ready to dust your work surface before kneading – just use some of the remaining flour you've measured out.

❧ In large bowl, dissolve sugar in warm water. Sprinkle in yeast; let stand until frothy, about 10 minutes. Stir in milk and oil. Stir in 3¾ cups (925 mL) of the flour and salt to form shaggy, moist dough.

❧ Turn out onto lightly floured surface. Knead, dusting with as much of the remaining flour as necessary to prevent sticking, until smooth and elastic, about 8 minutes. Form into ball; place in greased bowl, turning to grease all over. Cover with plastic wrap; let rise in warm place until doubled in bulk, 1½ to 2 hours.

❧ Dust rimless baking sheet with cornmeal; set aside.

❧ Punch down dough; form into ball. Place on prepared pan; cover with damp clean tea towel and let rise in warm place until not quite doubled in bulk, about 1 hour.

❧ Spray loaf with water. With sharp knife, cut three ½-inch (1 cm) deep intersecting slashes across top of loaf. Bake in centre of 450°F (230°C) oven for 10 minutes, spraying loaf 3 more times with water. Reduce heat to 400°F (200°C); bake until instant-read thermometer registers 195°F to 200°F (90°C to 100°C) and loaf is golden and sounds hollow when tapped on bottom, about 40 minutes. Transfer to rack; let cool.

Makes 1 loaf, 16 slices. | PER SLICE: about 165 cal, 4 g pro, 4 g total fat (1 g sat. fat), 28 g carb, 1 g fibre, 1 mg chol, 293 mg sodium. % RDI: 2% calcium, 13% iron, 1% vit A, 40% folate.

VARIATIONS

Seedy Crusty Crown Loaf: Reduce flour to 3¾ cups (925 mL). Knead ¼ cup (50 mL) each poppy seeds and lightly toasted sesame seeds into dough before first rise. Sprinkle loaf with 1 tbsp (15 mL) each raw sesame seeds and poppy seeds before slashing.

Crusty Sandwich or Dinner Rolls: Make dough as directed for Crusty Crown Loaf or Seedy Crusty Crown Loaf through to end of first rise.

❧ Grease 2 rimless baking sheets; set aside. Punch down dough. Divide into 8 pieces for sandwich rolls, 16 pieces for dinner rolls. Shape each into ball, stretching and pinching dough underneath to smooth tops; place, seam side down, on prepared pans. Cover with damp clean tea towel; let rise in warm place until not quite doubled in bulk, about 45 minutes. Whisk 1 egg with 1 tbsp (15 mL) water; brush over rolls.

↪ Bake in centre of 400°F (200°C) oven until golden and rolls sound hollow when tapped on bottoms, about 20 minutes for dinner rolls, 25 minutes for sandwich rolls. Transfer to rack; let cool. Makes 8 sandwich or 16 dinner rolls.

Whole Wheat Sourdough Bread

Although it's not a last-minute project – the starter and the bread need time to develop the distinctive tangy taste – this crusty, chewy loaf is actually easy to make and well worth the time.

Half	batch Sourdough Starter (recipe, opposite)	Half	1¾ cups	whole wheat bread flour	425 mL
1 cup	warm water	250 mL	2 tsp	salt	10 mL
2 cups	white bread flour (approx)	500 mL	1 tbsp	cornmeal	15 mL
			1	egg	1

In large bowl, combine sourdough starter with ¾ cup (175 mL) of the warm water; stir until smooth. With wooden spoon, beat in 1½ cups (375 mL) of the white bread flour until smooth. Cover with plastic wrap; let rise at room temperature for at least 12 hours or for up to 24 hours. Stir in remaining water.

Stir in whole wheat bread flour and salt; turn out onto floured surface. Knead, dusting with as much of the remaining white bread flour as necessary to prevent sticking, until smooth and elastic, about 8 minutes. Place in greased bowl, turning to grease all over. Cover with plastic wrap; let rise in warm place until tripled in bulk, about 2 hours.

Dust rimless baking sheet with cornmeal; set aside.

Punch down dough; turn out onto floured surface. Knead about 10 times to remove air bubbles. Cover with clean tea towel; let rest for 10 minutes. Press into ½-inch (1 cm) thick circle. Fold dough 1½ inches (4 cm) down from top, pressing down with hands. Repeat folding, pressing into torpedo-shaped loaf. Pinch seams and ends to seal.

Place loaf, seams side down, on prepared pan. Cover with clean tea towel; let rise until doubled in bulk, about 1½ hours.

Whisk egg with 1 tbsp (15 mL) water; brush over loaf. Using serrated knife, cut ½-inch (1 cm) deep slashes in top. Bake in centre of 425°F (220°C) oven until golden and loaf sounds hollow when tapped on bottom, 35 to 40 minutes. Transfer to rack; let cool.

Makes 1 loaf, 12 slices. | PER SLICE: about 182 cal, 6 g pro, 1 g total fat (0 g sat. fat), 37 g carb, 3 g fibre, 16 mg chol, 390 mg sodium. % RDI: 1% calcium, 14% iron, 1% vit A, 19% folate.

VARIATIONS

White Sourdough Bread: Omit whole wheat bread flour and increase white bread flour to 3¼ cups (800 mL).

Rye Sourdough Bread: Replace whole wheat bread flour with equal amount dark or light rye bread flour.

Boule (round loaf): Line 12-cup (3 L) bowl with clean tea towel. Dust with white bread flour. Shape dough into ball instead of torpedo shape; place, seam side up, in prepared bowl. Let rise as directed. Place, seam side down, on baking sheet; cut crisscross slashes in top.

Sourdough Starter

Before cake and granular yeasts were commercially available, spongy sourdough starter was the leavener that raised bread. If you feed the starter regularly, you can enjoy making sourdough bread for years to come, even sharing it with bread-baking friends and family.

2½ cups	all-purpose flour	625 mL
1 cup	warm water	250 mL
¼ tsp	active dry yeast	1 mL
½ cup	water or milk	125 mL

SOURDOUGH STARTER FEED:

1¼ cups	all-purpose flour	300 mL
¾ cup	water or milk	175 mL

➤ In 8-cup (2 L) container, mix 2 cups (500 mL) of the flour, warm water and yeast. Cover with plastic wrap; let stand at room temperature until tripled in volume, about 8 hours or for up to 24 hours. Refrigerate for 3 days. Stir in water or milk and remaining flour. Cover and refrigerate for 3 more days.

➤ Divide starter in half; place 1 half in large bowl to make bread (recipes, opposite).

➤ **SOURDOUGH STARTER FEED:** To feed the remaining starter, stir in flour and water or milk. Refrigerate for at least 2 days or for up to 1 week. **Note:** Starter must be divided and fed once a week in same manner; if not making bread, dispose of half of the starter and feed remainder.

HOW TO MIX

➤ A heavy-duty stand mixer, fitted with the paddle attachment, can take the work out of the preliminary mixing of the proofed yeast, liquid and some of the dry ingredients. Change to the dough hook when dough becomes too stiff to mix, and use it to do the kneading if you want to save your arm muscles for other tasks.

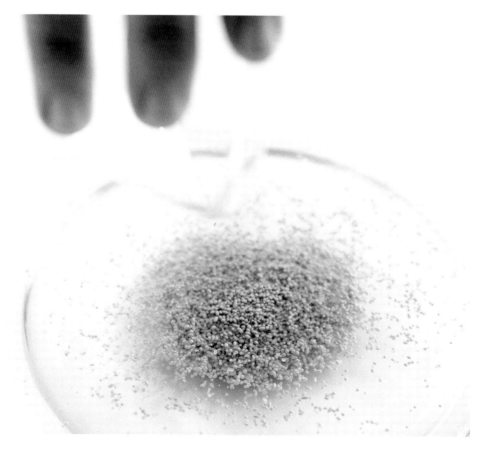

Oats and Molasses Bread

Baking bread from scratch is one of the most satisfying endeavours: kneading the dough, watching it rise, smelling it bake, then slathering a warm slice or two with butter.

STICKY DOUGHS

❯ Doughs containing rye flour, rolled oats, or whole wheat or whole grain flour are stickier than those made with just white wheat flour. If you go overboard with flour on the board while you're kneading, doughs made with these flours will absorb more flour than strictly necessary. The result? A dry loaf. Try kneading in a large bowl for the first few minutes and put up with a little stickiness to avoid adding excess flour.

1¼ cups	boiling water	300 mL
¾ cup	large-flake rolled oats	175 mL
⅓ cup	fancy molasses	75 mL
2 tbsp	butter, softened	25 mL
1	egg, beaten	1
1 tsp	granulated sugar	5 mL
½ cup	warm water	125 mL
1 tbsp	active dry yeast	15 mL

3 cups	all-purpose flour (approx)	750 mL
1 cup	whole wheat flour	250 mL
1¾ tsp	salt	9 mL

TOPPING:

1	egg, beaten	1
2 tbsp	large-flake rolled oats	25 mL

In heatproof bowl, stir boiling water with rolled oats; let stand until water is absorbed, about 15 minutes. Stir in molasses, butter and egg.

Meanwhile, in large bowl, dissolve sugar in warm water. Sprinkle in yeast; let stand until frothy, about 10 minutes. Stir in oat mixture. Stir in 2½ cups (625 mL) of the all-purpose flour, whole wheat flour and salt to form sticky dough.

Turn out onto floured surface. Knead, adding only as much of the remaining flour as necessary to prevent sticking, until smooth and elastic, about 5 minutes. Place in greased bowl, turning to grease all over. Cover with plastic wrap; let rise in warm place until doubled in bulk, about 1 hour.

Grease two 8- x 4-inch (1.5 L) loaf pans; set aside.

Punch down dough; divide in half. On floured surface, pat each half into 11- x 8-inch (28 x 20 cm) rectangle. Starting at narrow end, roll up each into cylinder; pinch edge and ends to seal. Fit, seam side down, into prepared pans. (Or shape each into round, stretching and pinching dough underneath to smooth top. Bake on large greased baking sheet.) Cover with clean tea towel; let rise in warm place until doubled in bulk, about 1 hour.

TOPPING: Brush loaves with egg; sprinkle with oats. Bake in centre of 375°F (190°C) oven until loaves sound hollow when tapped on bottoms, about 40 minutes. Transfer to racks; let cool.

Makes 2 loaves, 12 slices each. | PER SLICE: about 114 cal, 3 g pro, 2 g total fat (1 g sat. fat), 21 g carb, 1 g fibre, 19 mg chol, 185 mg sodium. % RDI: 2% calcium, 10% iron, 2% vit A, 16% folate.

Bread Machine Variation (dough only): Into pan of 2-lb (1 kg) bread machine, place (in order) molasses mixture, water, sugar, salt, all of the all-purpose flour, whole wheat flour and 1¼ tsp (6 mL) bread machine yeast. Choose dough setting. Shape and bake as directed.

Crunchy Crisscross Bread

This rustic loaf is hearty and flavourful, with a mix of different grains, including crunchy millet, which you can find in health food stores, health food sections of supermarkets, or bulk food outlets. Flaxseeds, whole and ground, are an excellent alternative.

DUST OFF YOUR BREAD MACHINE

❯ Use your bread machine to make dough, then shape it by hand and bake in the oven. Dough made in a bread machine tends to be puffier and more voluminous than hand-kneaded dough.

To adapt your favourite recipe for use in the bread machine, first check the maximum amount of flour your machine will hold. Adjust the recipe accordingly and do not exceed that amount.

Have all ingredients at room temperature, adding them to the pan in the order suggested. Always make sure the yeast is on top.

Open the lid and look at the dough as it begins its first mix and knead. If it is too dry and firm, and if the machine is straining, add a little liquid, a few drops or small spoonfuls at a time, until the dough is smooth and the machine is working normally. Similarly, if the dough is too wet, add a touch more flour near the end of kneading.

½ tsp	granulated sugar	2 mL		2½ cups	all-purpose flour (approx)	625 mL
1 cup	warm water	250 mL		¾ cup	whole wheat flour	175 mL
2 tsp	active dry yeast	10 mL		¼ cup	quick-cooking rolled oats	50 mL
2 tbsp	liquid honey	25 mL		¼ cup	each cornmeal and natural bran	50 mL
2 tbsp	butter, melted	25 mL		¼ cup	millet or sesame seeds	50 mL
1	egg	1		1 tsp	salt	5 mL

In large bowl, dissolve sugar in warm water. Sprinkle in yeast; let stand until frothy, 10 minutes. Whisk in honey, butter and egg. With wooden spoon, stir in 2 cups (500 mL) of the all-purpose flour, whole wheat flour, oats, cornmeal, bran, millet and salt until smooth. Gradually stir in enough of the remaining flour to form slightly sticky dough.

Turn out onto floured surface; knead, dusting with as much of the remaining flour as necessary to prevent sticking, until smooth and elastic, 8 to 10 minutes. Place in greased bowl, turning to grease all over. Cover with plastic wrap; let rise in warm place until doubled in bulk, about 1½ hours.

Grease rimless baking sheet; set aside.

Punch down dough; turn out onto floured surface. Knead into round loaf, stretching dough down all around and pinching underneath. Dust top with flour; place on pan. Cover with clean tea towel; let rise in warm place until doubled in bulk, 45 to 60 minutes.

Using serrated knife, slash shallow grid pattern on top of loaf. Bake in centre of 375°F (190°C) oven until golden and loaf sounds hollow when tapped on bottom, about 45 minutes. Transfer to rack; let cool.

Makes 1 loaf, 24 slices. | PER SLICE: about 113 cal, 3 g pro, 2 g total fat (1 g sat. fat), 21 g carb, 2 g fibre, 12 mg chol, 109 mg sodium. % RDI: 1% calcium, 8% iron, 1% vit A, 10% folate.

Bread Machine Variation (dough only): Into pan of 2-lb (1 kg) bread machine, place (in order) water, sugar, salt, honey, butter, beaten egg, all of the all-purpose and whole wheat flours, oats, cornmeal, bran, millet and yeast. Choose dough setting. Shape; bake as directed.

VARIATION

Crisscross Flax Bread: Omit bran. Replace cornmeal with ¼ cup (50 mL) ground flaxseeds; replace millet with ¼ cup (50 mL) whole flaxseeds. Increase second rise time to 60 to 75 minutes. Bake as directed.

Hazelnut Honey Bread

This rustic baguette is called *pain aux noix* in France. It begins with a soupy, fermented yeast, flour and water starter, called a *poolish*, which develops its distinctive tanginess. Spraying the oven with water creates steam, which adds an artisan-style crust.

½ cup	warm water	125 mL
¾ tsp	active dry yeast	4 mL
2½ cups	all-purpose flour (approx)	625 mL
1 cup	whole wheat flour	250 mL
¾ cup	each sliced and finely chopped hazelnuts	175 mL
½ cup	milk	125 mL

⅓ cup	liquid honey	75 mL
2 tbsp	butter, melted	25 mL
2 tsp	salt	10 mL
STARTER:		
¾ tsp	active dry yeast	4 mL
½ cup	warm water	125 mL
¾ cup	all-purpose flour	175 mL

SALT CONTENT

> Resist the temptation to play around with the amount of salt in a bread recipe. Salt is necessary for taste, and it plays a key role in encouraging the formation of gluten, which, in turn, regulates the yeast.

❧ **STARTER:** In bowl, sprinkle yeast over warm water; let stand for 1 minute. Stir with wooden spoon until yeast is dissolved. Add flour; stir until smooth, about 2 minutes. Cover with plastic wrap; let stand in warm place until bubbly and doubled in bulk, about 4 hours.

❧ Pour warm water into large bowl. Sprinkle in yeast; let stand for 1 minute. Stir with wooden spoon until dissolved. Stir starter and scrape into yeast mixture. Add 2 cups (500 mL) of the all-purpose flour, whole wheat flour, sliced and chopped hazelnuts, milk, ¼ cup (50 mL) of the honey, butter and salt; stir until soft ragged dough forms.

❧ Turn out onto floured surface; knead, dusting with as much of the remaining flour as necessary to prevent sticking, until smooth and elastic, about 10 minutes. Place in greased bowl, turning to grease all over. Cover with plastic wrap; let rise in warm place until doubled in bulk, 1½ to 2 hours.

❧ Line large rimless baking sheet with parchment paper or grease; set aside.

❧ Punch down dough; turn out onto lightly floured surface. Knead into ball. Divide in half; shape each into ball. Gently pull each into 11- x 8-inch (28 x 20 cm) rectangle. Starting at narrow end, diagonally roll up each into cylinder; pinch along bottoms and ends to seal. Transfer to prepared baking sheet, seam sides down and spaced well apart. Using serrated knife, cut 3 diagonal slashes in top of each loaf. Cover with clean tea towel; let rise until doubled in bulk, about 1 hour.

❧ Stir remaining honey with 1 tbsp (15 mL) warm water; brush over loaves. Place baking sheet in centre of 400°F (200°C) oven. With cold water, spray walls and floor of oven (avoiding oven light bulb) until steam fills oven, 10 seconds. Quickly close oven door to trap steam; wait for 5 minutes, then repeat spraying. Bake until loaves are golden and sound hollow when tapped on bottoms, 25 to 30 minutes. Transfer to rack; let cool.

Makes 2 loaves, 16 slices each. | PER SLICE: about 112 cal, 3 g pro, 4 g total fat (1 g sat. fat), 16 g carb, 1 g fibre, 3 mg chol, 153 mg sodium. % RDI: 1% calcium, 7% iron, 1% vit A, 12% folate.

Gunn's Cheese Onion Buns

It's a rare customer who goes into Gunn's, one of Winnipeg's most durable Jewish bakeries, and doesn't come out with more items than were on the shopping list – such as these scrumptious melt-in-the-mouth buns.

⅓ cup	granulated sugar	75 mL
1⅓ cups	warm milk	325 mL
2 tsp	active dry yeast	10 mL
2	eggs	2
¼ cup	vegetable oil	50 mL
1½ tsp	salt	7 mL
4½ cups	all-purpose flour (approx)	1.125 L
4 tsp	butter, melted	20 mL
2 cups	shredded old Cheddar cheese	500 mL
2 tbsp	poppy seeds	25 mL
1	small onion, thinly sliced	1
¼ cup	mayonnaise	50 mL

❧ In small bowl, dissolve 4 tsp (20 mL) of the sugar in warm milk. Sprinkle in yeast; let stand until frothy, about 10 minutes.

❧ Meanwhile, in large bowl and using electric mixer, beat eggs. Remove 2 tbsp (25 mL) of the beaten egg; reserve in small airtight container in refrigerator. Add remaining sugar to beaten eggs in bowl; beat until thick and pale yellow, about 2 minutes. Stir in yeast mixture, oil and salt. With wooden spoon, stir in enough of the flour to make firm, slightly sticky dough.

❧ Turn out onto lightly floured surface; knead, adding as much of the remaining flour as necessary to prevent sticking, until smooth and elastic, 10 to 12 minutes. Place in greased bowl, turning to grease all over. Cover with plastic wrap; let rise in warm place until doubled in bulk, about 2 hours.

❧ Line 2 rimmed baking sheets with parchment paper; set aside.

❧ Punch down dough; turn out onto lightly floured surface. Divide in half. Roll out each half into 12- x 8-inch (30 x 20 cm) rectangle. Brush each with half of the melted butter, leaving ½-inch (1 cm) border uncovered; sprinkle each with half each of the cheese and poppy seeds. Brush edges lightly with reserved beaten egg.

❧ Starting at long side, roll up; pinch seam to seal. Cut into 2-inch (5 cm) thick slices; place, about 2 inches (5 cm) apart, on prepared pans. Press to flatten to 1-inch (2.5 cm) thickness. Cover with clean tea towel and let rise in warm place until doubled in bulk, 1½ to 2 hours.

❧ Brush lightly with reserved beaten eggs; sprinkle with onion. Top each with 1 tsp (5 mL) mayonnaise. Bake in top and bottom thirds of 375°F (190°C) oven, switching and rotating pans halfway through, until golden and buns sound hollow when tapped on bottoms, 25 to 30 minutes. Transfer to rack; let cool.

Makes 12 large buns. | PER BUN: about 390 cal, 12 g pro, 18 g total fat (6 g sat. fat), 44 g carb, 2 g fibre, 58 mg chol, 462 mg sodium. % RDI: 18% calcium, 19% iron, 9% vit A, 55% folate.

Whole Wheat Hamburger Buns

What better way to show off Canada's top-quality hard wheat than in large buns for hamburgers or more petite rolls for dinner?

1¼ cups	milk	300 mL		2 cups	whole wheat flour	500 mL
3 tbsp	liquid honey	50 mL		2 cups	all-purpose flour (approx)	500 mL
2 tbsp	vegetable oil	25 mL				
1½ tsp	salt	7 mL		¼ cup	sunflower seeds or flaxseeds	50 mL
¼ cup	warm water	50 mL				
1	pkg instant dry yeast (or 2¼ tsp/11 mL)	1		1	egg yolk	1

❧ In small saucepan, heat together milk, all but 1 tsp (5 mL) of the honey, the oil, and salt until honey is melted; let cool to lukewarm.

❧ Meanwhile, in large bowl, dissolve remaining honey in warm water. Sprinkle in yeast; let stand until frothy, about 10 minutes. Whisk in milk mixture. Stir in all of the whole wheat flour, 1½ cups (375 mL) of the all-purpose flour and 2 tbsp (25 mL) of the sunflower seeds to form soft, sticky dough.

❧ Turn out onto lightly floured surface; knead, adding as much of the remaining flour as necessary to prevent sticking, until smooth and elastic, about 10 minutes. Place in greased bowl, turning to grease all over. Cover with plastic wrap; let rise in warm place until doubled in bulk, about 1 hour.

❧ Line rimless baking sheet with parchment paper or grease; set aside.

❧ Punch down dough; turn out onto floured surface. Roll into log; divide into 8 pieces. Shape each into ball, stretching and pinching dough underneath to smooth tops. Place, 2 inches (5 cm) apart, on prepared pan; let rest for 5 minutes. Flatten to 1-inch (2.5 cm) thickness. Cover and let rise in warm place for 20 minutes. Flatten and press buns to 4-inch (10 cm) diameter; cover and let rise for 25 to 30 minutes.

❧ Whisk egg yolk with 1 tbsp (15 mL) water; without pressing, brush over tops. Sprinkle with remaining sunflower seeds. Bake in centre of 375°F (190°C) oven until golden and buns sound hollow when tapped on bottoms, 20 minutes. Transfer to rack; let cool. (Make-ahead: Wrap each in plastic wrap; freeze in airtight containers for up to 1 month.)

Makes 8 buns. | PER BUN: about 324 cal, 10 g pro, 8 g total fat (1 g sat. fat), 55 g carb, 6 g fibre, 28 mg chol, 453 mg sodium. % RDI: 6% calcium, 23% iron, 3% vit A, 39% folate.

VARIATION

Whole Wheat Dinner Rolls with Sunflower Seeds: Divide log into 12 pieces; shape as directed but do not flatten. Let rise until doubled in bulk, 30 to 45 minutes. Bake as directed, reducing baking time to about 15 minutes.

Soft Pretzels

These large pretzels pair up perfectly with mustard, wurst and a stein of your favourite ale. Enjoy them fresh; better still, warm from the oven, as they stale quickly.

SHAPING SOFT PRETZELS

The final move is to cross ends to opposite side of circle. Start with the end on the left in the photo.

1 tsp	granulated sugar	5 mL
1½ cups	warm water	375 mL
1	pkg active dry yeast (or 2¼ tsp/11 mL)	1
2 tsp	vegetable oil	10 mL
4 cups	all-purpose flour (approx)	1 L

1 tsp	salt	5 mL
2 tbsp	baking soda	25 mL
TOPPING:		
1	egg, beaten	1
2 tsp	coarse salt	10 mL

In large bowl, dissolve sugar in ¼ cup (50 mL) of the warm water. Sprinkle in yeast; let stand until frothy, about 10 minutes. Stir in remaining water and oil. Stir in 3 cups (750 mL) of the flour and salt to make sticky dough.

Turn out onto lightly floured surface; knead, adding as much of the remaining flour as necessary to make firm dough, until smooth and elastic, about 10 minutes. Place in greased bowl, turning to grease all over. Cover with plastic wrap; let rise in warm place until doubled in bulk, about 1 hour.

Line 2 rimless baking sheets with parchment paper or grease; set aside.

Punch down dough. Cut into 8 pieces. On lightly floured surface, roll each piece into 20-inch (50 cm) rope. Form into circle, crossing left end over right end above circle, 3 inches (8 cm) from ends. Pick up ends and cross left end over right end again. Lift ends to opposite side of circle, overlapping circle by ¼ inch (5 mm) to create pretzel shape; press to seal. Place on prepared pans. Cover with clean tea towel; let rise in warm place for 15 minutes.

Add baking soda to large wide shallow saucepan of boiling water. Boil pretzels, 3 at a time, turning over once with slotted spatula, until puffed and set, about 1 minute. Using spatula, transfer to rack; let cool.

TOPPING: Return 4 pretzels to each prepared pan. Brush with egg; sprinkle with salt. Bake in top and bottom thirds of 400°F (200°C) oven, switching and rotating pans halfway through, until golden and pretzels sound hollow when tapped on bottoms, 25 to 30 minutes. Transfer to rack; let cool just until warm. **(Make-ahead: Let cool. Wrap each in plastic wrap and freeze in airtight container for up to 2 weeks. Reheat to serve.)**

Makes 8 large pretzels. | PER PRETZEL: about 252 cal, 8 g pro, 2 g total fat (trace sat. fat), 49 g carb, 2 g fibre, 23 mg chol, 684 mg sodium. % RDI: 1% calcium, 22% iron, 1% vit A, 70% folate.

Multigrain Loaf

This loaf, with its lovely wheaty flavour, even crumb and rustic artisanal look, will make even novices into confirmed bread bakers. You do have to begin the day before to mix the flour, water and yeast starter, but all three loaves – multigrain, whole wheat and white – are worth it. For all three, we used Robin Hood Best for Bread flours.

4 cups	multigrain bread flour	1 L		1 cup	warm water	250 mL
1 cup	warm water	250 mL		1½ tsp	active dry yeast	7 mL
2 tbsp	buckwheat honey	25 mL		1 cup	multigrain bread flour	250 mL
1½ tsp	fine sea salt	7 mL		**TOPPING:**		
STARTER:				½ tsp	multigrain bread flour	2 mL
1 tsp	granulated sugar	5 mL				

❧**STARTER:** In large bowl, dissolve sugar in warm water. Sprinkle in yeast; let stand until frothy, about 10 minutes. Stir in flour, stirring until mixture is consistency of thick pancake batter, about 2 minutes. Cover with plastic wrap; let stand in warm place until bubbly and puffy, and wheaty aroma develops, 8 to 12 hours.

❧ Stir in 3¼ cups (800 mL) of the flour, warm water, honey and salt to make soft sticky dough.

❧ Turn out onto generously floured surface; knead, dusting with as much of the remaining flour as necessary to prevent sticking, until smooth and elastic, about 8 minutes. Form into ball; place in greased bowl, turning to grease all over. Cover with plastic wrap; let rise in warm place until doubled in bulk, 1 to 1½ hours.

❧ Grease 9- x 5-inch (2 L) loaf pan; set aside.

❧ Punch down dough. Shape into ball; cover and let rest for 10 minutes. Press into 11- x 8-inch (28 x 20 cm) rectangle. Starting at short end, roll up into cylinder; pinch along bottom and ends to seal. Fit, seam side down, into prepared pan. Cover with clean tea towel and let rise in warm place until doubled in bulk, 1 to 1½ hours.

❧**TOPPING:** Dust top of loaf with flour. Slash top lengthwise down centre, starting and ending about 1 inch (2.5 cm) from edges of pan. Bake in centre of 375°F (190°C) oven until instant-read thermometer registers 215°F (101°C) and loaf is golden and sounds hollow when tapped on bottom, 50 to 60 minutes. Transfer to rack; let cool.

Makes 1 loaf, 12 slices. | PER SLICE: about 219 cal, 8 g pro, 1 g total fat (trace sat. fat), 45 g carb, 4 g fibre, 0 mg chol, 290 mg sodium. % RDI: 2% calcium, 19% iron, 2% vit C, 11% folate.

VARIATIONS

Unbleached White Loaf: Replace multigrain bread flour with unbleached white bread flour. Replace buckwheat honey with mild liquid honey.

Whole Wheat Loaf: Replace multigrain bread flour with whole wheat bread flour.

IDEAL BREAD PANS
❯ Choose shiny, heavy bread or loaf pans for a crisp, lighter crust. Darker pans, especially nonstick ones, absorb more heat and darken crusts excessively.

Frangipane Buns

Frangipane is a sweet almond paste as rich and seductive as the cinnamon filling in Gooey Cinnamon Buns (recipe, page 235).

	Sweet Yeast Dough (recipe, page 232)	
FRANGIPANE:		
1 cup	whole unblanched almonds	250 mL
⅓ cup	granulated sugar	75 mL
1 tbsp	all-purpose flour	15 mL
¼ cup	butter, softened	50 mL

1	egg	1
¾ tsp	almond extract	4 mL
TOPPING:		
1	egg, beaten	1
¼ cup	sliced almonds	50 mL
1 tbsp	icing sugar	15 mL

❧ Line 13- x 9-inch (3.5 L) metal cake pan with double layer of parchment paper; set aside.

❧ **FRANGIPANE:** In food processor, finely chop almonds. Add sugar and flour; pulse until combined. Add butter, egg and almond extract; pulse until smooth and pasty, about 30 seconds. Transfer to bowl. **(Make-ahead: Cover and refrigerate for up to 1 day.)**

❧ Punch down Sweet Yeast Dough. On lightly floured surface, roll out into 18- x 14-inch (45 x 35 cm) rectangle. Leaving 1-inch (2.5 cm) border, spread frangipane evenly over dough, mounding slightly on 1 long side. Starting with mounded side, tightly roll up; pinch seam to seal.

❧ With serrated knife, cut roll into 12 slices. Arrange, cut side up, in prepared pan. **(Make-ahead: Cover with plastic wrap and refrigerate for up to 12 hours. Loosen wrap and let come to room temperature before continuing, about 1 hour.)** Cover with clean tea towel; let rise in warm place until doubled in bulk, about 45 minutes.

❧ **TOPPING:** Brush with egg; sprinkle with almonds. Bake in centre of 375°F (190°C) oven until golden and rolls sound hollow when tapped on bottoms, 20 to 25 minutes. Let cool in pan on rack for 5 minutes. Transfer to rack; let cool. Dust with icing sugar. **(Make-ahead: Wrap in plastic wrap and overwrap in heavy-duty foil; freeze for up to 3 weeks.)**

Makes 12 buns. | PER BUN: about 374 cal, 10 g pro, 17 g total fat (6 g sat. fat), 46 g carb, 3 g fibre, 83 mg chol, 275 mg sodium. % RDI: 5% calcium, 20% iron, 9% vit A, 52% folate.

Sweet Yeast Dough

Making the dough in a bread machine makes it slightly puffier than dough made by hand. But it is effortless and convenient. A stand mixer with dough hook is almost as hands-off as the bread machine but does require tending.

THE RIGHT TEMPERATURE

❯ Bring eggs to room temperature before adding to yeast mixture.

½ cup	milk	125 mL	1	pkg active dry yeast (or 2¼ tsp/11 mL)	1
¼ cup	granulated sugar	50 mL	2	eggs	2
¼ cup	butter	50 mL	4 cups	all-purpose flour (approx)	1 L
1 tsp	salt	5 mL			
¼ cup	warm water	50 mL			

❧ In small saucepan, heat together milk, all but 2 tsp (10 mL) of the sugar, the butter and salt until butter is melted; let cool to lukewarm.

❧ Meanwhile, in large bowl, dissolve remaining sugar in warm water. Sprinkle in yeast; let stand until frothy, about 10 minutes. Whisk in milk mixture along with eggs. Stir in 3¼ cups (800 mL) of the flour, about 1 cup (250 mL) at a time, to form soft shaggy dough.

❧ Turn out onto lightly floured surface; knead, adding as much of the remaining flour as necessary to prevent sticking, until smooth and elastic, about 10 minutes.

❧ Place in large greased bowl, turning to grease all over. Cover with plastic wrap; let rise in warm place until doubled in bulk, about 1½ hours.

Makes 2 lb (1 kg).

Bread Machine Variation (dough only): Into pan of 2-lb (1 kg) bread machine add (in order) water, milk, beaten eggs, melted butter, sugar, salt, all of the flour and bread machine yeast. Choose dough setting. Shape and bake as directed.

Stand Mixer Variation (dough only): In mixer bowl, prepare yeast mixture; let stand until frothy, about 10 minutes. With paddle attachment, stir in milk mixture, eggs and 3½ cups (875 mL) of the flour to make soft, sticky dough. With dough hook, mix on low speed for 8 minutes, scraping down bowl halfway through and adding enough of the remaining flour to make dough smooth and elastic.

Chocolate Cranberry Twist

While not quite the extreme bread of yeast baking, this spectacular twisted round does take time, and it is wise to reserve enough of it to enjoy the process. The sweet dough is so easy to work with.

⅓ cup	corn syrup	75 mL
¼ cup	packed brown sugar	50 mL
¾ cup	dried cranberries, dried sour cherries or raisins	175 mL
⅔ cup	chocolate chips	150 mL
⅓ cup	chopped pecans	75 mL
	Sweet Yeast Dough (recipe, opposite)	

1 tsp	cinnamon	5 mL
GLAZE:		
1	egg	1
ICING:		
¼ cup	icing sugar	50 mL
2 tsp	milk	10 mL
2 tsp	butter, melted	10 mL

❧ Grease 10-inch (3 L) springform pan; set aside.

❧ In bowl, mix corn syrup with brown sugar; stir in cranberries, chocolate chips and pecans. Punch down Sweet Yeast Dough; turn out onto lightly floured surface. Roll out into 18- x 11-inch (45 x 28 cm) rectangle. Spread filling over dough, pressing into surface; sprinkle with cinnamon.

❧ Starting at long edge, tightly roll up; pinch seam to seal. Place, seam side down, on work surface; cut in half lengthwise. Keeping cut sides up, twist halves together; place in prepared pan, shaping into ring. Pinch ends together to seal. Cover with clean tea towel; let rise in warm place until doubled in bulk, about 1 hour.

❧ GLAZE: Beat egg; brush over wreath. Bake in centre of 350°F (180°C) oven until golden, about 35 minutes. Run knife around edge of pan; transfer to rack. Let cool.

❧ ICING: Mix together icing sugar, milk and butter; drizzle over wreath. (**Make-ahead: Store in airtight container at room temperature for up to 1 day.**)

Makes 1 loaf, 16 slices. | PER SLICE: about 282 cal, 5 g pro, 9 g total fat (4 g sat. fat), 46 g carb, 2 g fibre, 50 mg chol, 202 mg sodium. % RDI: 3% calcium, 16% iron, 5% vit A, 2% vit C, 12% folate.

SHAPING A TWISTED WREATH

It's an act of faith to cut the dough all the way through; there is the worrisome danger of losing the filling.

If you keep the cut side up, especially when twisting, the filling will remain intact.

Support the dough as you arrange it in pan. Stretch if needed as you ease the two ends together. Pinch ends to seal.

Chocolate Cinnamon Buns

A rich chocolate dough and chocolate chunks in the cinnamon swirl turn this surprising twist on a classic into an even more irresistible treat. If you're more of a traditionalist, try the tried-and-true Gooey Cinnamon Buns variation that follows.

BLENDING COCOA WITH FLOUR

❯ Whenever cocoa powder and flour are combined, they need to be well blended. Use a sieve, flour sifter or whisk to combine, repeating the process, if necessary, until no streaks remain.

SWEET ICING

❯ Although it could be considered overkill, you can drizzle icing over the buns. Whisk 1 cup (250 mL) icing sugar with 3 tbsp (50 mL) milk or water until smooth; drizzle over buns once they have cooled (or else the icing will simply melt).

½ cup	milk	125 mL
¼ cup	granulated sugar	50 mL
¼ cup	butter	50 mL
1 tsp	salt	5 mL
½ cup	warm water	125 mL
1 tbsp	active dry yeast	15 mL
2	eggs	2
3½ cups	all-purpose flour (approx)	875 mL
½ cup	cocoa powder	125 mL

FILLING:		
¾ cup	butter	175 mL
1 cup	packed brown sugar	250 mL
½ cup	corn syrup	125 mL
¾ cup	chopped walnut or pecan halves	175 mL
6 oz	bittersweet chocolate, chopped	175 g
1 tbsp	cinnamon	15 mL

❧ In small saucepan, heat together milk, all but 1 tsp (5 mL) of the sugar, the butter and salt until butter is melted; let cool to lukewarm.

❧ Meanwhile, in large bowl, dissolve remaining sugar in warm water. Sprinkle in yeast; let stand until frothy, about 10 minutes. Whisk in milk mixture along with eggs.

❧ Into separate bowl, sift flour with cocoa powder; sift again. With electric mixer, gradually beat 1½ cups (375 mL) of the flour mixture into egg mixture; beat for 2 minutes. Stir in enough of the remaining flour mixture to make soft slightly sticky dough that comes away from side of bowl.

❧ Lightly sprinkle some of the remaining flour mixture onto work surface; turn out dough. Knead, sprinkling with as much of the remaining flour mixture as necessary to prevent sticking, until smooth and elastic, about 10 minutes. Place in large greased bowl, turning to grease all over. Cover with plastic wrap; let rise in warm place until doubled in bulk, 1 to 1½ hours.

❧ Grease 13- x 9-inch (3 L) glass baking dish; set aside.

❧ FILLING: In saucepan, melt butter over medium heat; remove 2 tbsp (25 mL) and set aside. Add ¼ cup (50 mL) of the sugar and the corn syrup to pan; heat until sugar is dissolved. Pour into prepared baking dish. Combine remaining sugar, walnuts, chocolate and cinnamon; set aside.

❧ Punch down dough; turn out onto lightly floured surface. Roll out into 18- x 14-inch (45 x 35 cm) rectangle. Brush with reserved butter, leaving ½-inch (1 cm) border uncovered; sprinkle with sugar mixture. Starting at long side, tightly roll up, pinching seam to seal. With serrated knife, cut into 15 pieces; place, cut side down, in baking dish. Cover with clean tea towel and let rise until doubled in bulk, about 1 hour.

❧ Bake in centre of 375°F (190°C) oven until tops sound hollow when tapped, about 25 minutes. Let stand for 3 minutes. Place flat serving tray over dish. Wearing oven mitts, grasp dish and tray; turn over. Lift off pan, scraping out remaining filling to drizzle over buns. **(Make-ahead: Let cool. Cover and store for up to 1 day. Rewarm in 350°F/180°C oven for about 10 minutes.)**

Makes 15 buns. | PER BUN: about 437 cal, 7 g pro, 24 g total fat (12 g sat. fat), 55 g carb, 4 g fibre, 64 mg chol, 313 mg sodium. % RDI: 5% calcium, 24% iron, 13% vit A, 30% folate.

....

VARIATION

Gooey Cinnamon Buns: Make dough as directed, replacing cocoa powder with ½ cup (125 mL) all-purpose flour. Whisk dry ingredients together instead of sifting. Omit filling.
❧ FILLING: In saucepan over medium heat, melt ¾ cup (175 mL) butter with ¾ cup (175 mL) packed brown sugar; whisk until sugar is dissolved. Pour into prepared baking dish; sprinkle with ½ cup (125 mL) coarsely chopped pecans. Melt additional ¼ cup (50 mL) butter; set aside. Combine additional ¾ cup (175 mL) packed brown sugar, ½ cup (125 mL) coarsely chopped pecan halves and 1 tbsp (15 mL) cinnamon.
❧ Roll out dough as directed. Brush with all but 2 tbsp (25 mL) of the melted butter, leaving ½-inch (1 cm) border; sprinkle with sugar mixture. Roll up as directed; brush with remaining butter. With serrated knife, cut into 15 pieces; place in baking dish. Let rise, bake and serve as directed.

CINNAMON BUN SECRETS

● The mix of sugar and butter at the bottom of the baking dish becomes the buns' delectable topping.
● The melted butter brushed over the dough holds the dry filling in place.
● Sprinkle filling evenly; your fingers are ideal for this step.
● Roll firmly but without stretching the dough. Use both hands on the roll to keep it even.
● Pinch seam firmly to keep the buns together as you transfer them from work surface to baking dish.

Hot Cross Buns

One a penny, two a penny, hot cross buns. Save a penny and make hot cross buns for everyone who loves the heavenly spice fragrance of this traditional Easter treat.

⅓ cup	granulated sugar	75 mL	1½ tsp	nutmeg	7 mL
¾ cup	milk	175 mL	½ tsp	ground cloves	2 mL
½ cup	butter	125 mL	⅔ cup	dried currants	150 mL
½ tsp	salt	2 mL	½ cup	chopped candied mixed peel	125 mL
¼ cup	warm water	50 mL	**GLAZE:**		
1	pkg active dry yeast (or 2¼ tsp/11 mL)	1	2 tbsp	corn syrup	25 mL
2	eggs	2	1 tbsp	water	15 mL
4¾ cups	all-purpose flour (approx)	1.175 L	**ICING:**		
			1 cup	icing sugar	250 mL
2 tbsp	cinnamon	25 mL	4 tsp	water (approx)	20 mL

❧ In saucepan, heat all but 1 tsp (5 mL) of the sugar, the milk, butter and salt over medium heat until butter is melted; let cool to lukewarm.

❧ Meanwhile, in large bowl, dissolve remaining sugar in warm water. Sprinkle in yeast; let stand until frothy, about 10 minutes. Whisk in milk mixture along with eggs.

❧ In separate bowl, whisk together 4¼ cups (1.05 L) of the flour, cinnamon, nutmeg and cloves. Using electric mixer, beat 1½ cups (375 mL) of the flour mixture into yeast mixture; beat until smooth, about 2 minutes. Using wooden spoon, stir in enough of the remaining flour to make soft, slightly sticky dough.

❧ Turn out onto lightly floured surface; knead, adding as much of the remaining flour mixture as necessary to prevent sticking, until smooth and elastic, about 8 minutes. Place in greased bowl, turning to grease all over. Cover with plastic wrap; let rise in warm place until doubled in bulk, 1½ to 2 hours.

❧ Line large rimless baking sheet with parchment paper or grease; set aside.

❧ Punch down dough; turn out onto lightly floured surface. Knead in currants and peel. Cover with clean tea towel; let rest for 5 minutes. Shape into 16-inch (40 cm) log; with serrated knife, cut into 12 pieces. Shape each into ball, stretching and pinching dough underneath to smooth tops. Place, 2 inches (5 cm) apart, on prepared pan. Flatten with hands to 1-inch (2.5 cm) thickness. Cover with clean tea towel; let rise until doubled in bulk, about 1 hour.

❧ Bake in centre of 375°F (190°C) oven until browned and buns sound hollow when tapped on bottoms, 20 to 25 minutes. Transfer to rack; let cool. **(Make-ahead: Store in airtight container at room temperature for up to 1 day or wrap each and freeze in airtight container for up to 2 weeks.)**

❧ **GLAZE:** In small microwaveable bowl, microwave corn syrup with water at high until boiling, about 30 seconds; brush over buns.

~ICING: Whisk icing sugar with water, adding up to 2 tsp (10 mL) more water if necessary to make thick icing that holds its shape when piped. Using piping bag fitted with round tip or plastic bag with corner snipped, pipe cross on top of each cooled bun.

Makes 12 buns. | PER BUN: about 393 cal, 7 g pro, 10 g total fat (5 g sat. fat), 71 g carb, 3 g fibre, 53 mg chol, 182 mg sodium. % RDI: 5% calcium, 24% iron, 9% vit A, 2% vit C, 56% folate.

Traditional Challah

The Jewish Sabbath meal is traditionally graced with challah – a braided egg bread. For the Jewish New Year, the challah is shaped into a crown, with the addition of raisins as an extra guarantee of a special and lucky year.

BRAIDING CHALLAH

A four-rope braid gives this glossy egg bread a beautiful elegance. Start by securely pinching the ends together. Weave the ropes as described, using the step photos as a guide. Weave the ropes firmly together, without stretching, so there are no gaps between the twists.

2 tsp	granulated sugar	10 mL	2	eggs, lightly beaten	2
½ cup	warm water	125 mL	2	egg yolks	2
1	pkg active dry yeast (or 2¼ tsp/11 mL)	1	¼ cup	butter, melted, or vegetable oil	50 mL
3½ cups	all-purpose flour (approx)	875 mL	¾ cup	golden raisins	175 mL
1 tsp	salt	5 mL	**TOPPING:**		
¼ cup	liquid honey	50 mL	1	egg yolk, lightly beaten	1
			1 tbsp	sesame seeds	15 mL

In large bowl, dissolve sugar in warm water. Sprinkle in yeast; let stand until frothy, about 10 minutes. With wooden spoon, stir in 3 cups (750 mL) of the flour and salt; stir in honey, eggs, egg yolks and butter until soft sticky dough forms.

Turn out onto lightly floured surface; knead, adding as much of the remaining flour as necessary to prevent sticking, until smooth and elastic, about 10 minutes. Place in greased bowl, turning to grease all over. Cover with plastic wrap; let rise in warm place until doubled in bulk, about 1 hour.

Line large rimless baking sheet with parchment paper or grease; set aside.

Punch down dough; knead in raisins. Cover with clean tea towel and let rest for 5 minutes.

TO MAKE BRAID: Divide dough into quarters; roll each into 18-inch (45 cm) rope. Place ropes side by side on prepared pan; pinch together at 1 end. With pinched opposite you, start at pinched end. *Move second rope from left over rope on right. Move far right rope over 2 ropes on left. Move far left rope over 2 ropes on right. Repeat from * until braid is complete; tuck ends under braid and pinch to seal.

TO MAKE CROWN: Roll out dough into 30-inch (76 cm) rope. Holding 1 end in place, wind remaining rope around end to form fairly tight spiral that is slightly higher in centre. Transfer to prepared pan.

Cover braid or crown loaf with damp clean tea towel; let rise in warm place until doubled in bulk, about 1 hour.

TOPPING: Stir egg yolk with 1 tsp (5 mL) water; brush lightly over dough. Sprinkle with sesame seeds. Bake in centre of 350°F (180°C) oven until golden and loaf sounds hollow when tapped on bottom, 35 to 45 minutes. Transfer to rack; let cool.

Makes 1 loaf, 16 slices. | PER SLICE: about 189 cal, 5 g pro, 5 g total fat (2 g sat. fat), 31 g carb, 1 g fibre, 69 mg chol, 175 mg sodium. % RDI: 2% calcium, 12% iron, 5% vit A, 35% folate.

Bread Machine Variation (dough only): Replace active dry yeast with quick-rising (instant) dry yeast. Into pan of 2-lb (1 kg) bread machine, add (in order) water, honey, sugar, butter, eggs, egg yolks, salt, all of the flour and yeast. Choose dough setting. When complete, remove from pan. Knead in raisins; cover with clean tea towel and let rest for 5 minutes. Shape and bake as directed.

MAKING A CROWN

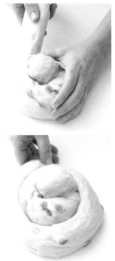

Use one hand to anchor the end of the dough log in centre. Wind log into a fairly tight spiral around centre, keeping centre slightly higher to form crown shape.

Bon Ton Bakery Cinnamon Bread

This swirly cinnamon loaf originated more than 50 years ago at the Bon Ton Bakery in the west end of Edmonton. Test Kitchen Specialist Adell Shneer, a native of Edmonton, is the sleuth who persuaded current Bon Ton owner Hilton Dinner to share the recipe. The best part of each slice is the subject of hot debate: is it the centre swirl or the slightly gooey bottom? That's yours to decide.

⅓ cup	granulated sugar	75 mL	1 tsp	salt	5 mL
1 cup	warm water	250 mL	⅓ cup	butter	75 mL
2½ tsp	active dry yeast	12 mL	FILLING:		
1	egg	1	1 cup	granulated sugar	250 mL
1 tsp	vanilla	5 mL	1 tbsp	cinnamon	15 mL
1 tsp	lemon juice	5 mL	GLAZE:		
3½ cups	white bread flour (approx)	875 mL	1	egg, beaten	1

༈ In large bowl, dissolve 1 tsp (5 mL) of the sugar in warm water. Sprinkle in yeast; let stand until frothy, about 10 minutes. Whisk in egg, vanilla and lemon juice.

༈ In separate bowl, whisk together 3¼ cups (800 mL) of the flour, remaining sugar and salt. Using pastry cutter, cut in butter until in pea-size pieces. Using wooden spoon, stir into yeast mixture to form soft dough.

༈ Turn out onto lightly floured surface. Knead, adding as much of the remaining flour as necessary to prevent sticking, until smooth and elastic, about 8 minutes. Place in greased bowl, turning to grease all over. Cover with plastic wrap; let rise in warm place until doubled in bulk, about 1 hour.

༈ Grease two 8- x 4-inch (1.5 L) loaf pans; set aside.

༈ Punch down dough. Divide in half. On lightly floured surface, roll each half out into 14- x 8-inch (35 x 20 cm) rectangle. Brush with 2 tbsp (25 mL) water, leaving 1-inch (2.5 cm) border along 1 short end.

༈ FILLING: In small bowl, whisk sugar with cinnamon; sprinkle half over each rectangle. Starting at short end without border, roll up jelly roll–style; pinch seams to seal. Fit, seam sides down, into prepared pans. Cover with clean tea towel and let rise in warm place until doubled in bulk, about 1 hour.

༈ GLAZE: Brush egg over loaves. Bake in centre of 375°F (190°C) oven until deep brown and loaves sound hollow when tapped on bottoms, 25 to 30 minutes. Transfer to racks; let cool. **(Make-ahead: Store in airtight container at room temperature for up to 2 days or overwrap in heavy-duty foil and freeze for up to 2 weeks.)**

Makes 2 loaves, 10 to 12 slices each. | PER EACH OF 12 SLICES: about 137 cal, 2 g pro, 3 g total fat (1 g sat. fat), 24 g carb, 1 g fibre, 16 mg chol, 102 mg sodium. % RDI: 1% calcium, 6% iron, 1% vit A, 13% folate.

Rum Raisin Loaf

This is perfect for the start of a special day or to use for French toast for brunch.

1 cup	raisins	250 mL	½ cup	sour cream	125 mL
¼ cup	dark rum	50 mL	1 tsp	vanilla	5 mL
⅓ cup	granulated sugar	75 mL	½ tsp	each grated lemon and orange rind	2 mL
½ cup	warm water	125 mL			
1 tbsp	active dry yeast	15 mL	3¾ cups	all-purpose flour (approx)	925 mL
⅓ cup	butter, melted	75 mL	½ tsp	salt	2 mL
2	eggs	2	1	egg yolk, lightly beaten	1

❧ Place raisins in small microwaveable bowl; pour rum over top. Cover and microwave at high for 1 minute. Let cool.

❧ Meanwhile, in large bowl, dissolve ½ tsp (2 mL) of the sugar in warm water. Sprinkle in yeast; let stand until frothy, about 10 minutes. Whisk in butter and remaining sugar. Whisk in eggs, 1 at a time. Whisk in sour cream, vanilla and lemon and orange rinds until smooth.

❧ Stir in 3 cups (750 mL) of the flour, 1 cup (250 mL) at a time, and salt to form sticky dough. Knead in ½ cup (125 mL) more of the remaining flour. Turn out onto lightly floured surface; knead, adding as much of the remaining flour as necessary to prevent sticking, until smooth and elastic, about 8 minutes. Place in greased bowl, turning to grease all over. Cover with plastic wrap; let rise until doubled in bulk, about 1½ hours.

❧ Grease two 8- x 4-inch (1.5 L) loaf pans; set aside.

❧ Punch down dough; turn out onto lightly floured surface. Drain raisins, reserving rum. Pat raisins dry; knead into dough. Cover with clean tea towel and let rest for 5 minutes.

❧ Divide dough in half. Divide each half into thirds; roll each third into 16-inch (40 cm) rope. Braid ropes together; pinch ends to seal. Place in prepared pans. Cover with clean tea towel; let rise in warm place until doubled in bulk, about 1 hour.

❧ Brush loaves with egg yolk. Bake in centre of 400°F (200°C) oven until golden and loaves sound hollow when tapped on bottoms, about 30 minutes. Brush with reserved rum, if desired. Let cool. (Make-ahead: Wrap in plastic wrap and store at room temperature for up to 1 day or overwrap in heavy-duty foil and freeze for up to 2 weeks.)

Makes 2 loaves, 12 slices each. | PER SLICE: about 144 cal, 3 g pro, 4 g total fat (2 g sat. fat), 24 g carb, 1 g fibre, 34 mg chol, 83 mg sodium. % RDI: 1% calcium, 9% iron, 4% vit A, 25% folate.

Bread Machine Variation (dough only): Into pan of 2-lb (1 kg) bread machine, add (in order) water, butter, beaten eggs, sour cream, vanilla, lemon and orange rinds, sugar, salt, 3½ cups (875 mL) all-purpose flour and bread machine yeast. Choose dough setting. Knead in raisins, shape and bake as directed.

Croatian Poppy Seed Roll

Makovnjača is a sweet traditional Croatian bread served at Easter. Its characteristic soft crust is achieved by covering the hot loaf for 20 minutes.

¾ cup	milk	175 mL	¾ cup	milk	175 mL
¼ cup	granulated sugar	50 mL	⅓ cup	granulated sugar	75 mL
1 tbsp	active dry yeast	15 mL	3 tbsp	liquid honey	50 mL
¼ cup	butter	50 mL	2 tbsp	dried currants or chopped raisins	25 mL
2	eggs	2	2 tbsp	butter	25 mL
2¾ cups	all-purpose flour (approx)	675 mL	1 tsp	grated lemon rind	5 mL
2 tsp	grated lemon rind	10 mL	¼ tsp	cinnamon	1 mL
¼ tsp	salt	1 mL	1 tbsp	amber rum or water	15 mL
POPPY SEED FILLING:			**TOPPING:**		
1 cup	poppy seeds	250 mL	1	egg	1

❧ In microwaveable bowl or saucepan, warm milk. Pour 2 tbsp (25 mL) into separate bowl; add 1 tsp (5 mL) of the sugar and stir until dissolved. Sprinkle in yeast; let stand until frothy, about 20 minutes.

❧ Meanwhile, add butter and remaining sugar to remaining milk; heat, stirring, just until butter is melted. Let cool to lukewarm; whisk in eggs and yeast mixture.

❧ In large bowl, whisk together 2½ cups (625 mL) of the flour, lemon rind and salt. Make well in centre; add milk mixture. With wooden spoon, stir to form soft, slightly sticky dough that comes away from side of bowl.

❧ Turn out onto floured surface; knead, adding as much of the remaining flour as necessary to prevent sticking, until smooth and elastic, about 2 minutes. Place in greased bowl, turning to grease all over. Cover with plastic wrap and let rise in warm place until doubled in bulk, about 1 hour.

❧ **POPPY SEED FILLING:** Meanwhile, in clean coffee grinder, grind poppy seeds. In saucepan, bring milk, sugar and honey to boil. Stir in poppy seeds, currants, butter, lemon rind and cinnamon; return to boil. Reduce heat to medium; cook, stirring often, until fairly dry and stiff, about 8 minutes. Stir in rum; let cool for 10 minutes.

❧ Line large rimless baking sheet with parchment paper or grease; set aside.

❧ Punch down dough. Turn out onto floured surface. Roll out into 14- x 12-inch (35 x 30 cm) rectangle. Leaving ½-inch (1 cm) border uncovered, spread filling over dough. Starting at long side, roll up; pinch seam to seal. Using metal spatulas, place roll, diagonally and seam side down, on prepared pan. Cover loosely with greased plastic wrap; let rise in warm place until doubled in bulk, about 1 hour.

❧ **TOPPING:** Whisk egg; gently brush about half over dough. Bake in centre of 350°F (180°C) oven until golden and loaf sounds hollow when tapped on bottom, about

30 minutes. Transfer baking sheet to rack; drape clean tea towel over loaf and let cool for 20 minutes. Uncover and remove parchment paper; let cool on rack before slicing.

Makes 1 loaf, 18 slices. | PER SLICE: about 209 cal, 5 g pro, 9 g total fat (3 g sat. fat), 28 g carb, 2 g fibre, 43 mg chol, 80 mg sodium. % RDI: 13% calcium, 14% iron, 5% vit A, 2% vit C, 29% folate.

....

VARIATION

Croatian Walnut Roll (Orehnjača): In food processor, blend together 2¼ cups (550 mL) chopped walnut halves; ⅓ cup (75 mL) granulated sugar; 1 egg; ¼ cup (50 mL) butter, melted; 2 tbsp (25 mL) dried currants or raisins; 1 tbsp (15 mL) amber rum or water; and 1 tbsp (15 mL) liquid honey. Do not cook. Use in place of poppy seed filling.

Christmas Stollen

Fragrant with spices and peel and dotted with cherries, nuts and raisins, stollen is a traditional German Christmas bread that's enjoyed around the world.

SHAPING STOLLEN

Press firmly on centre of dough log to create two thick raised borders on both sides of a trough.

1¼ cups	milk	300 mL	1 cup	raisins	250 mL
½ cup	granulated sugar	125 mL	½ cup	candied mixed peel	125 mL
2	pkg active dry yeast (or 4½ tsp/22 mL)	2	½ cup	candied cherries, chopped	125 mL
2	eggs	2	½ cup	toasted slivered almonds	125 mL
5 cups	all-purpose flour (approx)	1.25 L	1 tsp	grated lemon rind	5 mL
1½ tsp	salt	7 mL	1	egg white, lightly beaten	1
Pinch	each cinnamon, nutmeg and ground cardamom	Pinch	¼ cup	butter, melted	50 mL
¾ cup	unsalted butter, softened	175 mL		Icing sugar	

Beaten egg white is the glue that will hold the stollen together.

Fold bottom half of dough upward over trough toward top edge, aligning raised borders side by side. Press together firmly to make sure the stollen will not come apart when it rises and bakes.

❧ In saucepan, heat milk with 1 tsp (5 mL) of the sugar to lukewarm (110°F to 112°F/ 43°C to 44°C); remove from heat. Sprinkle in yeast; let stand until frothy, about 10 minutes. Whisk in eggs.

❧ In large bowl, whisk together 3 cups (750 mL) of the flour, remaining sugar, salt, cinnamon, nutmeg and cardamom; add yeast mixture and stir until smooth. Drop in softened butter all at once, stirring with wooden spoon until blended. Stir in remaining flour to make soft, somewhat lumpy dough.

❧ Turn out onto lightly floured surface; knead, adding up to 3 tbsp (50 mL) more flour if necessary, until smooth and elastic, 10 to 12 minutes. Lightly dust with flour; cover with clean tea towel and let rest for 5 minutes. Meanwhile, in small bowl, stir together raisins, candied peel and cherries, almonds and lemon rind.

❧ Flatten dough into rectangle; sprinkle two-thirds with one-half of the raisin mixture. Fold dough over in thirds; knead until raisin mixture is evenly distributed, about 4 minutes. Cover with clean tea towel and let rest for 5 minutes. Repeat with remaining raisin mixture. Place dough in greased bowl, turning to grease all over. Cover with plastic wrap; let rise in warm place until doubled in bulk, about 1½ hours.

❧ Line 2 large rimless baking sheets with parchment paper or grease; set aside.

❧ Punch down dough; divide in half. On lightly floured surface, shape each half into 8-inch (20 cm) long log. With long side closest, roll out middle section of each log to ½-inch (1 cm) thickness, leaving 1-inch (2.5 cm) border unrolled at top and bottom.

❧ Brush egg white over each piece of rolled-out dough; fold bottom half of dough up almost to top, aligning raised borders side by side. Place on prepared pans. Cover with clean tea towels; let rise in warm place until doubled in bulk, about 1 hour.

❧ Bake in top and bottom thirds of 350°F (180°C) oven, rotating and switching pans halfway through, until golden and loaves sound hollow when tapped on bottoms, about 45 minutes. Transfer to rack; brush all over with melted butter. Let cool. Dust all over with icing sugar. (Make-ahead: Wrap in plastic wrap and store at room temperature for up to 3 days or overwrap in heavy-duty foil and freeze for up to 1 month.)

Makes 2 loaves, 10 slices each. | PER SLICE: about 302 cal, 6 g pro, 12 g total fat (6 g sat. fat), 44 g carb, 2 g fibre, 44 mg chol, 213 mg sodium. % RDI: 4% calcium, 14% iron, 10% vit A, 2% vit C, 40% folate.

Pizza Dough

The dough for this crisp, airy crust is a dream to work, especially after a 24-hour rest. By then, its gluten has relaxed, making the dough easy to roll out. To make the pizzas that follow, use this dough or the same weight of purchased dough.

3 cups	all-purpose flour (approx)	750 mL	1 tsp	salt	5 mL
2 tsp	quick-rising (instant) dry yeast	10 mL	1¼ cups	hot (120°F/50°C) water	300 mL
			1 tbsp	extra-virgin olive oil	15 mL

❧ In bowl, combine 2¾ cups (675 mL) of the flour, yeast and salt. With wooden spoon, gradually stir in water and oil until ragged dough forms, using hands if necessary.

❧ Turn out onto lightly floured surface; knead, adding as much of the remaining flour, 1 tbsp (15 mL) at a time, as necessary to prevent sticking, until smooth and elastic, about 8 minutes. Place in greased bowl, turning to grease all over; cover with plastic wrap.

❧ PIZZA TONIGHT: Let rise in warm place until doubled in bulk, about 1 hour.

❧ PIZZA LATER: Let rise in refrigerator for 1 day. Or freeze in large resealable freezer bag for up to 1 month; let thaw and rise in refrigerator overnight.

Makes about 1½ lb (750 g) dough, enough for one 14-inch (35 cm) pizza base.

Bread Machine Variation: Into pan of 2-lb (1 kg) bread machine, place (in order) water, oil, salt, all of the flour and yeast. Choose dough setting.

VARIATIONS

Multigrain Pizza Dough: Substitute 1¾ cups (425 mL) multigrain bread flour and 1⅔ cups (400 mL) all-purpose flour (approx) for the all-purpose flour. Combine dry ingredients, reserving 2 tbsp (25 mL) of the all-purpose flour to dust work surface. Add ¼ cup (50 mL) mixed seeds (such as flax, sunflower and sesame) to the dry ingredients. Mix; let rise as directed.

Middle Eastern Flatbread: Line 2 large rimless baking sheets with parchment paper; set aside. Punch down Pizza Dough; turn out onto lightly floured surface. Knead into ball; flatten into rough circle. Cut into 6 wedges; gently stretch or roll out each into ¼-inch (5 mm) thick irregular triangle. Place on prepared baking sheets; cover with clean tea towel and let rise for 15 minutes.

❧ Use prepared zaatar or combine 2 tsp (10 mL) toasted sesame seeds, ¾ tsp (4 mL) each ground sumac and dried thyme, and ¼ tsp (1 mL) coarse salt. Whisk together 2 tbsp (25 mL) extra-virgin olive oil, 1 tbsp (15 mL) lemon juice and 1 tbsp (15 mL) zaatar or spice mixture; brush over dough. Bake in bottom third of 425°F (220°C) oven until golden, about 10 minutes. Serve hot.

Three-Cheese Spinach Pizza

Spinach adds a flavour twist to this classic cheese combo. We prefer fresh spinach, but you can also use 1 package (10 oz/300 g) frozen, thawed and drained. Smoked provolone or Cheddar cheese are options instead of the Gorgonzola cheese.

	Pizza Dough (recipe, opposite)		1 cup	shredded mozzarella cheese	250 mL
1 tbsp	extra-virgin olive oil	15 mL	⅓ cup	grated Parmesan cheese	75 mL
1	clove garlic, thinly sliced	1	4 oz	Gorgonzola cheese, crumbled or cubed	125 g
¼ tsp	pepper	1 mL			
1	bunch spinach (8 oz/250 g), trimmed, cooked and squeezed dry (see tip, right)	1			

❧ Grease 14-inch (35 cm) pizza pan; set aside.

❧ On lightly floured surface, roll out dough into 14-inch (35 cm) round; centre on prepared pan. Brush with oil; sprinkle with garlic, pepper and spinach. Top with mozzarella, Parmesan and Gorgonzola cheeses.

❧ Bake in bottom third of 425°F (220°C) oven until cheese is bubbly and crust is golden and slightly puffed, about 20 minutes.

Makes 8 slices. | PER SLICE: about 328 cal, 14 g pro, 13 g total fat (7 g sat. fat), 38 g carb, 2 g fibre, 30 mg chol, 669 mg sodium. % RDI: 23% calcium, 24% iron, 34% vit A, 5% vit C, 74% folate.

QUICK COOKING SPINACH

❯ Cook trimmed spinach with just the water clinging to leaves in large covered saucepan over medium-high heat, stirring once or twice, until wilted. Scrape into sieve; let cool enough to handle. Squeeze or press out liquid.

Clockwise from top:
Mushroom Fontina Pizza
(opposite), Three-Cheese
Spinach Pizza (page 247),
Calabrese Potato Provolone
Pizza (page 250) and Grilled
Eggplant and Fresh
Mozzarella Pizza (page 251)

Mushroom Fontina Pizza

The woodsy flavour of this topping works beautifully with the multigrain dough. For a stylish finish, drizzle with truffle or porcini oil or good extra-virgin olive oil before serving.

6 cups	mushrooms, stemmed (1 lb/500 g)	1.5 L	2 tbsp	chopped fresh parsley	25 mL
1 tbsp	extra-virgin olive oil	15 mL		Multigrain Pizza Dough (recipe, page 246)	
1	small onion, minced	1	2 tbsp	chopped fresh thyme	25 mL
2	cloves garlic, minced	2	1½ cups	shredded Fontina cheese	375 mL
¼ tsp	each salt and pepper	1 mL			

DRIED HERB OPTION

❯ To replace fresh thyme with dried, use one-third as much called for – in this case, reducing from 2 tbsp (25 mL) to 2 tsp (10 mL).

❧ In food processor, pulse mushrooms into coarse paste; set aside.

❧ In large skillet, heat oil over medium heat; fry onion, garlic, salt and pepper, stirring occasionally, until onion is softened, about 5 minutes.

❧ Stir in mushroom paste; cook, stirring, until liquid is evaporated, about 15 minutes. Stir in parsley. **(Make-ahead: Let cool. Refrigerate in airtight container for up to 1 day.)**

❧ Grease 14-inch (35 cm) pizza pan; set aside.

❧ On lightly floured surface, roll out dough into 14-inch (35 cm) round; centre on prepared pan. Spread with mushroom mixture; sprinkle with thyme and Fontina cheese.

❧ Bake in bottom third of 425°F (220°C) oven until cheese is bubbly and crust is golden and slightly puffed, about 20 minutes.

Makes 8 slices. | PER SLICE: about 351 cal, 15 g pro, 14 g total fat (5 g sat. fat), 44 g carb, 5 g fibre, 25 mg chol, 533 mg sodium. % RDI: 14% calcium, 28% iron, 7% vit A, 8% vit C, 42% folate.

Calabrese Potato Provolone Pizza

Here's a pizza to please the meat-and-potato lovers. Dried Calabrese sausage is an Italian salami with a bit of heat, but other sliced quality salami will do.

1	small Yukon Gold potato	1	3 oz	Calabrese sausage, thinly sliced	90 g
	Pizza Dough (recipe, page 246)		7	fresh sage leaves, chopped	7
1 cup	Tomato Pizza Sauce (recipe, below)	250 mL	1½ cups	shredded provolone cheese	375 mL

↬ Peel potato. Preferably using mandolin, slice into paper-thin rounds. **(Make-ahead: Place in airtight container; cover with water. Refrigerate for up to 1 day. Drain; pat dry.)**

↬ Grease 14-inch (35 cm) pizza pan; set aside.

↬ On floured surface, roll out dough into 14-inch (35 cm) round; centre on prepared pan. Spread with tomato sauce. Layer potato, sausage and sage on top; top with cheese.

↬ Bake in bottom third of 425°F (220°C) oven until cheese is bubbly and crust is golden and slightly puffed, about 20 minutes.

Makes 8 slices. | PER SLICE: about 325 cal, 13 g pro, 11 g total fat (5 g sat. fat), 42 g carb, 2 g fibre, 22 mg chol, 652 mg sodium. % RDI: 17% calcium, 24% iron, 6% vit A, 15% vit C, 57% folate.

Tomato Pizza Sauce

Homemade tomato pizza sauce is much more flavourful than the commercial variety. This makes enough for two pizzas, doubles easily for more and freezes well, too.

1	can (28 oz/796 mL) tomatoes	1	¼ tsp	dried oregano	1 mL
			½ tsp	wine vinegar	2 mL
2 tbsp	extra-virgin olive oil	25 mL	Pinch	each salt, pepper and granulated sugar	Pinch
1	small onion, minced	1			
2	cloves garlic, minced	2			

↬ Drain tomatoes, reserving juice; seed and chop. Set aside.

↬ In saucepan, heat oil over medium heat; fry onion, garlic and oregano, stirring occasionally, until onion is translucent, about 5 minutes.

↬ Add tomatoes and reserved juice, vinegar, salt, pepper and sugar; simmer until thickened, about 20 minutes. Let cool for 5 minutes.

↬ Transfer to food processor; blend until smooth. **(Make-ahead: Refrigerate in airtight container for up to 1 week or freeze for up to 1 month.)**

Makes about 2 cups (500 mL). | PER 1 CUP (250 ML): about 208 cal, 4 g pro, 14 g total fat (2 g sat. fat), 21 g carb, 4 g fibre, 0 mg chol, 518 mg sodium. % RDI: 13% calcium, 30% iron, 5% vit A, 92% vit C, 13% folate.

Grilled Eggplant and Fresh Mozzarella Pizza

Look for fresh mozzarella and bocconcini cheeses in sealed bags or tubs of water at deli counters. For a delicious splurge, use buffalo mozzarella, a flavourful fresh mozzarella made from water-buffalo milk. If neither is available, use regular mozzarella.

8 oz	fresh mozzarella or bocconcini cheese	250 g
1	small eggplant (12 oz/ 375 g), thinly sliced	1
2 tbsp	vegetable oil	25 mL
¼ tsp	each salt and pepper	1 mL
	Pizza Dough (recipe, page 246)	

1 cup	Tomato Pizza Sauce (recipe, opposite)	250 mL
¼ cup	fresh basil leaves	50 mL
6	anchovy fillets (or 1 tbsp/ 15 mL drained capers)	6

SKIP THE GRILL
❯ You can also broil eggplant on a foil-lined baking sheet, turning once, until golden and translucent, about 5 minutes.

❧ Drain and pat mozzarella dry; cut into ¼-inch (5 mm) thick rounds. Arrange on towel-lined tray; let stand for 30 minutes.

❧ Meanwhile, brush eggplant with oil; sprinkle with salt and pepper. Place on greased grill over medium-high heat; close lid and grill, turning once, until tender, about 10 minutes. **(Make-ahead: Refrigerate in airtight container for up to 1 day.)**

❧ Grease 14-inch (35 cm) pizza pan; set aside.

❧ On lightly floured surface, roll out dough into 14-inch (35 cm) round; centre on prepared pan. Spread with tomato sauce; sprinkle with basil. Top with eggplant, anchovies and mozzarella.

❧ Bake in bottom third of 425°F (220°C) oven until cheese is bubbly and crust is golden and slightly puffed, about 20 minutes.

Makes 8 slices. | PER SLICE: about 346 cal, 13 g pro, 14 g total fat (5 g sat. fat), 43 g carb, 3 g fibre, 24 mg chol, 552 mg sodium. % RDI: 19% calcium, 23% iron, 6% vit A, 13% vit C, 60% folate.

Potato Rosemary Focaccia

The mashed potatoes in the dough give this focaccia a light texture. You need to boil and mash 3 baking potatoes, about 1 lb (500 g) total, for the dough.

2½ tsp	granulated sugar	12 mL
1 cup	warm water	250 mL
1	pkg active dry yeast (or 2¼ tsp/11 mL)	1
2 tbsp	extra-virgin olive oil	25 mL
2 cups	cooled mashed potatoes	500 mL
1 tsp	salt	5 mL
3½ cups	all-purpose flour (approx)	875 mL
1 tbsp	cornmeal	15 mL

TOPPING:

¼ cup	extra-virgin olive oil	50 mL
2 tbsp	chopped fresh rosemary (or 2 tsp/10 mL crumbled dried rosemary)	25 mL
1	clove garlic, minced	1
1 tsp	kosher salt	5 mL
½ tsp	pepper	2 mL
2	red potatoes (8 oz/250 g), thinly sliced	2

In large bowl, dissolve sugar in warm water. Sprinkle in yeast; let stand until frothy, about 10 minutes. Stir in oil.

In separate bowl, mix mashed potatoes with salt; stir into yeast mixture. Stir in enough of the flour to form slightly sticky dough.

Turn out onto lightly floured surface. Knead, dusting surface with as much of the remaining flour as necessary to prevent sticking, until smooth and elastic, about 8 minutes. Place in greased bowl, turning to grease all over. Cover with plastic wrap; let rise in warm place until doubled in bulk, about 1 hour.

Grease 15- x 10-inch (40 x 25 cm) rimmed baking sheet; sprinkle evenly with cornmeal. Punch down dough; press evenly into prepared pan. Let rise until puffed slightly higher than edge of pan, about 45 minutes.

TOPPING: In small bowl, whisk together oil, rosemary, garlic, salt and pepper. Gently press fingertips into dough to make indentations all over; brush half of the oil mixture over top. Arrange sliced potatoes over top, overlapping if necessary. Brush remaining oil mixture over potatoes.

Bake in bottom third of 375°F (190°C) oven until crust is golden and potatoes are tender, 30 to 40 minutes. Run knife around edges to loosen. Transfer to rack; let cool. Cut into squares.

Makes 12 squares. | PER SQUARE: about 245 cal, 5 g pro, 7 g total fat (1 g sat. fat), 40 g carb, 2 g fibre, 0 mg chol, 386 mg sodium. % RDI: 1% calcium, 14% iron, 7% vit C, 27% folate.

VARIATION

Herbed Focaccia: Omit potato topping. Brush dough with extra-virgin olive oil; top with crumbled dried sage or rosemary and sea salt. Reduce baking time by about 5 minutes.

Naan

Just right for serving with curries, this flatbread goes well with any kind of stew or chili, too.

1 tsp	granulated sugar	5 mL
1 cup	warm water	250 mL
1	pkg active dry yeast (or 2¼ tsp/11 mL)	1
3¾ cups	all-purpose flour (approx)	925 mL
1 tsp	salt	5 mL
½ tsp	baking powder	2 mL

¼ cup	plain yogurt	50 mL
¼ cup	butter, melted	50 mL
TOPPING:		
1 tbsp	minced garlic	15 mL
1 tbsp	sesame seeds	15 mL
2 tbsp	butter, melted	25 mL

RELAX!

> If the dough becomes too stretchy during shaping, cover it lightly and let it rest for a few minutes.

In small bowl, dissolve sugar in warm water. Sprinkle in yeast; let stand until frothy, about 10 minutes.

In large bowl, whisk together 3¼ cups (800 mL) of the flour, salt and baking powder; make well in centre. Pour yeast mixture, yogurt and butter into well; stir, gradually incorporating flour mixture, to form soft, slightly sticky dough.

Turn out onto lightly floured surface; knead, adding as much of the remaining flour as necessary to prevent sticking, until smooth and elastic, about 8 minutes. Place in greased bowl, turning to grease all over. Cover with plastic wrap; let rise in warm place until doubled in bulk, about 1 hour.

Turn out onto lightly floured surface; form into log. Divide into 8 pieces. Gently stretch each into scant ¼-inch (5 mm) thick teardrop shape. Cover with clean tea towel and let rest for 10 minutes.

TOPPING: Sprinkle dough with garlic and sesame seeds. Place on electric griddle or in cast-iron skillet or griddle over medium-high heat. Bake, turning once, until puffed and golden, 5 minutes. Brush with butter. Wrap in tea towel to keep soft; serve warm.

Makes 8 pieces. | PER PIECE: about 309 cal, 7 g pro, 10 g total fat (6 g sat. fat), 47 g carb, 2 g fibre, 24 mg chol, 374 mg sodium. % RDI: 3% calcium, 21% iron, 8% vit A, 66% folate.

Crisp Seedy Cracker Bread

Truly an ancient form of bread, even without yeast, these crackling crackers add pizzazz to a bread basket. As you might imagine, they pair up beautifully with dips and spreads – and cheeses, too!

3¾ cups	all-purpose flour (approx)	925 mL	1	egg white, beaten	1
			⅓ cup	sesame seeds or poppy seeds	75 mL
1 tsp	salt	5 mL			
1½ cups	water	375 mL	½ tsp	sea salt	2 mL

↜ Grease 2 rimless baking sheets; set aside.

↜ In food processor, pulse 3½ cups (875 mL) of the flour with salt until combined. With motor running, add water in steady stream until dough forms ball. Pulse in as much of the remaining flour as necessary, 1 tbsp (15 mL) at a time, until dough is no longer sticky. Whirl for 1 minute.

↜ Turn out onto lightly floured surface; knead into ball. Cover with bowl or plastic wrap; let rest for 30 minutes.

↜ Divide dough into 6 pieces. Leaving remaining pieces covered with plastic wrap, roll out 1 piece into very thin 14- x 9-inch (35 x 23 cm) rectangle; place on 1 of the prepared pans. Brush lightly with some of the egg white; sprinkle lightly with about one-sixth each of the sesame seeds and salt.

↜ Bake in centre of 500°F (260°C) oven, turning baking sheet halfway through, until edges are browned and golden brown blisters appear all over, 7 to 9 minutes. Let cool on rack.

↜ Repeat with remaining dough, egg white, seeds and salt. Break into long shards.

(Make-ahead: Store in airtight container for up to 1 week.)

Makes about 48 pieces. | PER PIECE: about 42 cal, 1 g pro, 1 g total fat (0 g sat. fat), 8 g carb, trace fibre, 0 mg chol, 66 mg sodium. % RDI: 4% iron, 10% folate.

Roll the dough as paper-thin as possible. It is still strong enough to lift onto a greased baking sheet.

The thin layer of egg white pretty well anchors all of the seed topping. But do expect some sprinkles as you break the finished cracker bread into shards.

Crispy Breadsticks with Sea Salt and Sesame Seeds

Sea salt adds a burst of crunch to these breadsticks. Serve with dips or as part of an Italian antipasto platter with olives, salami, grilled vegetables and Romano cheese.

1 tsp	granulated sugar	5 mL	2 tsp	salt	10 mL
1½ cups	warm water	375 mL	**TOPPING:**		
1	pkg active dry yeast (or 2¼ tsp/11 mL)	1	1	egg	1
			⅓ cup	toasted sesame seeds	75 mL
3 tbsp	extra-virgin olive oil	50 mL	1 tbsp	coarse sea salt	15 mL
1 tbsp	liquid honey	15 mL			
3¾ cups	all-purpose flour (approx)	925 mL			

↳ In large bowl, dissolve sugar in ¼ cup (50 mL) of the warm water. Sprinkle in yeast; let stand until frothy, about 10 minutes. Add remaining warm water, oil and honey. With wooden spoon, stir in 3½ cups (875 mL) of the flour and salt until shaggy dough forms.

↳ Turn out onto lightly floured surface; knead, adding as much of the remaining flour as necessary to prevent sticking, until smooth and elastic, 8 to 10 minutes. Place in greased bowl, turning to grease all over. Cover with plastic wrap; let rise in warm place until doubled in bulk, about 1 hour.

↳ Line 2 rimless baking sheets with parchment paper or grease; set aside.

↳ Punch down dough; turn out onto floured surface. Divide in half; pat each half out into 8- x 5-inch (20 x 12 cm) square. Cover with clean tea towel; let rest for 10 minutes.

↳ Cut each square crosswise to make 16 strips. On unfloured surface, roll each strip by hand into 16-inch (40 cm) long stick.

↳ **TOPPING:** In small bowl, whisk egg with 1 tbsp (15 mL) water. On sheet of waxed paper longer than sticks, combine sesame seeds with sea salt. Brush sticks with egg mixture; roll each in salt mixture to coat. Place, 1 inch (2.5 cm) apart, on prepared pans. Bake in top and bottom thirds of 450°F (230°C) oven, rotating and switching pans halfway through, until golden, about 15 minutes. Transfer to racks; let cool.

(Make-ahead: Wrap in plastic wrap and store at room temperature for up to 2 days; recrisp in 350°F/180°C oven for about 10 minutes.)

Makes 32 pieces. | PER PIECE: about 79 cal, 2 g pro, 2 g total fat (trace sat. fat), 12 g carb, 1 g fibre, 6 mg chol, 292 mg sodium. % RDI: 6% iron, 12% folate.

Bread Machine Variation (dough only): Into pan of 2-lb (1 kg) bread machine, place (in order) all of the water, sugar, oil, honey, 4 cups (1 L) all-purpose flour and 1¼ tsp (6 mL) bread machine yeast. Choose dough setting. Shape and bake as directed.

Rye Crackers

The caraway-rye combination makes these crackers an excellent base for smoked or pickled fish – or funky flavoured Gouda or Havarti cheeses.

1 tbsp	caraway seeds	15 mL		1⅓ cups	all-purpose flour (approx)	325 mL
¼ tsp	granulated sugar	1 mL		1 tsp	salt	5 mL
1¼ cups	warm water	300 mL		1 tbsp	vegetable oil	15 mL
1 tsp	active dry yeast	5 mL				
1¼ cups	rye flour	300 mL				

❧ In small skillet, toast caraway seeds over medium heat, shaking pan occasionally, until fragrant, 3 to 5 minutes. Transfer to clean coffee grinder or mortar and pestle; grind to fine powder. Set aside.

❧ In large bowl, dissolve sugar in warm water. Sprinkle in yeast; let stand until frothy, about 10 minutes. With wooden spoon, stir in rye flour, 1 cup (250 mL) of the all-purpose flour, ground caraway seeds and salt to form shaggy dough.

❧ Turn out onto floured surface; knead, adding only as much of the remaining flour as necessary to prevent sticking, until smooth and elastic, about 5 minutes. Form into ball. Place in large greased bowl, turning to grease all over. Cover with plastic wrap; let rise in warm place until almost doubled in bulk, about 1½ hours.

❧ Lightly grease 2 rimless baking sheets; set aside.

❧ Punch down dough; turn out onto lightly floured surface. Divide into 12 pieces. Dusting with only as much all-purpose flour as necessary to prevent sticking, roll out each piece as thinly as possible into long rectangle with rounded edges. Transfer to prepared pans; prick all over with fork. Let stand for 15 minutes.

❧ Bake in top and bottom thirds of 400°F (200°C) oven, rotating and switching pans halfway through, until crisp, 10 to 12 minutes. Transfer to racks; brush with oil. Let cool. (**Make-ahead: Store in airtight container at room temperature for up to 1 week or freeze for up to 1 month.**) Break each into 4 pieces.

Makes 48 pieces. | PER PIECE: about 27 cal, 1 g pro, trace total fat (0 g sat. fat), 5 g carb, 1 g fibre, 0 mg chol, 48 mg sodium. % RDI: 3% iron, 5% folate.

Chapter 5

Quick Breads

Quick breads are just that – fast to mix and just as fast to bake. Unlike raised yeast breads, they require no kneading and rising time. Thanks to leaveners – baking powder and baking soda are the most common – quick breads emerge from the oven hot, feathery light and inviting the addition of butter and jam (or marmalade, honey, peanut butter or cheese; it's up to you).

In addition to their time-crunch and sensual appeals, quick breads are often an entry route beginners take before flouring their hands to make pastry or launching into a layer cake. And they are as variable as they are fast. Like an artist with a palette full of colours to choose from, you can change the spice or stir in dried cherries instead of raisins and turn a classic into a novelty. They please in the morning, afternoon and evening, or, depending on the variety, can make a fabulous dessert or accompany savoury courses.

This chapter is organized around two major quick bread categories: scones and biscuits (with Irish Soda Bread and Welsh Cakes included) and muffins and loaves. A bonus popover recipe finishes off the chapter.

A word of advice: This is the kind of chapter that gets splattered with batter as family members try out the recipes. Slip the book into a cookbook stand or have a sheet of firm clear plastic or plastic wrap handy to keep the pages tidy. On the other hand, if you want future generations to know which recipes you baked most, signalled by copious splats, go easy on the plastic.

Steps to First-Class Biscuits and Scones

❯ Press firmly on the pastry blender, moving around the bowl, to cut the butter into small pieces and coat each bit with dry ingredients. Stop when the mixture looks crumbly but still has some larger, pea-size pieces of butter.

❯ As you add liquid ingredients, simultaneously toss dry ingredients up from the bottom of the bowl. Steady the bowl on a folded towel or damp dish cloth wrapped like a nest around the bottom of the bowl.

❯ *Ragged* is the best word you can use to describe the texture of perfectly mixed biscuit or scone dough.

❯ A few gentle pushes and pulls with a floured hand will bring the slightly sticky biscuit dough together on a floured work surface. Avoid leaving your hands on the dough – this melts the butter, reducing flakiness.

❯ Pat or roll out into 10- x 7-inch (25 x 18 cm) rectangle; cut the dough in half lengthwise, then make three cuts crosswise to make six squares. Cut squares from corner to corner to form 12 triangular biscuits or scones.

❯ Transfer to parchment paper–lined or flour-dusted rimless baking sheet.

❯ Brush tops of biscuits with milk or cream, or an egg wash made by mixing 1 egg or egg yolk with 1 tbsp (15 mL) water or milk.

❯ Sprinkle with coarse or regular granulated sugar for a glittery finish.

❯ Baking biscuits or scones in the centre of a hot oven, usually 400°F (200°C), guarantees a light, golden, flaky result.

EQUIPMENT FOR QUICK BREADS

- Shiny metal rimless baking sheets

- Muffin pans, with cups about 2¾ inches (7 cm) in diameter and ⅓- to ½-cup (75 to 125 mL) capacity

- Miniature muffin or tart pans, with cups about 1¾ inches (4.5 cm) in diameter and 2-tbsp (25 mL) capacity

- Shiny metal loaf pans: 8- x 4-inch (1.5 L) and 9- x 5-inch (2 L)

- Cast-iron skillet: 10-inch (25 cm)

- Popover pan

- Ice cream scoop (disher) with release mechanism: 2⅝-inch (6.25 cm) for ½-cup (125 mL) portions, and larger sizes as desired

- Biscuit cutter or graduated set of round cookie cutters

- Wooden rolling pin

- Pastry blender

The Easy-Mix Muffin Method

> This is also the mixing method to use for quick bread loaves.

> Start by preparing the muffin cups. Grease with a pastry brush and butter, brush or spray with oil, or line with paper liners. Arrange the oven rack in the centre position and preheat the oven (most muffins bake at 375°F/190°C).

> Choose a large bowl in which to whisk dry ingredients together – this bowl will hold all the batter, so size counts.

> There's no need to beat eggs separately; whisk them with the liquids before pouring over the dry ingredients.

> Now sprinkle the add-ins onto the unmixed dry and wet ingredients. Feel free to improvise with them, interchanging dried fruits, such as slivered apricots, golden and other raisins, currants, dried cherries, cranberries and more. Or mix them up with chopped walnut halves, pecans, hazelnuts or slivered almonds. Chocolate chips are a delightful indulgence.

> Use just a few deft strokes to bring the dry and wet ingredients together. Overstirring creates tough, tunnel-filled muffins. Stir just until there are no streaks or pockets of the dry ingredients.

> A ½-cup (125 mL) ice-cream scoop with a release mechanism is the most efficient way to fill muffin cups equally. Or use two large spoons, one to scoop the batter and the second to push it down into the cup.

> Since the leavening starts to work as soon as the wet and dry ingredients are combined, get the muffins into the pan and the oven as fast as possible.

> When muffins are finished baking, set the pan on a rack for a few minutes. If you've greased the pan, run a knife around each muffin to loosen. Transfer to rack to cool, or simply tilt muffins up to cool right in the pan.

Our Finest Buttermilk Scones

These scones, also known as biscuits, are an indulgence any time of day. In a hurry? Cut them into squares or triangles. When you're not so pressed for time, cut out rounds, rerolling the scraps.

2½ cups	all-purpose flour	625 mL	½ cup	cold butter, cubed	125 mL
2 tbsp	granulated sugar	25 mL	1 cup	buttermilk	250 mL
2½ tsp	baking powder	12 mL	1	egg	1
½ tsp	each baking soda and salt	2 mL			

❧ Line large rimless baking sheet with parchment paper or dust with flour; set aside.

❧ In large bowl, whisk together flour, sugar, baking powder, baking soda and salt. Using pastry blender, cut in butter until crumbly. In separate bowl, whisk buttermilk with egg; pour over flour mixture. Stir with fork to make soft ragged dough.

❧ With lightly floured hands, press dough into ball. On floured surface, knead gently 10 times. Pat out into 10- x 7-inch (25 x 18 cm) rectangle; trim edges to straighten.

❧ Cut rectangle into 6 squares; cut each diagonally in half. Place on prepared pan. Bake in centre of 400°F (200°C) oven until golden, 18 to 20 minutes. Transfer to rack; let cool. (Make-ahead: Store in airtight container at room temperature for up to 1 day or wrap each in plastic wrap and freeze in airtight container for up to 2 weeks.)

Makes 12 scones. | PER SCONE: about 189 cal, 4 g pro, 9 g total fat (5 g sat. fat), 23 g carb, 1 g fibre, 37 mg chol, 289 mg sodium. % RDI: 6% calcium, 9% iron, 8% vit A, 26% folate.

SWEET VARIATIONS

Apricot Almond Scones: Sprinkle ¾ cup (175 mL) chopped dried apricots over ingredients just before stirring together. Shape and bake as directed. After scones have cooled, drizzle with Almond Icing (recipe, opposite). Sprinkle with ¼ cup (50 mL) toasted sliced almonds.

Cherry White Chocolate Scones: Sprinkle 1 cup (250 mL) dried cherries, halved, and 3 oz (90 g) white chocolate, chopped, over ingredients just before stirring together. Shape and bake as directed. If you like, you can drizzle cooled scones with 2 oz (60 g) white chocolate, melted; let stand until set, about 1 hour.

Dried Fruit and Lemon Scones: Add 2 tsp (10 mL) grated lemon rind to dry ingredients. Sprinkle ½ cup (125 mL) dried currants, raisins, dried blueberries, dried cranberries, chopped dried cherries, chopped dried apricots or chopped prunes over ingredients just before stirring together. Shape and bake as directed.

Lemon Poppy Seed Scones: Add 1 tbsp (15 mL) grated lemon rind and 4 tsp (20 mL) poppy seeds to dry ingredients. Shape and bake as directed. After scones have cooled, drizzle with Lemon Icing (recipe, opposite).

Mini Strawberry Shortcakes: Add 1 tbsp (15 mL) grated lemon rind to dry ingredients. Pat out into scant ¾-inch (2 cm) thick round. Using 1¾-inch (4.5 cm) floured round or fluted cookie cutter, cut out rounds. Brush with 1 egg, beaten; sprinkle with granulated sugar. Bake for about 12 minutes. Let cool. Split and fill with 2 cups (500 mL) sliced strawberries, sweetened to taste; top with 1 cup (250 mL) whipping cream, softly whipped.

Oat Scones: Substitute ½ cup (125 mL) large-flake rolled oats for ½ cup (125 mL) of the flour. Add 1 tsp (5 mL) cinnamon to dry ingredients. Sprinkle ½ cup (125 mL) raisins or dried currants over ingredients just before stirring together. Shape and bake as directed.

SAVOURY VARIATIONS

Bacon Tomato Scones: Reduce sugar to 1 tbsp (15 mL). Add ½ tsp (2 mL) dried basil to dry ingredients. Sprinkle ½ cup (125 mL) each crumbled cooked bacon and chopped drained oil-packed sun-dried tomatoes over ingredients just before stirring together. Shape as directed. Brush scones with 1 egg, beaten. Bake as directed.

Cheddar Scones: Omit sugar. Add ¼ tsp (1 mL) cayenne pepper to dry ingredients. Sprinkle 1 cup (250 mL) shredded old Cheddar cheese over ingredients just before stirring together. Shape as directed. Brush scones with 1 egg, beaten; sprinkle with ½ cup (125 mL) shredded old Cheddar cheese. Bake as directed. Aged Gouda is a grand alternative to Cheddar.

Smoked Cheese and Oregano Scones: Reduce sugar to 1 tbsp (15 mL). Add 1 tsp (5 mL) dried oregano to dry ingredients. Sprinkle 1 cup (250 mL) shredded smoked provolone, Gouda or Cheddar cheese over ingredients just before stirring together. Shape as directed. Brush scones with 1 egg, beaten; sprinkle with ½ cup (125 mL) shredded smoked provolone, Gouda or Cheddar cheese. Bake as directed.

Almond Icing

1 cup	icing sugar	250 mL	Dash	almond extract	Dash
2 tbsp	milk	25 mL			

⤚ Stir together icing sugar, milk, almond extract and up to 1 tsp (5 mL) water if necessary to make thin icing. Drizzle over warm scones for a sheer glaze or over cooled scones for an opaque finish.

Makes ⅓ cup (75 mL).

VARIATION

Lemon Icing: Use lemon juice instead of milk. Omit almond extract.

Walnut Chocolate Fudge Scones

The trick here is to whisk the cocoa thoroughly with the dry ingredients. A perfect blend with no streaks is ideal.

2 cups	all-purpose flour	500 mL
½ cup	cocoa powder	125 mL
¼ cup	packed brown sugar	50 mL
2½ tsp	baking powder	12 mL
½ tsp	each baking soda and salt	2 mL
½ cup	cold butter, cubed	125 mL
1 cup	buttermilk	250 mL
1	egg	1

1 tsp	vanilla	5 mL
¾ cup	chopped toasted walnut halves	175 mL

FUDGE ICING:

1 cup	icing sugar	250 mL
2 tbsp	cocoa powder	25 mL
2 tbsp	milk (approx)	25 mL
1 tsp	vanilla	5 mL

❧ Line large rimless baking sheet with parchment paper or dust with flour; set aside.

❧ In large bowl, whisk together flour, cocoa, brown sugar, baking powder, baking soda and salt. Using pastry blender, cut in butter until crumbly. In separate bowl, whisk together buttermilk, egg and vanilla; pour over flour mixture. Sprinkle with walnuts; stir with fork to make soft ragged dough.

❧ With lightly floured hands, press dough into ball. On floured surface, knead gently 10 times. Pat out into 10- x 7-inch (25 x 18 cm) rectangle; trim edges to straighten.

❧ Cut rectangle into 6 squares; cut each diagonally in half. Place on prepared pan. Bake in centre of 400°F (200°C) oven until tops are firm to the touch, 18 to 20 minutes. Transfer to rack; let cool.

❧ **FUDGE ICING:** In small bowl, sift sugar with cocoa. Add milk and vanilla; whisk until smooth, adding up to 1 tsp (5 mL) more milk if necessary to make spreadable. Spread over scones; let stand until set, about 1 hour. **(Make-ahead: Store in airtight container at room temperature for up to 1 day or wrap each in plastic wrap and freeze in airtight container for up to 2 weeks.)**

Makes 12 scones. | PER SCONE: about 270 cal, 5 g pro, 14 g total fat (6 g sat. fat), 34 g carb, 2 g fibre, 41 mg chol, 307 mg sodium. % RDI: 7% calcium, 15% iron, 8% vit A, 17% folate.

Pumpkin Spice Scones

This scone is for pumpkin lovers. Canned pumpkin, not pie filling, yields more pumpkin than you need for these scones. Freeze the remaining purée for Pumpkin Spice Muffins (recipe, page 283) or Pumpkin Crème Brûlée (recipe, page 303).

(recipe, page 283) or Pumpkin Crème Brûlée (recipe, page 303).

SCONE SHAPES

ROUNDS: Pat dough into ½-inch (1 cm) thick round. Using 2½-inch (6 cm) floured cutter, cut out shapes, dipping cutter into flour between cuts. Repat and cut scraps, forming last scraps into the cook's biscuit. Bake for about 15 minutes.

WEDGES: On prepared baking sheet, pat dough out into ½-inch (1 cm) thick round. Cut like a pie into 8 to 12 triangular wedges. No need to separate the wedges, but do increase baking time to about 25 minutes.

SQUARES: On pan, pat out dough as directed. Cut into 12 squares. Separate to bake.

2½ cups	all-purpose flour	625 mL
⅓ cup	packed brown sugar	75 mL
2½ tsp	baking powder	12 mL
½ tsp	baking soda	2 mL
½ tsp	each ground ginger, cinnamon and salt	2 mL
Pinch	ground cloves	Pinch
½ cup	cold butter, cubed	125 mL
¾ cup	buttermilk	175 mL

½ cup	canned pumpkin purée	125 mL
1	egg	1
1 tsp	vanilla	5 mL

CINNAMON ICING:

1 cup	icing sugar	250 mL
2 tbsp	milk	25 mL
¼ tsp	cinnamon	1 mL

- Line large rimless baking sheet with parchment paper or dust with flour; set aside.
- In large bowl, whisk together flour, brown sugar, baking powder, baking soda, ginger, cinnamon, salt and cloves. Using pastry blender, cut in butter until crumbly. In separate bowl, whisk together buttermilk, pumpkin purée, egg and vanilla; pour over flour mixture. Stir with fork to make soft ragged dough.
- With lightly floured hands, press dough into ball. On floured surface, knead gently 10 times. Pat out into 10- x 7-inch (25 x 18 cm) rectangle; trim edges to straighten.
- Cut rectangle into 6 squares; cut each diagonally in half. Place on prepared pan. Bake in centre of 400°F (200°C) oven until golden, 18 to 20 minutes. Transfer scones to rack; let cool.
- **CINNAMON ICING:** In small bowl, whisk together sugar, milk, cinnamon and up to 1 tsp (5 mL) water if necessary to make spreadable. Spread over scones; let stand until set, about 1 hour. **(Make-ahead: Store in airtight container at room temperature for up to 1 day or wrap each in plastic wrap and freeze in airtight container for up to 2 weeks.)**

Makes 12 scones. | PER SCONE: about 239 cal, 4 g pro, 9 g total fat (5 g sat. fat), 37 g carb, 1 g fibre, 40 mg chol, 302 mg sodium. % RDI: 6% calcium, 11% iron, 28% vit A, 2% vit C, 16% folate.

Apricot Scone Wreath

The freeze-ahead feature of this scone wreath makes it a handy recipe for brunches and house-guest weekends.

2½ cups	all-purpose flour	625 mL		2	eggs	2
2 tbsp	granulated sugar	25 mL		⅓ cup	apricot or cherry jam	75 mL
2½ tsp	baking powder	12 mL		½ cup	finely chopped toasted walnut halves	125 mL
½ tsp	baking soda	2 mL		**GLAZE:**		
½ tsp	salt	2 mL		⅓ cup	icing sugar	75 mL
½ cup	cold butter, cubed	125 mL		1 tbsp	orange juice	15 mL
1 cup	buttermilk	250 mL				

Line large rimmed baking sheet with parchment paper; set aside.

In large bowl, whisk together flour, sugar, baking powder, baking soda and salt. Using pastry blender, cut in butter until crumbly. In separate bowl, whisk buttermilk with 1 of the eggs; pour over flour mixture. Stir with fork to make soft ragged dough.

With lightly floured hands, press dough into ball. On floured surface, knead gently 10 times. Roll out into 16- x 10-inch (40 x 25 cm) rectangle. Spread with jam, leaving ½-inch (1 cm) border at 1 long side uncovered. Sprinkle with walnuts. Starting at covered long side, roll up dough; pinch edges to seal.

Using serrated knife, cut into 1-inch (2.5 cm) thick slices. Arrange, cut side up and overlapping, in 9-inch (23 cm) circle on prepared pan. **(Make-ahead: Freeze until firm. Wrap in plastic wrap then heavy-duty foil; freeze for up to 1 week. Unwrap and return to baking sheet; thaw in refrigerator. Add 10 minutes to baking time.)**

In small bowl, lightly beat remaining egg; brush over wreath. Bake in centre of 400°F (200°C) oven until golden, about 15 minutes. Transfer to rack.

GLAZE: Meanwhile, in small bowl, whisk icing sugar with orange juice until smooth; drizzle over wreath while still warm from oven.

Makes 12 servings. | PER SERVING: about 259 cal, 5 g pro, 12 g total fat (6 g sat. fat), 33 g carb, 1 g fibre, 56 mg chol, 312 mg sodium. % RDI: 6% calcium, 11% iron, 9% vit A, 2% vit C, 21% folate.

VARIATIONS

Savoury Ham and Jarlsberg Wreath: Replace jam with ¼ cup (50 mL) Dijon mustard. Replace walnuts with 1 cup (250 mL) shredded Jarlsberg cheese, ½ cup (125 mL) diced Black Forest ham and 2 green onions, chopped. Omit glaze.

Savoury Roasted Red Pepper and Goat Cheese Wreath: Replace jam with ½ cup (125 mL) soft goat cheese. Replace walnuts with ⅓ cup (75 mL) each finely chopped roasted sweet red pepper and pitted black olives. Omit glaze. Sprinkle with 2 tbsp (25 mL) chopped fresh parsley after baking.

Sweet Milk Baking Powder Biscuits

Plump, light biscuits are a simple pleasure. Enjoy them with butter and jam, or make them into a breakfast sandwich (see variation, below).

2 cups	all-purpose flour	500 mL	¾ cup	milk		175 mL
1 tbsp	baking powder	15 mL		Granulated sugar (optional)		
½ tsp	salt	2 mL				
½ cup	cold butter, cubed	125 mL				

❧ Line large rimless baking sheet with parchment paper or dust with flour; set aside.

❧ In large bowl, whisk together flour, baking powder and salt. Using pastry blender, cut in butter until crumbly. Pour all but 2 tbsp (25 mL) of the milk over top, stirring with fork to form soft ragged dough.

❧ Turn out onto floured surface. With lightly floured hands, knead gently until dough comes together. Pat or roll out to ½-inch (1 cm) thickness. Using 2¼-inch (5.5 cm) floured cutter, cut out rounds. Place on prepared pan. Gather up scraps and repat dough; cut out more rounds, pressing remaining scraps into final (cook's) biscuit.

❧ Brush tops with remaining milk; sprinkle with sugar (if using). Bake in centre of 400°F (200°C) oven until golden, 18 to 20 minutes. Transfer to rack; let cool. (**Make-ahead: Store in airtight container at room temperature for up to 12 hours. Or wrap each in plastic wrap and freeze in airtight container for up to 2 weeks; thaw and reheat in 350°F/180°C oven for 10 minutes.**)

Makes 12 biscuits. | PER BISCUIT: about 155 cal, 3 g pro, 8 g total fat (5 g sat. fat), 17 g carb, 1 fibre, 22 mg chol, 234 mg sodium. % RDI: 6% calcium, 7% iron, 8% vit A, 20% folate.

....

VARIATION

Breakfast Biscuits: Using 3¼-inch (8.5 cm) round cutter, cut dough into 6 large biscuits. Bake as directed. While still hot, split and sandwich with bacon and fried or scrambled eggs. Add a slice of cheese if you like.

PREPPING BUTTER FOR BISCUITS AND SCONES

Cubing is the usual way to ready cold butter for cutting into dry ingredients. Evenly sized pieces blend more evenly.

Shredding the butter is another alternative. Because shreds are smaller than cubes, there is less cutting in later. Hold butter in its wrapper or foil; shred, using large holes on box grater. This is especially effective if you freeze your butter first – there's less risk of the butter melting as you shred. You can shred the butter right over the dry ingredients, toss together, then proceed with stirring in the wet ingredients.

Spud Island Biscuit Fingers

Potatoes lend flavour and moisture to a traditional P.E.I. specialty: biscuits. The biscuits are just as tasty without the cheese and cayenne.

CRUSTY VS. SOFT SIDES

❯ FOR CRUSTY SIDES:
Bake biscuits and scones 1 to 2 inches (2.5 to 5 cm) apart on rimless baking sheet and let them cool on a rack.

❯ FOR SOFT SIDES:
Bake biscuits or scones in metal cake pan with sides touching. Cover lightly with clean tea towel while still hot to soften their exteriors.

2¼ cups	all-purpose flour	550 mL	½ cup	cold butter, cubed	125 mL
1 tbsp	granulated sugar	15 mL	¾ cup	shredded Gouda cheese	175 mL
2 tsp	baking powder	10 mL	1 cup	buttermilk	250 mL
1 tsp	baking soda	5 mL	¾ cup	mashed potatoes	175 mL
½ tsp	salt	2 mL	1	egg yolk	1
¼ tsp	cayenne pepper	1 mL			

❧ Dust rimless baking sheet generously with all-purpose flour; set aside.

❧ In large bowl, whisk together flour, sugar, baking powder, baking soda, salt and cayenne pepper. With pastry blender, cut in butter until crumbly with a few larger pieces. Sprinkle with ½ cup (125 mL) of the cheese.

❧ In separate bowl, whisk buttermilk with potatoes until smooth; pour over dry ingredients. With fork, toss together until soft ragged dough forms. Turn out onto floured surface; knead 3 or 4 times until dough holds together. Pat out into 9- x 6-inch (23 x 15 cm) rectangle. Cut lengthwise in half; cut crosswise in sixths to make 12 finger-shaped biscuits.

❧ Arrange on prepared pan. Brush with egg yolk; sprinkle with remaining cheese. Bake in centre of 400°F (200°C) oven until golden, about 18 minutes.

Makes 12 biscuits. | PER BISCUIT: about 208 cal, 5 g pro, 11 g total fat (6 g sat. fat), 23 g carb, 1 g fibre, 50 mg chol, 397 mg sodium. % RDI: 9% calcium, 9% iron, 9% vit A, 2% vit C, 16% folate.

VARIATION

Sweet Potato Biscuit Fingers: Substitute mashed cooked sweet potatoes for mashed potatoes. Reduce all-purpose flour to 2 cups (500 mL) and buttermilk to ¾ cup (175 mL), adding up to 2 tsp (10 mL) more buttermilk if there are dry patches in bowl.

Welsh Cakes

Spices – often both nutmeg and mace – and currants make these griddle "cakes" distinctive and different from scones or baking powder biscuits.

1⅔ cups	all-purpose flour	400 mL	½ cup	cold butter, cubed	125 mL
½ cup	granulated sugar	125 mL	⅓ cup	dried currants	75 mL
¾ tsp	baking powder	4 mL	¼ cup	candied mixed peel or dried currants	50 mL
½ tsp	each salt and nutmeg	2 mL			
¼ tsp	each baking soda and ground mace or nutmeg	1 mL	1	egg	1
			¼ cup	milk	50 mL

In large bowl, whisk together flour, sugar, baking powder, salt, nutmeg, baking soda and mace. With pastry blender, cut in butter until crumbly. Stir in currants and peel. In separate bowl, whisk egg with milk; pour over dry ingredients. Toss with fork to make soft ragged dough.

With floured hands, press into flat square. On well-floured surface, roll out dough to ¼-inch (5 mm) thickness. With floured 2-inch (5 cm) round cutter, cut out shapes, rerolling scraps.

Bake on lightly greased griddle or in skillet over medium heat or in electric skillet at 300°F (150°C) until light brown on both sides and no longer doughy inside, about 6 minutes. **(Make-ahead: Let cool. Layer between waxed paper in airtight container and store at room temperature for up to 1 day or freeze for up to 2 weeks.)**

Makes about 40 cakes. | PER CAKE: about 59 cal, 1 g pro, 3 g total fat (2 g sat. fat), 9 g carb, trace fibre, 12 mg chol, 68 mg sodium. % RDI: 1% calcium, 2% iron, 2% vit A, 5% folate.

Maritime Brown Bread

What sets this chewy bread with rich molasses flavour apart is the cooking method and container: the bread is steamed in large tomato cans. It's traditionally served with baked beans, but you can enjoy it with just about any savoury entrée. It's also tasty toasted and buttered. If you like, add ¾ cup (175 mL) raisins, chopped dates or chopped dried apricots.

1 cup	whole wheat flour	250 mL		1½ cups	buttermilk, at room temperature	375 mL
1 cup	dark or light rye flour	250 mL		¾ cup	fancy molasses	175 mL
1 cup	cornmeal	250 mL		½ cup	unsweetened applesauce	125 mL
1½ tsp	baking soda	7 mL				
1 tsp	salt	5 mL				

❧ Grease two 28-oz (796 mL) tomato cans. Grease two 8-inch (20 cm) squares of parchment paper or foil; set aside.

❧ In large bowl, whisk together whole wheat and rye flours, cornmeal, baking soda and salt. In separate bowl, whisk together buttermilk, molasses and applesauce; pour over flour mixture. Stir just until blended. Divide between prepared cans. Cover tops with prepared paper, greased side down and leaving 1-inch (2.5 cm) pleat for bread to expand; tie securely with string, about 1 inch (2.5 cm) below rim.

❧ Place cans on steamer rack or heatproof trivet in deep pot or Dutch oven just large enough to accommodate width and depth of cans. Pour in enough boiling water to come halfway up sides of cans. Cover and return to boil over medium heat; reduce heat and simmer until cake tester inserted in centre comes out clean, about 2½ hours. Top up steaming water with boiling water if the level drops. Remove from cans; let cool on racks. **(Make-ahead: Wrap in plastic wrap and store at room temperature for up to 5 days. Or overwrap in heavy-duty foil and freeze for up to 2 weeks.)**

Makes 2 loaves, 10 slices each. | PER SLICE: about 109 cal, 3 g pro, 1 g total fat (trace sat. fat), 24 g carb, 2 g fibre, 1 mg chol, 227 mg sodium. % RDI: 5% calcium, 9% iron, 2% vit C, 4% folate.

BANNOCK

❯ Bannock is a quick-bread cousin of biscuits and scones. Due to its name and ingredients, bannock is usually associated with Scotland. But it has become a staple for aboriginal peoples on this continent, whose ancestors were using wild ingredients to make a form of bannock prior to the arrival of Europeans.

In its most basic form, contemporary bannock is made from flour, fat, leavening, salt and water. To that ingredient list, you can add dried milk powder, rolled oats, cornmeal, milk, raisins, currants and/or blueberries – whatever is at hand. It is traditionally baked in a skillet over an open fire wrapped around a green stick or in the oven, but a slightly different version is fried into crisp, puffed pillows.

Irish Soda Bread

A loaf of bread takes too long to make, so why bother? Irish soda bread says phooey to this idea. With baking soda instead of yeast, you can bake a loaf in less than an hour.

2 cups	all-purpose flour	500 mL		1½ cups	buttermilk	375 mL
1 cup	whole wheat flour	250 mL		¼ cup	vegetable oil	50 mL
2 tbsp	flaxseeds or sesame seeds	25 mL		**TOPPING:**		
2 tbsp	granulated sugar	25 mL		1 tbsp	all-purpose flour	15 mL
1 tsp	each baking soda and salt	5 mL				

❧ Line rimmed baking sheet with parchment paper or grease; set aside.

❧ In large bowl, whisk together all-purpose and whole wheat flours, flaxseeds, sugar, baking soda and salt. In separate bowl, whisk buttermilk with oil; pour over dry ingredients. Stir with fork to make soft ragged dough.

❧ With floured hands, press dough into ball. On floured surface, knead gently 10 times. Place on prepared pan; gently pat out into 6-inch (15 cm) circle.

❧ TOPPING: Sprinkle flour over loaf. With sharp knife, score large X on top.

❧ Bake in centre of 375°F (190°C) oven until golden and cake tester inserted in centre comes out clean, about 45 minutes.

Makes 1 loaf, 16 slices. | PER SLICE: about 136 cal, 4 g pro, 5 g total fat (trace sat. fat), 21 g carb, 2 g fibre, 1 mg chol, 242 mg sodium. % RDI: 3% calcium, 8% iron, 5% folate.

VARIATIONS

Cheese and Onion Soda Bread: Omit flaxseeds and topping. Add 1 cup (250 mL) shredded old Cheddar cheese, ¼ cup (50 mL) chopped green onions and pinch cayenne pepper to dry ingredients.

Honey Apricot Soda Bread: Omit sugar, flaxseeds and topping. Increase all-purpose flour to 2¼ cups (550 mL). Add ½ cup (125 mL) each chopped dried apricots and raisins to dry ingredients. Add ⅓ cup (75 mL) liquid honey to liquid ingredients. After baking, let soda bread stand on rack for 15 minutes. Mix ½ cup (125 mL) icing sugar with 2 tbsp (25 mL) orange juice until smooth; drizzle over loaf.

Carrot Pineapple Loaf

There's nothing earnest about this carrot-flecked loaf. The icing and whimsical marzipan carrots do push it into the let's-fuss-a-little category of cakes, but when you don't have time, leave the loaf unadorned or just go for the cream cheese icing. Any way, the loaf is still delicious.

2 cups	all-purpose flour	500 mL
2 tsp	baking powder	10 mL
1 tsp	baking soda	5 mL
½ tsp	salt	2 mL
2	eggs	2
1 cup	granulated sugar	250 mL
½ cup	vegetable oil	125 mL
2 tsp	finely grated orange rind	10 mL
1 tsp	vanilla	5 mL
2 cups	grated carrots	500 mL
1	can (14 oz/398 mL) crushed pineapple, drained	1

½ cup	sweetened shredded or flaked coconut	125 mL

CREAM CHEESE ICING:

2 tbsp	each cream cheese and butter, softened	25 mL
¼ tsp	vanilla	1 mL
¾ cup	icing sugar	175 mL

MARZIPAN CARROTS:

1 oz	marzipan	30 g
	Green and orange paste food colouring	
1 tsp	chocolate wafer cookie crumbs	5 mL

❧ Line 9- x 5-inch (2 L) loaf pan with double layer of parchment paper; set aside.

❧ In large bowl, whisk together flour, baking powder, baking soda and salt. In separate large bowl, beat eggs with sugar until light and fluffy; beat in oil, orange rind and vanilla. Pour over dry ingredients; stir just until moistened. Stir in carrots, pineapple and coconut. Scrape into prepared pan; smooth top.

❧ Bake in centre of 350°F (180°C) oven until cake tester inserted in centre comes out clean, about 1 hour. Let cool in pan on rack for 15 minutes. Transfer to rack; let cool. **(Make-ahead: Wrap in plastic wrap and store at room temperature for up to 2 days or overwrap in heavy-duty foil and freeze for up to 2 weeks. Thaw.)**

❧ **CREAM CHEESE ICING:** In bowl, beat cream cheese with butter; beat in vanilla. Beat in sugar in 2 additions until smooth. Spread over top of loaf.

❧ **MARZIPAN CARROTS:** Tint 1 tsp (5 mL) of the marzipan green, then tint remainder orange, kneading to combine. Divide orange marzipan into 7 balls; roll each into carrot shape and score with knife to resemble carrot. Shape green marzipan into carrot tops. With toothpick, make hole in each carrot and attach top.

❧ Using handle of wooden spoon, make 3 holes lengthwise along centre of icing and loaf. Insert 3 of the carrots, leaving leafy tops and bit of orange sticking out. Arrange remaining carrots on top. Sprinkle cookie crumbs around each carrot to resemble earth.

Makes 1 loaf, 16 slices. | PER SLICE: about 254 cal, 3 g pro, 11 g total fat (3 g sat. fat), 37 g carb, 1 g fibre, 29 mg chol, 228 mg sodium. % RDI: 3% calcium, 7% iron, 25% vit A, 3% vit C, 17% folate.

Banana Pecan Loaf

For full banana flavour, let the bananas ripen to the very speckled fragrant stage. When you are packing up slices for lunches and freezing some for breakfasts, don't forget to save one to nibble on with an afternoon latte or chai.

1½ cups	all-purpose flour	375 mL		¼ cup	vegetable oil	50 mL
1 tsp	baking powder	5 mL		2	eggs	2
1 tsp	baking soda	5 mL		1 tsp	vanilla	5 mL
½ tsp	salt	2 mL		¾ cup	chopped pecans	175 mL
1 cup	mashed very ripe bananas (2 large)	250 mL		**GLAZE:**		
1 cup	packed brown sugar	250 mL		¼ cup	icing sugar	50 mL
½ cup	sour cream	125 mL		1 tbsp	milk	15 mL

↜ Line 9- x 5-inch (2 L) loaf pan with double layer of parchment paper or grease; set aside.

↜ In large bowl, whisk together flour, baking powder, baking soda and salt. In separate large bowl, whisk together bananas, brown sugar, sour cream, oil, eggs and vanilla; scrape over dry ingredients. Sprinkle with pecans; stir just until combined.

↜ Scrape into prepared pan; smooth top. Bake in centre of 350°F (180°C) oven until cake tester inserted in centre comes out clean, about 1 hour. Let cool in pan on rack for 15 minutes. Transfer to rack; let cool. (**Make-ahead: Wrap in plastic wrap and store at room temperature for up to 3 days or overwrap in heavy-duty foil and freeze for up to 2 weeks.**)

↜ GLAZE: In bowl, whisk icing sugar with milk until smooth. Brush over top of loaf. Let stand until set, about 30 minutes.

Makes 1 loaf, 16 slices. | PER SLICE: about 201 cal, 3 g pro, 9 g total fat (1 g sat. fat), 29 g carb, 1 g fibre, 26 mg chol, 186 mg sodium. % RDI: 3% calcium, 8% iron, 2% vit A, 2% vit C, 14% folate.

Old-Fashioned Date and Nut Loaf

You can use the traditional block of dates found in the baking section of your supermarket. Just ensure that they are pliable and glistening. Buying already-chopped walnuts may seem like a smart shortcut, but, too often, the ones sold in bags in your baking aisle are rancid. It's better to buy higher-quality halves to chop yourself – they cost a bit more but are worth every penny.

¾ cup	water	175 mL		1	egg	1
1½ cups	chopped pitted dates	375 mL		1 cup	milk	250 mL
2 cups	all-purpose flour	500 mL		¼ cup	butter, melted, or vegetable oil	50 mL
½ cup	packed brown sugar	125 mL				
2½ tsp	baking powder	12 mL		1 tsp	vanilla	5 mL
½ tsp	baking soda	2 mL		1 cup	chopped walnut halves	250 mL
½ tsp	salt	2 mL				

USE YOUR FINGERS

❯ Whisking dry ingredients together is easy when you're working with granulated sugar, but slightly-more-flavourful brown sugar may be a bit clumpy. You may need to use your fingers to rub it evenly into the flour mixture. Be sure to squash or, if they're rock-hard, remove any lumps.

☙ Line 9- x 5-inch (2 L) loaf pan with double layer of parchment paper or grease; set aside.

☙ In large microwaveable bowl, microwave water at high until boiling, about 1 minute. Add dates. Microwave at high, stirring twice, until mushy, about 5 minutes. (Or, in saucepan, cook water with dates over medium heat, stirring often, until mushy, about 8 minutes.) Let cool.

☙ Meanwhile, in separate large bowl, whisk together flour, brown sugar, baking powder, baking soda and salt; set aside.

☙ Add egg, milk, butter and vanilla to date mixture; whisk until combined. Scrape over dry ingredients; sprinkle with ¾ cup (175 mL) of the walnuts and stir just until combined.

☙ Scrape into prepared pan; smooth top. Sprinkle with remaining walnuts. Bake in centre of 350°F (180°C) oven until cake tester inserted in centre comes out clean, about 1 hour. Let cool in pan on rack for 15 minutes. Transfer to rack; let cool. (**Make-ahead: Wrap in plastic wrap and store at room temperature for up to 3 days or overwrap in heavy-duty foil and freeze for up to 2 weeks.**)

Makes 1 loaf, 16 slices. | PER SLICE: about 215 cal, 4 g pro, 9 g total fat (3 g sat. fat), 33 g carb, 2 g fibre, 20 mg chol, 193 mg sodium. % RDI: 6% calcium, 9% iron, 4% vit A, 19% folate.

Cheddar and Sage Skillet Cornbread

Slightly coarse cornmeal adds a pleasing crunchy texture to cornbread. No multigrain flour? Use ⅓ cup (75 mL) each all-purpose flour and whole wheat flour. Be sure to measure out all the ingredients before you put the skillet in the hot oven. There's just enough time to mix them while the butter melts and the skillet heats.

2 tbsp	butter	25 mL		½ tsp	salt	2 mL
1¾ cups	medium-grind cornmeal	425 mL		2	eggs	2
				1½ cups	milk	375 mL
⅔ cup	multigrain flour	150 mL		1 cup	shredded old Cheddar cheese	250 mL
1 tbsp	granulated sugar	15 mL				
2 tsp	baking powder	10 mL		1 tbsp	chopped fresh sage (or 1 tsp/5 mL dried)	15 mL

❧ Place butter in 10-inch (25 cm) ovenproof cast-iron skillet. Heat in centre of 450°F (230°C) oven until smoking, about 6 minutes.

❧ Meanwhile, in large bowl, whisk together cornmeal, flour, sugar, baking powder and salt. In separate bowl, beat eggs until foamy; whisk in milk. Pour over cornmeal mixture. Add half of the cheese and the sage; stir just until combined.

❧ Scrape batter into hot pan; sprinkle with remaining cheese.

❧ Bake until golden and firm to the touch, about 25 minutes. Let cool in pan on rack for 5 minutes. If desired, invert onto rack; invert top side up. Eat while still hot or let cool. **(Make-ahead: Store in airtight container at room temperature for up to 2 days or wrap in plastic wrap and freeze in airtight container for up to 2 weeks.)**

Makes 8 to 12 servings. | PER EACH OF 12 SERVINGS: about 188 cal, 7 g pro, 7 g total fat (4 g sat. fat), 24 g carb, 2 g fibre, 48 mg chol, 242 mg sodium. % RDI: 12% calcium, 6% iron, 8% vit A, 20% folate.

Blueberry Streusel Muffins

Canada is the world's largest producer of wild blueberries, so it's no surprise that blueberry muffins are a Canadian favourite. Fresh blueberries are best (you can use cultivated ones, too), but you can also stir in frozen berries straight from the freezer so they don't colour the batter. Make sure to have the buttermilk and butter at room temperature before mixing the batter; if they are fridge-cold, the butter will clump and not mix in evenly.

2 cups	all-purpose flour	500 mL
1 cup	packed brown sugar	250 mL
¾ tsp	baking soda	4 mL
½ tsp	salt	2 mL
1	egg	1
1 cup	buttermilk	250 mL
¼ cup	butter, melted	50 mL
1 tsp	vanilla	5 mL
½ tsp	grated lemon rind	2 mL

1 cup	fresh or frozen wild blueberries, or cultivated blueberries	250 mL

STREUSEL:

3 tbsp	packed brown sugar	50 mL
3 tbsp	sliced almonds	50 mL
3 tbsp	all-purpose flour	50 mL
Pinch	grated nutmeg	Pinch
1 tbsp	butter, melted	15 mL

❧ Line 12 muffin cups with paper liners or grease; set aside.

❧ STREUSEL: In bowl, mix brown sugar, almonds, flour and nutmeg; drizzle with butter. Toss with fork; set aside.

❧ In large bowl, whisk together flour, brown sugar, baking soda and salt. In separate bowl, whisk together egg, buttermilk, butter, vanilla and lemon rind; pour over dry ingredients. Sprinkle with blueberries; stir just until dry ingredients are moistened.

❧ Spoon into prepared muffin cups; sprinkle with streusel. Bake in centre of 375°F (190°C) oven until tops are firm to the touch, about 25 minutes. Let cool in pan on rack for 5 minutes. Transfer to rack; let cool. (**Make-ahead: Store in airtight container at room temperature for up to 1 day or wrap each in plastic wrap and freeze in airtight container for up to 2 weeks.**)

Makes 12 muffins. | PER MUFFIN: about 240 cal, 4 g pro, 7 g total fat (4 g sat. fat), 42 g carb, 1 g fibre, 30 mg chol, 241 mg sodium. % RDI: 5% calcium, 11% iron, 5% vit A, 2% vit C, 23% folate.

VARIATION

Raspberry Streusel Muffins: Replace blueberries with fresh or frozen raspberries.

Banana Chocolate Chip Muffins

Chocolate chips are indeed an indulgence in muffins. So if you are feeling virtuous, replace them with chopped nuts.

2½ cups	all-purpose flour	625 mL		1 cup	buttermilk	250 mL
1 cup	packed brown sugar	250 mL		1 cup	mashed very ripe bananas (2 large)	250 mL
1½ tsp	baking powder	7 mL		⅓ cup	vegetable oil	75 mL
1 tsp	baking soda	5 mL		1 tsp	vanilla	5 mL
½ tsp	salt	2 mL		¾ cup	chocolate chips	175 mL
2	eggs	2				

❧ Line 12 muffin cups with paper liners or grease; set aside.

❧ In large bowl, whisk together flour, brown sugar, baking powder, baking soda and salt. In separate bowl, beat eggs; whisk in buttermilk, bananas, oil and vanilla. Pour over dry ingredients. Sprinkle with chocolate chips; stir just until dry ingredients are moistened.

❧ Spoon into prepared muffin cups, filling three-quarters full. Bake in centre of 375°F (190°C) oven until tops are firm to the touch, 20 to 25 minutes. Let cool in pan on rack for 5 minutes. Transfer to rack; let cool. **(Make-ahead: Store in airtight container at room temperature for up to 2 days or wrap each in plastic wrap and freeze in airtight container for up to 2 weeks.)**

Makes 12 muffins. | PER MUFFIN: about 305 cal, 5 g pro, 11 g total fat (3 g sat. fat), 50 g carb, 2 g fibre, 32 mg chol, 264 mg sodium. % RDI: 6% calcium, 14% iron, 2% vit A, 2% vit C, 16% folate.

TESTING FOR MUFFIN DONENESS

❯ Always check muffins 5 minutes before the time specified in the recipe.

❯ Trust your senses. Can you smell a toasty, grainy fragrance? Do the muffins feel firm to a light touch in the centre? Can you see that a cake tester or skewer inserted into the centre comes out clean? If you answer yes to all of these questions, the muffins are ready to come out of the oven.

Applesauce Bran Muffins

Use your homemade applesauce or put it on the shopping list so you can make these moist, healthy snacks. Wrapped and frozen, big muffins like these make excellent quickie breakfasts and tuck very nicely into lunch bags.

BUTTERMILK SUBSTITUTES

❯ Commercially available buttermilk is made by combining pasteurized skim milk with a lactic acid bacterial culture and fermenting it at a low temperature to create a thick, tart liquid. When there's no buttermilk in your fridge, substitute one of the following.

● Pour 1 tbsp (15 mL) lemon juice or white, cider or white wine vinegar into a glass measuring cup. Add enough milk to measure 1 cup (250 mL); stir. Let stand for 10 minutes; stir again.

● Combine equal parts plain yogurt and milk, both lower fat if desired.

● Whisk ¼ cup (50 mL) buttermilk powder (available in bulk food stores) with 1 cup (250 mL) cold water. Or whisk the buttermilk powder into the dry ingredients and add water to the liquid ingredients.

1	egg	1	1 cup	natural wheat bran	250 mL
1 cup	applesauce	250 mL	2 cups	all-purpose flour	500 mL
⅔ cup	buttermilk	150 mL	1 tsp	baking soda	5 mL
⅓ cup	packed brown sugar	75 mL	1 tsp	cinnamon	5 mL
¼ cup	fancy molasses	50 mL	½ tsp	salt	2 mL
¼ cup	vegetable oil	50 mL	1 cup	raisins	250 mL
1 tsp	vanilla	5 mL			

❧ Line 12 muffin cups with paper liners or grease; set aside.

❧ In large bowl, whisk together egg, applesauce, buttermilk, brown sugar, molasses, oil and vanilla until well blended. Stir in bran; let stand until softened and some of the liquid is absorbed, about 5 minutes.

❧ In separate large bowl, whisk together flour, baking soda, cinnamon and salt; pour applesauce mixture over dry ingredients. Sprinkle with raisins; stir just until dry ingredients are moistened.

❧ Spoon into prepared muffin cups, filling to top. Bake in centre of 375°F (190°C) oven until golden and tops are firm to the touch, about 25 minutes. Let cool in pan on rack for 5 minutes. Transfer to rack; let cool. (**Make-ahead: Store in airtight container at room temperature for up to 2 days or wrap each in plastic wrap and freeze in airtight container for up to 2 weeks.**)

Makes 12 muffins. | PER MUFFIN: about 229 cal, 4 g pro, 6 g total fat (1 g sat. fat), 43 g carb, 4 g fibre, 17 mg chol, 225 mg sodium. % RDI: 5% calcium, 16% iron, 1% vit A, 3% vit C, 22% folate.

Pumpkin Spice Muffins

Instead of an icing, these pumpkin pie–spiced muffins are dressed up with a complementary maple spread. In a hurry? Omit spread and serve as is or with butter.

1¾ cups	all-purpose flour	425 mL
¾ cup	packed brown sugar	175 mL
1½ tsp	baking powder	7 mL
1 tsp	cinnamon	5 mL
½ tsp	baking soda	2 mL
½ tsp	salt	2 mL
½ tsp	ground ginger	2 mL
¼ tsp	ground cloves	1 mL
¼ tsp	nutmeg	1 mL
½ cup	chopped walnut halves	125 mL

2	eggs	2
¾ cup	canned pumpkin purée	175 mL
¼ cup	vegetable oil	50 mL
1 tsp	vanilla	5 mL

MAPLE CREAM CHEESE SPREAD:

Half	pkg (8 oz/250 g pkg) regular or light cream cheese, softened	Half
1 tbsp	icing sugar	15 mL
1 tbsp	maple syrup	15 mL
¼ tsp	vanilla	1 mL

Line 12 muffin cups with paper liners or grease; set aside.

In large bowl, whisk together flour, brown sugar, baking powder, cinnamon, baking soda, salt, ginger, cloves and nutmeg; mix in ¼ cup (50 mL) of the walnuts.

In separate bowl, whisk together eggs, pumpkin purée, oil and vanilla; pour over dry ingredients. Stir just until dry ingredients are moistened.

Spoon into prepared muffin cups. Sprinkle with remaining walnuts. Bake in centre of 375°F (190°C) oven until golden and tops are firm to the touch, 20 to 25 minutes. Let cool in pan on rack for 5 minutes. Transfer to rack; let cool. **(Make-ahead: Store in airtight container at room temperature for up to 2 days or wrap each in plastic wrap and freeze in airtight container for up to 2 weeks.)**

MAPLE CREAM CHEESE SPREAD: In bowl, beat cream cheese until light; beat in icing sugar, maple syrup and vanilla until blended. **(Make-ahead: Cover and refrigerate for up to 2 days.)** Serve muffins with spread.

Makes 12 muffins. | PER MUFFIN: about 253 cal, 5 g pro, 12 g total fat (3 g sat. fat), 32 g carb, 1 g fibre, 42 mg chol, 224 mg sodium. % RDI: 5% calcium, 12% iron, 36% vit A, 2% vit C, 14% folate.

FREEZING AND THAWING MUFFINS

> To freeze muffins, we recommend wrapping each one individually in plastic wrap, then enclosing the wrapped muffins in a rigid airtight container or a resealable plastic bag. Muffins will stay perfectly fresh for about 2 weeks in the freezer.

> To thaw, let stand for 2 hours at room temperature – perfect timing if you're slipping a frozen muffin into a lunch bag. To speed things up, unwrap frozen muffin, place on microwaveable plate, cover and microwave at high for about 20 seconds.

Date Orange Muffins

While dates are top-notch in these crunchy-topped moist muffins, you have other options: golden raisins; dried currants, cherries or cranberries; or slivered dried apricots.

2 cups	all-purpose flour	500 mL	½ cup	milk	125 mL
½ cup	granulated sugar	125 mL	¼ cup	vegetable oil	50 mL
2 tbsp	grated orange rind	25 mL	1 tsp	vanilla	5 mL
2 tsp	baking powder	10 mL	1 cup	chopped pitted dates	250 mL
1 tsp	baking soda	5 mL	TOPPING:		
½ tsp	salt	2 mL	¼ cup	granulated sugar	50 mL
1	egg	1	1 tbsp	grated orange rind	15 mL
½ cup	orange juice	125 mL			

↜ Line 12 muffin cups with paper liners or grease; set aside.

↜ In large bowl, whisk together flour, sugar, orange rind, baking powder, baking soda and salt. In separate bowl, beat egg; whisk in orange juice, milk, oil and vanilla. Pour over dry ingredients. Sprinkle with dates; stir just until dry ingredients are moistened. Spoon into prepared muffin cups, filling three-quarters full.

↜ **TOPPING:** Stir sugar with orange rind; sprinkle 1 tsp (5 mL) over each cup. Bake in centre of 375°F (190°C) oven until firm to the touch, about 20 minutes. Let cool in pan on rack for 5 minutes. Transfer to rack; let cool. **(Make-ahead: Store in airtight container at room temperature for up to 2 days or wrap each in plastic wrap and freeze in airtight container for up to 2 weeks.)**

Makes 12 muffins. | PER MUFFIN: about 223 cal, 3 g pro, 5 g total fat (1 g sat. fat), 41 g carb, 2 g fibre, 248 mg sodium. % RDI: 4% calcium, 8% iron, 2% vit A, 10% vit C, 12% folate.

Prairie Honey Oatmeal Muffins

These wholesome muffins are a nutritious start to the day or a tasty pick-me-up snack. The recipe makes 10 muffins; fill the remaining muffin cups with water to prevent the pan from warping.

AVOID A STICKY MESS, HONEY

❯ Before measuring sticky sweeteners, such as honey, molasses, or corn or maple syrup, lightly grease the measuring cup. They'll slide in and give an accurate measurement, then slide out just as easily.

❯ When a recipe calls for vegetable oil and a sticky sweetener, as this one does, simply measure the oil first, then the sweetener. No need to grease the measuring cup.

1 cup	large-flake rolled oats	250 mL
1 cup	buttermilk	250 mL
1 cup	whole wheat flour	250 mL
1½ tsp	baking powder	7 mL
½ tsp	each baking soda and cinnamon	2 mL
¼ tsp	salt	1 mL
⅓ cup	each vegetable oil and liquid honey	75 mL
¼ cup	packed brown sugar	50 mL
1	egg	1
⅓ cup	roasted unsalted sunflower seeds	75 mL

❧ Line 10 muffin cups with paper liners or grease; set aside.

❧ In large bowl, stir oats with buttermilk; let stand for 15 minutes. Meanwhile, in separate large bowl, whisk together flour, baking powder, baking soda, cinnamon and salt.

❧ Whisk oil, honey, brown sugar and egg into buttermilk mixture; scrape over dry ingredients. Sprinkle with ¼ cup (50 mL) of the sunflower seeds; stir just until dry ingredients are moistened.

❧ Spoon into prepared muffin cups; sprinkle with remaining sunflower seeds. Bake in centre of 375°F (190°C) oven until tops are firm to the touch, about 17 minutes. Let cool in pan on rack for 5 minutes. Transfer to rack; let cool. **(Make-ahead: Store in airtight container at room temperature for up to 3 days or wrap each in plastic wrap and freeze in airtight container for up to 2 weeks.)**

Makes 10 muffins. | PER MUFFIN: about 241 cal, 6 g pro, 11 g total fat (1 g sat. fat), 32 g carb, 3 g fibre, 19 mg chol, 191 mg sodium. % RDI: 6% calcium, 11% iron, 1% vit A, 10% folate.

Carrot Oatmeal Muffins

This muffin has lots of variations – both inside and on top – for different tastes.

1½ cups	all-purpose flour	375 mL		1 cup	milk	250 mL
1 cup	quick-cooking rolled oats (not instant)	250 mL		1	egg	1
				¼ cup	vegetable oil	50 mL
½ cup	packed brown sugar	125 mL		1 tsp	vanilla	5 mL
1 tbsp	baking powder	15 mL		1	carrot, grated	1
½ tsp	cinnamon or ground ginger	2 mL		½ cup	chopped walnut halves (optional)	125 mL
¼ tsp	salt	1 mL				

᠊᠊ Line 12 muffin cups with paper liners or grease; set aside.

᠊᠊ In large bowl, whisk together flour, oats, brown sugar, baking powder, cinnamon and salt. In separate bowl, whisk together milk, egg, oil and vanilla; pour over dry ingredients. Sprinkle with carrot, and walnuts (if using); stir just until dry ingredients are moistened.

᠊᠊ Spoon into prepared muffin cups. Bake in centre of 375°F (190°C) oven until firm to the touch, about 20 minutes. Let cool in pan on rack for 5 minutes. Transfer to racks; let cool. (Make-ahead: Store in airtight container at room temperature for up to 1 day or wrap each in plastic wrap and freeze in airtight container for up to 2 weeks.)

Makes 12 muffins. | PER MUFFIN: about 182 cal, 4 g pro, 6 g total fat (1 g sat. fat), 28 g carb, 1 g fibre, 17 mg chol, 145 mg sodium. % RDI: 7% calcium, 10% iron, 12% vit A, 17% folate.

VARIATIONS

Apple Raisin Oatmeal Muffins: Replace carrot with 1 apple, peeled and grated; replace walnuts with ½ cup (125 mL) raisins.

Crunchy-Top Carrot Oatmeal Muffins: In small bowl, mix 2 tbsp (25 mL) granulated sugar with pinch cinnamon; sprinkle over muffins before baking.

Orange-Glazed Carrot Oatmeal Muffins: In small bowl, mix ¾ cup (175 mL) icing sugar with 2 tbsp (25 mL) orange juice. Drizzle over cooled muffins.

Sweet Oat–Topped Carrot Oatmeal Muffins: In bowl, mix ¼ cup (50 mL) packed brown sugar with ¼ cup (50 mL) quick-cooking rolled oats; sprinkle over muffins before baking.

Tropical Fruit Oatmeal Muffins: Replace carrot with ¾ cup (175 mL) mixed dried tropical fruit (chopped into ½-inch/1 cm pieces if necessary); replace walnuts with ¼ cup (50 mL) sweetened shredded or flaked coconut.

Glazed Apple Cinnamon Puff

Not quite a soufflé, not quite a crêpe, this intriguing baked pancake, also known as a "Dutch baby" or German pancake, relies entirely on eggs to puff it into a crusty and tender case for fruit. Before preheating the oven, place racks in centre and bottom positions. The puff is baked on the centre one, and the other one should be out of the way so that the top of the puff doesn't touch it. The apples retain their heat, so caution young children.

3	large apples, peeled and cored (about 1½ lb/750 g)	3	¾ cup	milk	175 mL
			1 tbsp	granulated sugar	15 mL
⅓ cup	butter, melted	75 mL	Pinch	salt	Pinch
3	eggs	3	¼ cup	packed brown sugar	50 mL
¾ cup	all-purpose flour	175 mL	¼ tsp	cinnamon or nutmeg	1 mL

➤ Cut apples into scant ½-inch (1 cm) thick slices; set aside.

➤ In blender or food processor, blend 2 tbsp (25 mL) of the butter, the eggs, flour, milk, sugar and salt until smooth. Set batter aside.

➤ In 10-inch (25 cm) cast-iron or ovenproof heavy-bottomed skillet, heat remaining butter over medium heat. Add brown sugar, cinnamon and apples; cook, stirring occasionally, until apples are golden and tender, about 15 minutes.

➤ Pour batter over apples. Bake in centre of 425°F (220°C) oven until puffed and edge is browned, about 20 minutes.

➤ If desired, invert onto serving plate, scraping any remaining apples and syrup onto puff. Serve immediately.

Makes 6 servings. | PER SERVING: about 284 cal, 6 g pro, 14 g total fat (8 g sat. fat), 36 g carb, 2 g fibre, 123 mg chol, 119 mg sodium. % RDI: 6% calcium, 9% iron, 14% vit A, 5% vit C, 20% folate.

Sky-High Popovers

Unlike Yorkshire pudding, which must be made at the last minute, these crisp and easy popovers can be made ahead and reheated just before serving, leaving you free for last-minute gravy making when roast beef is on the menu.

2	eggs	2	1 cup	all-purpose flour	250 mL
1 cup	milk	250 mL	½ tsp	salt	2 mL

❧ Generously grease 8 muffin cups or cups of popover pan; set aside.

❧ In large bowl, whisk eggs with milk; stir in flour and salt until blended but still lumpy. Spoon into prepared muffin cups, filling three-quarters full.

❧ Place in centre of cold oven. Heat oven to 450°F (230°C); bake for 25 minutes. With skewer, puncture each popover; bake for 10 minutes or until golden, crisp and puffed. **(Make-ahead: Let cool. Store in airtight container at room temperature for up to 8 hours. Reheat in 325°F/160°C oven for 5 to 10 minutes.)**

Makes 8 popovers. | PER POPOVER: about 90 cal, 4 g pro, 2 g total fat (1 g sat. fat), 13 g carb, 1 g fibre, 49 mg chol, 171 mg sodium. % RDI: 4% calcium, 6% iron, 3% vit A, 18% folate.

Chapter 6

Spoon Desserts

While cakes, tarts and pies are all desserts, and you can eat them with a spoon, there is one grouping of this sweet finale to dinner that we can rightly call "spoon desserts." These are the easy-to-slip-down confections that require only a spoon to get to the heart of the dish. They are our friends the cobblers, crisps, crumbles and crunchy-topped fruit dishes; the self-saucing puddings that are all gooey beneath a spongy cake topping; the custards, including those with an air of French sophistication, such as crème caramel and crème brûlée; bread puddings that belie their thrifty heritage; and representatives of the trifle world.

The ingredients and the way spoon desserts are put together are varied, but they all share one trait: their sheer ease of preparation. None requires the skill that rolling out pie pastry does, nor the preparation and fiddling time demanded by a layer cake.

Spoon desserts, in short, are satisfying pleasures without fuss. They offer variety and a comfortable old-fashionedness that feels as right today as it ever has.

- Glass baking dishes:
  8-inch (2 L) square
  and 13- x 9-inch (3 L)

- Shiny metal cake pan:
  13- x 9-inch (3.5 L)

- Ramekins or custard
  cups, with ¾- to 1-cup
  (175 to 250 mL) capacity

- Heatproof oval baking
  dish: 6-cup (1.5 L)

- Bundt or tube pan:
  10-inch (3 L)

- Springform pan:
  9-inch (2.5 L)

- Shallow roasting pan

- Tongs

- Sieve

- Citrus zester

- Small kitchen torch,
  optional but
  recommended

Crisp Techniques

❯ Start by preparing the fruit, which should be fully ripe and juicy. You can play around with the combinations, such as in Apple Crisp (recipe, page 298), keeping in mind what's in season locally.

❯ Choose a shallow ovenproof dish, an attractive one that goes from oven to table. Make sure it has plenty of room to spread out the fruit and provides space for the all-important crunchy, golden brown topping.

❯ Work the softened butter into the mix of flour and brown sugar with a fork or your fingertips. The topping should look evenly crumbly when you're done.

❯ For a special, crunchy touch, add chopped pecan or walnut halves or slivered almonds to the topping.

❯ Sprinkle topping evenly over the fruit. Using your fingers will give you the best control over distribution.

❯ Serve these desserts still warm from the oven or reheat in 350°F (180°C) oven just until the heat revives the topping and warms up the fruit and juices.

Crème Caramel Techniques

❯ Start with a heavy-bottomed 2-quart (2 L) saucepan. Set a clean pastry brush in a measuring cup half-full of cold water beside the stove. Beside it, set out the baking dish for the Orange Lime Crème Caramel (recipe, page 301) and have a pair of oven mitts handy for later.

❯ To make the caramel topping, bring the sugar and water to a boil, stirring just until the sugar dissolves. Brush down side of pan above the boiling sugar with the wet pastry brush. This washes away any crystals that form above the boiling syrup.

❯ Don't leave the boiling syrup at any time while making caramel. It takes just a few minutes to go from clear to golden – and even less time to go from amber to burnt.

❯ Keep brushing the side of the saucepan with the brush dipped in cold water as the syrup turns from golden to deep amber. Swirl the pan from time to time to blend the darker caramel with the lighter.

❯ Stand safely back as you pour the boiling syrup into the baking dish. Working quickly, tilt the dish back, forth and sideways to encourage the caramel to coat the entire bottom of the dish.

Warm Apricot Cobbler

Fresh apricots have such a short season. Let them shine in this tender biscuit-topped cobbler.

CHECKING COBBLERS FOR DONENESS

❯ Slip the tip of a knife under the centremost biscuit and tip it up to get a look underneath. If the underside still looks doughy, let it bake a few minutes longer.

6 cups	sliced pitted apricots	1.5 L		¼ cup	granulated sugar	50 mL
½ cup	granulated sugar	125 mL		4 tsp	baking powder	20 mL
2 tbsp	all-purpose flour	25 mL		½ tsp	baking soda	2 mL
1 tsp	grated lemon rind	5 mL		¼ tsp	salt	1 mL
4 tsp	lemon juice	20 mL		⅓ cup	cold butter, cubed	75 mL
½ tsp	ground cardamom or nutmeg	2 mL		½ cup	buttermilk	125 mL

BISCUIT TOPPING:

1½ cups	all-purpose flour	375 mL

GLAZE:

1 tbsp	milk	15 mL
1 tbsp	granulated sugar	15 mL

❧ Grease 8-inch (2 L) square glass baking dish or 8-cup (2 L) shallow casserole or gratin dish; set aside.

❧ In large bowl, toss together apricots, sugar, flour, lemon rind and juice, and cardamom until coated. Scrape into prepared baking dish; set aside.

❧ BISCUIT TOPPING: In large bowl, whisk together flour, sugar, baking powder, baking soda and salt; with pastry blender, cut in butter until crumbly. Add buttermilk all at once, stirring with fork to make soft, slightly sticky dough; gather into ball.

❧ On lightly floured surface, knead dough about 10 times or until smooth. Pat out into circle about ½ inch (1 cm) thick. Using 3-inch (8 cm) round fluted cookie cutter, cut out rounds, rerolling and cutting scraps. (Or shape dough into 8-inch/20 cm square; cut into 6 pieces.) Arrange over fruit.

❧ GLAZE: Brush rounds lightly with milk; sprinkle with sugar. Bake in 375°F (190°C) oven until centre biscuit is no longer doughy underneath, about 40 minutes. Serve warm. (Make-ahead: Let cool. Set aside for up to 8 hours. Reheat to serve.)

Makes 6 servings. | PER SERVING: about 372 cal, 6 g pro, 11 g total fat (7 g sat. fat), 64 g carb, 3 g fibre, 33 mg chol, 494 mg sodium. % RDI: 11% calcium, 16% iron, 26% vit A, 13% vit C, 21% folate.

....

VARIATIONS

Blueberry Raspberry Cobbler: Replace apricot mixture with 4 cups (1 L) fresh raspberries, 3 cups (750 mL) fresh blueberries, ⅓ cup (75 mL) granulated sugar, 2 tbsp (25 mL) cornstarch and 1 tbsp (15 mL) lemon juice.

Peach Berry Cobbler: Replace apricot mixture with 6 cups (1.5 L) sliced peeled peaches, 1 cup (250 mL) raspberries or blueberries, ⅓ cup (75 mL) granulated sugar, 2 tbsp (25 mL) all-purpose flour and 1 tbsp (15 mL) lemon juice.

Plum Cobbler: Replace apricot mixture with 7 cups (1.75 L) sliced plums, ⅓ cup (75 mL) packed brown sugar, 1 tbsp (15 mL) cornstarch, and pinch cinnamon, nutmeg or ground cloves (optional).

MORE CRUMBLES

❯ Double or multiply the amount of crumble topping you make and store the excess in an airtight container in the freezer, ready for last-minute crumbles or to sprinkle over muffins.

Juicy Fruit Crumble

This crumble topping works with all manner of fruits and flavour combinations. It makes the perfect simple dessert year-round, with whatever fruit is in season or on hand.

	Fruit filling (see Variations, below)	
CRUMBLE TOPPING:		
1 cup	large-flake rolled oats	250 mL
½ cup	all-purpose flour	125 mL

⅓ cup	packed brown sugar	75 mL
¼ tsp	cinnamon	1 mL
Pinch	salt	Pinch
⅓ cup	butter, softened	75 mL

❧ Grease 8-inch (2 L) square glass baking dish; set aside.

❧ **CRUMBLE TOPPING:** In bowl, whisk together oats, flour, brown sugar, cinnamon and salt. With fork, mash in butter until crumbly.

❧ Spread fruit filling evenly in prepared baking dish; sprinkle with crumble topping. Bake in centre of 350°F (180°C) oven until bubbly, fruit is tender and topping is crisp and golden, 40 to 60 minutes. Serve warm. **(Make-ahead: Let cool. Set aside for up to 8 hours. Reheat to serve.)**

Makes 6 servings. | PER SERVING (USING APPLE CINNAMON FILLING): about 347 cal, 4 g pro, 12 g total fat (7 g sat. fat), 60 g carb, 4 g fibre, 27 mg chol, 79 mg sodium. % RDI: 3% calcium, 13% iron, 9% vit A, 7% vit C, 14% folate.

VARIATIONS

Apple Cinnamon Filling: In large bowl, combine 8 cups (2 L) sliced peeled apples, ¼ cup (50 mL) granulated sugar, 2 tbsp (25 mL) all-purpose flour and ½ tsp (2 mL) cinnamon.

Apple Plum Filling: In large bowl, combine 4 cups (1 L) sliced plums, 2 cups (500 mL) sliced peeled apples, ⅓ cup (75 mL) packed brown sugar, 2 tbsp (25 mL) all-purpose flour and ¼ tsp (1 mL) each nutmeg and cinnamon.

Apple Quince Filling: In large bowl, combine 5 cups (1.25 L) sliced peeled apples, 3 cups (750 mL) thinly sliced peeled quinces, ¼ cup (50 mL) granulated sugar, 1 tbsp (15 mL) all-purpose flour and 1 tbsp (15 mL) lemon juice.

Blueberry Peach Filling: In large bowl, combine 6 cups (1.5 L) sliced peeled peaches, 2 cups (500 mL) blueberries, ¼ cup (50 mL) granulated sugar, 3 tbsp (50 mL) all-purpose flour and 1 tbsp (15 mL) lemon juice.

Bumbleberry Filling: In large bowl, combine 3 cups (750 mL) diced peeled apples; 2 cups (500 mL) quartered strawberries; 1 cup (250 mL) each raspberries, blueberries and blackberries; ¼ cup (50 mL) granulated sugar; and 3 tbsp (50 mL) all-purpose flour.

Mincemeat Pear Filling: In large bowl, combine 1 jar (700 mL) all-fruit mincemeat; 2 firm ripe pears, peeled and grated; 1 cup (250 mL) chopped dried figs or whole golden raisins; and 1 tsp (5 mL) finely grated orange rind.

Pear Cranberry Filling: In large bowl, combine 6 cups (1.5 L) diced peeled pears, 2 cups (500 mL) fresh or thawed frozen cranberries, ¼ cup (50 mL) granulated sugar and 3 tbsp (50 mL) all-purpose flour.

Strawberry Rhubarb Filling: In large bowl, combine 6 cups (1.5 L) fresh or thawed frozen sliced rhubarb, 2 cups (500 mL) sliced strawberries, ½ cup (125 mL) granulated sugar, 3 tbsp (50 mL) all-purpose flour and ½ tsp (2 mL) finely grated orange rind.

Rhubarb Banana Crumble

Here's a way to savour the sweet tropical flavour of bananas that goes beyond slicing them onto your cereal or waiting until they're spotty enough to make into muffins.

5 cups	sliced fresh or thawed frozen rhubarb	1.25 L	¼ cup	quick-cooking rolled oats	50 mL
⅓ cup	granulated sugar	75 mL	¼ cup	each granulated and packed brown sugar	50 mL
2 tbsp	all-purpose flour	25 mL	¼ tsp	cinnamon	1 mL
3	bananas, sliced	3	⅓ cup	unsalted butter, softened	75 mL
CRUMBLE TOPPING:			¼ cup	chopped walnut halves	50 mL
⅓ cup	all-purpose flour	75 mL	¼ cup	pine nuts (optional)	50 mL

➜ Grease 8-inch (2 L) square glass baking dish; set aside.

➜ In bowl, toss together rhubarb, sugar and flour. Scrape into prepared baking dish; cover with foil. Bake in 400°F (200°C) oven, stirring once, until almost tender, about 25 minutes. Arrange bananas over top.

➜ **CRUMBLE TOPPING:** Meanwhile, in bowl, whisk together flour, oats, granulated and brown sugars, and cinnamon. With fork, mash in butter until crumbly. Mix in walnuts, and pine nuts (if using). Sprinkle over bananas.

➜ Bake, uncovered, in 350°F (180°C) oven until bubbly and topping is golden, about 25 minutes. Serve warm. **(Make-ahead: Let cool. Set aside for up to 8 hours. Reheat to serve.)**

Makes 6 to 8 servings. | PER EACH OF 8 SERVINGS: about 267 cal, 3 g pro, 11 g total fat (5 g sat. fat), 43 g carb, 3 g fibre, 20 mg chol, 8 mg sodium. % RDI: 7% calcium, 7% iron, 8% vit A, 15% vit C, 13% folate.

ROLLED OATS

> Rolled oats are a whole grain, made from hulled oat kernels that have been steamed then flattened. When a baking recipe calls for rolled oats, choose either large-flake, often referred to as old-fashioned, or quick-cooking rolled oats. They are interchangeable. However, large-flake are recommended for their chewy texture and the attractive ragged look they give to cookies, squares and crumbles.

The word *oatmeal* is often used when referring to rolled oats, as in Oatmeal Cookies (recipe, page 35), but oatmeal is in fact ground oat kernels or groats. Oatmeal also refers to the porridge made from rolled, ground or cut oats.

In baking, avoid both instant oats and coarse-textured steel-cut, Irish or Scottish oats. These are, for different reasons, suitable for porridge but not at all for baking.

Apple Crisp

There's plenty of crunchy crisp atop the sliced apple foundation – even for crisp lovers who claim to never get enough.

COMPANIONS FOR CRISPS, CRUMBLES AND BETTIES

❯ Creamy embellishments add richness, texture and sweetness, which complement the crunchy toppings and tart fruit of these desserts. Try vanilla ice cream; frozen yogurt; whipped cream; pouring cream or Crème Anglaise (recipe, page 328); yogurt, especially thickened Greek, Balkan-style and vanilla yogurt, or goat or sheep's milk yogurt; sour cream; or crème fraîche. Check our Sauces & Garnishes chapter (pages 316 to 339) for more inspiration.

❯ For juicy fruit crisps and crumbles featuring apples or pears, take a cue from apple pie and serve a slice of old Cheddar or Gouda cheese alongside.

8 cups	sliced peeled apples (about 6 large, 2½ lb/ 1.25 kg)	2 L
¼ cup	granulated sugar	50 mL
2 tbsp	all-purpose flour	25 mL
½ tsp	cinnamon	2 mL

TOPPING:

1 cup	all-purpose flour	250 mL
¾ cup	packed brown sugar	175 mL
½ cup	butter, softened	125 mL

❧ Grease 8-inch (2 L) square glass baking dish; set aside.

❧ In large bowl, toss together apples, sugar, flour and cinnamon. Arrange evenly in prepared baking dish.

❧ **TOPPING:** In separate bowl, whisk flour with brown sugar. Using fork, mash in butter until crumbly. Sprinkle over apple mixture.

❧ Bake in centre of 350°F (180°C) oven until bubbly, topping is golden and fruit is translucent and tender, about 1 hour. Serve warm. **(Make-ahead: Let cool. Set aside for up to 8 hours. Reheat to serve.)**

Makes 6 servings. | PER SERVING: about 428 cal, 3 g pro, 16 g total fat (10 g sat. fat), 72 g carb, 3 g fibre, 41 mg chol, 120 mg sodium. % RDI: 4% calcium, 13% iron, 14% vit A, 7% vit C, 22% folate.

VARIATIONS

Almond Cherry Crisp: Replace apple mixture with 4 cups (1 L) drained thawed pitted sour cherries or pitted fresh black cherries, 2 cups (500 mL) diced peeled apples, ⅓ cup (75 mL) granulated sugar, 3 tbsp (50 mL) all-purpose flour for sour cherries (or 2 tbsp/25 mL for black cherries) and 2 tsp (10 mL) lemon juice. Add ¾ cup (175 mL) slivered almonds to topping.

Pear Cranberry Crisp: Replace apple mixture with 4 cups (1 L) sliced peeled pears, 2 cups (500 mL) fresh or frozen cranberries, ¼ cup (50 mL) liquid honey and 2 tbsp (25 mL) all-purpose flour. Add ½ cup (125 mL) chopped pecans to topping.

Plum Apple Crisp: Replace apple mixture with 4 cups (1 L) sliced plums, 2 cups (500 mL) sliced peeled apples, ⅓ cup (75 mL) packed brown sugar and 2 tbsp (25 mL) all-purpose flour.

Strawberry Rhubarb Crisp: Replace apple mixture with 4 cups (1 L) sliced fresh or thawed frozen rhubarb, 2 cups (500 mL) halved strawberries, ⅓ cup (75 mL) packed brown sugar and 2 tbsp (25 mL) all-purpose flour.

Pear Cranberry Crisp

Apple Brown Betty

This is an authentic old-fashioned dessert – apples layered with fresh bread crumbs and lemon. It's absolutely heavenly with warm Rum-Spiked Crème Anglaise (recipe, page 328) or vanilla ice cream. To make fresh crumbs, trim crusts, tear bread into chunks and chop in food processor until about the size of raw long-grain rice.

3 cups	coarse fresh bread crumbs	750 mL	2 tsp	finely grated lemon rind	10 mL
			½ tsp	cinnamon	2 mL
⅓ cup	butter, melted	75 mL	Pinch	each ground allspice and nutmeg	Pinch
8 cups	thickly sliced peeled apples (about 8 apples, 3 lb/1.5 kg)	2 L	¼ cup	apple juice or water	50 mL
⅔ cup	packed brown sugar	150 mL	2 tbsp	lemon juice	25 mL

➤ Grease 8-inch (2 L) square glass baking dish; set aside.

➤ In bowl, toss bread crumbs with butter; spread one-quarter in prepared baking dish.

➤ In large bowl, toss together apples, brown sugar, lemon rind, cinnamon, allspice and nutmeg; spread half over crumb base in dish. Top with another quarter of the bread crumb mixture; spread remaining apple mixture over top. Drizzle with apple juice and lemon juice. Sprinkle with remaining bread crumb mixture.

➤ Bake in centre of 375°F (190°C) oven until golden and apples are tender, about 45 minutes. (**Make-ahead: Let cool. Cover and set aside for up to 8 hours. Reheat, if desired.**)

Makes 6 to 8 servings. | PER EACH OF 8 SERVINGS: about 258 cal, 2 g pro, 9 g total fat (5 g sat. fat), 46 g carb, 3 g fibre, 24 mg chol, 172 mg sodium. % RDI: 4% calcium, 7% iron, 8% vit A, 13% vit C, 6% folate.

SETTING UP A HOT WATER BATH (A.K.A. *BAIN MARIE*)

➤ Baked custards such as crème caramel and crème brûlée require a hot water bath with a constant temperature no higher than 212°F (100°C) so that their egg-rich mixtures do not overheat and split.

● Choose a large shallow pan that holds the baking dish(es) comfortably. It should allow room for the water to circulate around the dish(es) and be deep enough for the water to come halfway up the sides of the baking dish(es). A roasting pan is often the best choice.

● The safest way to manage a hot water bath is to fill it when it's already on the oven rack. Place the custard-filled baking dish(es) in the larger pan. Then, pull the centre rack of the oven out about halfway for the pan to rest on securely. Set the pan on the rack and, avoiding the baking dish(es), pour hot water into the pan until it comes halfway up the sides of the baking dish(es). Gently and slowly push the rack back into the oven, being careful not to slop any of the water into the custard.

● When the custard is baked, turn off the oven and gently pull out the centre rack. Lift out the baking dish(es). For small baking dishes, such as custard cups or ramekins, use tongs to transfer them to a rack on a tray. With the oven off and its door ajar, let the water cool until it's safe to pour out.

Orange Lime Crème Caramel

This traditional custard dessert baked in a caramel-coated mould has a surprising burst of citrus. Reducing the milk with the sugar gives the custard a desirable thickness and richness.

½ cup	granulated sugar	125 mL	½ cup	granulated sugar	125 mL
CUSTARD:			Pinch	salt	Pinch
4 cups	milk	1 L	4	eggs	4
2	strips each orange and lime rind	2	6	egg yolks	6

❧ Set out 6-cup (1.5 L) oval baking dish and large shallow pan, such as roasting pan; set aside.

❧ In deep heavy saucepan, stir sugar with 2 tbsp (25 mL) water over medium heat until dissolved, brushing down side of pan with pastry brush dipped in cold water. Bring to boil over medium-high heat; boil, without stirring but brushing down side of pan often, until deep amber, about 7 minutes. Pour caramel into prepared baking dish, tilting and swirling dish to coat bottom. Set baking dish in large shallow pan.

❧ CUSTARD: In separate heavy saucepan, heat milk and orange and lime rinds over medium heat until bubbles form around edge. Stir in sugar and salt; simmer until reduced to 3½ cups (875 mL), about 15 minutes. Remove orange and lime rinds.

❧ Meanwhile, in bowl, whisk eggs with egg yolks; slowly whisk in hot milk. Pour into caramel-coated dish.

❧ Pour enough hot water into roasting pan to come halfway up side of baking dish. Bake in centre of 350°F (180°C) oven until knife inserted in centre comes out clean, about 1 hour. Transfer baking dish to rack and let cool. (Make-ahead: Cover and refrigerate for up to 2 days. Place dish in warm water for 5 minutes before inverting.)

❧ To serve, run knife around edge of custard; place rimmed serving platter on top and invert.

Makes 8 servings. | PER SERVING: about 240 cal, 9 g pro, 9 g total fat (3 g sat. fat), 31 g carb, trace fibre, 255 mg chol, 97 mg sodium. % RDI: 16% calcium, 6% iron, 17% vit A, 3% vit C, 17% folate.

VARIATION

Vanilla Crème Caramel: Omit orange and lime rinds. Stir 2 tsp (10 mL) vanilla into egg and hot milk mixture.

Classic Crème Brûlée

Pumpkin Crème Brûlée

From the first crunch of the crackle topping to the last bite of the creamy pumpkin custard, this sinfully pleasing dessert makes a splendid ending to a fall – or any season – dinner. Canned pumpkin purée (not pie filling) relieves the cook of making the purée from scratch.

1½ cups	canned pumpkin purée	375 mL
1 tsp	vanilla	5 mL
½ tsp	cinnamon	2 mL
¼ tsp	each nutmeg and ground ginger	1 mL
2 cups	whipping cream	500 mL
8	egg yolks	8
⅓ cup	granulated sugar	75 mL
CRACKLE TOPPING:		
½ cup	granulated sugar	125 mL

↜ Arrange eight 6-oz (175 mL) ramekins or custard cups in large shallow pan, such as roasting pan; set aside.

↜ In large bowl, whisk together pumpkin purée, vanilla, cinnamon, nutmeg and ginger; set aside.

↜ In saucepan, heat cream until steaming. In bowl, whisk egg yolks with granulated sugar; slowly whisk in cream. Whisk into pumpkin mixture. Pour into prepared custard cups. Pour enough hot water into pan to come halfway up sides of cups.

↜ Bake in centre of 350°F (180°C) oven until edges are set but centres still jiggle and knife inserted in centres comes out creamy, about 35 minutes. Transfer cups to rack; let cool. Cover and refrigerate until chilled and set, about 2 hours. **(Make-ahead: Refrigerate for up to 2 days.)**

↜ **CRACKLE TOPPING:** Pat custards dry; sprinkle evenly with sugar. Holding small kitchen torch so end of flame touches sugar, heat until sugar bubbles and turns dark amber. Chill, uncovered, for at least 30 minutes before serving. **(Make-ahead: Refrigerate for up to 3 hours.)**

Makes 8 servings. | PER SERVING: about 357 cal, 5 g pro, 26 g total fat (15 g sat. fat), 27 g carb, 1 g fibre, 280 mg chol, 36 mg sodium. % RDI: 8% calcium, 11% iron, 119% vit A, 3% vit C, 15% folate.

VARIATIONS

Apple Butter Crème Brûlée: Replace pumpkin purée with ½ cup (125 mL) apple butter. Increase whipping cream to 2½ cups (625 mL).

Classic Crème Brûlée: Omit pumpkin, cinnamon, nutmeg and ginger. Whisk egg yolks with sugar; whisk in 3 cups (750 mL) steaming hot cream and 1½ tsp (7 mL) vanilla.

BRÛLÉE SUCCESS

This custard continues to firm up when removed from the oven, so when you test for doneness, the knife inserted into the centre should come out still a little creamy.

A home-kitchen torch, available at kitchenware shops, is superior to any other method of caramelizing an even layer of sugar. The tip of the flame touches the sugar, causing it to warm, bubble and brown. Move the flame around to evenly caramelize tops.

No torch? Broil the crèmes brûlées (in flameproof dishes). Rearrange them during broiling to ensure that the sugar caramelizes evenly without burning.

Vanilla Pots de Crème with Cranberry Port Compote

These little creamy custards are a stylish make-ahead dessert. Bring the flavours of fall into play with a ruby red compote to serve over top. For the rest of the year, try the Rhubarb Cherry Compote variation (below), berries or macerated sliced peaches or nectarines.

2 cups	10% cream	500 mL
1 cup	whipping cream	250 mL
8	egg yolks	8
⅓ cup	granulated sugar	75 mL
1 tbsp	vanilla	15 mL

CRANBERRY PORT COMPOTE:		
1 cup	ruby port	250 mL
½ cup	granulated sugar	125 mL
1	cinnamon stick, halved	1
1½ cups	fresh or frozen cranberries	375 mL

➤ Arrange eight 6-oz (175 mL) ramekins or custard cups in large shallow pan, such as roasting pan; set aside.

➤ **CRANBERRY PORT COMPOTE:** In saucepan, bring port, sugar and cinnamon stick to boil over medium heat; boil until syrupy and reduced to ⅔ cup (150 mL), about 13 minutes. Add cranberries; simmer, stirring occasionally, until split and slightly wrinkled but still whole, about 6 minutes. Let cool and chill. **(Make-ahead: Cover and refrigerate for up to 2 days.)**

➤ In saucepan, heat 10% and whipping creams over medium heat until bubbles form around edge. In bowl, whisk egg yolks with sugar; gradually whisk in cream, then vanilla. Skim off foam. Pour into ramekins. Pour enough boiling water into roasting pan to come halfway up sides of ramekins.

➤ Bake in centre of 325°F (160°C) oven until knife inserted in centres comes out clean, about 35 minutes. Transfer ramekins to rack; let cool. Cover and refrigerate until chilled. **(Make-ahead: Refrigerate for up to 1 day.)** Serve with compote.

Makes 8 servings. | PER SERVING: about 346 cal, 5 g pro, 22 g total fat (12 g sat. fat), 30 g carb, 1 g fibre, 261 mg chol, 46 mg sodium. % RDI: 10% calcium, 6% iron, 23% vit A, 3% vit C, 13% folate.

VARIATION

Vanilla Pots de Crème with Rhubarb Cherry Compote: Omit Cranberry Port Compote. In small saucepan, combine 1 cup (250 mL) cut (½-inch/1 cm pieces) fresh or frozen rhubarb, 1 cup (250 mL) frozen or drained jarred pitted sour cherries, ¼ cup (50 mL) granulated sugar and 1 tsp (5 mL) lemon juice; bring to boil over medium-high heat, stirring often. Reduce heat, cover and simmer for 7 minutes, stirring occasionally. Uncover and simmer until rhubarb breaks down, about 3 minutes. Scrape into bowl; refrigerate until cold, about 1 hour. **(Make-ahead: Cover and refrigerate for up to 2 days.)**

Knock-Your-Socks-Off Chocolate Bread Pudding

Bread pudding was born out of thrift – not a virtue when you're choosing the best-quality chocolate to snuggle into a rich custardy pudding. You can also push the deliciousness envelope by adding dried sour cherries along with the chocolate; they add a nice tart bite. Serve with Rum-Spiked Crème Anglaise (recipe, page 328).

10 cups	cubed (1 inch/2.5 cm) egg bread (challah), crusts removed (about one 680 g loaf)	2.5 L	2 cups	whipping cream	500 mL
			4	eggs	4
			3	egg yolks	3
6 oz	coarsely chopped good-quality bittersweet chocolate	175 g	¾ cup	granulated sugar	175 mL
			1 tsp	vanilla	5 mL
2 cups	milk	500 mL	¼ tsp	salt	1 mL

LEFTOVER EGG WHITES

❯ Check the index under "egg whites" for ways to use up any leftovers. Think along the lines of angel food cakes and meringues.

❧ Grease 13- x 9-inch (3 L) glass baking dish. Spread bread cubes and chocolate in baking dish; set aside.

❧ In large bowl, whisk together milk, cream, eggs, egg yolks, ⅔ cup (150 mL) of the sugar, vanilla and salt. Pour over bread cubes and chocolate. Let stand until almost all of the liquid is absorbed, pressing gently with rubber spatula if necessary, about 40 minutes. **(Make-ahead: Cover with plastic wrap and refrigerate for up to 12 hours.)** Sprinkle with remaining sugar.

❧ Place baking dish in large roasting pan; fill pan with enough hot water to come 1 inch (2.5 cm) up sides of baking dish. Bake in centre of 350°F (180°C) oven until puffed and knife inserted in centre comes out clean, 40 to 45 minutes.

Makes 12 servings. | PER SERVING: about 402 cal, 9 g pro, 25 g total fat (14 g sat. fat), 37 g carb, 2 g fibre, 182 mg chol, 244 mg sodium. % RDI: 11% calcium, 14% iron, 20% vit A, 19% folate.

Blueberry Bread Pudding

This bread pudding takes its inspiration from the one served at Pictou Lodge Resort in Nova Scotia. Serve with Whisky Sauce (recipe, page 320).

6	eggs	6	1 tsp	vanilla	5 mL
2 cups	18% cream	500 mL	12 cups	cubed white home-style sandwich bread, about 1½ loaves (675 g each), crusts trimmed off	3 L
1 cup	granulated sugar	250 mL			
1 cup	whipping cream	250 mL			
1 cup	milk	250 mL	2 cups	fresh blueberries	500 mL
1 tbsp	maple extract	15 mL	½ cup	finely chopped pecans	125 mL

USING FROZEN BLUEBERRIES

❯ To make this pudding a year round treat, substitute frozen wild blueberries for fresh and do not assemble ahead of baking. Spoon half of the bread mixture into prepared baking dish. Sprinkle with still-frozen wild blueberries. Top with remaining bread mixture. Increase baking time by about 5 minutes.

↪ Grease 13- x 9-inch (3 L) glass baking dish; set aside.

↪ In large bowl, whisk eggs. Whisk in 18% cream, all but 2 tbsp (25 mL) of the sugar, the whipping cream, milk, maple extract and vanilla. Add bread and blueberries; stir gently but thoroughly to moisten evenly. Scrape into prepared baking dish. **(Make-ahead: Cover and refrigerate for up to 8 hours; add 10 minutes to baking time.)**

↪ Toss pecans with remaining sugar; sprinkle over bread mixture. Bake in centre of 375°F (190°C) oven until puffed, golden and tip of knife inserted in centre comes out clean, about 45 minutes. Let cool in pan on rack for 15 minutes to serve hot or for up to 1 hour to serve warm.

Makes 8 to 10 servings. | PER EACH OF 10 SERVINGS: about 459 cal, 10 g pro, 26 g total fat (12 g sat. fat), 48 g carb, 2 g fibre, 174 mg chol, 290 mg sodium. % RDI: 14% calcium, 13% iron, 20% vit A, 5% vit C, 25% folate.

Blueberry Pudding Cake

Pudding cakes, self-saucing puddings or hasty puddings – these two-layer desserts hark back to a time when a baked dessert was de rigueur at every meal. Now these puddings have a new charm for special occasions, served warm in a bowl with a nice oval of premium vanilla ice cream melting seductively into the cake top and juicy fruit underpinnings.

3 cups	fresh blueberries	750 mL	2	eggs	2
⅔ cup	granulated sugar	150 mL	1 tsp	grated lemon rind	5 mL
¾ cup	water	175 mL	½ tsp	vanilla	2 mL
¼ cup	lemon juice	50 mL	1¼ cups	all-purpose flour	300 mL
CAKE TOPPING:			1½ tsp	baking powder	7 mL
½ cup	butter, softened	125 mL	Pinch	salt	Pinch
¾ cup	granulated sugar	175 mL	½ cup	milk	125 mL

❧ Grease 8-inch (2 L) square glass baking dish; add blueberries and toss with ⅓ cup (75 mL) of the sugar. Set aside.

❧ CAKE TOPPING: In large bowl, beat butter with sugar until light. Beat in eggs, 1 at a time, beating well after each. Beat in lemon rind and vanilla.

❧ In separate bowl, whisk together flour, baking powder and salt. Add to butter mixture alternately with milk, making 3 additions of dry ingredients and 2 of milk. Scrape evenly over blueberries; smooth top. Set aside.

❧ In small saucepan, bring water, lemon juice and remaining sugar to boil, stirring until sugar is dissolved; pour evenly over batter. Bake in centre of 350°F (180°C) oven until bubbly around edges and cake is firm to the touch, 50 minutes. Let cool slightly before serving. (Make-ahead: Set aside at room temperature for up to 8 hours; reheat, if desired.)

Makes 8 servings. | PER SERVING: about 369 cal, 5 g pro, 13 g total fat (8 g sat. fat), 60 g carb, 2 g fibre, 78 mg chol, 164 mg sodium. % RDI: 5% calcium, 9% iron, 13% vit A, 15% vit C, 22% folate.

VARIATIONS

Blueberry Pudding Cake with frozen blueberries: Replace fresh blueberries with frozen wild blueberries. Add 1 tbsp (15 mL) cornstarch to blueberry and sugar mixture. Increase baking time by 15 minutes.

Raspberry Pudding Cake: Replace blueberries with 6 cups (1.5 L) frozen raspberries. Thaw berries in sieve over bowl to catch juice. When completely thawed, pour juice into measuring cup. Add enough water to make 1 cup (250 mL). Substitute for water and lemon juice to make liquid for pouring over batter.

Rhubarb Pudding Cake: Replace blueberries with frozen or fresh sliced rhubarb. Add 1 tbsp (15 mL) cornstarch to rhubarb and sugar mixture. Substitute 1 cup (250 mL) orange juice for water and lemon juice to make liquid for pouring over batter. Substitute orange rind for lemon rind in cake. If using frozen rhubarb, increase baking time by 15 minutes.

Maple Pudding Chômeur

This wickedly sweet cake-pudding combo is a favourite in Canada wherever there are cooks with French heritage. The sauce starts out as maple syrup and water poured over the batter but ends up gooey and delicious on the bottom after baking. Serve warm with ice cream or whipped cream.

MAPLE SYRUP

❯ For the most distinct maple flavour in baking, choose darker grades, such as No. 2 Amber or No. 1 Medium.

1 cup	all-purpose flour	250 mL		½ cup	raisins	125 mL
½ cup	granulated sugar	125 mL		SAUCE:		
4 tsp	baking powder	20 mL		1½ cups	water	375 mL
¼ tsp	nutmeg	1 mL		1 cup	maple syrup	250 mL
¾ cup	milk	175 mL		2 tbsp	butter, melted	25 mL
¼ cup	butter, melted	50 mL		1 tsp	cornstarch	5 mL
1 tsp	finely grated lemon rind	5 mL				

❧ Grease 8-inch (2 L) square glass baking dish; set aside.

❧ In bowl, whisk together flour, sugar, baking powder and nutmeg. In separate bowl, whisk together milk, butter and lemon rind; pour over dry ingredients. Sprinkle with raisins; stir just until combined. Spread in prepared baking dish.

❧ SAUCE: In bowl, whisk together water, maple syrup, butter and cornstarch; pour over batter. Bake in centre of 350°F (180°C) oven until golden and firm to the touch, 40 to 45 minutes. Let cool slightly before serving. (Make-ahead: Set aside at room temperature for up to 8 hours. Reheat, if desired.)

Makes 8 servings. | PER SERVING: about 326 cal, 3 g pro, 9 g total fat (6 g sat. fat), 60 g carb, 1 g fibre, 29 mg chol, 237 mg sodium. % RDI: 11% calcium, 11% iron, 9% vit A, 2% vit C, 10% folate.

Sticky Date Pudding with Irish Whiskey Toffee Sauce

You won't have any trouble getting rid of extra servings of this toothsome cake and whiskey-laced sauce. There is no reason not to replace the Irish whiskey with a blended Scotch, brandy or rum.

1½ cups	water	375 mL
1⅓ cups	chopped pitted dates	325 mL
2 tsp	baking soda	10 mL
1 cup	butter, softened	250 mL
½ cup	granulated sugar	125 mL
4	eggs	4
1 tsp	vanilla	5 mL
2½ cups	all-purpose flour	625 mL

2 tsp	baking powder	10 mL
IRISH WHISKEY TOFFEE SAUCE:		
¾ cup	butter	175 mL
1¼ cups	packed dark brown sugar	300 mL
¾ cup	whipping cream	175 mL
¼ cup	Irish whiskey (such as Bushmills or Jameson)	50 mL

꙳ Grease 10-inch (3 L) Bundt or tube pan; dust with flour; set aside.

꙳ In saucepan, bring water, dates and baking soda to boil; let cool.

꙳ In large bowl, beat butter with sugar until light and fluffy; beat in eggs, 1 at a time, beating well after each. Beat in vanilla. In separate bowl, whisk flour with baking powder; stir into butter mixture alternately with date mixture, making 2 additions of dry ingredients and 1 of date mixture. Scrape into prepared pan; smooth top. Bake in centre of 350°F (180°C) oven for 45 minutes.

꙳ **IRISH WHISKEY TOFFEE SAUCE:** Meanwhile, in saucepan, melt butter over medium heat; stir in brown sugar until dissolved. Add cream and bring to simmer; simmer, stirring occasionally, until thickened slightly, about 5 minutes. Stir in whiskey; keep warm.

꙳ Remove cake from oven; using skewer, poke about 40 holes all over cake; pour ⅓ cup (75 mL) warm toffee sauce evenly over top. Return to oven; bake until cake tester inserted in centre comes out clean, about 15 minutes. Let cool in pan on rack for 10 minutes.

꙳ Invert cake onto flat rimmed plate. Poke another 40 holes all over; pour ⅓ cup (75 mL) more sauce over cake. (**Make-ahead: Let cool. Wrap in plastic wrap; store in airtight container at room temperature for up 2 days. Cover remaining sauce and refrigerate for up to 2 days. Reheat to serve.**)

꙳ To serve, rewarm remaining sauce if necessary; drizzle over slices of cake.

Makes 12 servings. | PER SERVING: about 585 cal, 6 g pro, 34 g total fat (21 g sat. fat), 66 g carb, 3 g fibre, 152 mg chol, 488 mg sodium. % RDI: 7% calcium, 15% iron, 30% vit A, 29% folate.

Apple Dumplings with Rum Butterscotch Sauce

This is just the kind of dessert you will never find in a restaurant. And who would want to, given how simple the steps are to make it – and your reputation – at home?
Avoid supersize apples, instead choosing ones that fit comfortably into the baking dish and provide a satisfying but not overwhelming portion.

Using an apple corer or melon baller, carve out the core, making sure there's enough space for the sugar and pecans.

6	apples (about 2¼ lb/1.125 kg), peeled and cored	6
¼ cup	packed brown sugar	50 mL
¼ cup	chopped pecans	50 mL
SAUCE:		
1 cup	packed brown sugar	250 mL
½ cup	amber or dark rum	125 mL
¾ tsp	ground ginger	4 mL
3 tbsp	butter	50 mL
DOUGH:		
2 cups	all-purpose flour	500 mL
2 tsp	baking powder	10 mL
½ tsp	salt	2 mL
¾ cup	cold butter, cubed	175 mL
½ cup	milk	125 mL

Brush the edges of the dough to ensure a good seal. Pull up the dough one side at a time and pinch together gently.

The pastry forms a neat package around the apples.

↜ Grease 13- x 9-inch (3 L) glass baking dish; set aside.

↜ SAUCE: In small saucepan, bring 1½ cups (375 mL) water, brown sugar, rum and ginger to boil, stirring until sugar is dissolved. Reduce heat and simmer for 2 minutes. Remove from heat; stir in butter. Set aside.

↜ DOUGH: In bowl, whisk together flour, baking powder and salt. With pastry blender, cut in butter until crumbly. Add milk all at once; stir until dough begins to clump together. Press into ball.

↜ Turn out onto floured surface. Roll out into 21- x 14-inch (53 x 35 cm) rectangle; cut into six 7-inch (18 cm) squares. Place apple in centre of each. Divide sugar and pecans evenly among apple cavities. Brush edges of each pastry square with water; bring up corners of dough over apple to meet in centre; pinch edges to seal. Place, 1 inch (2.5 cm) apart, in prepared baking dish. Pour sauce over pastry-covered apples.

↜ Bake in 375°F (190°C) oven for 40 minutes. Spoon sauce over pastry; bake until pastry is golden and apples are tender, about 10 minutes longer. Serve warm.
(Make-ahead: Let cool and set aside for up to 4 hours. Reheat to serve.)

Makes 6 servings. | PER SERVING: about 696 cal, 6 g pro, 33 g total fat (19 g sat. fat), 95 g carb, 3 g fibre, 78 mg chol, 525 mg sodium. % RDI: 12% calcium, 22% iron, 26% vit A, 7% vit C, 40% folate.

Tiramisu

This Italian dessert – part trifle, part fresh cheesecake – became a favourite in the 1980s and lingers fondly on menus of restaurants such as Grano in Toronto. It's also a bestseller at Pusateri's, Toronto's premier fine-food grocery store. This recipe is originally from Grano and uses homemade cake, but you can substitute store-bought giant ladyfingers.

½ cup	ground espresso or dark roast coffee beans	125 mL		2 tsp	baking powder	10 mL
3 tbsp	coffee liqueur	50 mL		**MASCARPONE FILLING:**		
1 tbsp	granulated sugar	15 mL		1½ cups	whipping cream	375 mL
CAKE:				3	egg yolks	3
5	eggs	5		3 tbsp	granulated sugar	50 mL
1½ cups	granulated sugar	375 mL		1	tub (475 g) mascarpone cheese, softened	1
2½ cups	sifted cake-and-pastry flour	625 mL		1 tbsp	cocoa powder	15 mL

❧ Line 13- x 9-inch (3.5 L) metal cake pan with parchment paper; set aside.

❧ CAKE: In large bowl and using electric mixer, beat eggs with sugar until doubled in volume and batter falls in ribbons when beaters are lifted, 10 to 12 minutes. Sift flour with baking powder over egg mixture; gently fold in.

❧ Scrape into prepared pan. Bake in centre of 375°F (190°C) oven until cake springs back when lightly touched in centre and sides pull away from pan, 20 to 25 minutes. Let cool in pan on rack for 10 minutes. Transfer to rack; let cool. Peel off paper.

❧ Combine ground espresso with 3 cups (750 mL) boiling water; let stand for 5 minutes. Using coffee filter or double layer of damp cheesecloth in sieve, strain into bowl. Stir in coffee liqueur and sugar; let cool.

❧ MASCARPONE FILLING: Whip cream until soft peaks form; set aside.

❧ In large heatproof bowl set over saucepan of simmering water, beat egg yolks with sugar until pale and thickened, about 3 minutes. Remove from heat. Fold in mascarpone and one-quarter of the whipped cream. Fold in remaining whipped cream.

❧ Cut cake horizontally in half; trim edges. Place 1 layer in bottom of 13- x 9-inch (3.5 L) metal cake pan. Soak with half of the coffee mixture; spread with half of the mascarpone mixture. Repeat with remaining cake, coffee mixture and mascarpone mixture. Dust with cocoa. Refrigerate for 4 hours. (Make-ahead: Cover; refrigerate for up to 12 hours.)

Makes 16 servings. | PER SERVING: about 402 cal, 6 g pro, 25 g total fat (15 g sat. fat), 39 g carb, trace fibre, 169 mg chol, 81 mg sodium. % RDI: 7% calcium, 12% iron, 12% vit A, 15% folate.

VARIATION

Quick-to-Make Tiramisu: Replace cake with 2 pkg (each 150 g) giant ladyfingers (about 26). Use 13 ladyfingers per layer; dip ladyfingers into coffee mixture.

Strawberry Trifle

Do make this dessert when strawberries are in season. Berries are red through and through, are a manageable size and they taste of early summer sunshine. A trifle is also a canvas for painting, so feel free to change the fruit according to the season. Raspberries, wild blueberries and peaches are delicious, too, and go well with raspberry jam accents.

1 cup	whipping cream	250 mL		2 tbsp	granulated sugar	25 mL
⅔ cup	seedless raspberry jam or strawberry jam	175 mL		**CAKE:**		
1 cup	halved strawberries	250 mL		4	eggs, separated	4
CUSTARD:				¼ tsp	cream of tartar	1 mL
¼ cup	granulated sugar	50 mL		⅔ cup	granulated sugar	150 mL
3 tbsp	cornstarch	50 mL		1 tsp	grated orange rind	5 mL
3	eggs	3		2 tbsp	orange juice	25 mL
2 cups	milk	500 mL		1 tsp	vanilla	5 mL
2 tsp	vanilla	10 mL		1 cup	sifted cake-and-pastry flour	250 mL
MACERATED STRAWBERRIES:				¼ tsp	baking powder	1 mL
3 cups	sliced strawberries	750 mL		¼ tsp	salt	1 mL
⅓ cup	sweet sherry or orange juice	75 mL				

❧ CAKE: Grease side of 9-inch (2.5 L) springform pan; line bottom with parchment paper. Set aside.

❧ In large bowl, beat egg whites with cream of tartar until soft peaks form. Beat in half of the sugar, 1 tbsp (15 mL) at a time, until stiff peaks form; set aside.

❧ In separate large bowl, beat egg yolks with remaining sugar until thick and pale, about 2 minutes. Beat in orange rind and juice, and vanilla. In separate bowl, whisk together flour, baking powder and salt. Add to egg yolk mixture; stir just until combined. Stir in about one-quarter of the egg whites; fold in remaining whites. Scrape into prepared pan; smooth top.

❧ Bake in centre of 325°F (160°C) oven until cake springs back when lightly touched and cake tester inserted in centre comes out clean, 40 to 45 minutes. Let cool in pan on rack for 10 minutes. Remove side of pan; invert cake onto rack. Remove bottom of pan; let cool. Peel off paper.

❧ CUSTARD: In bowl, whisk sugar with cornstarch. Whisk in eggs and ½ cup (125 mL) of the milk.

❧ Heat remaining milk in saucepan over medium heat until small bubbles form around edge of pan; gradually whisk about half into egg mixture. Scrape back into pan; cook, stirring, until thickened enough to mound on spoon, about 5 minutes. Strain into bowl; stir in vanilla. Place plastic wrap directly on surface. Refrigerate custard until chilled, about 4 hours.

❧ MACERATED BERRIES: Meanwhile, in bowl, stir together strawberries, sherry and sugar. Cover and refrigerate for 1 hour. Strain berries, reserving liquid.

❧ In bowl, whip ½ cup (125 mL) of the whipping cream; fold into custard.

❧ Cut cake horizontally into thirds; brush each of the layers with reserved berry liquid. Spread 1 cut side of each layer with jam. Trimming edges if necessary, fit 1 cake layer, jam side up, into bottom of 12-cup (3 L) glass trifle bowl. Top with one-third of the macerated berries and one-third of the custard. Repeat layers twice.

❧ Cover and refrigerate for at least 4 hours. **(Make-ahead: Refrigerate for up to 1 day.)**

❧ Whip remaining cream. Spread over top; top with halved strawberries.

Makes 12 servings. | PER SERVING: about 314 cal, 7 g pro, 11 g total fat (6 g sat. fat), 47 g carb, 2 g fibre, 137 mg chol, 121 mg sodium. % RDI: 8% calcium, 10% iron, 14% vit A, 58% vit C, 20% folate.

BUILDING A TRIFLE

● Start by preparing the fruit; here, macerating strawberries to infuse them with flavour and to create a syrup to brush over the cake. Moistness is what a trifle is all about.

● Many trifles call for store-bought pound or angel food cake. Frankly, a freshly baked cake tastes so much better.

● Instead of cubing the cake, cut horizontally into thirds; spread each layer with a complementary flavoured jam. Seedless raspberry is our favourite.

● Layer cake and spoon in fillings and cream carefully so that layers are clearly defined. Smooth the custard layers with an offset spatula or back of a spoon.

● Seal the bowl with plastic wrap and let the trifle mellow in the refrigerator. There the juicy fruit, custard and syrup will bring the cake to the brink of utter tenderness. This rest period, a minimum of four hours, makes trifle a good make-ahead dessert.

Chapter 7

Sauces & Garnishes

The art of embellishing desserts has clicked up a notch in the last couple of decades. We can thank pastry chefs for the inspiration: plates dusted with icing sugar or cocoa, crème anglaise puddled under slices of cake or pooled beside tarts, drizzles and dots of caramel sauce, fruit purées, crème fraîche and piped whipped cream…you name it, they've done it.

This level of artful arrangement of dessert plates may not always be possible in a home kitchen, even on company-over occasions. But there are sauces and decorative garnishes that are easily doable and add pizzazz to almost any dessert. Try some and discover how to make a dessert that's not just a nice last course but rather an eye-popping, taste-bud-tempting, reputation-making finale.

Working with Eggs

> Eggs are one of the essentials of baking. They gloss and glaze breads, pastries and quick breads. They provide the leavening power for foam cakes, such as sponge and angel food, and enrich everything they go into. Eggs and egg yolks thicken puddings, such as crème brûlée; stiffen fillings; firm up muffins; and provide lustre and substance to sauces, like the ones in this chapter.

> A Clean Break

Cracking an egg is easy, but keeping bits of shell out of the bowl can be tough. If they fall in, use the edge of a half-shell to scoop them out and discard.

> To Separate Eggs

● It is easier to separate cold eggs than room-temperature eggs.

● Set out three bowls: one for whites, one for yolks and one over which to crack the eggs (a.k.a. the "just-in-case bowl"). In our photo, we used a liquid measuring cup for the whites bowl, in preparation for making an angel food cake.

● Crack egg; over the just-in-case bowl, pull shells apart, keeping the half holding the yolk upright and letting the white around the yolk and the white from the other shell drip into the bowl.

● Carefully pour yolk from one half-shell into the other, again letting the white drip into the bowl. Repeat until as much of the white as possible has been separated from the yolk. Slide the yolk into the yolk bowl; pour the white from the just-in-case bowl into the whites bowl or liquid measuring cup.

● Continue with more eggs, always using that just-in-case bowl for the first step. That way, if a yolk breaks and mixes in with its white, you can set them aside without ruining a whole batch of whites. Simply pour the yolk-white combo into an airtight container to use for muffins or scrambled eggs.

● Practice does make perfect, but if all this sounds too complicated, there are egg separators available at cookware and department stores. You can also buy pasteurized egg whites in cartons in supermarket dairy cases. We have found them reliable, but they beat up to a slightly lower volume than fresh egg whites.

EQUIPMENT FOR SAUCES & GARNISHES

● Heavy-bottomed saucepans: 2-quart (2 L) and 3-quart (3 L)

● Whisk attachment for hand or stand mixer, optional but recommended

● Shiny metal loaf pan: 5¾- x 3¼-inch (625 mL)

● Small fine sieve

● Large shiny metal rimmed baking sheet

● Silicone baking mat

● Plastic squeeze bottles

Tempering Eggs

> If cold eggs are added to hot liquids, there is a real danger they will cook on contact; i.e., scramble instead of combining with liquid into a silky custard. Tempering warms up cold eggs and allows them to be incorporated into hot mixtures smoothly without curds.

● In bowl, whisk eggs until evenly yellow.

● While whisking the eggs, gradually pour in the hot liquid. The amount of liquid should be roughly half of the volume of the eggs. Whisk in additional hot liquid, up to about one-third of the liquid.

● For crème anglaise or other stirred custards, whisk the warmed eggs and liquid back into the pan with the remaining liquid and cook over low heat, stirring constantly, until the custard thickens enough to coat the back of a spoon, at about 180°F (82°C)

● For baked puddings with a custard base, such as bread pudding or crème caramel, whisk all of the hot liquid into the eggs before pouring into the baking dish(es).

Whisky Sauce

This very grown-up whisky-laced sauce is addictive. Spoon it warm over Blueberry Bread Pudding (recipe, page 306) for a divine dessert.

1	egg	1	⅓ cup	unsalted butter, melted	75 mL
½ cup	granulated sugar	125 mL	¼ cup	whisky	50 mL
1 tsp	cornstarch	5 mL			

~ In heatproof bowl, whisk together egg, sugar and cornstarch until smooth; whisk in butter. Set over saucepan of simmering water; cook, whisking, until thick enough to coat back of spoon, about 4 minutes. Remove from heat; whisk in whisky. **(Make-ahead: Let cool. Cover and refrigerate for up to 1 day. Reheat in heatproof bowl over saucepan of hot but not boiling water.)**

Makes about 1¼ cups (300 mL). | PER 2 TBSP (25 mL): about 112 cal, 1 g pro, 7 g total fat (4 g sat. fat), 10 g carb, 0 g fibre, 35 mg chol, 7 mg sodium. % RDI: 1% iron, 6% vit A, 1% folate.

Raspberry Sauce

This gorgeous scarlet sauce is often referred to on restaurant menus as a *coulis*.

3	pkg (each 300 g) frozen unsweetened raspberries, thawed	3	1 tbsp	raspberry-flavoured liqueur (optional)	15 mL
¾ cup	instant dissolving (fruit/berry) sugar	175 mL			

~ In food processor or blender, purée raspberries; press through fine sieve into bowl to remove seeds. Whisk in sugar, and raspberry liqueur (if using). **(Make-ahead: Refrigerate in airtight container for up to 3 days.)**

Makes 2½ cups (625 mL). | PER 2 TBSP (25 mL): about 41 cal, trace pro, trace total fat (0 g sat. fat), 10 g carb, 0 g fibre, 0 mg chol, 0 mg sodium. % RDI: 1% calcium, 1% iron, 1% vit A, 15% vit C, 4% folate.

VARIATION

Blackberry Sauce: Replace raspberries with ripe fresh or frozen blackberries.

Mango Sauce

If you're making this sauce in the spring, when mangoes are in season, choose yellower, kidney-shaped Ataulfo mangoes for the most luscious flavour. They have a silky texture and a smaller pit and are less fibrous than many of the larger red-and-green mangoes.

4	small mangoes, peeled, pitted and chopped (about 3 cups/750 mL)	4	¼ cup	granulated sugar	50 mL
			2 tbsp	each lime juice and orange juice	25 mL

In food processor, purée together mangoes, sugar, lime juice and orange juice; press through fine sieve into small bowl to remove any fibres. **(Make-ahead: Refrigerate in airtight container for up to 2 days.)**

Makes about 1¾ cups (425 mL). | PER 2 TBSP (25 mL): about 37 cal, trace pro, trace total fat (0 g sat. fat), 9 g carb, 0 g fibre, 0 mg chol, 1 mg sodium. % RDI: 1% iron, 14% vit A, 18% vit C, 3% folate.

Macerated Strawberry Sauce

Fresh summer strawberries get extra zing from a bit of orange-flavoured liqueur. This sauce lends its fabulous fruit flavour and bright red colour beautifully to Orange White Chocolate Strawberry Shortcake (recipe, page 108).

2 cups	sliced strawberries	500 mL	2 tbsp	orange-flavoured liqueur	25 mL
2 tbsp	granulated sugar	25 mL			

In bowl, combine strawberries, sugar and liqueur; let stand for 30 minutes.

Makes 2 cups (500 mL). | PER 2 TBSP (25 mL): about 20 cal, trace pro, trace total fat (0 g sat. fat), 4 g carb, trace fibre, 0 mg chol, 0 mg sodium. % RDI: 1% iron, 20% vit C, 2% folate.

MANGO CUTTING MADE EASY

- Slice mango lengthwise through flesh on each side of the long slim pit in the centre.
- Lay the two halves, or "cheeks," on cutting board. With knife, score the flesh of each half in crosshatch pattern, carefully cutting to, but not through, skin.
- Gently push against the skin so that the cubes on the cut side pop upward.
- Slice off sections at the skin. Voilà – chopped mango, fast.
- It's the cook's reward to nibble off the juicy tidbits remaining on the pit.
- Mangoes freeze well, in cubes or puréed.

Blueberry Sauce

With its fresh blueberries, this sauce adds a spoonful of summer over pound cake, rice pudding or creamy custard.

| ¼ cup | granulated sugar | 50 mL | 2 tsp | cornstarch | 10 mL |
| ¼ cup | orange juice | 50 mL | 1 cup | blueberries | 250 mL |

In small saucepan, bring sugar and orange juice to boil, stirring until sugar is dissolved. In small bowl, blend cornstarch with 2 tbsp (25 mL) water; stir into pan along with blueberries. Cook, stirring, until boiling and thickened, about 2 minutes. **(Make-ahead: Set aside at room temperature for up to 1 hour.)**

Makes about 1 cup (250 mL). | PER 2 TBSP (25 mL): about 40 cal, trace pro, 0 g total fat (0 g sat. fat), 10 g carb, trace fibre, 0 mg chol, 1 mg sodium. % RDI: 7% vit C, 1% folate.

STORING SAUCES

❯ Use a jar to store sauces in the refrigerator. Dress up the jar or make it a decorative one for a lovely gift.

Silky Bittersweet Chocolate Sauce

This sauce is an all-time favourite, either thick and cold or easy-pour consistency at room temperature. To serve hot, increase chocolate to 8 oz (250 g).

| 1¼ cups | whipping cream | 300 mL | 6 oz | bittersweet chocolate, chopped | 175 g |
| 3 tbsp | corn syrup | 50 mL | | | |

In saucepan, bring cream and corn syrup to boil; remove from heat. Whisk in chocolate until smooth and melted. Let stand until thickened, about 15 minutes. **(Make-ahead: Refrigerate in airtight container for up to 5 days.)**

Makes about 2 cups (500 mL). | PER 2 TBSP (25 mL): about 127 cal, 1 g pro, 12 g total fat (8 g sat. fat), 6 g carb, 2 g fibre, 24 mg chol, 13 mg sodium. % RDI: 2% calcium, 5% iron, 6% vit A.

VARIATION

Silky Mocha Sauce: Add 2 tsp (10 mL) espresso powder or instant coffee granules along with chopped chocolate.

Chocolate Raspberry Sauce

Pour this rich sauce over ice cream, puddle it under a piece of cake or enjoy it with fresh berries.

REHEATING
CHOCOLATE
SAUCES

❯ Gentle heat is required. Warm the sauce in a heatproof bowl over a saucepan with 2 inches (5 cm) barely simmering water, stirring often.

1 cup	whipping cream	250 mL	6 oz	bittersweet chocolate, chopped	175 g
¼ cup	thawed raspberry cocktail concentrate	50 mL			

In small saucepan, bring cream and raspberry concentrate just to boil. Add chocolate; whisk until smooth and melted. Let stand until thickened, about 15 minutes. **(Make-ahead: Refrigerate in airtight container for up to 5 days. Reheat before serving.)**

Makes about 1¾ cups (425 mL). | PER 2 TBSP (25 mL): about 133 cal, 1 g pro, 11 g total fat (6 g sat. fat), 9 g carb, 1 g fibre, 22 mg chol, 6 mg sodium. % RDI: 2% calcium, 4% iron, 6% vit A.

Brandy Fudge Sauce

Milk chocolate lightens the flavour of this wickedly silky sauce.

1¼ cups	whipping cream	300 mL	2 oz	milk chocolate, chopped	60 g
¼ cup	brandy	50 mL	2 tbsp	butter, cubed	25 mL
3 tbsp	granulated sugar	50 mL			
8 oz	bittersweet chocolate, chopped	250 g			

In small saucepan, bring cream, brandy and sugar to boil, stirring occasionally until sugar is dissolved. Remove from heat.

Add bittersweet and milk chocolates and butter; whisk until smooth and chocolate is melted. **(Make-ahead: Let cool. Refrigerate in airtight container for up to 5 days. Reheat before serving.)**

Makes about 2 cups (500 mL). | PER 1 TBSP (15 mL): about 90 cal, 1 g pro, 8 g total fat (5 g sat. fat), 5 g carb, 1 g fibre, 14 mg chol, 11 mg sodium. % RDI: 1% calcium, 4% iron, 4% vit A.

VARIATION

Fudge Sauce: Substitute ¼ cup (50 mL) milk and 2 tsp (10 mL) vanilla for brandy.

Dulce de Leche

Sometimes translated from Spanish as "milk candy" or "milk jam," this trendy Latin American delicacy is milk mixed with caramel that's then boiled until rich and gooey. It's delicious over almost everything. Made with goat's milk, it is known as *cajeta* in Mexico.

2	cans (each 385 mL) 2% evaporated milk	2	1 tbsp	cornstarch	15 mL
			½ tsp	baking soda	2 mL
1¼ cups	milk	300 mL	1 cup	granulated sugar	250 mL

In large heavy saucepan, bring evaporated milk and ¾ cup (175 mL) of the milk to boil. In bowl, whisk together remaining milk, cornstarch and baking soda; whisk into boiling milk mixture. Reduce heat to low; simmer, stirring occasionally to prevent sticking and boiling over.

Meanwhile, in large heavy-bottomed stockpot, stir sugar with ¾ cup (175 mL) water over medium heat until dissolved. Brush down side of pot with pastry brush dipped in cold water. Bring to boil; boil, without stirring but brushing down side of pan often, until light golden, about 15 minutes. Remove caramel from heat. Set large fine sieve over pot, resting on rim.

Standing back and averting face, slowly pour milk mixture through sieve into caramel; whisk vigorously until caramel is dissolved. Return to heat; simmer, stirring occasionally, until dark golden and thick enough to coat back of wooden spoon, 1 to 1½ hours. To remove any lumps, strain through fine sieve and funnel into large glass jar. Let cool. **(Make-ahead: Refrigerate for up to 6 months.)**

Makes about 2 cups (500 mL). | PER 2 TBSP (25 mL): about 107 cal, 4 g pro, 1 g total fat (1 g sat. fat), 20 g carb, 0 g fibre, 6 mg chol, 104 mg sodium. % RDI: 15% calcium, 1% iron, 4% vit A, 7% vit C, 2% folate.

Caramel Sauce

Creamy and almost sinful, caramel sauce is the perfect sweet topping for ice cream, cakes or cheesecakes, especially our New York Cheesecake (recipe, page 143).

1½ cups	granulated sugar	375 mL	¼ cup	butter	50 mL
⅔ cup	whipping cream	150 mL			

➥ In heavy saucepan, stir sugar with ⅓ cup (75 mL) water over medium heat until dissolved, brushing down side of pan with pastry brush dipped in cold water. Bring to boil; boil vigorously, without stirring but brushing down side of pan often, until dark amber, about 6 minutes. Remove from heat.

➥ Standing back and averting face, add cream; whisk until smooth. Whisk in butter until smooth. Let cool. **(Make-ahead: Refrigerate in airtight container for up to 1 week; rewarm to liquefy.)**

Makes about 1¼ cups (300 mL). | PER 2 TBSP (25 mL): about 209 cal, trace pro, 10 g total fat (6 g sat. fat), 30 g carb, 0 g fibre, 33 mg chol, 39 mg sodium. % RDI: 1% calcium, 9% vit A.

VARIATION

Bourbon Caramel Sauce: Whisk ¼ cup (50 mL) bourbon and 1 tsp (5 mL) lemon juice into finished hot sauce. Return pan to heat; simmer for 4 minutes.

Crème Anglaise

This velvety pouring custard is fantastic drizzled on puddings, apple crisp, bread pudding and fruit, or pooled under or poured over cake and fruit pies.

1 cup	whipping cream or 18% cream	250 mL	¼ cup	granulated sugar	50 mL
1 cup	milk	250 mL	6	egg yolks	6
			1 tsp	vanilla	5 mL

In saucepan, heat together cream, milk and half of the sugar over medium heat until steaming and bubbles form around edge.

Meanwhile, in bowl, whisk egg yolks with remaining sugar. Whisk in about half of the hot cream mixture in thin stream; stir back into pan. Cook over low heat, stirring constantly, until thick enough to coat back of spoon, about 5 minutes.

Strain into clean bowl; stir in vanilla. Place plastic wrap directly on surface; let cool. Refrigerate until cold, at least 1 hour. **(Make-ahead: Refrigerate for up to 3 days.)**

Makes about 2 cups (500 mL). | PER 2 TBSP (25 mL): about 91 cal, 2 g pro, 8 g total fat (4 g sat. fat), 4 g carb, 0 g fibre, 97 mg chol, 16 mg sodium. % RDI: 3% calcium, 1% iron, 9% vit A, 5% folate.

VARIATIONS

Eggnog Crème Anglaise: Omit vanilla. Stir 2 tbsp (25 mL) dark rum and ¼ tsp (1 mL) grated nutmeg into finished sauce.

Orange Whisky Crème Anglaise: Omit vanilla. Add 1 tsp (5 mL) grated orange rind to cream mixture before heating. Stir 2 tbsp (25 mL) whisky into finished sauce.

Rum-Spiked Crème Anglaise: Stir 2 tbsp (25 mL) to ¼ cup (50 mL) rum into finished sauce.

Vanilla Bean Crème Anglaise: Omit vanilla. Slit 1 vanilla bean; with side of knife, scrape out seeds. Add seeds and bean halves to cream mixture before heating. When straining, be sure to retain the vanilla bean seeds in the sauce. Remove bean halves before serving; pat dry and use to flavour a canister of granulated sugar.

SECRETS OF SILKY CUSTARD SAUCES

No matter how carefully a stirred custard is cooked, there will be some tiny lumps. Strain through a fine sieve to remove them.

● To prevent a skin from forming on the surface of the custard as it cools, lay a piece of plastic wrap directly on the surface.

Raspberry Red Wine Sauce

Heavenly scented with raspberry and vanilla, this wine reduction is a sophisticated addition to fresh berries or peaches, or any creamy dessert or angel food cake.

1	bottle (750 mL) dry red wine	1	⅔ cup	granulated sugar	150 mL
1	can (275 mL) frozen raspberry cocktail concentrate, thawed	1	2 tsp	vanilla	10 mL

In large saucepan over medium heat, stir together wine, raspberry concentrate and sugar; bring to boil. Boil gently until reduced to 1½ cups (375 mL), about 30 minutes. Remove from heat; stir in vanilla. Pour into glass jar; refrigerate until chilled, about 1 hour. **(Make-ahead: Refrigerate for up to 3 weeks.)**

Makes about 1½ cups (375 mL). | PER 2 TBSP (25 mL): about 118 cal, trace pro, 0 g total fat (0 g sat. fat), 26 g carb, 0 g fibre, 0 mg chol, 3 mg sodium. % RDI: 1% calcium, 2% iron, 2% folate.

HAVE A SUNDAE PARTY
❯ Choose a selection of sauces – chocolate, caramel and fruit-based ones – and offer to guests with complementary ice creams and sorbets. For kids, add candies and sprinkles; for adults, toasted nuts and sliced fruit are fun.

VARIATION

Cranberry Red Wine Sauce: Increase sugar to 1¼ cups (300 mL). Substitute 1 can (275 mL) frozen cranberry cocktail concentrate for raspberry cocktail concentrate. Boil gently until reduced to 2 cups (500 mL), about 45 minutes.

Fancy Cranberry Sauce Topping

Ruby red, with the sweet-tart zing of cranberries, this compote is fabulous over cheesecake, especially New York Cheesecake (recipe, page 143). Spoon about ½ cup (125 mL) over cheesecake, then refrigerate for 2 hours. Serve remainder alongside.

1	bag (340 g) fresh or frozen cranberries	1	½ cup	water	125 mL
			1 tbsp	cornstarch	15 mL
¾ cup	granulated sugar	175 mL	½ cup	port	125 mL

In saucepan, bring cranberries, sugar and water to boil; reduce heat and simmer until saucy and berries pop but still retain shape, about 8 minutes.

Whisk cornstarch into port until dissolved; gently stir into cranberry mixture and return to boil. Simmer until compote clears and thickens, about 1 minute. Scrape into large glass jar. Let cool slightly; cover and refrigerate until cold, about 2 hours. **(Make-ahead: Refrigerate for up to 5 days.)**

Makes about 2 cups (500 mL). | PER 2 TBSP (25 mL): about 59 cal, 0 g pro, 0 g total fat (0 g sat. fat), 13 g carb, 1 g fibre, 0 mg chol, 1 mg sodium. % RDI: 4% vit C.

Raspberry Orange Sauce

Just a little bit tart, this robust topping comes alive on ice cream, especially alongside a thick chocolate sauce.

SUGARED FRUIT GARNISHES

❯ Frosted and sparkling, these pretty decorations take desserts to a spectacular new level.

❧ In small saucepan, bring ½ cup (125 mL) granulated sugar and ⅓ cup (75 mL) water to full rolling boil. Let cool to room temperature.

❧ Dip washed, dried whole berries, red and white currants, golden Cape gooseberries (physalis or ground cherries) or clusters of small grapes into syrup, letting excess drip back into pan. Roll in granulated sugar. Let dry on parchment or waxed paper–lined rimmed baking sheet. Use as soon as possible.

1	pkg (600 g) frozen unsweetened raspberries, thawed and drained	1	3 tbsp	orange-flavoured liqueur or orange juice	50 mL
¼ cup	raspberry jam	50 mL	1 tbsp	liquid honey	15 mL
			1 tsp	lemon juice	5 mL

❧ In food processor, purée together raspberries, jam, liqueur, honey and lemon juice; press through fine sieve to remove seeds. **(Make-ahead: Refrigerate in airtight container for up to 5 days.)**

Makes about 2 cups (500 mL). | PER 1 TBSP (15 mL): about 19 cal, trace pro, trace total fat (0 g sat. fat), 4 g carb, 0 g fibre, 0 mg chol, 1 mg sodium. % RDI: 1% iron, 7% vit C, 2% folate.

Sour Cherry and Vodka Sauce

This fancy sauce is surprisingly easy to make. If using frozen cherries, let thaw in a sieve over a bowl to retain the juices. Serve warm over crêpes with a bit of mascarpone, cold over ice cream, or with pound or angel food cake.

2¼ cups	thawed frozen or canned sour cherries in juice	550 mL	2 tbsp	lemon juice	25 mL
			¼ cup	vodka	50 mL
½ cup	granulated sugar	125 mL	1 tsp	vanilla	5 mL

❧ Drain cherries, reserving juice. In saucepan, bring cherries, ¼ cup (50 mL) of the cherry juice, sugar and lemon juice to boil. Reduce heat and simmer until reduced to 1¾ cups (425 mL), 12 to 15 minutes. Stir in vodka and vanilla. Let cool slightly. **(Make-ahead: Let cool. Refrigerate in airtight container for up to 5 days. Reheat before using, if desired.)**

Makes about 2 cups (500 mL). | PER 2 TBSP (25 mL): about 43 cal, trace pro, trace total fat (trace sat. fat), 9 g carb, trace fibre, 0 mg chol, 1 mg sodium. % RDI: 1% iron, 2% vit A, 2% vit C.

Whipped Cream

Cream whips best when the cream, bowl and beaters are cold. It is important not to overwhip cream, as it may separate and curdle, turning to butter and buttermilk. Add flavourings or sweeteners, such as sugar, at the beginning.

1 cup	whipping cream	250 mL	½ tsp	vanilla	2 mL
2 tbsp	sugar	25 mL			

🍂 In bowl, whip together cream, sugar and vanilla until stiff peaks form.

Makes about 2 cups (500 mL). | PER 2 TBSP (25 mL): about 55 cal, trace pro, 5 g total fat (3 g sat. fat), 2 g carb, 0 g fibre, 19 mg chol, 5 mg sodium. % RDI: 1% calcium, 6% vit A.

VARIATIONS

Citrus Whipped Cream: Omit vanilla. Add 1 tsp (5 mL) finely grated lemon, orange or lime rind to cream mixture. Whip as directed.

Cocoa Whipped Cream: Sift 2 tbsp (25 mL) cocoa powder over cream mixture. Cover and refrigerate for 30 minutes; stir. Whip as directed.

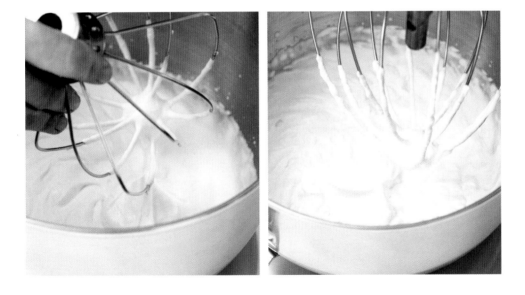

Stabilized Whipped Cream

Adding melted gelatin to whipped cream allows it to be made ahead and held in the refrigerator for up to 1 day. This is especially useful in cakes and trifles that need to be assembled in advance.

GARNISHING WITH FRESH FLOWERS

❯ Add colour, whimsy and charm to desserts with a scattering of pretty petals and blossoms.

● Use unsprayed flowers from your garden or favourite florist.

● Edible flowers include: borage, carnations, cornflowers, daylilies, chrysanthemums, geraniums, gladioli, lavender, marigolds, nasturtiums, pansies, pinks (dianthus), sweet peas, violas and violets.

● Pick flowers early in the day. Rinse blossoms, leaves and stems briefly in cool water; shake dry. Place in a pitcher of cold water and refrigerate until needed.

1 tsp	gelatin	5 mL	2 tbsp	icing sugar	25 mL
1 cup	whipping cream	250 mL			

🍃 In small saucepan, sprinkle gelatin over 2 tbsp (25 mL) cold water; let stand for 5 minutes. Warm over low heat, without stirring, until dissolved. Set aside.

🍃 In bowl, whip cream with icing sugar until soft peaks form. While beating, drizzle in gelatin mixture. Beat to desired stiffness.

Makes about 2 cups (500 mL). | PER 2 TBSP (25 mL): about 53 cal, trace pro, 5 g total fat (3 g sat. fat), 1 g carb, 0 g fibre, 19 mg chol, 6 mg sodium. % RDI: 1% calcium, 6% vit A.

Tangy Whipped Cream

This yogurt-infused topping, with a taste like that of crème fraîche, has a really lovely tang that complements all sorts of desserts.

1 cup	Balkan-style yogurt	250 mL	2 tbsp	icing sugar	25 mL
1 cup	whipping cream	250 mL			

🍃 Line sieve with damp cheesecloth; set over bowl. Add yogurt; let drain in refrigerator for 1 hour.

🍃 In bowl, whip cream with icing sugar until soft peaks form. Fold in drained yogurt.

Makes about 2½ cups (625 mL). | PER 2 TBSP (25 mL): about 53 cal, 1 g pro, 5 g total fat (3 g sat. fat), 2 g carb, 0 g fibre, 17 mg chol, 8 mg sodium. % RDI: 2% calcium, 5% vit A.

Candied Orange Rind

Dress up citrus desserts with a touch of sparkle. The flavour-rich peel from navel oranges, lemons and grapefruits make fabulous candied rind.

1	navel orange	1
1⅓ cups	granulated sugar	325 mL

❧ Using vegetable peeler, cut strips of rind from 1 orange. Cut lengthwise into thin shoelace-like strips.

❧ In saucepan, combine 1 cup (250 mL) of the sugar with ¼ cup (50 mL) water; bring to boil, stirring until sugar is dissolved. Boil for 1 minute.

❧ Add rind; simmer until translucent, about 6 minutes.

❧ With slotted spoon or tongs, remove rind, shaking off excess syrup. Immediately toss with remaining sugar, using fork to separate pieces. Let harden on plate. **(Make-ahead: Layer between waxed paper and store in airtight container at room temperature for up to 2 weeks.)**

Makes ⅓ cup (75 mL).

Syrup-Poached Lemon Rind

Cheery yellow strips of lemon rind make an elegant garnish, especially on our Lemon Dacquoise (recipe, page 151).

1	lemon	1	½ cup	lemon juice	125 mL
½ cup	granulated sugar	125 mL			

❧ With vegetable peeler or paring knife, cut strips of rind from top to bottom all around lemon. Cut lengthwise into thin strips, trimming to straighten edges.

❧ In small saucepan, combine sugar with lemon juice; bring to boil. Add rind and return to boil. Remove from heat; let cool. **(Make-ahead: Store rind in syrup in airtight container at room temperature for up to 1 week.)** Drain well.

Makes about ¼ cup (50 mL).

SPARKLY SUGARED FLOWERS

❯ Flowers such as violas, violets or borage, or petals from roses, make elegant garnishes when dressed in a glittery coat of sugar. Use atop celebration cakes or any dessert that requires a special flourish.

● If using roses, separate petals from flowers.

● Swish petals or flowers in barely lukewarm water with a touch of soap. Rinse in a bowl of barely lukewarm water and drain. Pat dry.

● In small bowl, whisk ¼ cup (50 mL) pasteurized egg white until foamy.

● Working with 1 petal or flower at a time, brush both sides with egg white. Sprinkle with granulated sugar to coat.

● Let dry on parchment or waxed paper–lined rimmed baking sheet, about 2 hours.

● Cover loosely with plastic wrap or layer between waxed paper in airtight container and store for up to 3 days.

Lemon Curd

The quantity of butter in this lemon curd helps it set up nicely and gives it a satiny richness.

4	egg yolks	4	⅓ cup	lemon juice	75 mL
½ cup	granulated sugar	125 mL	⅓ cup	cold butter, cubed	75 mL
1 tbsp	grated lemon rind	15 mL			

THE DONENESS TEST
❯ Like a stirred custard, or crème anglaise, lemon curd is done when it is thick enough to coat the back of a spoon (opposite).

➤ In heatproof bowl, whisk together egg yolks, sugar and lemon rind and juice; set over saucepan of simmering water. Cook, stirring, until mixture is thick enough to coat back of spoon and candy thermometer registers 160°F (71°C), 8 to 10 minutes.

➤ Remove from heat; stir in butter, 1 piece at a time, until smooth. Strain through fine sieve into airtight container. Place plastic wrap directly on surface. Refrigerate until cold and thick enough to mound firmly on spoon, about 2 hours. (**Make-ahead: Refrigerate for up to 1 day.**)

Makes about 1 cup (250 mL). | PER 2 TBSP (25 mL): about 149 cal, 2 g pro, 10 g total fat (6 g sat. fat), 13 g carb, 0 g fibre, 122 mg chol, 58 mg sodium. % RDI: 1% calcium, 2% iron, 11% vit A, 8% vit C, 7% folate.

Orange White Chocolate Curd

This curd is a delightful, creamy, fresh take on traditional lemon curd. It can lend its charming brightness to top fruit and desserts and is the luscious filling for Orange White Chocolate Strawberry Shortcake (recipe, page 108).

1 tsp	unflavoured gelatin	5 mL	1 tbsp	grated orange rind	15 mL
2	eggs	2	⅓ cup	orange juice	75 mL
2	egg yolks	2	2 tbsp	lemon juice	25 mL
⅓ cup	granulated sugar	75 mL	3 oz	white chocolate, chopped	90 g

➤ In small microwaveable bowl or saucepan, sprinkle gelatin over 1 tbsp (15 mL) cold water; let stand for 5 minutes. Microwave at high for 10 seconds, or warm over low heat until dissolved, about 1 minute.

➤ Meanwhile, in heatproof bowl, whisk together eggs, egg yolks, sugar, orange rind and juice, and lemon juice. Set over saucepan of simmering water; cook, whisking, until mixture is thick enough to mound on spoon, about 6 minutes.

➤ Remove from heat. Whisk in white chocolate until melted. Whisk in gelatin mixture; refrigerate, whisking occasionally, until curd mounds firmly on spoon, 15 to 20 minutes.

Makes 1½ cups (375 mL). | PER 2 TBSP (25 mL): about 87 cal, 2 g pro, 4 g total fat (2 g sat. fat), 11 g carb, 0 g fibre, 65 mg chol, 18 mg sodium. % RDI: 2% calcium, 1% iron, 3% vit A, 7% vit C, 5% folate.

Chocolate Garnishes

These cutouts, curls, shavings and shards make enough to decorate an 8-inch (20 cm) to 10-inch (25 cm) tart, cake or cheesecake. Place finished curls and cutouts on waxed paper–lined rimmed baking sheet. Cover lightly with waxed paper and refrigerate.

6 oz	bittersweet or semisweet chocolate	175 g

❧ **CHOPPING CHOCOLATE:** Using chef's knife, chop chocolate into almond-size pieces. In heatproof bowl over saucepan of hot (not boiling) water, melt chocolate until about three-quarters melted. Remove from heat. Stir until completely melted.

❧ **SPREADING CHOCOLATE:** Pour chocolate onto back of 15- x 10-inch (40 x 25 cm) rimmed baking sheet (do not use nonstick pan). With offset spatula or rubber spatula, spread evenly over pan. Refrigerate until set, about 15 minutes. Place baking sheet on large damp towel that extends beyond edge of sheet; let stand for 3 minutes.

SHORT ROUND CURLS: Brace pan against body. Holding bowl of teaspoon at 45-degree angle to pan and working toward yourself, scrape about 4 inches (10 cm) chocolate into curls. Refrigerate pan if chocolate begins to soften. Use toothpick or offset spatula to transfer curls, in single layer, to waxed paper–lined rimmed baking sheet. Refrigerate.

PENCIL-THIN CURLS: Refrigerate pan before spreading with melted chocolate. Brace pan against body. At opposite side of pan, hold large chef's knife at 90-degree angle to pan; hold top of blade firm and steady with other hand. Pull knife toward yourself, scraping chocolate into pencil-thin curls. If chocolate is too cold, it will be brittle; let stand for a few minutes until it curls nicely.

CUTOUTS: Line bottom of 15- x 10-inch (40 x 25 cm) rimmed baking sheet with parchment paper. Spread chocolate over half of parchment; refrigerate for 15 minutes. Let stand for 5 minutes. Using cookie cutter, cut out shapes; chill if necessary to firm up. Lift off with tip of knife or offset spatula.

BLOCK METHOD: Buy chocolate in blocks or pour melted dark, milk or white chocolate into foil-lined 5¾- x 3¼-inch (625 mL) loaf pan. Refrigerate until set, about 4 hours; unmould. Let stand for 20 minutes or until slightly softened.

SHAVINGS OR SHARDS: Holding chocolate with foil or parchment and bracing block comfortably at an angle, slowly draw blade of sharp vegetable peeler down side of block.

Piped Chocolate Garnishes

These pretty designs really stand out (and up!) on top of a cake. Create lacy trees, stars, hearts or other shapes to suit the occasion. Simple designs are often the most effective.

MAKING A
PAPER CONE

Cut 10-inch (25 cm) square of parchment paper. Cut in half diagonally to make 2 triangles. Place triangle with right angle closest to you. With hand holding 1 corner of long side of triangle, roll hand inward to begin forming cone, making the point at centre of long side.

Wrap other corner of parchment around cone. Fold top corner points down to hold cone shape firm. Snip off tip of cone.

2 oz	bittersweet, semisweet or white chocolate, chopped	60 g

❧ Make parchment paper cone (see Making a Paper Cone, left).

❧ Trace desired designs onto parchment paper or waxed paper. Turn paper over and place on rimmed baking sheet.

❧ In heatproof bowl over saucepan of hot (not boiling) water, melt chocolate. Let cool slightly. Pour into paper cone. Fold top of cone over to seal. Cut off tip to desired size.

❧ Holding cone gently between thumb and forefinger, trace chocolate over designs. Refrigerate until set, about 15 minutes. **(Make-ahead: Refrigerate for up to 1 day.)** Using offset spatula, transfer garnishes to dessert.

Chocolate Leaves

Use pesticide-free rose, lemon or basil leaves from your garden or florist. They look stunning arranged atop a layer cake, cheesecake, Bundt or angel food cake.

	Rose, lemon or basil leaves	
3 oz	bittersweet, semisweet or white chocolate, chopped	90 g

❧ Remove leaves from stems. Swish leaves in cool soapy water; rinse and blot dry.

❧ In heatproof bowl over saucepan of hot (not boiling) water, melt chocolate. Holding stem end of leaf between thumb and forefinger and supporting leaf on cutting board, brush chocolate over back of leaf. Place on waxed-paper lined rimmed baking sheet; refrigerate until firm, about 15 minutes.

❧ Brush second layer of chocolate over leaves; chill. Starting at stem end, gently peel away leaf; discard. **(Make-ahead: Layer between waxed paper in airtight container and refrigerate for up to 1 week.)**

Meringue Straws

Break these meringue straws into various lengths or use whole to decorate cakes, crèmes brûlées or plated desserts. Be careful – they're fragile.

2	egg whites	2	½ cup	granulated sugar	125 mL
Pinch	cream of tartar	Pinch			

❧ Line 2 large rimless baking sheets with silicone baking mats or parchment paper; set aside.

❧ In bowl, beat egg whites until foamy; beat in cream of tartar until soft peaks form. Beat in sugar, 2 tbsp (25 mL) at a time, until stiff glossy peaks form.

❧ Using piping bag fitted with ¼-inch (5 mm) plain tip, pipe twelve 9-inch (23 cm) long straws, 1 inch (2.5 cm) apart, onto prepared baking sheets.

❧ Bake in top and bottom thirds of 200°F (100°C) oven, switching and rotating pans halfway through, until dry and crisp, about 1 hour. Turn off oven; let stand in oven for 1 hour. Transfer to rack; let cool. **(Make-ahead: Store in airtight container at room temperature for up to 3 days.)**

Makes 24 pieces. | PER PIECE: about 17 cal, trace pro, 0 g total fat (0 g sat. fat), 4 g carb, 0 g fibre, 0 mg chol, 4 mg sodium.

VARIATION

Chocolate Meringue Straws: Fold 2 tbsp (25 mL) cocoa powder, sifted, into beaten egg whites.

Bake: To cook with dry heat in the oven. Never crowd items in the oven – the best results depend on the free circulation of heat. Keep an oven thermometer inside to check that the temperature setting is accurate. If it's not, adjust it until you reach the correct temperature.

Bake blind: To bake a pastry shell fully or partially before filling. This prevents the pastry from shrinking or blistering. Prick pastry all over at 1-inch (2.5 cm) intervals. Line with foil, pressing it so it hugs the pastry, then fill with pie weights or dried beans (reuse them over and over again). Once heat sets the pastry, in about 10 minutes, remove the foil and weights. Depending on the recipe, return to oven to finish baking or fill and bake. For more information, see page 173.

Batter: A flour and liquid mixture, often containing other ingredients, that is thin enough to pour. See also *Dough*, below.

Beat: To soften hard fats, incorporate air into a mixture, incorporate dry and wet ingredients, or smooth out batter. Beating is usually done with an electric mixer (we recommend a stand mixer).

Blend: To mix two or more ingredients until completely combined and smooth, using a spoon, whisk, mixer or blender.

Boil: To heat liquid to 212°F (100°C), at which point bubbles vigorously break the surface.

Caramelize: To cook sugar, or preferably a sugar-and-water mixture, until the sugar liquefies or dissolves, becomes syrupy and darkens from golden to rich brown. Use a heavy saucepan to make caramel. For step-by-step instructions, see page 326. *Caramelize* can also refer to the slow cooking of ingredients, such as onions, that concentrates and toasts their natural sugars.

Chill: To refrigerate until evenly cold. To speed the process for custards or other liquid mixtures, pour them into metal bowl; set in larger bowl containing ice cubes and water. Let chill, stirring and scraping down side of inner bowl frequently.

Chop: To cut into pieces about ½ inch (1 cm) square; not as uniform as cubing.

Cream: To beat butter with sugar until as light and fluffy as whipped cream in order to incorporate air.

Crimp: To pinch or press together two edges of pastry using fingers or fork. See also *Flute*, below.

Cube: To cut into medium-size, uniform cubes about ½ inch (1 cm) square.

Cut in: To break up a cold solid fat, such as butter or lard, into dry ingredients. Use a pastry blender until the mixture is crumbly with some larger pieces and each piece of fat is coated with dry ingredients. For fast results, use a food processor. You can use two knives, but the process is laborious.

Dice: To cut into small, uniform cubes about ¼ inch (5 mm) square.

Dough: A flour and liquid mixture, often including other ingredients, that is stiff enough to knead or shape with your hands. See also *Batter,* above.

Dust: To sprinkle a fine powder, such as icing sugar or cocoa powder, decoratively over a baked item. To dust, spoon icing sugar or cocoa into a fine sieve; over baked item, tap the side of the sieve, moving it over surface to cover evenly.

Flute: To form a decorative, grooved pleat around the edge of a pie or pastry. For step-by-step instructions, see page 156. See also *Crimp,* above.

Fold: To gently combine a light mixture filled with air, such as beaten egg whites or cream, into a heavier mixture, such as a batter, without deflating the lighter mixture. This is usually done in two stages. First, about one-third of the lighter mixture is incorporated to lighten the heavier mixture. This ensures that the second addition will blend in more easily and keep its airiness. Second, the rest of the lighter mixture is gently incorporated. The secret of folding is to never lift the spatula out of the mixture. For step-by-step instructions, see page 95.

Ganache: A rich chocolate mixture used as a cake covering, truffle filling or sauce. To make, pour boiling cream over chopped chocolate; whisk until chocolate is melted and smooth. With white chocolate, you may need to complete the melting process by warming the mixture in a heatproof bowl set over a saucepan of hot (not boiling) water.

Glaze: To create a shiny surface on baked goods. This can be done by brushing an egg wash (1 egg or egg yolk mixed with 1 tbsp/15 mL water) over bread, pastries or quick breads before baking. Or it can be done by drizzling or spreading a sweet syrup or thin icing over baked cakes, sweet rolls or cookies.

Grate: To use a box grater or rasp to cut foods such as citrus zest, bread crumbs or hard cheese into tiny bits. See also *Shred,* below.

Grease: To completely and generously cover inner or flat surface of cake pans or baking sheets with melted butter or oil. This prevents baked goods from sticking to the pan. Use a pastry brush. Vegetable oil spray is an easy alternative.

Infuse: To steep herbs, citrus peel, vanilla beans or spices in hot liquid to add flavour.

Knead: To use hands, a stand mixer or a bread machine to fold, push and turn dough, usually yeast-based, until it is firm, stretchy and no longer sticky. Kneading develops the gluten in the flour. For step-by-step instructions, see page 214.

Macerate: To let fruit soak in liquid, often alcoholic, to tenderize or flavour it, or to create a sauce-like topping.

Mince: To cut into very fine pieces, much smaller than chopping or dicing.

Mix: To use a spoon, fork, whisk or beaters to combine two or more ingredients.

Mousse: An airy sweet or savoury mixture usually lightened with egg whites or whipping cream, sometimes set with gelatin.

Pipe: To force an icing, thick batter or soft dough through the tip of a piping bag (or a sturdy plastic bag with the corner snipped off) to create a specific shape.

Plump: To hydrate dried fruit with liquid such as water, juice or alcohol. Soaking the fruit softens it and helps keep baked goods fresh – dry fruit will absorb the moisture around it, causing baked goods to go stale faster.

Preheat: To heat the oven ahead of time to ensure even heat and proper temperature during baking. Turn on the oven at least 10 minutes before it's needed. And check the oven before turning on the heat to ensure that the racks are in the right position and to determine if anything – like drying muffin tins – lurks unexpected inside.

Prick: To pierce pastry with a fork to prevent it from blistering or shrinking during baking. See also *Bake blind*, above.

Proof: To check that yeast is alive. To do so, recipes start by sprinkling yeast over slightly sweetened water and letting the mixture stand for 10 minutes. If it bubbles and increases in volume, that is proof that your bread will, too. If it doesn't, check the best-before date on the yeast package. If it hasn't expired, start again, making sure that the water is the temperature called for in the recipe. If it has expired, start again with freshly purchased yeast. For step-by-step instructions, see page 214.

Purée: To mash food until smooth using a food processor or blender, or by hand using a food mill or sieve.

Reduce: To boil down a liquid, usually over high heat and uncovered, to evaporate water, concentrating both the flavour and the texture.

Ribbon: When beating eggs with sugar, the stage reached when the batter falls into thin bands, or ribbons, when the beaters are lifted out. For more information, see page 140.

Scald: To heat milk or cream almost to the boiling point, or until bubbles form around edge of pan.

Score: To make shallow cuts in the surface of yeast breads in order to make an attractive design and to ensure even rising and baking. For bars or squares, phyllo pastries or strudels, scoring the surface before or after baking helps to delineate portions and makes final cuts cleaner and neater.

Scrape down: To push ingredients down, using a flexible rubber spatula, from the side of the mixer or food processor bowl back into the bulk of the batter.

Shred: To use a box grater to cut foods such as softer cheeses, fruit or vegetables into evenly sized strips. See also *Grate*, above.

Sift: To use a sieve or flour sifter to blend together dry ingredients and break up lumps in cocoa powder or icing sugar. This is a necessary step before measuring cake-and-pastry flour.

Simmer: To heat a liquid until bubbles rise from the bottom of the pan and break gently on the surface.

Stir: To mix ingredients together with a spoon, whisk or spatula using a circular motion.

Strain: To drain a mixture through a sieve to separate solids from liquid.

Temper: To gradually whisk a hot liquid mixture with beaten eggs or egg yolks to prevent them from scrambling on contact. For step-by-step instructions, see page 319.

Toss: To combine ingredients using a utensil such as a fork to lightly lift and let them fall. Rotate the bowl as you toss to evenly moisten, mix or coat.

Whip: To beat a liquid, such as cream, until soft or firm peaks form. Whip by hand with a whisk or use an electric mixer with a whisk attachment. For more information, see page 331.

Whirl: To turn ingredients rapidly in a food processor in order to combine, chop or purée them.

Whisk: To use a wire whisk to mix together dry ingredients, blend a mixture together or incorporate air into a batter.

Zest: To remove the flavourful coloured outer layer of citrus fruit. Use a box grater or rasp for a variety of dimensions, or a zester for longer strips.

High-Altitude Baking

❯ High elevations affect baking, so follow these guidelines to ensure perfect results.

● In high places, there is less atmospheric pressure, so leavening agents such as baking powder, baking soda and yeast release more and larger gas bubbles. These bubbles expand very quickly and then, before the heat of the oven has firmed them up, collapse, causing cakes and breads to fall. The solution for cake and quick bread batters is to reduce the baking powder or baking soda by ⅛ tsp (0.5 mL) for each 1 tsp (5 mL) called for in the recipe. This is less of an issue with cookies, as less leavening is generally the rule.

● The internal temperature of a cake baking at high altitude is lower, which means it will take longer than the time specified. Look for visual clues of doneness and increase baking time by a few minutes, but do not alter the oven temperature.

● Excessive sugar weakens a cake's structure. If the amount of sugar in the ingredient list is more than half the quantity of flour, reduce the sugar by 1 tbsp (15 mL) for every 1 cup (250 mL) called for.

● Since yeast doughs rise more quickly at high altitudes, rely more on visual clues than on suggested rising times to make sure that the dough has risen just until doubled in bulk. If you let it go longer, the bread will develop large air cells, causing it to fall during baking.

● At high altitudes, moisture evaporates at a lower temperature, which results in baked goods that are drier. It helps to line your cake and baking pans with parchment paper.

About Our Nutrition Information

❯ To meet nutrient needs each day, moderately active women 25 to 49 need about 1,900 calories, 51 g protein, 261 g carbohydrate, 25 to 35 g fibre and not more than 63 g total fat (21 g saturated fat). Men and teenagers usually need more. Canadian sodium intake of approximately 3,500 to 4,500 mg daily should be reduced. Percentage of recommended daily intake (% RDI) is based on the highest recommended intakes (excluding those for pregnant and lactating women) for calcium, iron, vitamins A and C, and folate.

Figures are rounded off. They are based on the first ingredient listed when there is a choice and do not include optional ingredients or those with no specified amounts.

ABBREVIATIONS:
cal = calories
pro = protein
carb = carbohydrate
sat. fat = saturated fat
chol = cholesterol

Photography

Christopher Campbell: pages 62, 194, 195 and 206.

Hasnain Dattu: pages 116 and 295.

Yvonne Duivenvoorden: pages 30, 51, 56, 63, 64, 87, 99, 102, 123, 128, 137, 141, 146, 149, 172, 182, 187, 193, 223, 230, 243, 248, 265, 275, 278, 307, 310 and 322.

Geoff George: pages 49 and 65.

Edward Pond: pages 4, 7, 12, 13, 14, 15, 16, 17, 18, 19, 24, 25, 32, 36, 40, 41, 43, 71, 76, 77, 90, 91, 93, 94, 95, 96, 105, 110, 111, 112, 113, 134, 135, 139, 140, 143, 144, 152, 153, 155, 156, 157, 160, 165, 168, 173, 176, 177, 184, 188, 201, 202, 203, 210, 212, 213, 215, 216, 217, 219, 221, 228, 233, 235, 237, 238, 239, 244, 245, 254, 255, 258, 259, 260, 261, 266, 269, 285, 290, 291, 292, 293, 299, 302, 303, 304, 312, 315, 316, 317, 318, 319, 326, 327, 328, 331, 334, 336, 337, 338 and 352.

David Scott: pages 80 and 268.

Food Styling

Julie Aldis: pages 99 and 182.

Donna Bartolini: pages 7, 12, 13, 14, 15, 16, 17, 18, 19, 24, 25, 32, 40, 41, 43, 71, 76, 77, 90, 91, 93, 94, 95, 96, 105, 110, 111, 112, 113, 116, 134, 135, 139, 140, 143, 144, 146, 152, 153, 155, 156, 157, 160, 165, 168, 173, 176, 177, 184, 188, 201, 203, 212, 213, 215, 216, 217, 219, 221, 233, 235, 237, 238, 239, 244, 245, 254, 255, 258, 259, 260, 261, 266, 269, 285, 290, 291, 292, 293, 295, 299, 302, 303, 304, 312, 315, 316, 317, 318, 319, 326, 327, 328, 331, 334, 336, 337 and 338.

Carol Dudar: pages 172 and 307.

Heather Howe: pages 62, 194, 195, 206, 210 and 228.

Lucie Richard: pages 30, 51, 56, 64, 80, 128, 149, 223, 243, 265, 268 and 275.

Claire Stancer: pages 123 and 278.

Claire Stubbs: pages 63, 87, 102, 137, 141, 187, 193, 230, 248, 310 and 322.

Rosemarie Superville: page 65.

Sandra Watson: page 202.

Nicole Young: page 49.

Props Styling

Marc-Philippe Gagné: pages 141, 295 and 322.

Maggi Jones: pages 7, 12, 13, 14, 15, 16, 17, 18, 19, 24, 25, 32, 40, 41, 43, 71, 76, 77, 90, 91, 93, 94, 95, 96, 105, 110, 111, 112, 113, 134, 135, 139, 140, 143, 144, 152, 153, 155, 156, 157, 160, 165, 168, 173, 176, 177, 184, 188, 201, 202, 203, 212, 213, 215, 216, 217, 219, 221, 233, 235, 237, 238, 239, 244, 245, 254, 255, 258, 259, 260, 261, 266, 269, 285, 290, 291, 292, 293, 299, 302, 303, 304, 312, 315, 316, 317, 318, 319, 326, 327, 328, 331, 334, 336, 337 and 338.

OK Props: pages 99 and 187.

Oksana Slavutych: pages 30, 49, 51, 56, 63, 64, 65, 80, 87, 102, 116, 123, 128, 137, 146, 149, 172, 182, 193, 223, 230, 243, 248, 265, 268, 275, 278, 307 and 310.

All recipes were developed by The Canadian Living Test Kitchen, except the following.

Donna Bartolini: pages 22, 65 and 200.

Edythe Diebel: page 118.

Emilie Dore: page 36.

Sharol Josephson: page 113.

Lesleigh Landry: page 73.

Rose Murray: pages 60, 284 and 306.

Christine Picheca: pages 29 and 32 (Pignoli).

Daphna Rabinovitch: pages 43, 112 and 129.

Emily Richards: pages 209 and 241.

Dufflet Rosenberg: page 117.

Adell Shneer: pages 240, 252 and 283.

Linda Stephen: pages 71 and 329 (Raspberry Red Wine Sauce).

Nicole Young: page 32 (Barazek).

Hand model, **Adell Shneer**
Appliances, courtesy of **KitchenAid Canada**

❯ Two formidable home economists set the standard for baking at *Canadian Living*: founding food editor Carol Ferguson and her associate, Margaret Fraser. They were not alone, as among the magazine's earliest contributors were respected authors, notably Bonnie Stern, Rose Murray, Anne Lindsay and Kay Spicer. Adding to this pool of talent was The Canadian Living Test Kitchen, staffed over the years with extraordinarily gifted bakers. Patsy Jamieson, Daphna Rabinovitch and Donna Bartolini all made their reputations as pastry chefs before they ever donned a crimson *CL* apron as Test Kitchen managers.

When it came time to create *The Complete Canadian Living Baking Book,* I called on Donna Bartolini, Test Kitchen food specialist Adell Shneer and senior food specialist Heather Howe to help shape the content. Adell and Heather also worked with me to develop new recipes and adaptations.

Many more Test Kitchen names come to mind when it comes to baking, among them the rest of the current staff: senior food specialist Alison Kent; food specialists Rheanna Kish, Soo Kim and Kate Dowhan; contributing editor Andrew Chase; food editor Gabrielle Bright; and web food editor Christine Picheca. It seems that almost everyone who has ever worked in our Test Kitchen has stirred something delicious into this book, including senior editor Beverley Renahan, who did her stirring at the computer.

Bringing the recipes alive on the pages of the magazine is our creative director, Michael Erb, who designed and shaped this easy-to-use and beautiful cookbook. He was assisted by Roy Gaiot and his associates in the *Canadian Living* art department, notably June Anderson. The many photographers, food stylists and props stylists we have worked with over the years (see page 351 for credits) all deserve our recognition for making the visuals of our baked goods as tempting and helpful as possible for both budding and seasoned bakers. Photographer Edward Pond and props stylist Maggi Jones, along with Adell Shneer and Donna Bartolini (this time in her food stylist's role), get special thanks for the new step-by-step and beauty shots, so enchantingly taken with spring sunshine beaming into the studio.

The production of the cookbook is a whole other story that goes beyond making the recipes and photography. Here, the extraordinarily organized and committed project editor Tina Anson Mine, with production coordinator Erin Poetschke, copy editors Karen Campbell-Sheviak, Austen Gilliland, Miriam Osborne and James Doyle, and editorial assistant Patrick Flynn, shaped and cajoled recipes into a cohesive cookbook. Tina checked and rechecked, as editors do, but with her special zeal, to make sure the recipes are accurate, consistent, easy to follow and enjoyable to read. She worked with Sharyn Joliat at Info Access to get the nutrional analysis; Gillian Watts on the comprehensive index; and creative director Michael Erb, Transcontinental Books publisher Jean Paré and production manager Marie-Suzanne Menier on all stages of production.

A word of thanks goes to Monsieur Paré as well as to Diane Hargrave of DHPR Communications Inc.; and Frances Bedford, Janet Joy Wilson, Marlene Fraser and Duncan Shields at Random House Canada for all they have done to assist *Canadian Living* cookbooks, past and present. And if that's the cake, the icing goes to *Canadian Living* editor-in-chief Susan Antonacci and group publisher Lynn Chambers.

Thanks to all for the essential ingredients – passion and commitment – they have brought to *The Complete Canadian Living Baking Book.*

Left to right: Senior food specialist Heather Howe and food specialist Adell Shneer